GENDER QUEER

A MEMOIR BY
MAIA KOBABE
COLORS BY PHOEBE KOBABE

ONI PRESS

COLORS BY PHOEBE KOBABE
SENSITIVITY READ BY MELANIE GILLMAN
EDITOR: ANDREA COLVIN
ASSISTANT EDITOR: GRACE BORNHOFT

GENDER QUEER: A MEMOIR, PUBLISHED MAY 2020 BY ONI-LION FORGE PUBLISHING GROUP, LLC.,
1319 SE MARTIN LUTHER KING JR. BLVD., SUITE 240, PORTLAND, OR 97214. GENDER QUEER: A MEMOIR
IS © 2022 MAIA KOBABE. ONI PRESS LOGO AND ICON TM & © 2022 ONI-LION FORGE PUBLISHING GROUP, LLC.
ALL RIGHTS RESERVED. ONI PRESS LOGO AND ICON ARTWORK CREATED BY KEITH A. WOOD.

THIS IS A WORK OF NON-FICTION.
EXCEPT WHERE PERMISSION HAS BEEN GIVEN, ALL NAMES HAVE BEEN CHANGED.

PRINTED IN CANADA.

ISBN: 978-1-5493-0400-2
EISBN: 978-1-5493-0751-5
LIBRARY OF CONGRESS CONTROL NUMBER: 2018958115

10 9 8 7 6

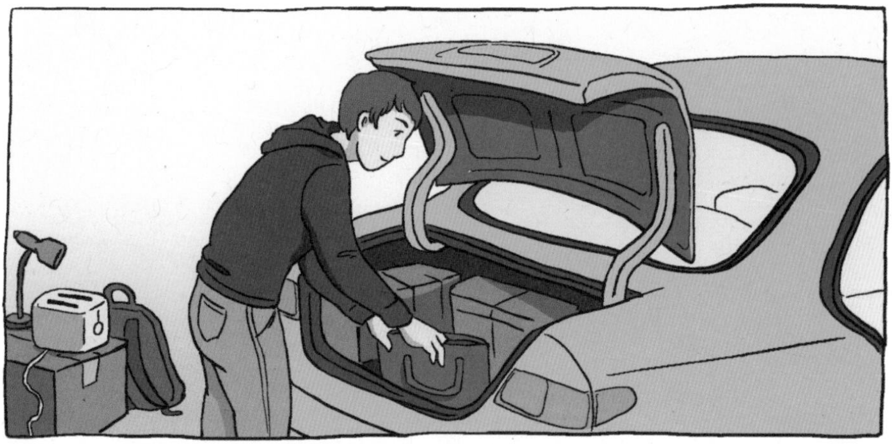

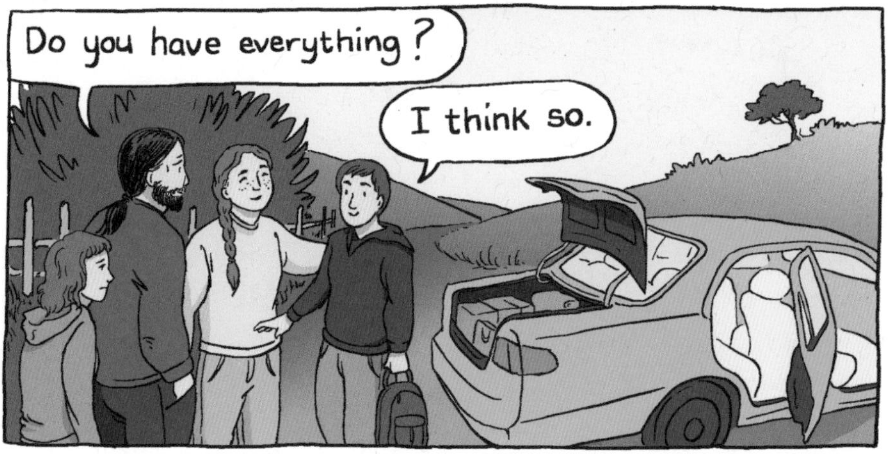
Do you have everything?
I think so.

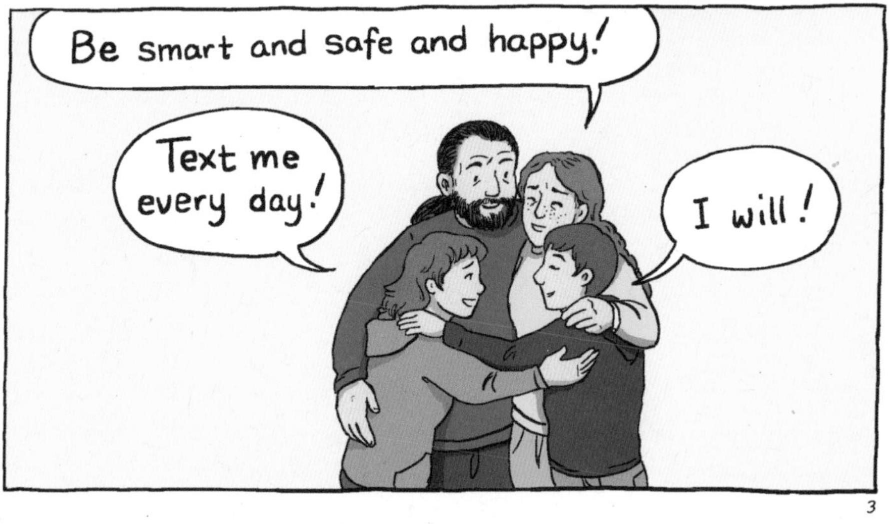
Be smart and safe and happy!
Text me every day!
I will!

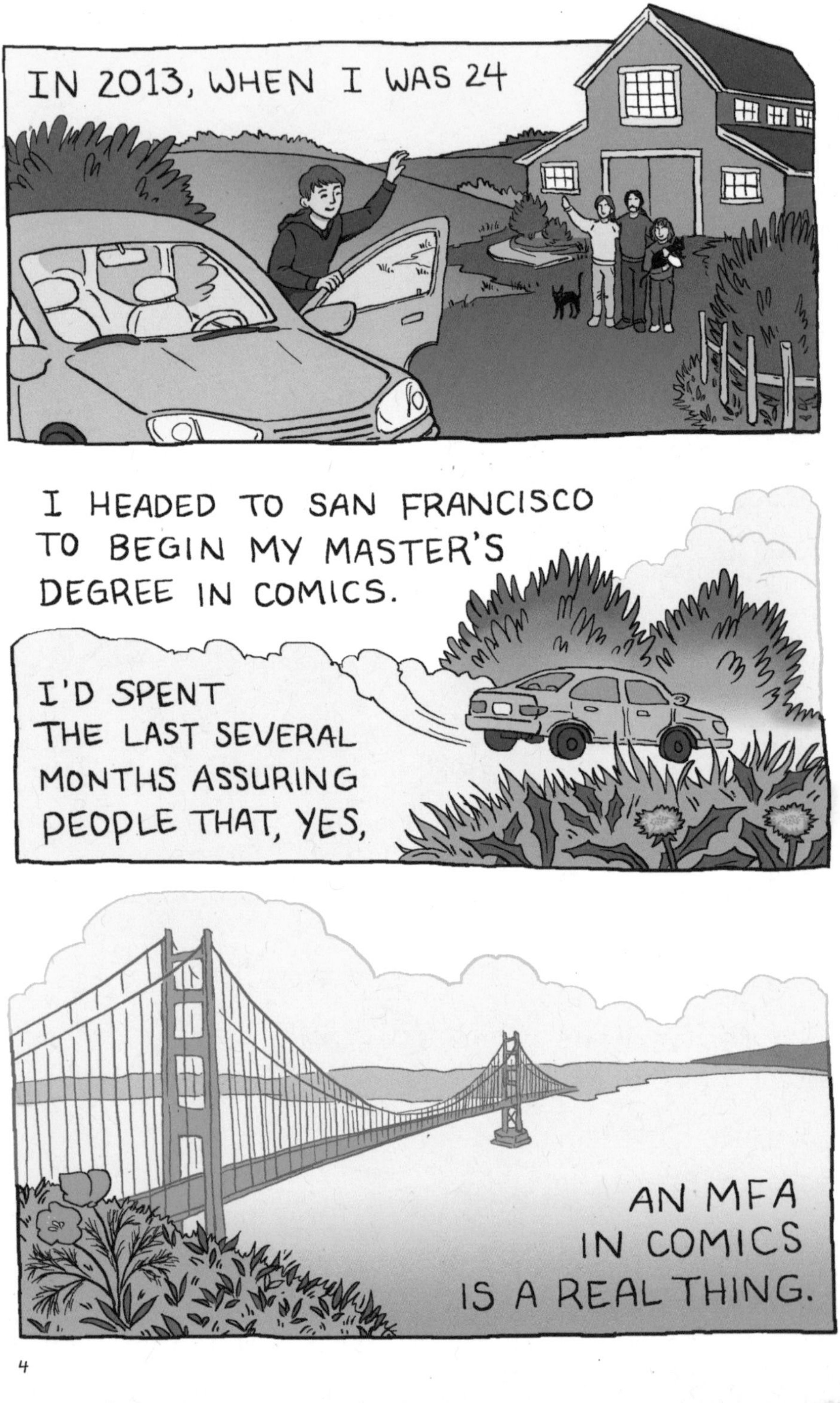
IN 2013, WHEN I WAS 24
I HEADED TO SAN FRANCISCO TO BEGIN MY MASTER'S DEGREE IN COMICS.
I'D SPENT THE LAST SEVERAL MONTHS ASSURING PEOPLE THAT, YES,
AN MFA IN COMICS IS A REAL THING.

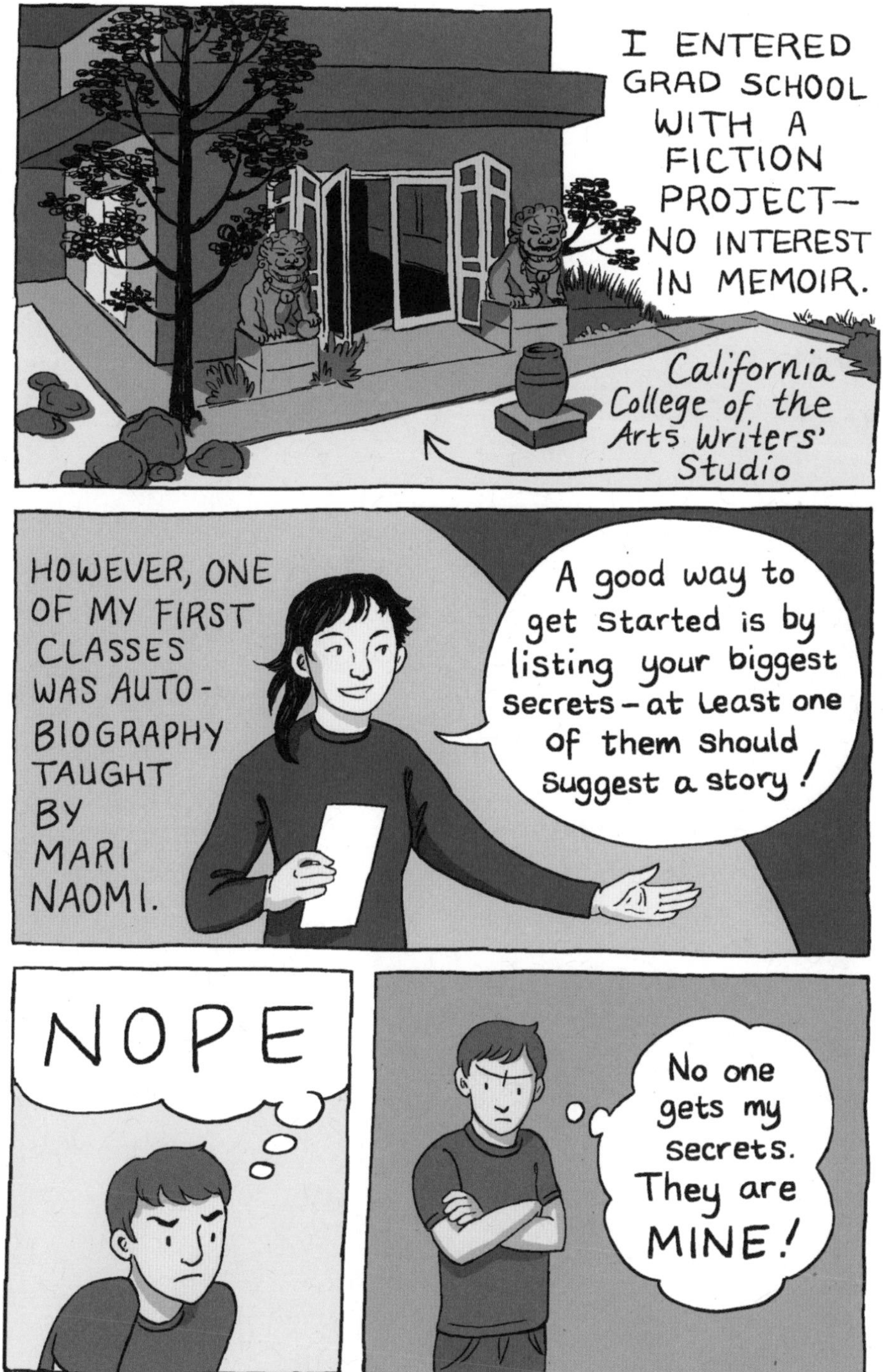
I ENTERED GRAD SCHOOL WITH A FICTION PROJECT— NO INTEREST IN MEMOIR.
California College of the Arts Writers' Studio
HOWEVER, ONE OF MY FIRST CLASSES WAS AUTO-BIOGRAPHY TAUGHT BY MARI NAOMI.
A good way to get started is by listing your biggest secrets—at least one of them should suggest a story!
NOPE
No one gets my secrets. They are MINE!

I STRUGGLED IN THIS CLASS.

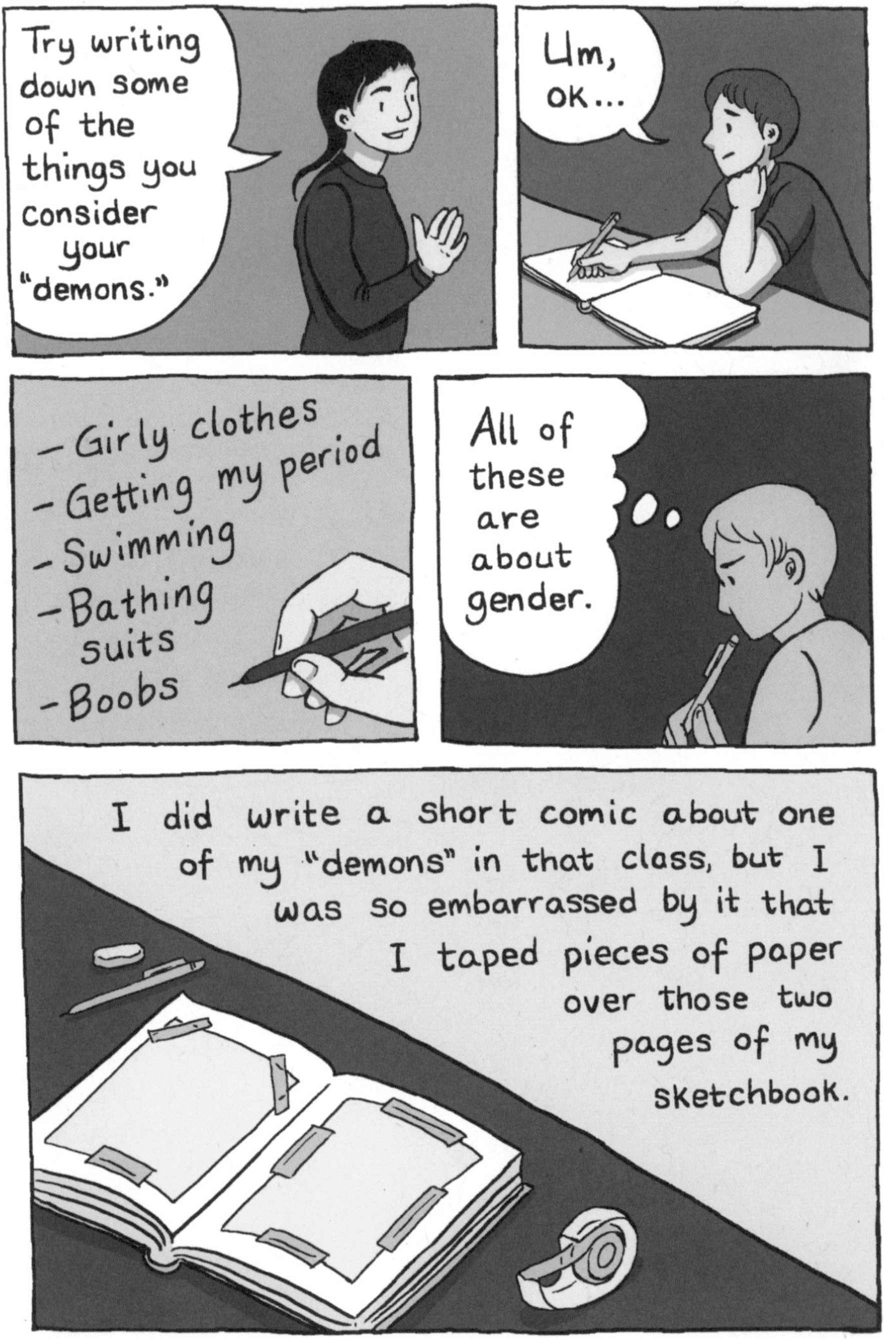
Try writing down some of the things you consider your "demons."
Um, ok...
-Girly clothes
-Getting my period
-Swimming
-Bathing suits
-Boobs
All of these are about gender.
I did write a short comic about one of my "demons" in that class, but I was so embarrassed by it that I taped pieces of paper over those two pages of my sketchbook.

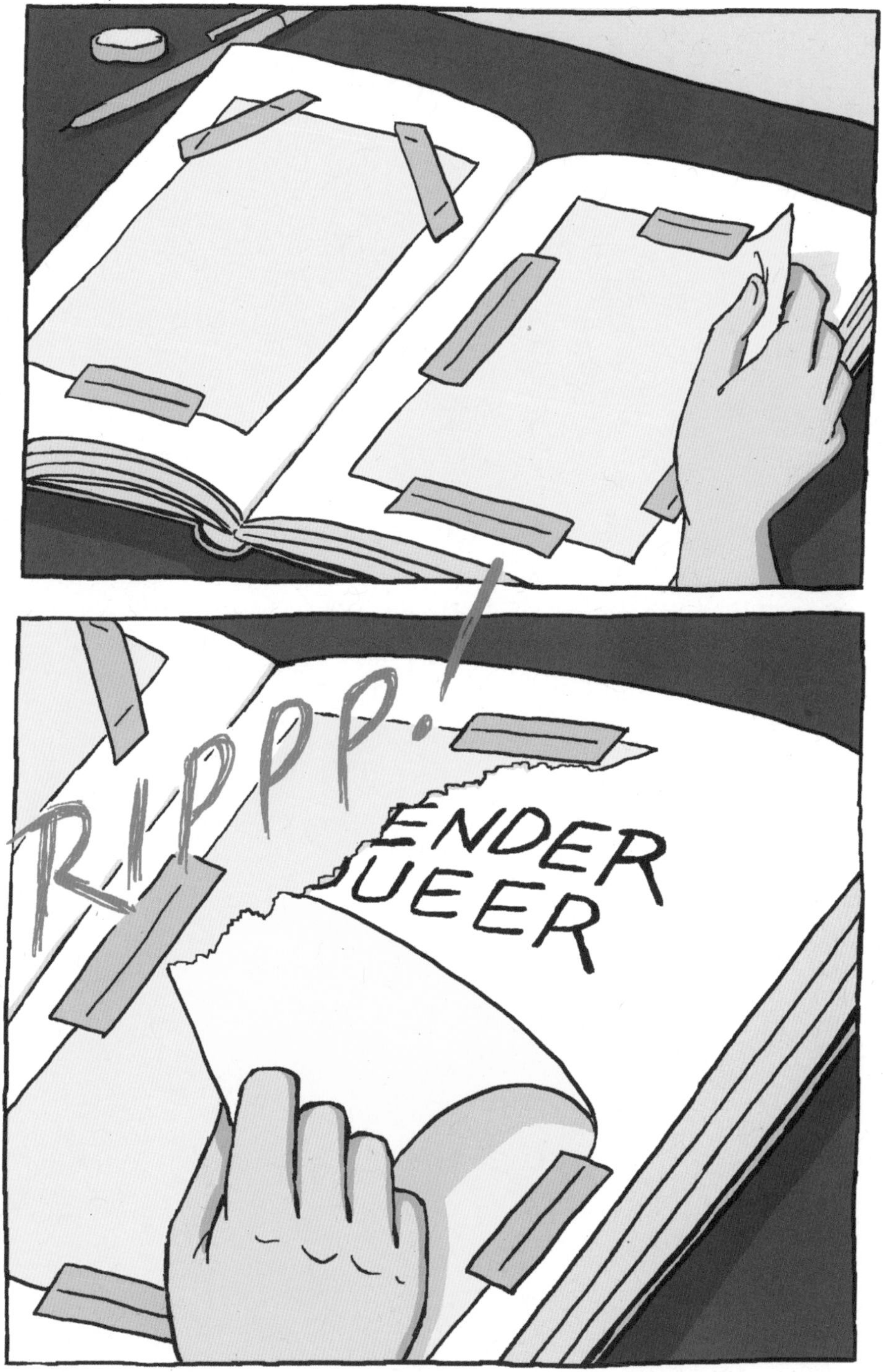
RIPPP!
ENDER
UEER

GENDER QUEER

a memoir

BY MAIA KOBABE

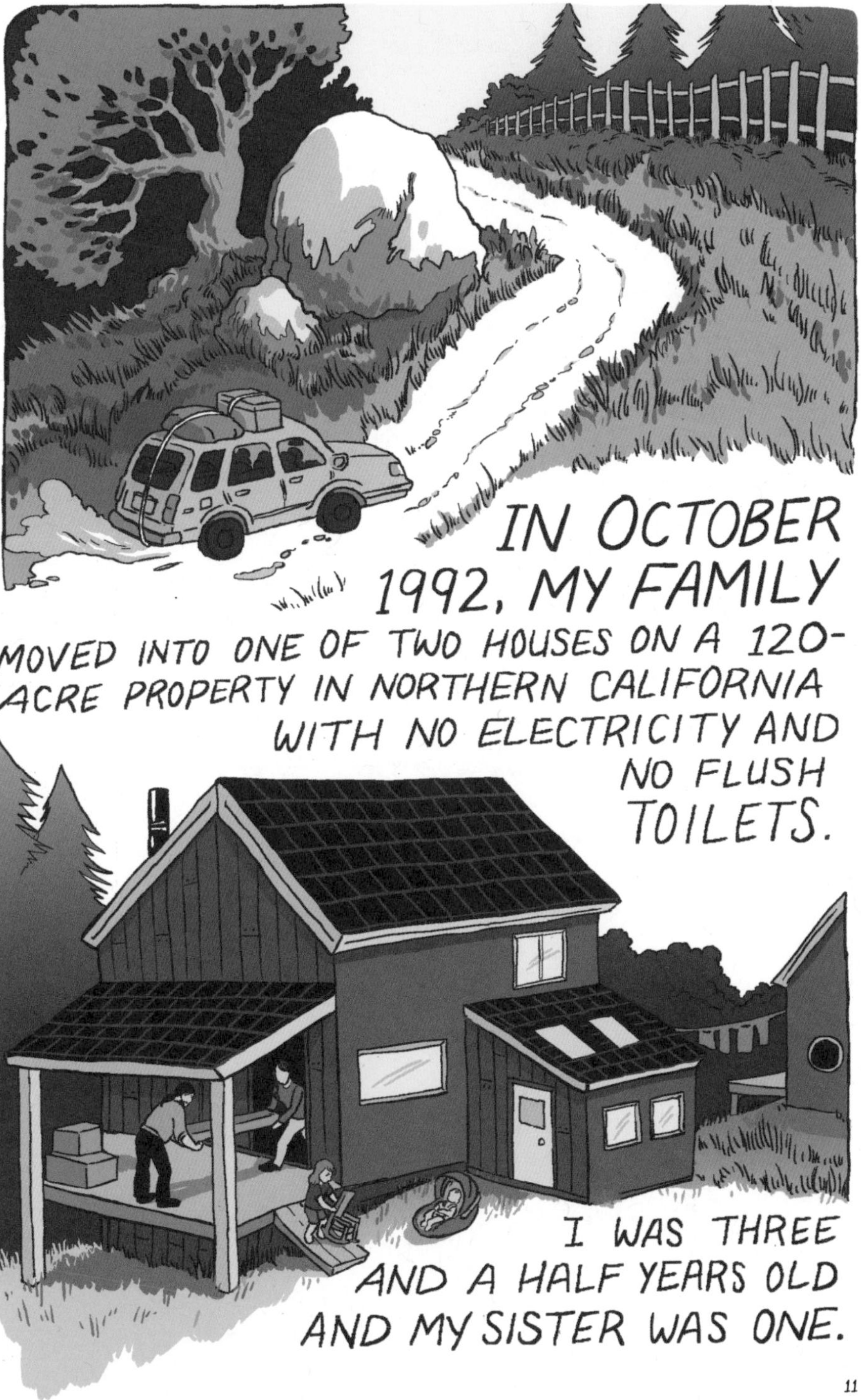
IN OCTOBER 1992, MY FAMILY
MOVED INTO ONE OF TWO HOUSES ON A 120-ACRE PROPERTY IN NORTHERN CALIFORNIA WITH NO ELECTRICITY AND NO FLUSH TOILETS.
I WAS THREE AND A HALF YEARS OLD AND MY SISTER WAS ONE.

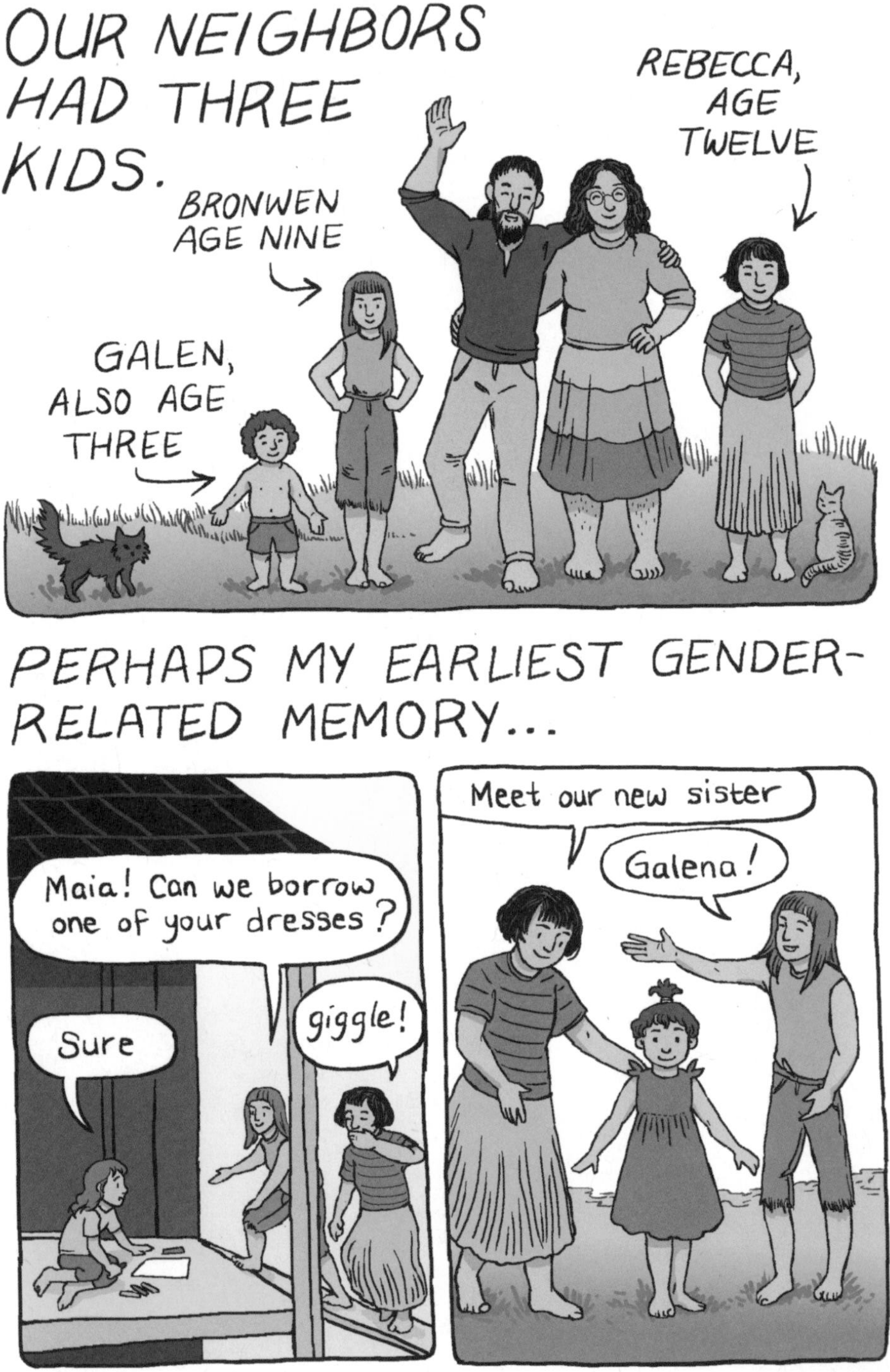
OUR NEIGHBORS HAD THREE KIDS.
REBECCA, AGE TWELVE
BRONWEN AGE NINE
GALEN, ALSO AGE THREE
PERHAPS MY EARLIEST GENDER-RELATED MEMORY...
Maia! Can we borrow one of your dresses?
Sure
giggle!
Meet our new sister
Galena!

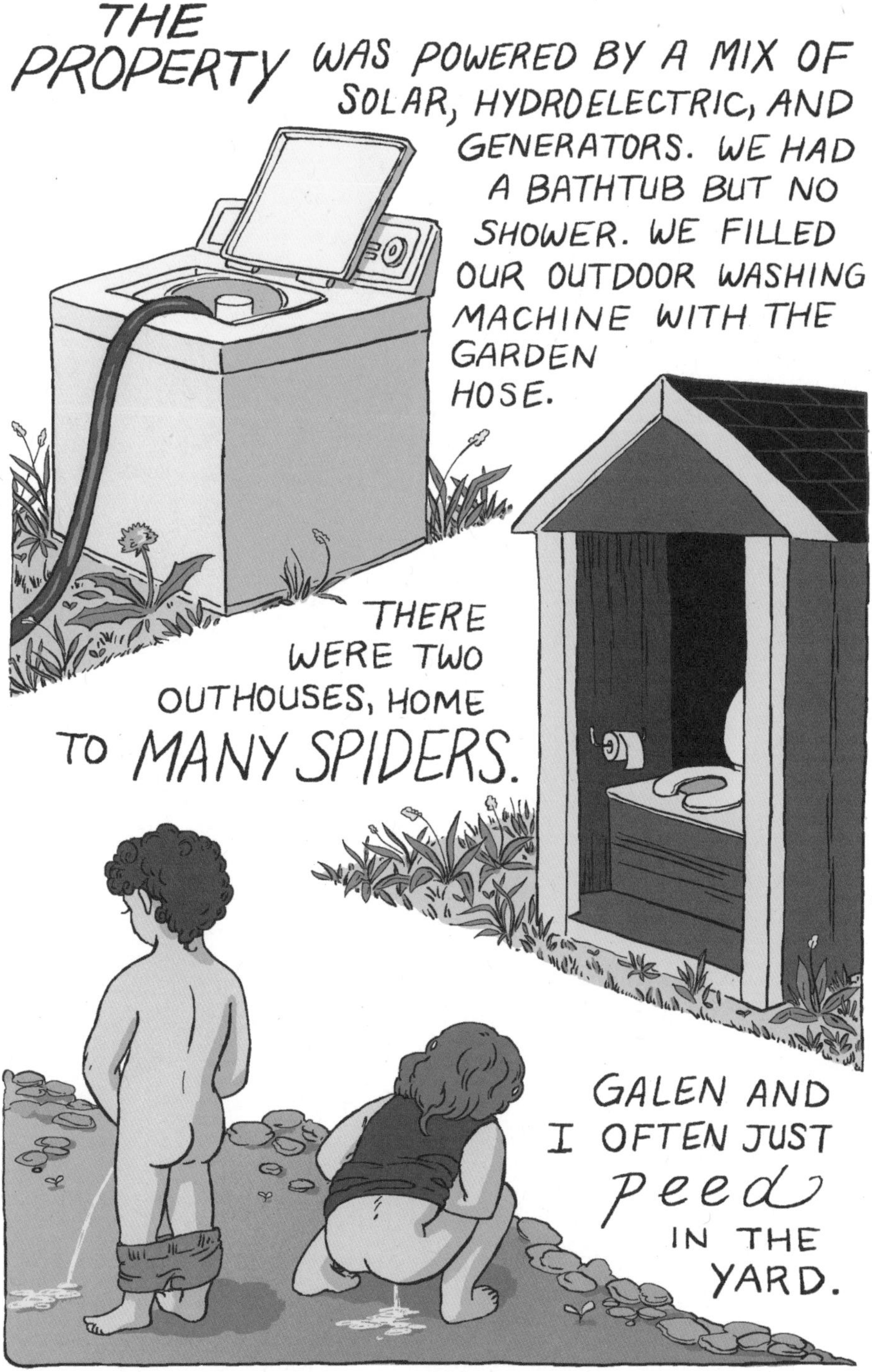
THE PROPERTY WAS POWERED BY A MIX OF SOLAR, HYDROELECTRIC, AND GENERATORS. WE HAD A BATHTUB BUT NO SHOWER. WE FILLED OUR OUTDOOR WASHING MACHINE WITH THE GARDEN HOSE.
THERE WERE TWO OUTHOUSES, HOME TO MANY SPIDERS.
GALEN AND I OFTEN JUST peed IN THE YARD.

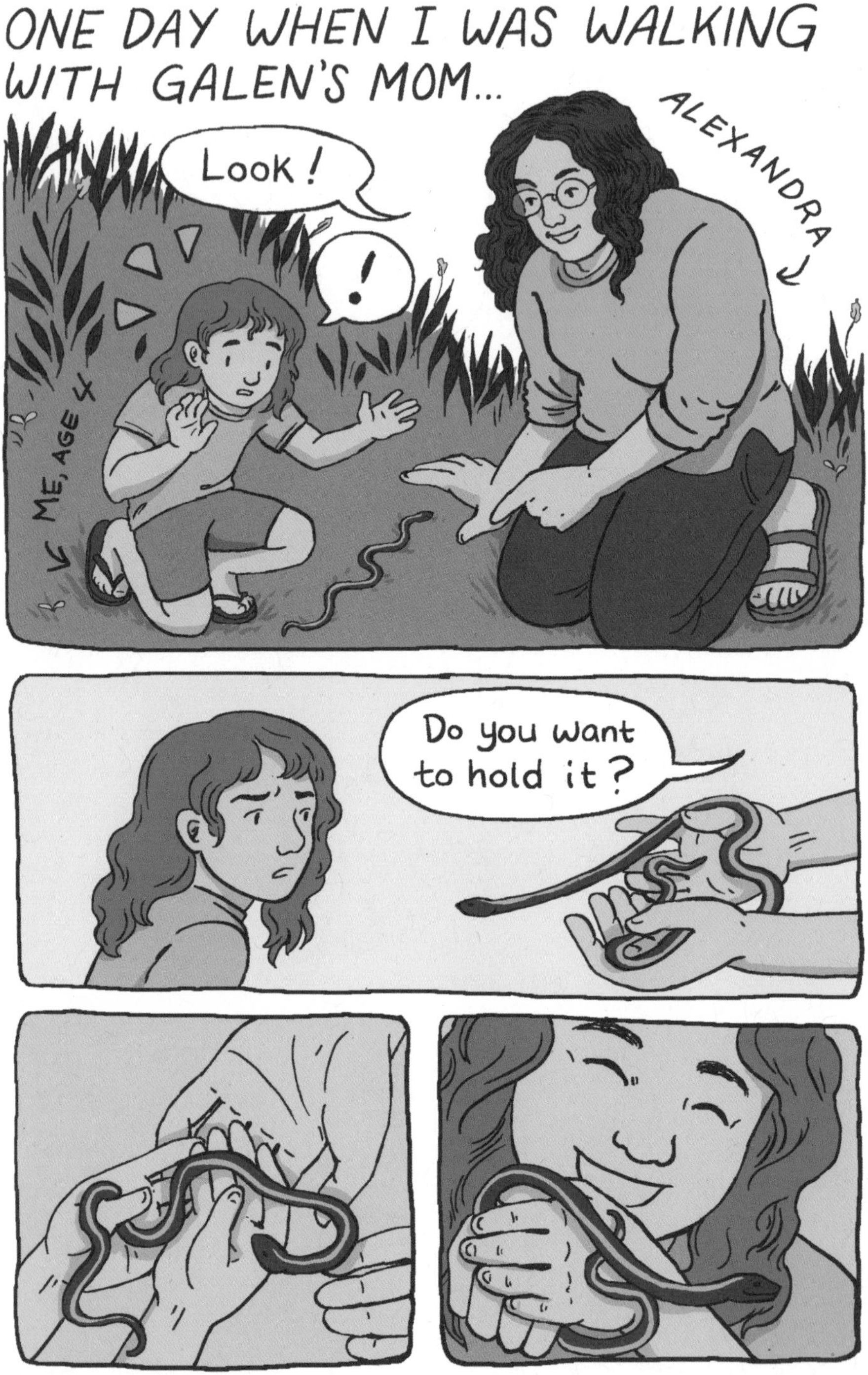
ONE DAY WHEN I WAS WALKING WITH GALEN'S MOM...
ALEXANDRA
Look!
!
ME, AGE 4
Do you want to hold it?

FOR MANY BIRTHDAYS AFTER I REQUESTED SNAKE-THEMED GIFTS:

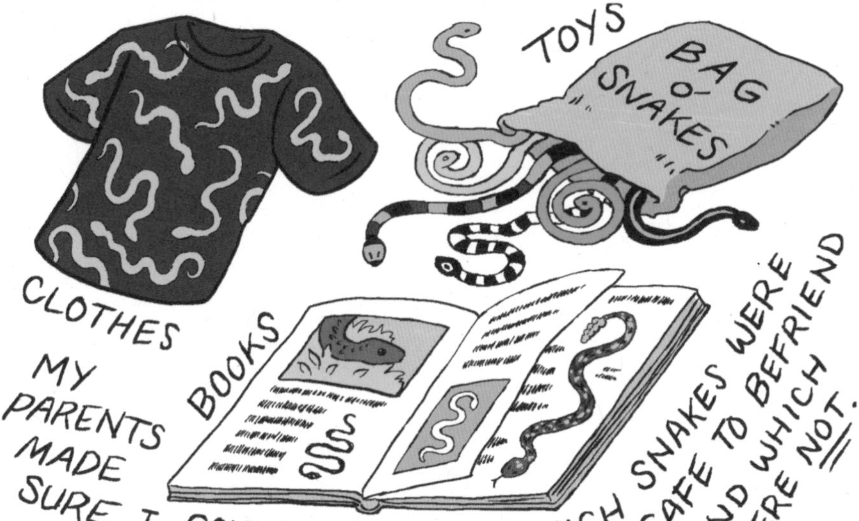
TOYS
BAG O- SNAKES
CLOTHES
BOOKS

MY PARENTS MADE SURE I COULD IDENTIFY WHICH SNAKES WERE SAFE TO BEFRIEND AND WHICH WERE NOT.

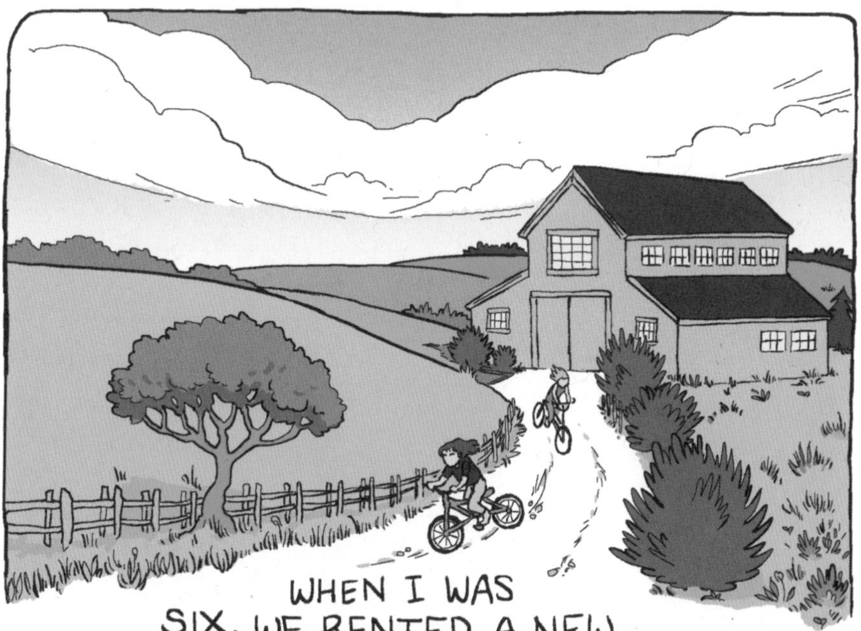

WHEN I WAS SIX, WE RENTED A NEW HOUSE AT THE END OF A MILE-LONG DRIVEWAY, SURROUNDED BY COW PASTURES.

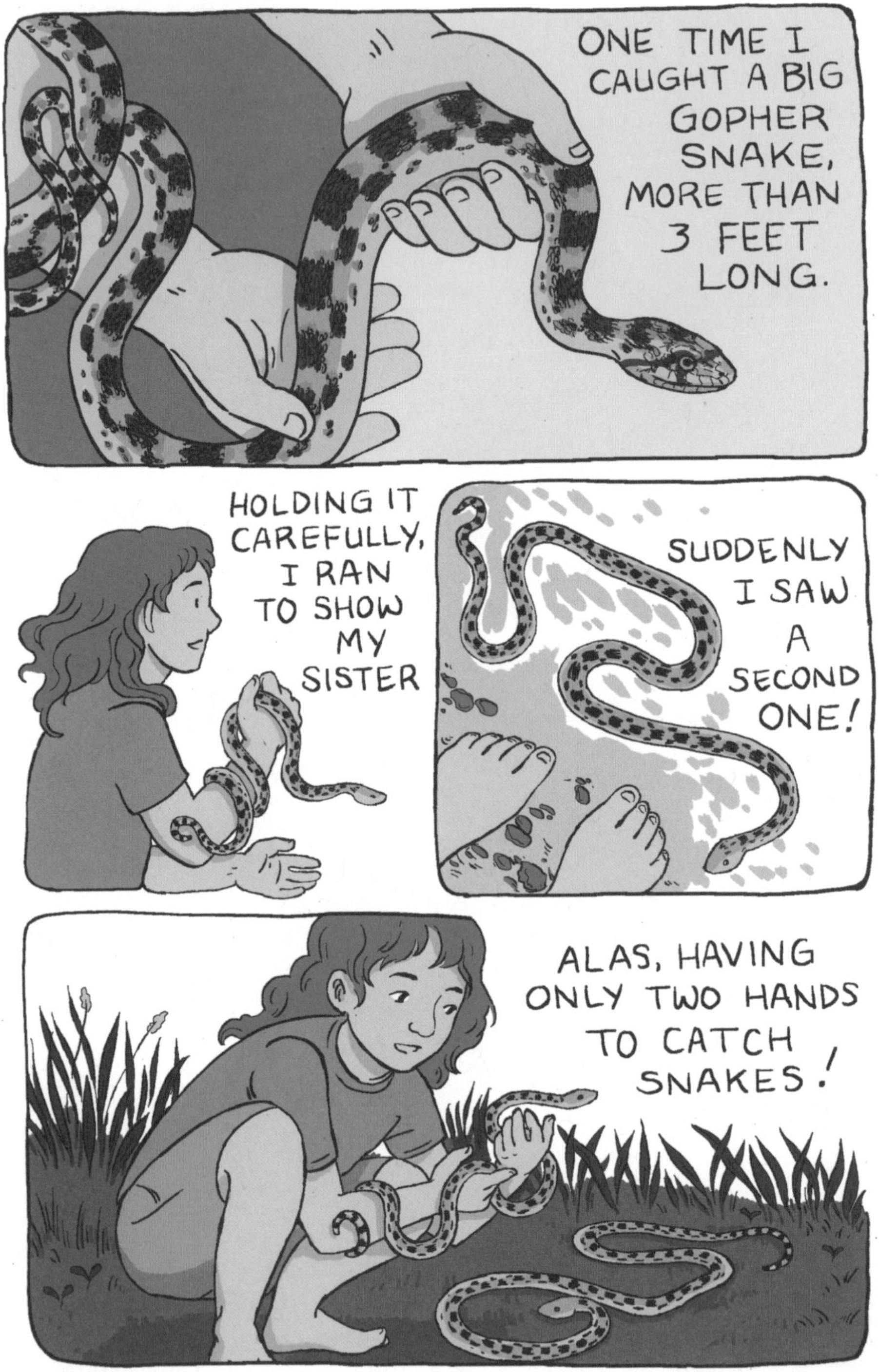
ONE TIME I CAUGHT A BIG GOPHER SNAKE, MORE THAN 3 FEET LONG.
HOLDING IT CAREFULLY, I RAN TO SHOW MY SISTER
SUDDENLY I SAW A SECOND ONE!
ALAS, HAVING ONLY TWO HANDS TO CATCH SNAKES!

NEITHER GALEN NOR I ATTENDED A PRESCHOOL OR A KINDERGARTEN. THE FIRST DAY OF FIRST GRADE WAS OUR FIRST TIME MIXING WITH OTHER KIDS OUR AGE.

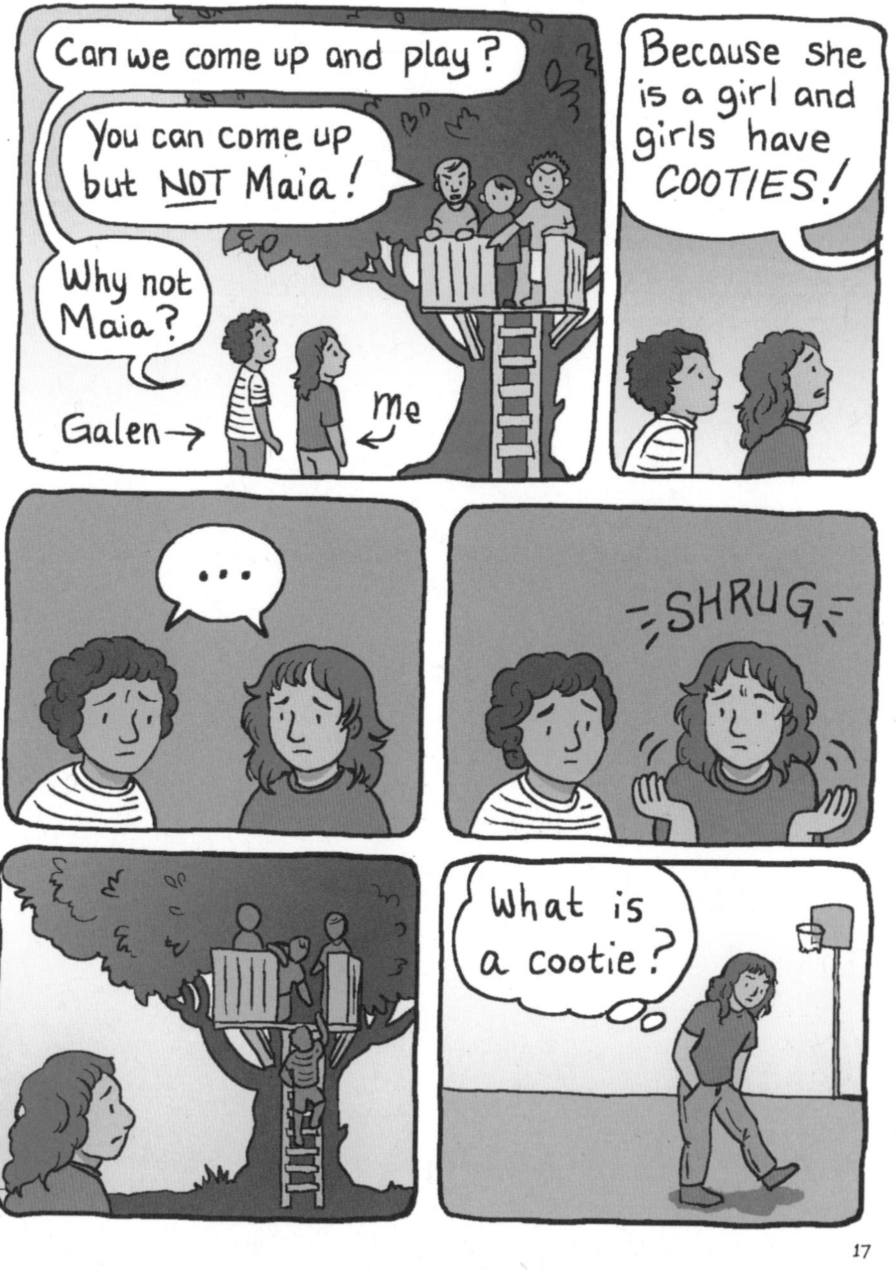

Can we come up and play?
You can come up but NOT Maia!
Why not Maia?
Galen
me
Because she is a girl and girls have COOTIES!
...
SHRUG
What is a cootie?

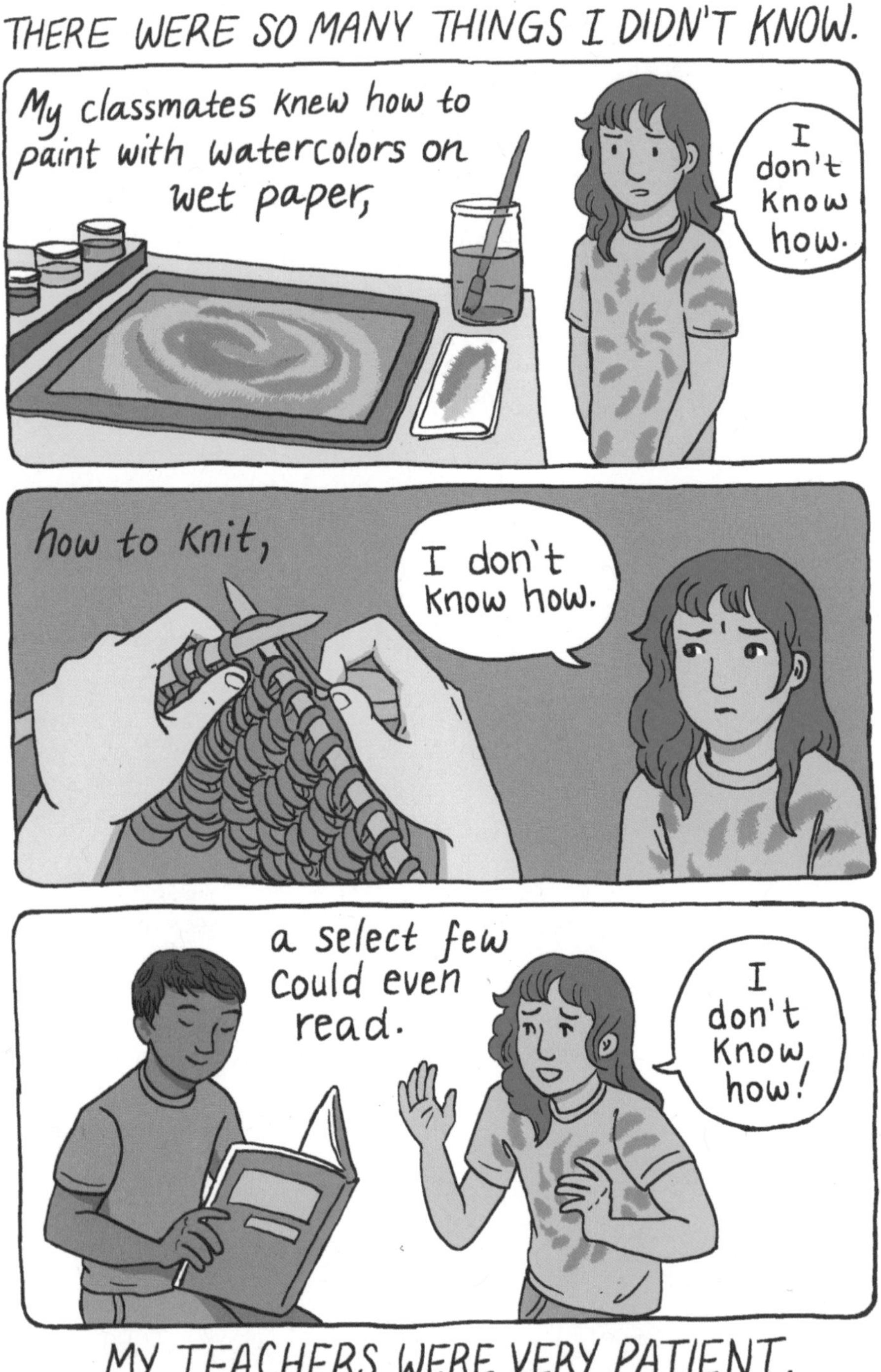
THERE WERE SO MANY THINGS I DIDN'T KNOW.
My classmates knew how to paint with watercolors on wet paper,
I don't know how.
how to knit,
I don't know how.
a select few could even read.
I don't know how!
MY TEACHERS WERE VERY PATIENT.

AT MY WALDORF ELEMENTARY SCHOOL

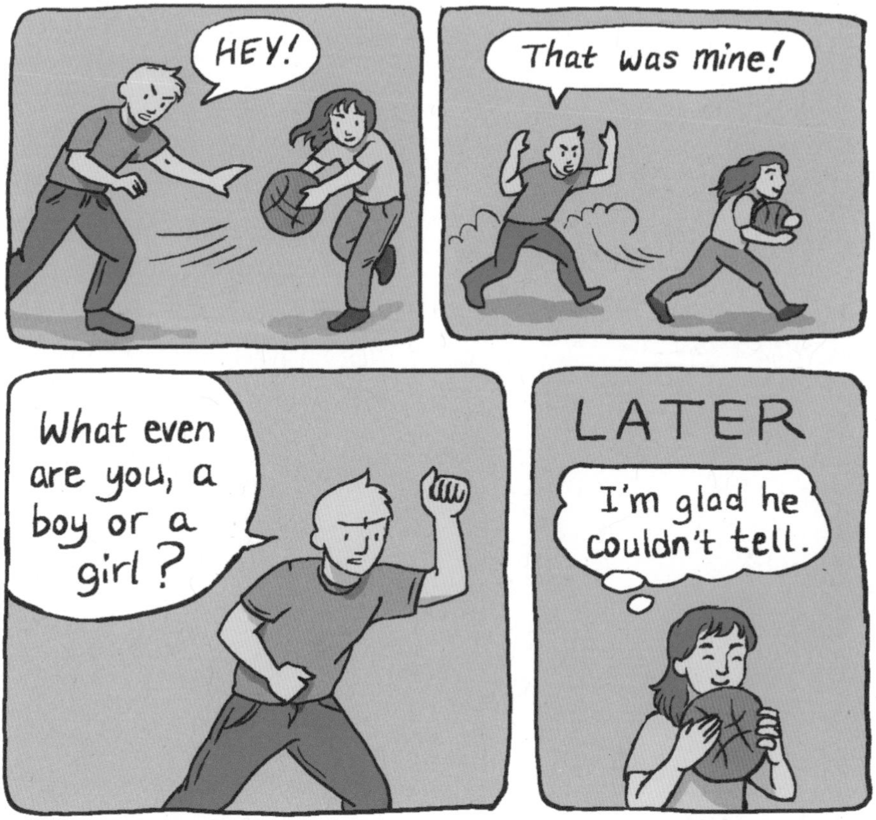
HEY!
That was mine!
What even are you, a boy or a girl?
LATER
I'm glad he couldn't tell.

IT WASN'T UNUSUAL FOR BOYS TO HAVE LONG HAIR

IN MY CLASS OF 18 STUDENTS FOUR BOYS HAD HAIR THAT BRUSHED THEIR SHOULDERS.

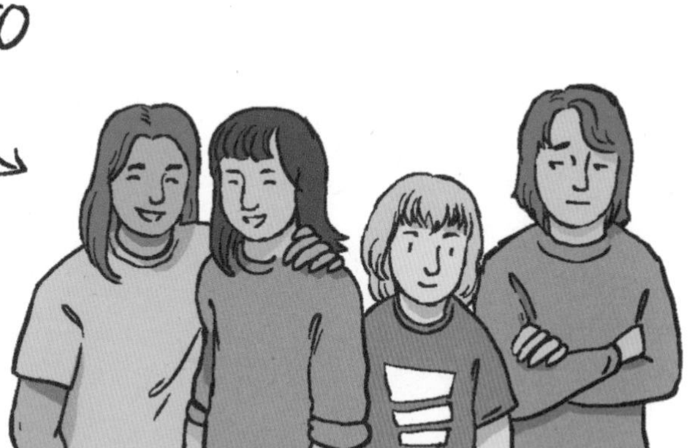

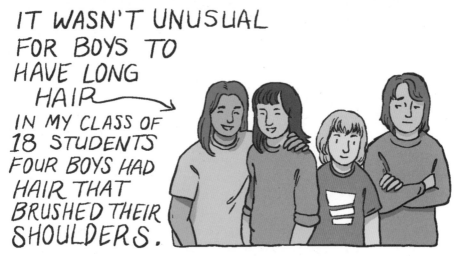

I REMEMBER A FIELD TRIP
I TOOK WITH MY CLASS IN THIRD GRADE

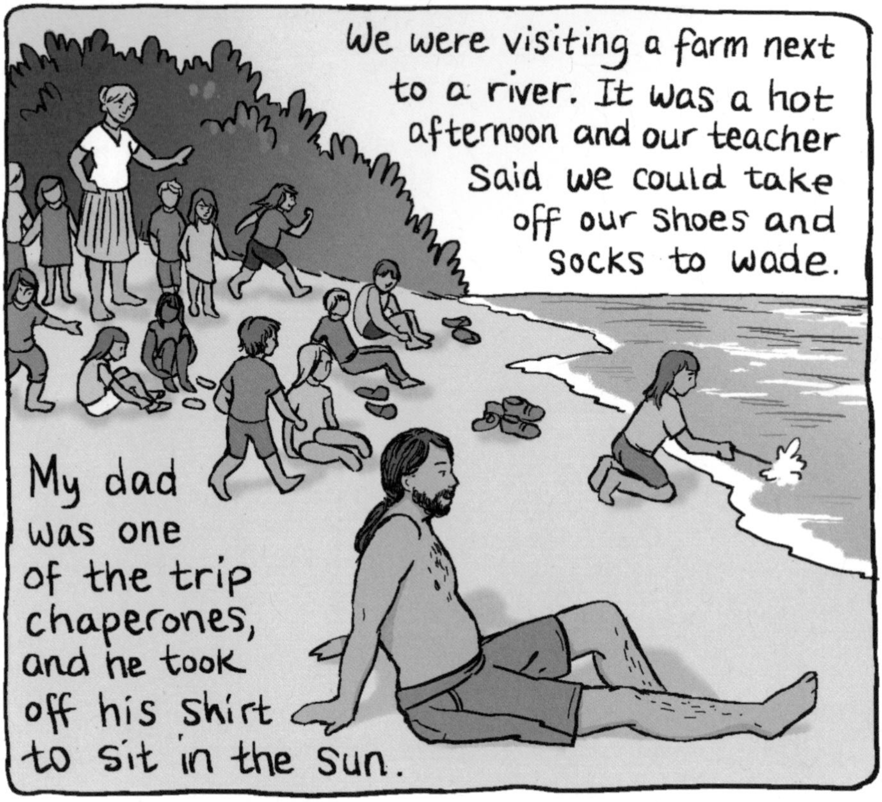
We were visiting a farm next to a river. It was a hot afternoon and our teacher said we could take off our shoes and socks to wade.
My dad was one of the trip chaperones, and he took off his shirt to sit in the sun.

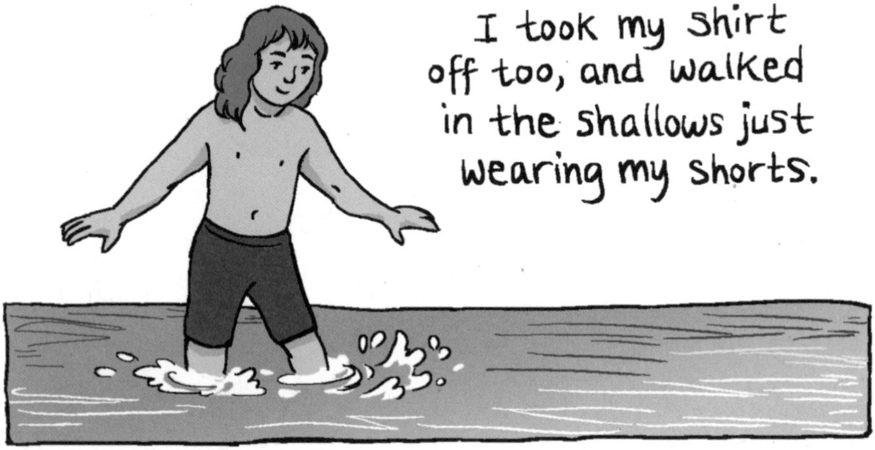
I took my shirt off too, and walked in the shallows just wearing my shorts.

SOME OF MY CLASSMATES NOTICED.

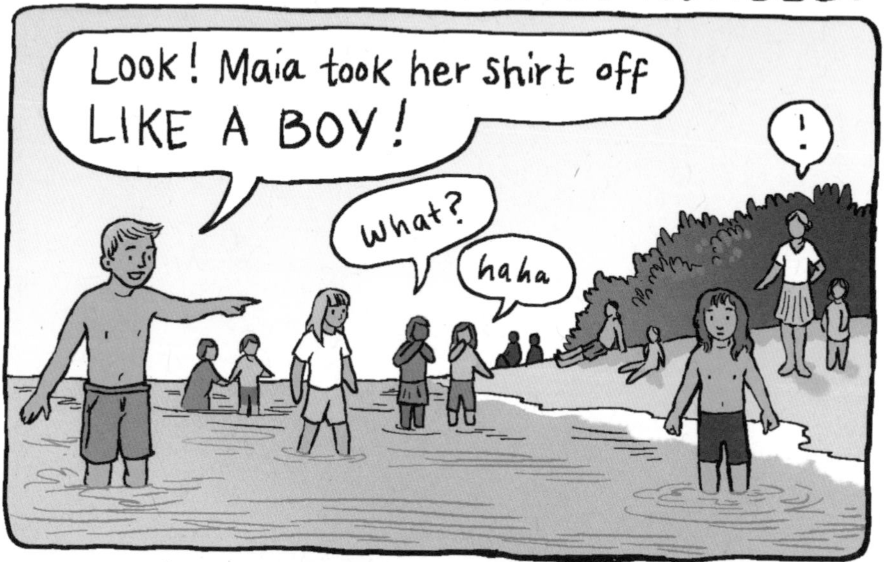
Look! Maia took her shirt off LIKE A BOY!
what?
haha
!

MY TEACHER INTERVENED.

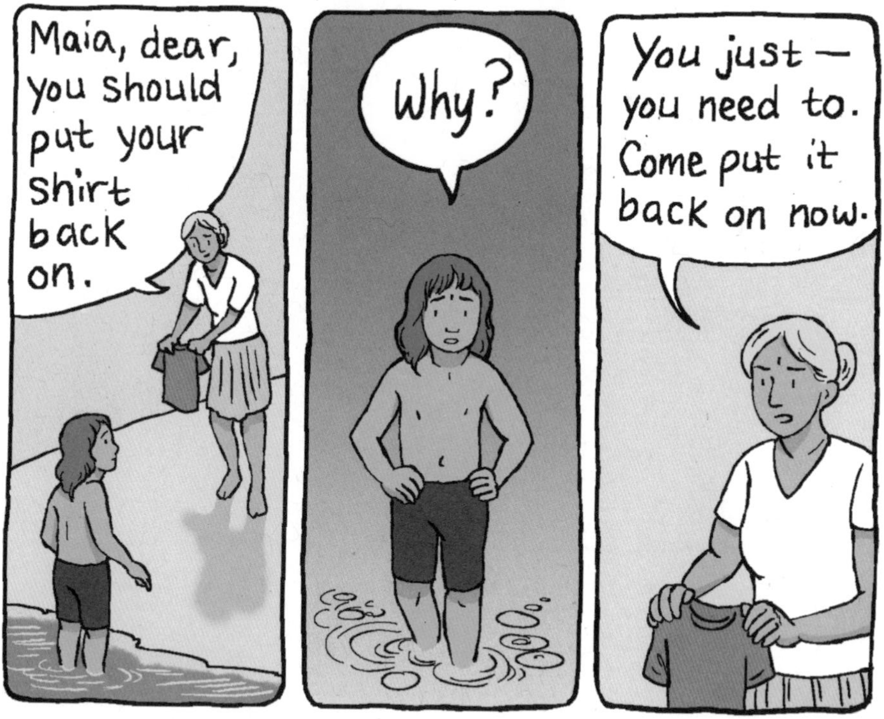
Maia, dear, you should put your shirt back on.
Why?
You just — you need to. Come put it back on now.

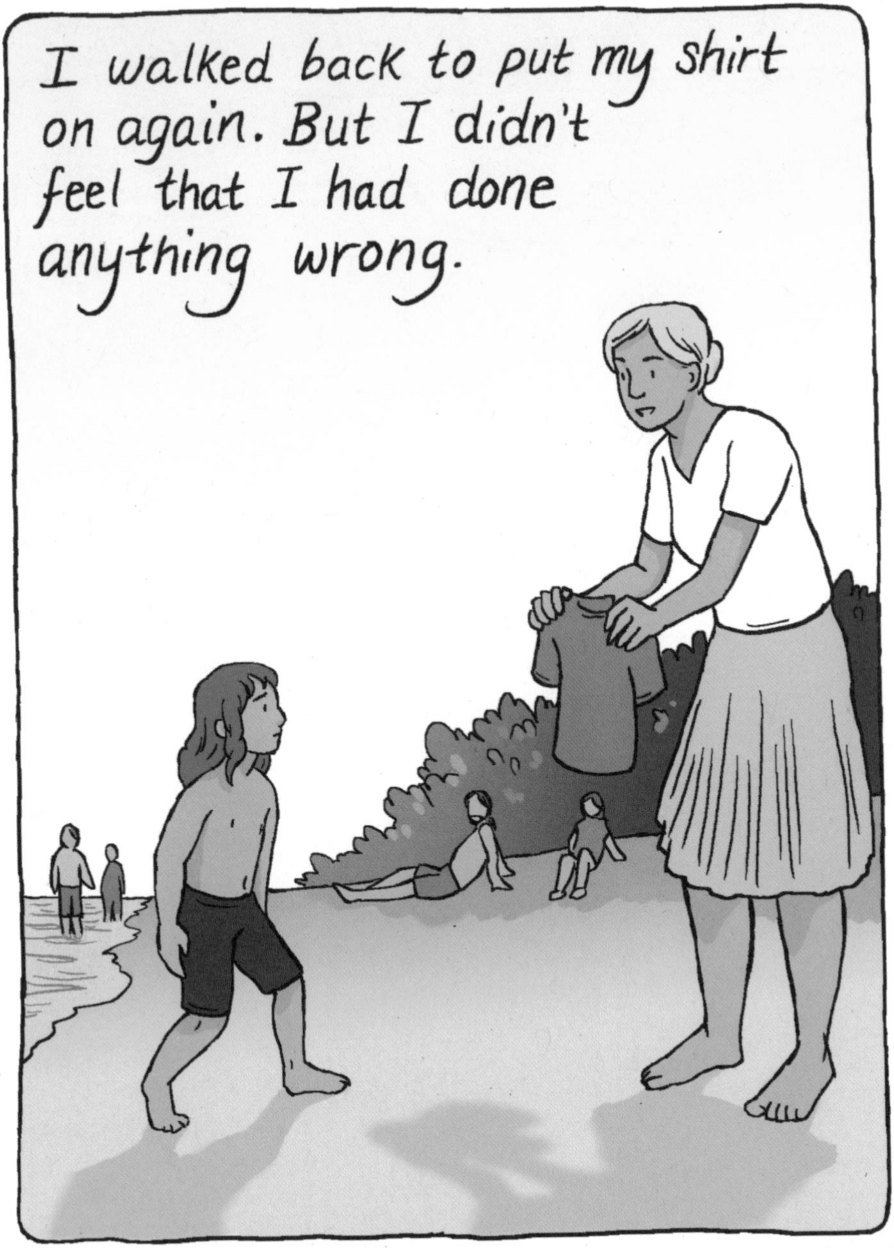
I walked back to put my shirt on again. But I didn't feel that I had done anything wrong.

It was everyone else being silly, NOT ME.

NEITHER OF MY PARENTS WERE INTERESTED IN ENFORCING GENDER ROLES

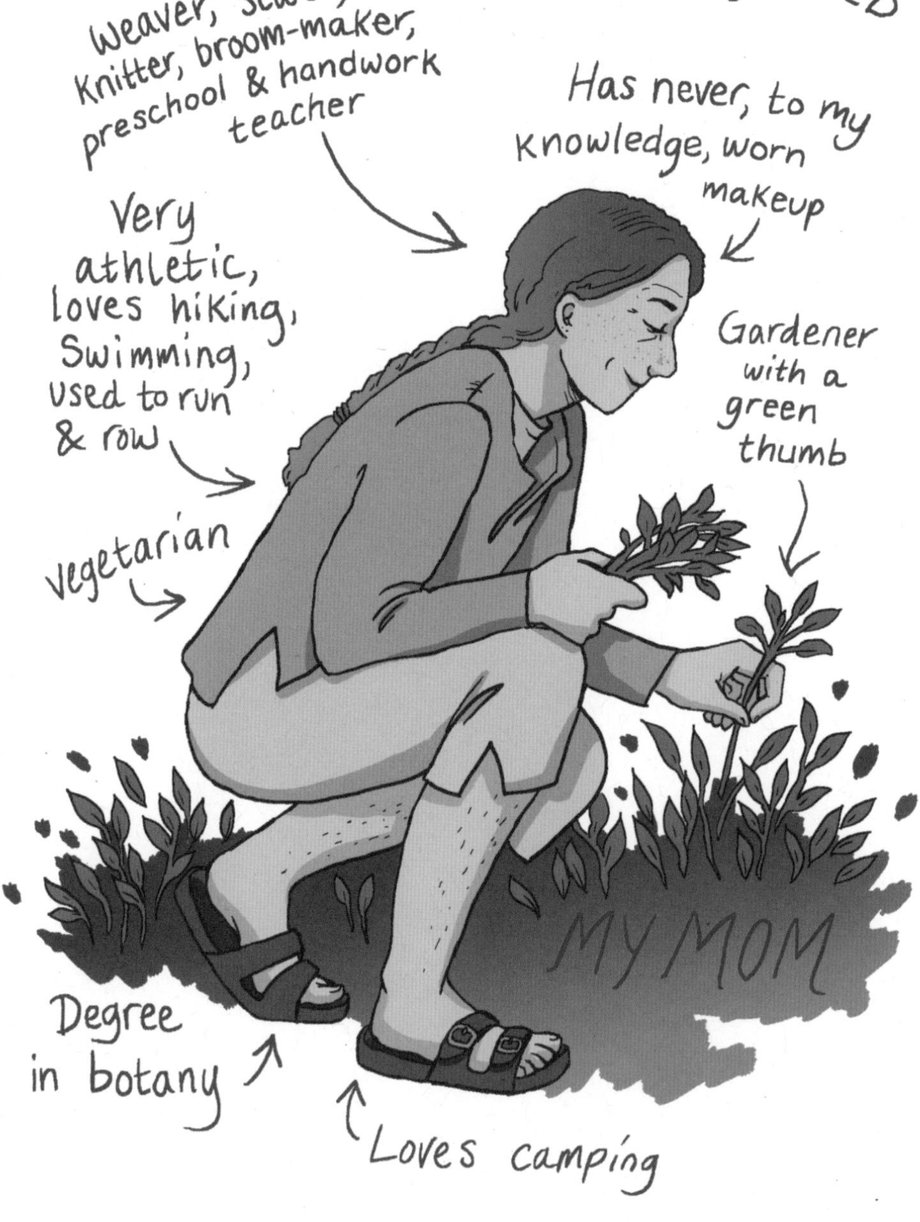
Weaver, sewer, knitter, broom-maker, preschool & handwork teacher
Has never, to my knowledge, worn makeup
Very athletic, loves hiking, swimming, used to run & row
Gardener with a green thumb
vegetarian
MY MOM
Degree in botany
Loves camping

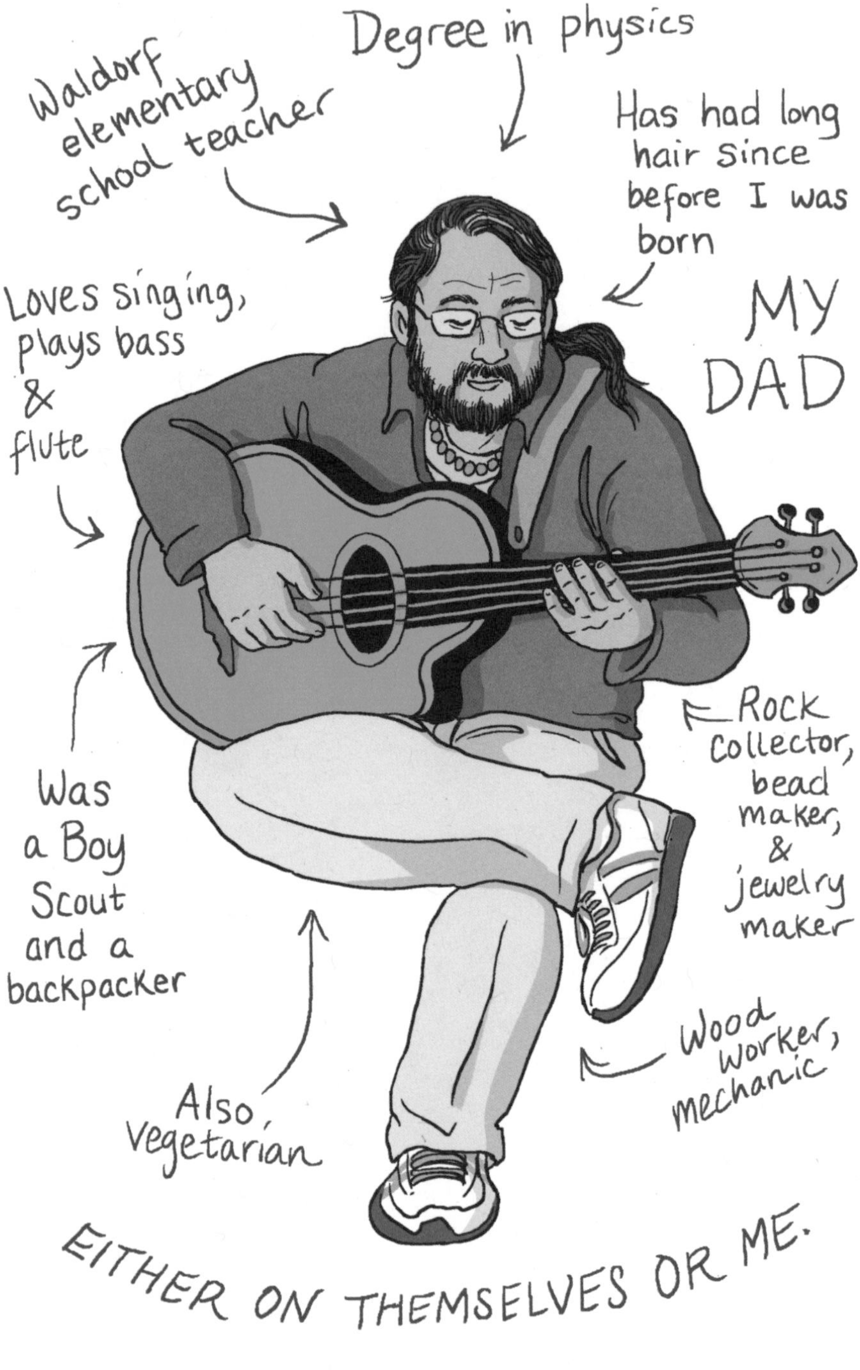
Degree in physics
Waldorf elementary school teacher
Has had long hair since before I was born
MY DAD
Loves singing, plays bass & flute
Was a Boy Scout and a backpacker
Rock collector, bead maker, & jewelry maker
Wood worker, mechanic
Also, vegetarian
EITHER ON THEMSELVES OR ME.

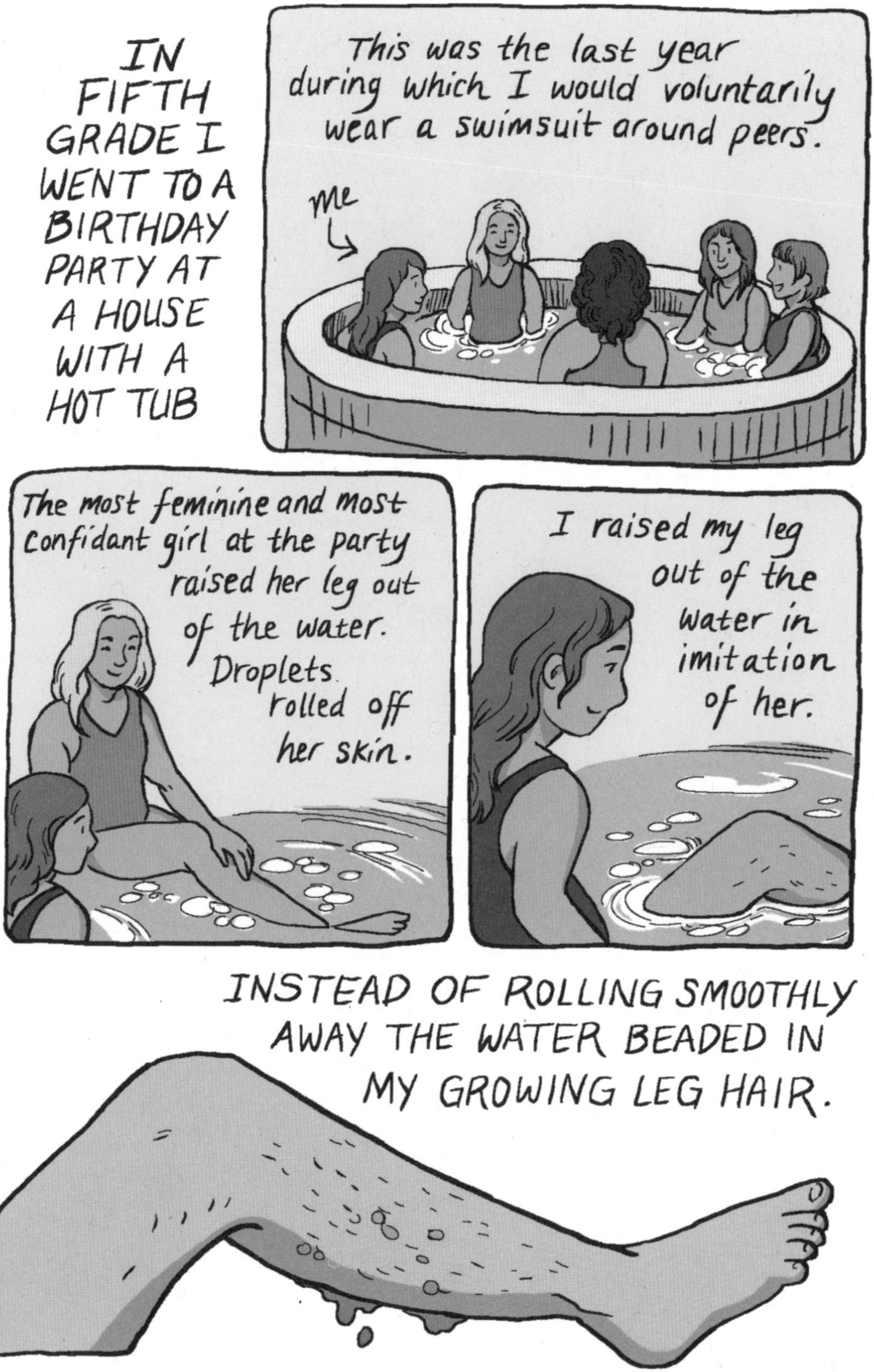
IN FIFTH GRADE I WENT TO A BIRTHDAY PARTY AT A HOUSE WITH A HOT TUB
This was the last year during which I would voluntarily wear a swimsuit around peers.
me
The most feminine and most confidant girl at the party raised her leg out of the water. Droplets rolled off her skin.
I raised my leg out of the water in imitation of her.
INSTEAD OF ROLLING SMOOTHLY AWAY THE WATER BEADED IN MY GROWING LEG HAIR.

I WAS GRUMPY AND EMBARRASSED TO ENCOUNTER YET ANOTHER THING I WAS APPARENTLY SUPPOSED TO KNOW BUT DIDN'T.

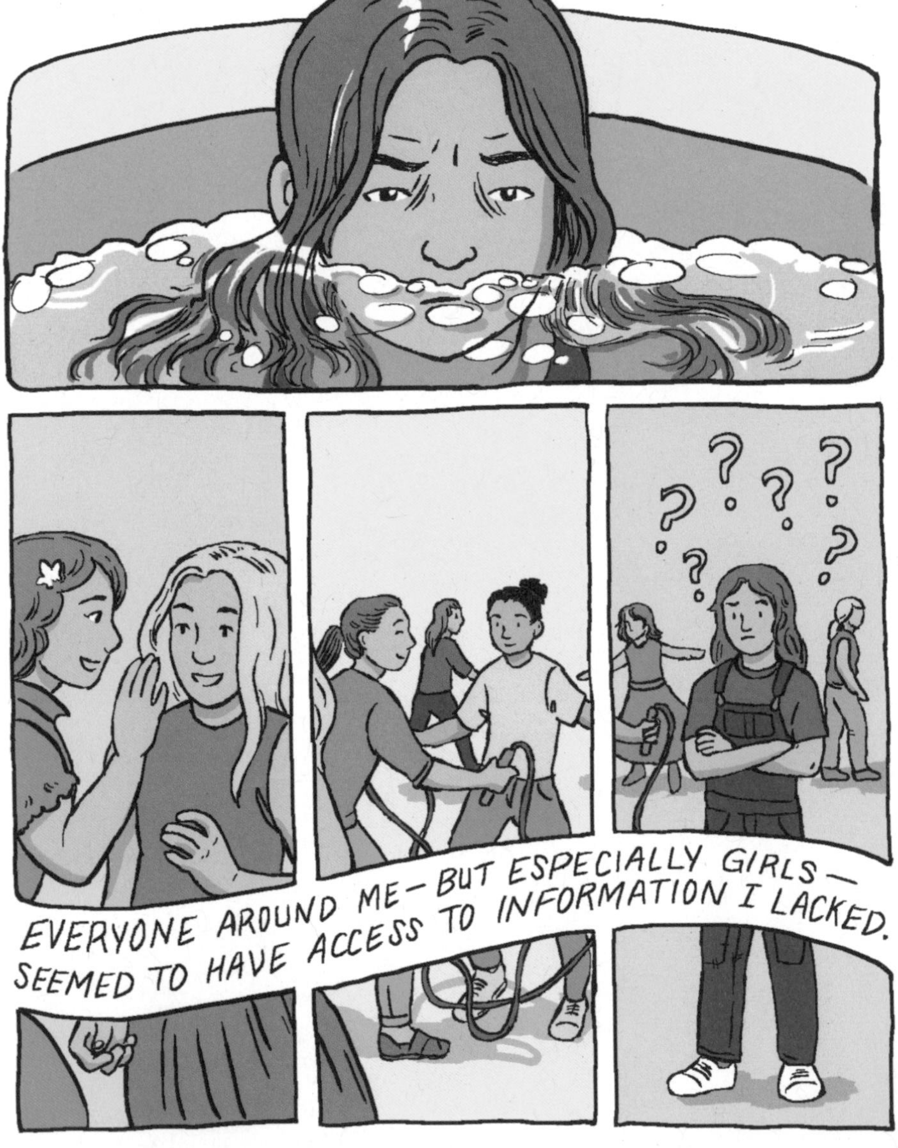

?
?
?
?
?
?
EVERYONE AROUND ME—BUT ESPECIALLY GIRLS—SEEMED TO HAVE ACCESS TO INFORMATION I LACKED.

This was both emotionally and literally true. AT 11 YEARS OLD I HAD NOT YET LEARNED TO READ.

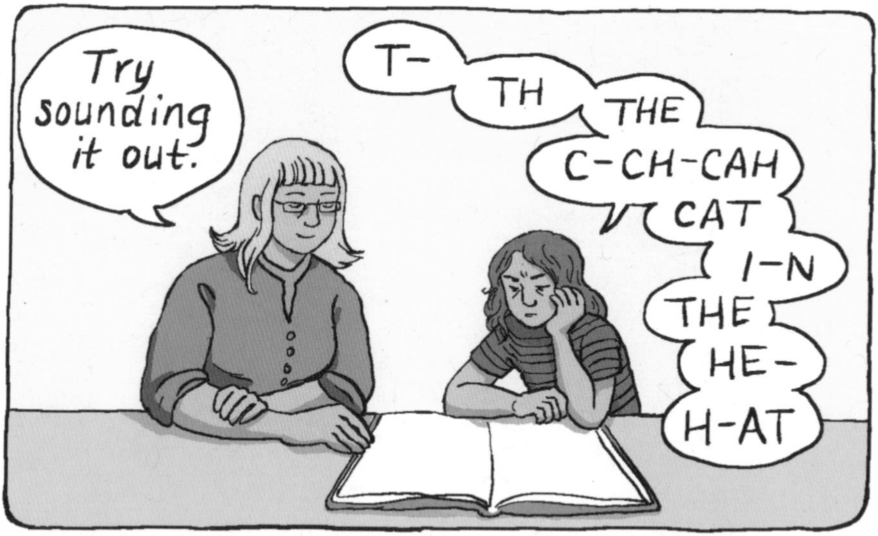
Try sounding it out.
T-
TH
THE
C-CH-CAH
CAT
I-N
THE
HE-
H-AT

I STARTED AFTER-SCHOOL TUTORING BUT MY PROGRESS WAS FRUSTRATINGLY SLOW. I HAD TWO CONSOLATIONS:

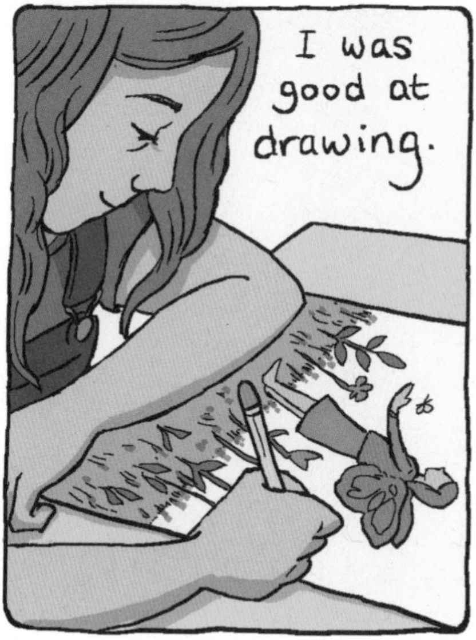
I was good at drawing.

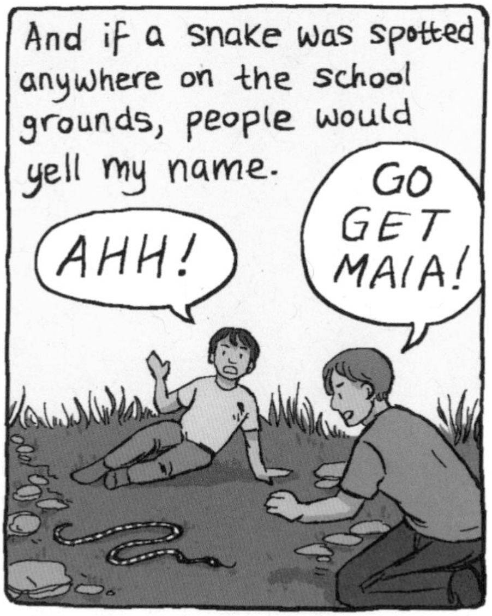
And if a snake was spotted anywhere on the school grounds, people would yell my name.
AHH!
GO GET MAIA!

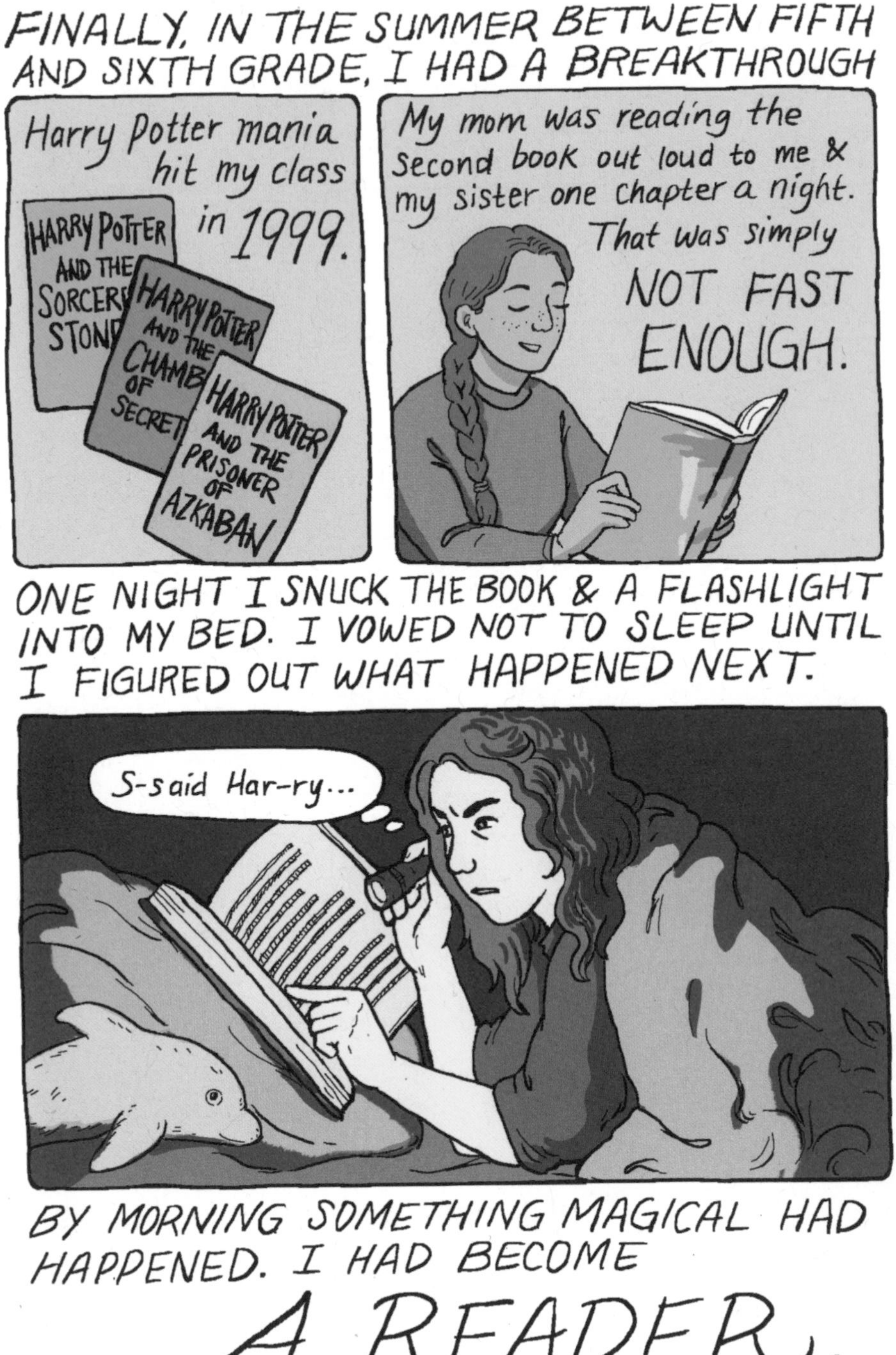
FINALLY, IN THE SUMMER BETWEEN FIFTH AND SIXTH GRADE, I HAD A BREAKTHROUGH
Harry Potter mania hit my class in 1999.
HARRY POTTER AND THE SORCERER'S STONE
HARRY POTTER AND THE CHAMBER OF SECRETS
HARRY POTTER AND THE PRISONER OF AZKABAN
My mom was reading the second book out loud to me & my sister one chapter a night.
That was simply NOT FAST ENOUGH.
ONE NIGHT I SNUCK THE BOOK & A FLASHLIGHT INTO MY BED. I VOWED NOT TO SLEEP UNTIL I FIGURED OUT WHAT HAPPENED NEXT.
S-said Har-ry...
BY MORNING SOMETHING MAGICAL HAD HAPPENED. I HAD BECOME
A READER.

A MUCH LESS WELCOME CHANGE WAS JUST AROUND THE CORNER.

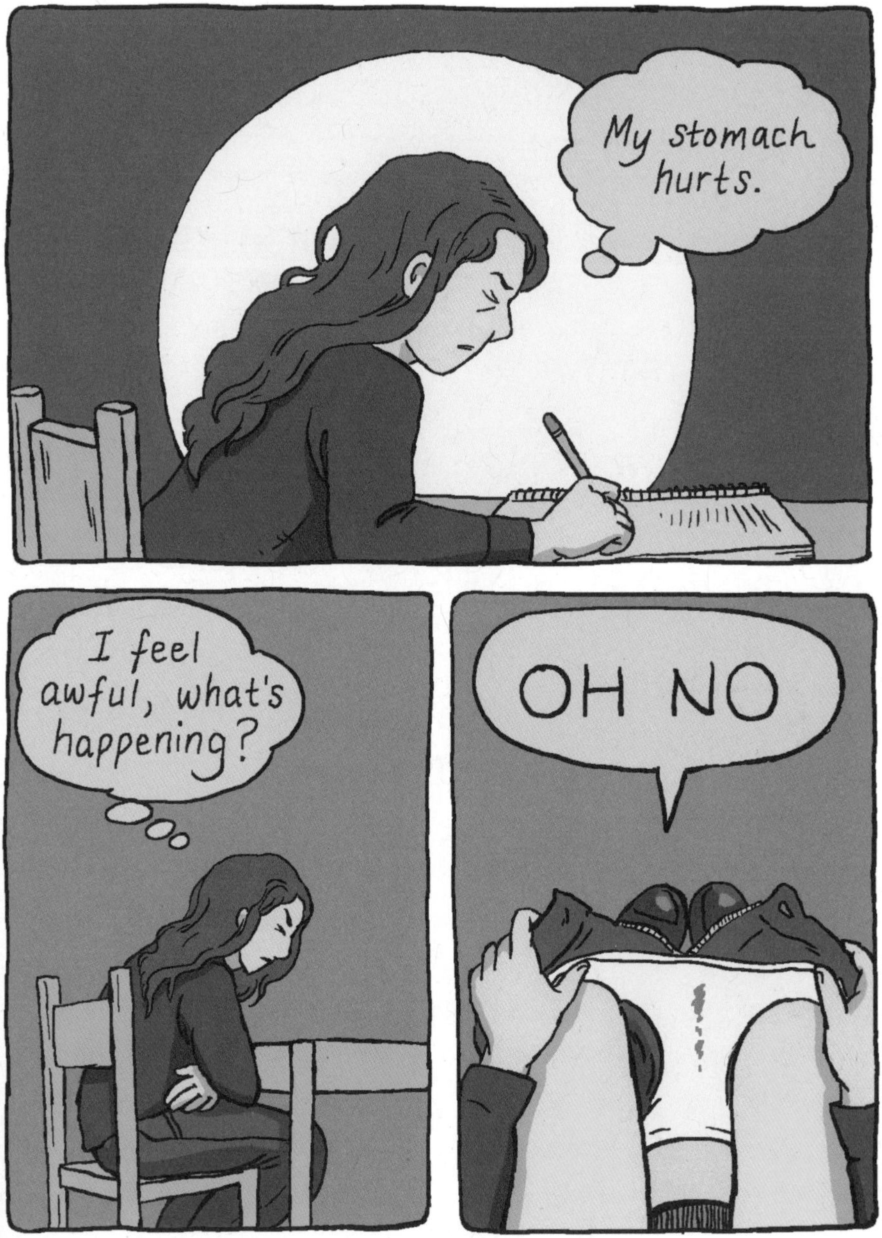
My stomach hurts.
I feel awful, what's happening?
OH NO

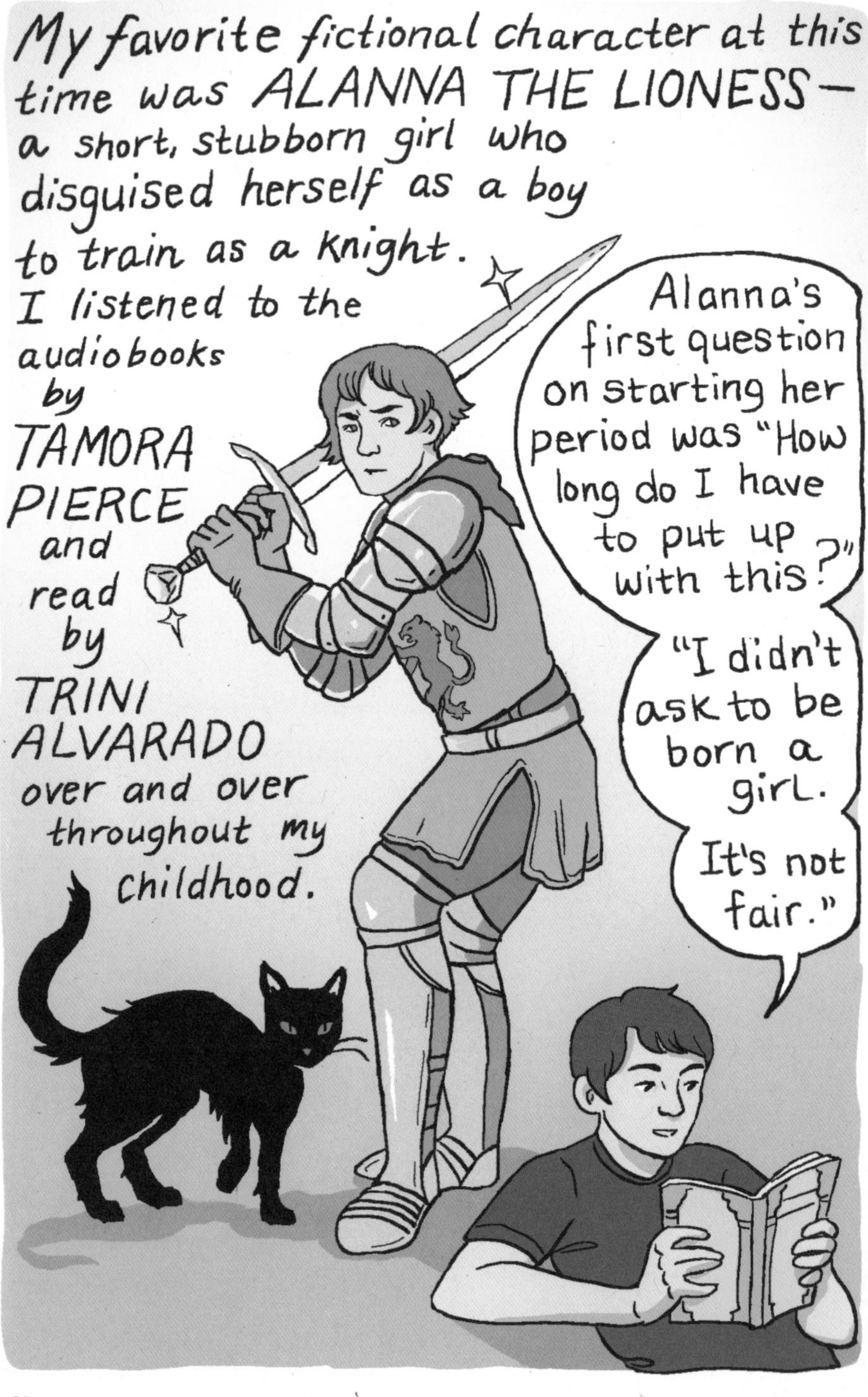
My favorite fictional character at this time was ALANNA THE LIONESS— a short, stubborn girl who disguised herself as a boy to train as a knight.
I listened to the audiobooks by TAMORA PIERCE and read by TRINI ALVARADO over and over throughout my childhood.
Alanna's first question on starting her period was "How long do I have to put up with this?"
"I didn't ask to be born a girl.
It's not fair."

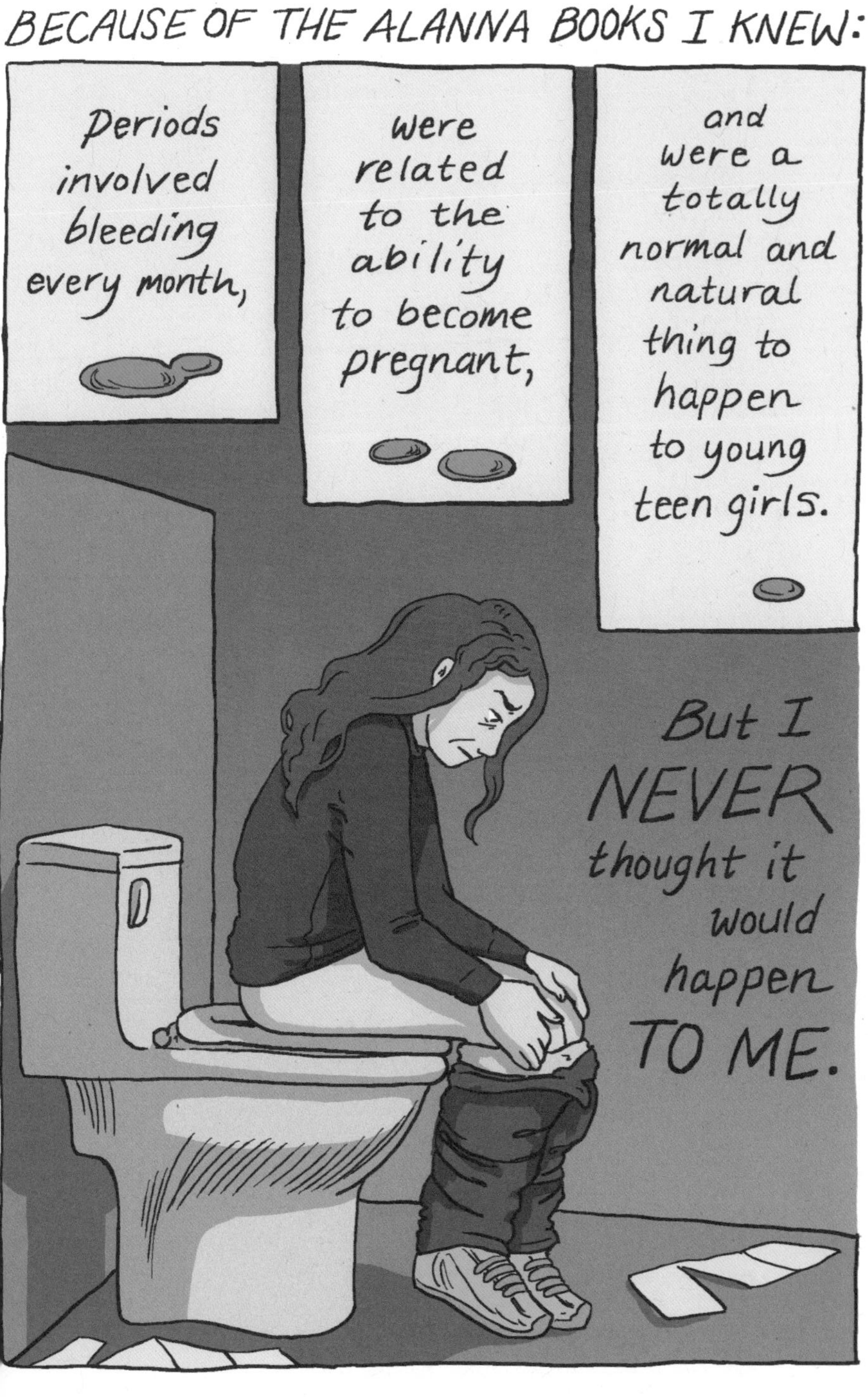
BECAUSE OF THE ALANNA BOOKS I KNEW:
Periods involved bleeding every month,
were related to the ability to become pregnant,
and were a totally normal and natural thing to happen to young teen girls.
But I NEVER thought it would happen TO ME.

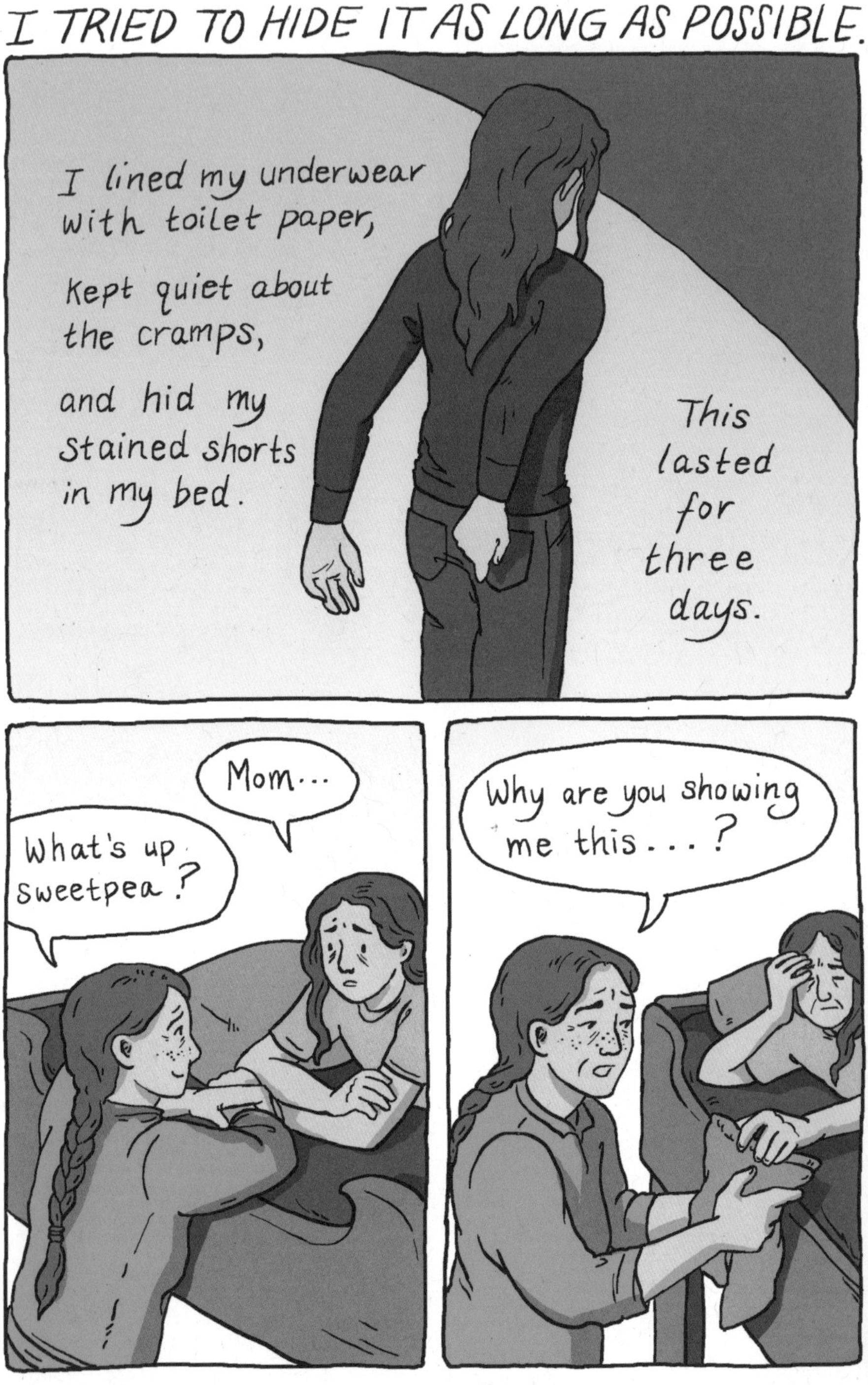
I TRIED TO HIDE IT AS LONG AS POSSIBLE.
I lined my underwear with toilet paper,
Kept quiet about the cramps,
and hid my stained shorts in my bed.
This lasted for three days.
Mom...
What's up sweetpea?
Why are you showing me this...?

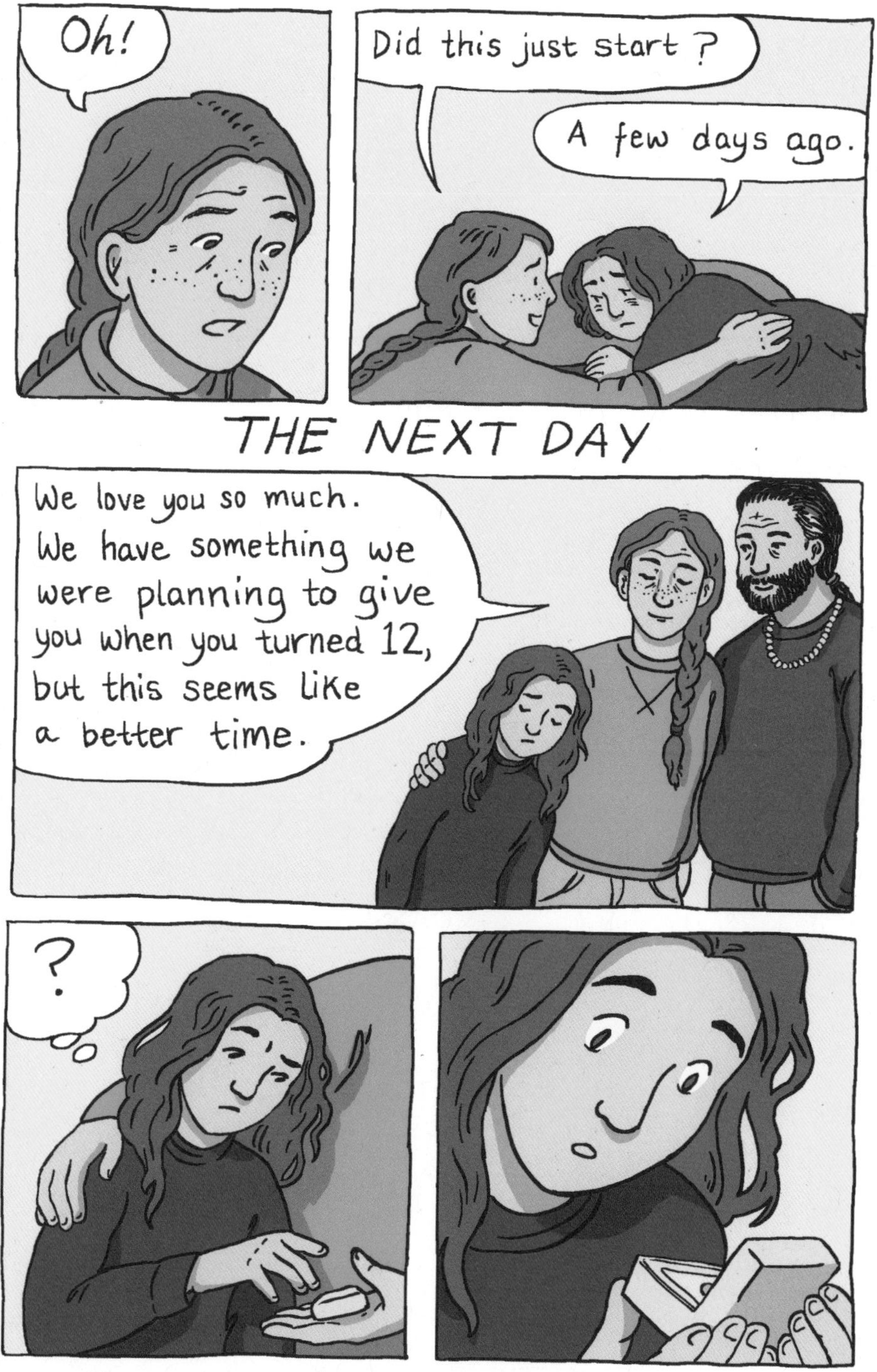
Oh!
Did this just start?
A few days ago.
THE NEXT DAY
We love you so much. We have something we were planning to give you when you turned 12, but this seems like a better time.
?

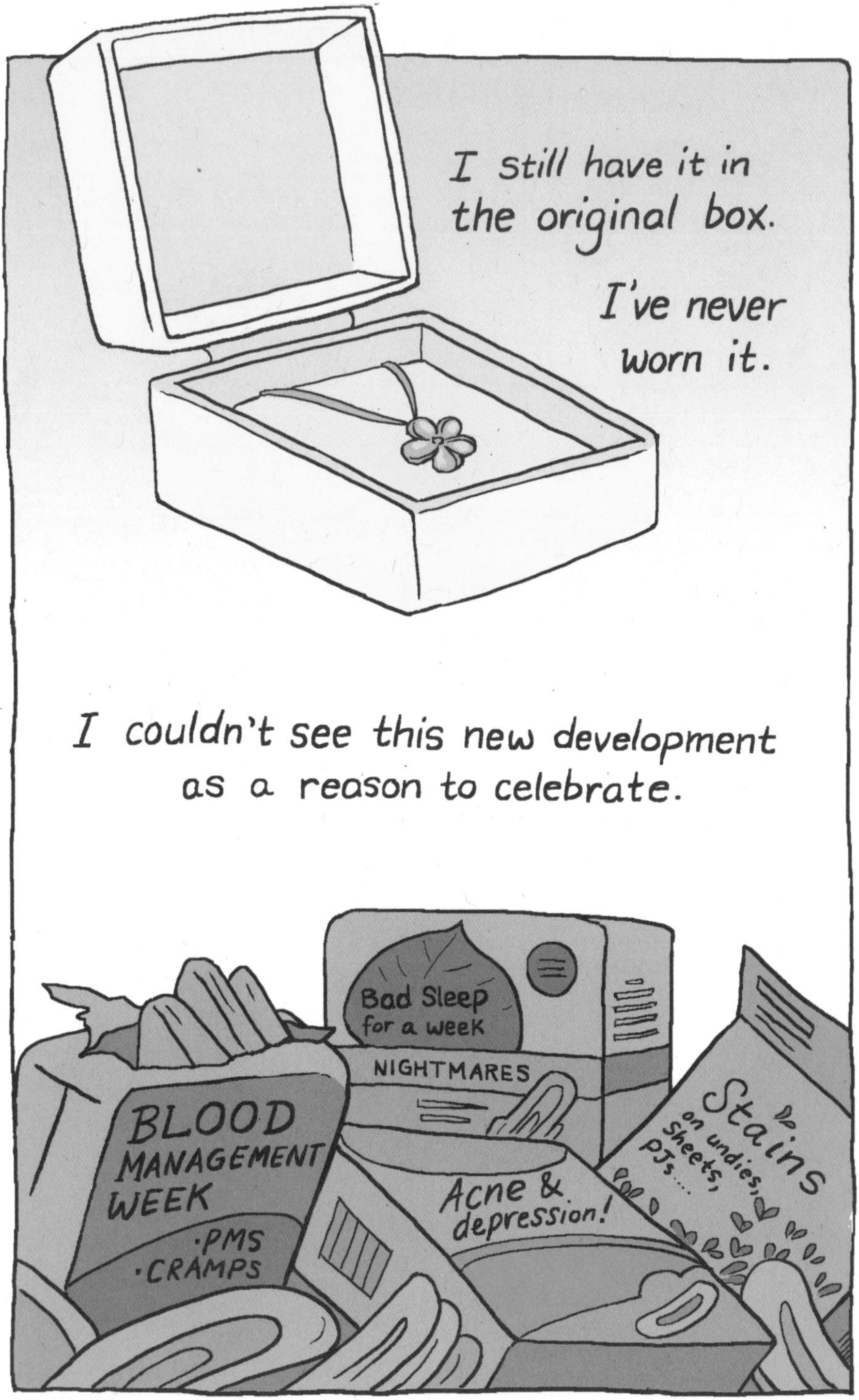
I still have it in the original box.
I've never worn it.
I couldn't see this new development as a reason to celebrate.
Bad Sleep for a week
NIGHTMARES
BLOOD MANAGEMENT WEEK
·PMS
·CRAMPS
Acne & depression!
Stains
on undies, Sheets, PJs....

HIDING MY PERIOD BECAME EXTREMELY IMPORTANT TO ME.

FOR TWO ENTIRE SCHOOL YEARS I SUCCESSFULLY AVOIDED EVER USING A SCHOOL BATHROOM.

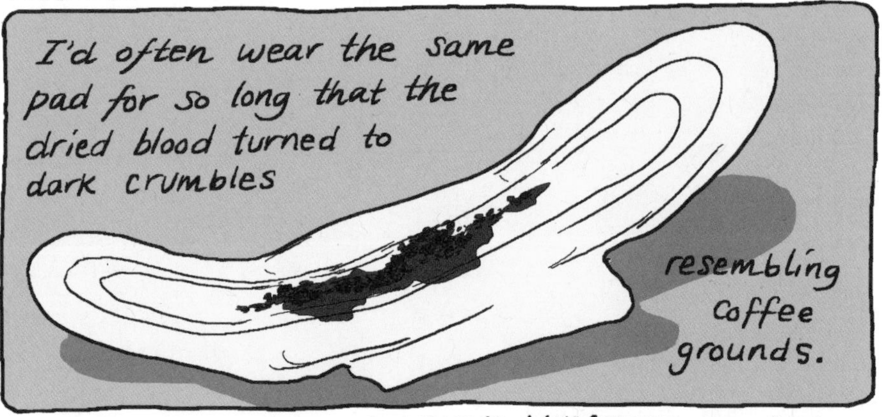
I'd often wear the same pad for so long that the dried blood turned to dark crumbles
resembling coffee grounds.

TO THIS DAY A HUGE NUMBER OF MY NIGHTMARES INVOLVE MENSTRUAL BLOOD.

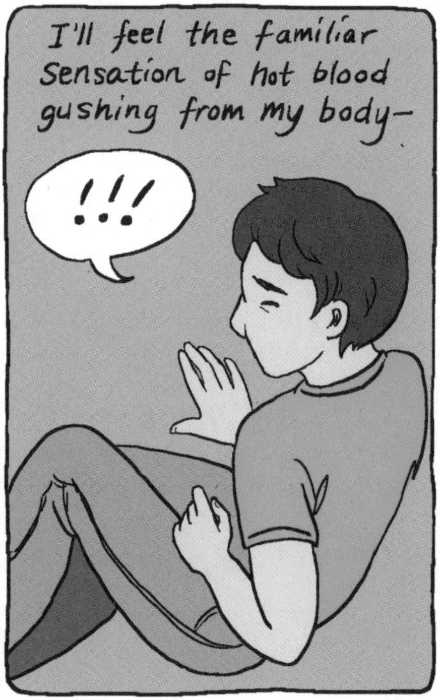
I'll feel the familiar sensation of hot blood gushing from my body–
!!!

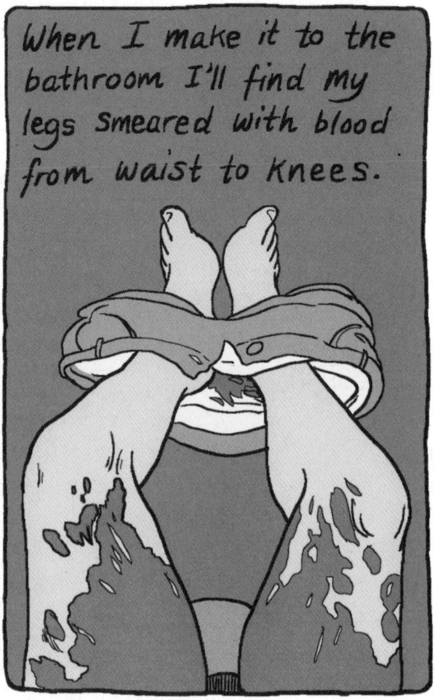
When I make it to the bathroom I'll find my legs smeared with blood from waist to knees.

OF COURSE I NEVER HAVE A PAD OR CLEAN CLOTHES.

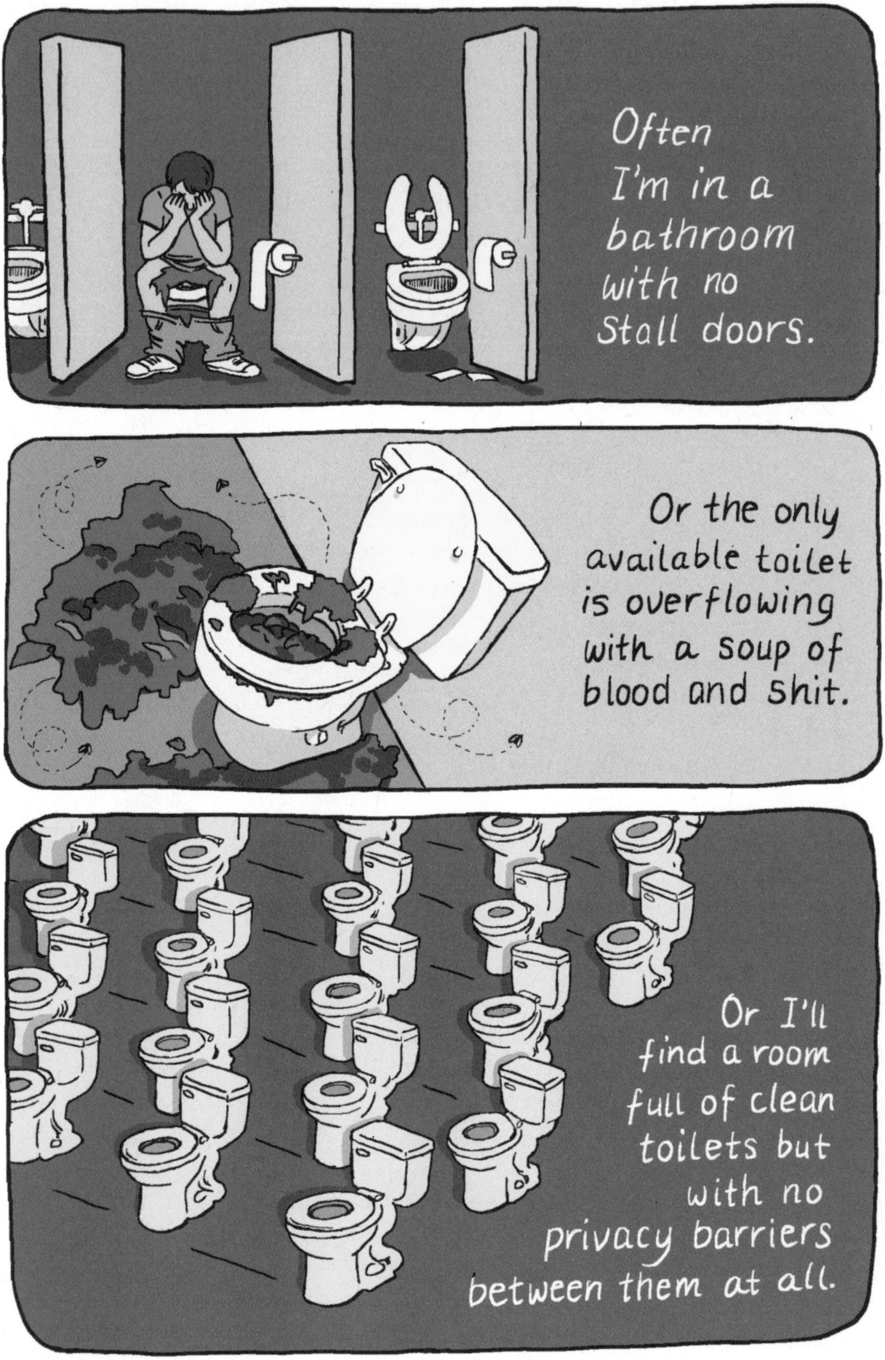
Often I'm in a bathroom with no Stall doors.
Or the only available toilet is overflowing with a soup of blood and shit.
Or I'll find a room full of clean toilets but with no privacy barriers between them at all.

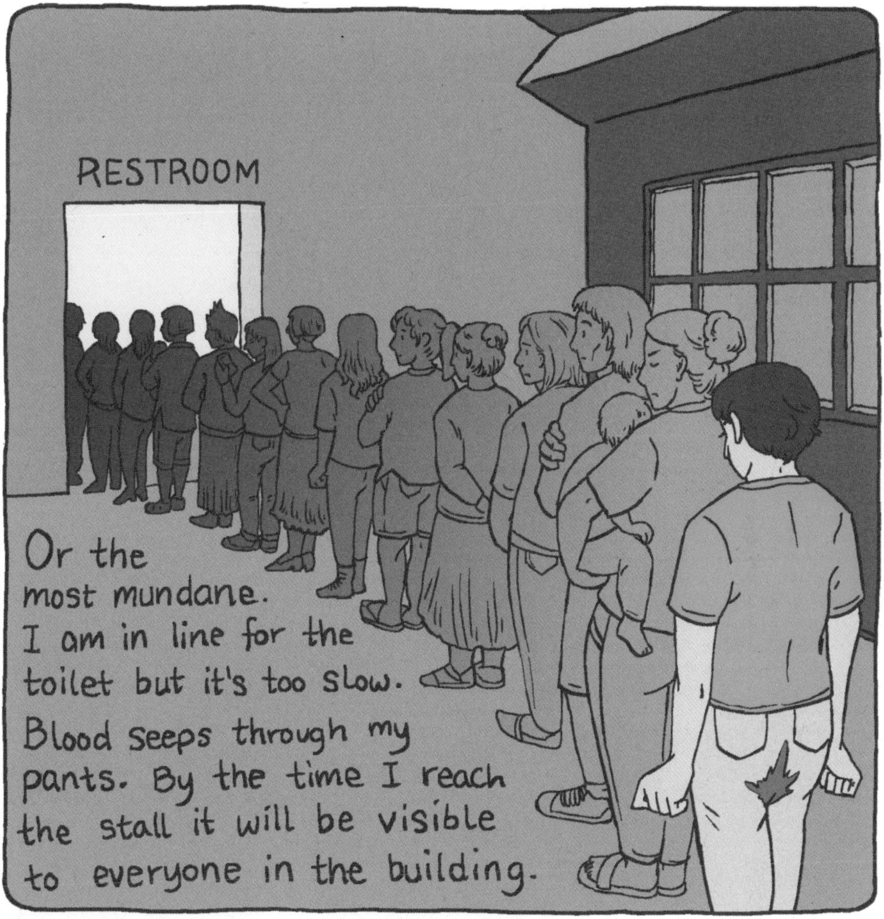
RESTROOM
Or the most mundane. I am in line for the toilet but it's too slow. Blood seeps through my pants. By the time I reach the stall it will be visible to everyone in the building.

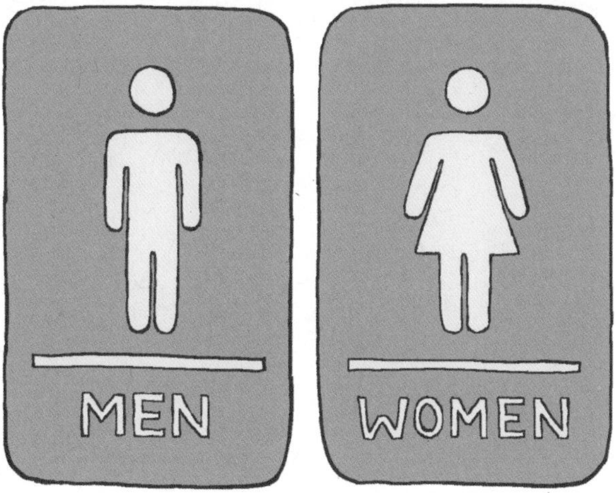
MEN
WOMEN

IT'S AMAZING I NEVER DEVELOPED A URINARY TRACT INFECTION.

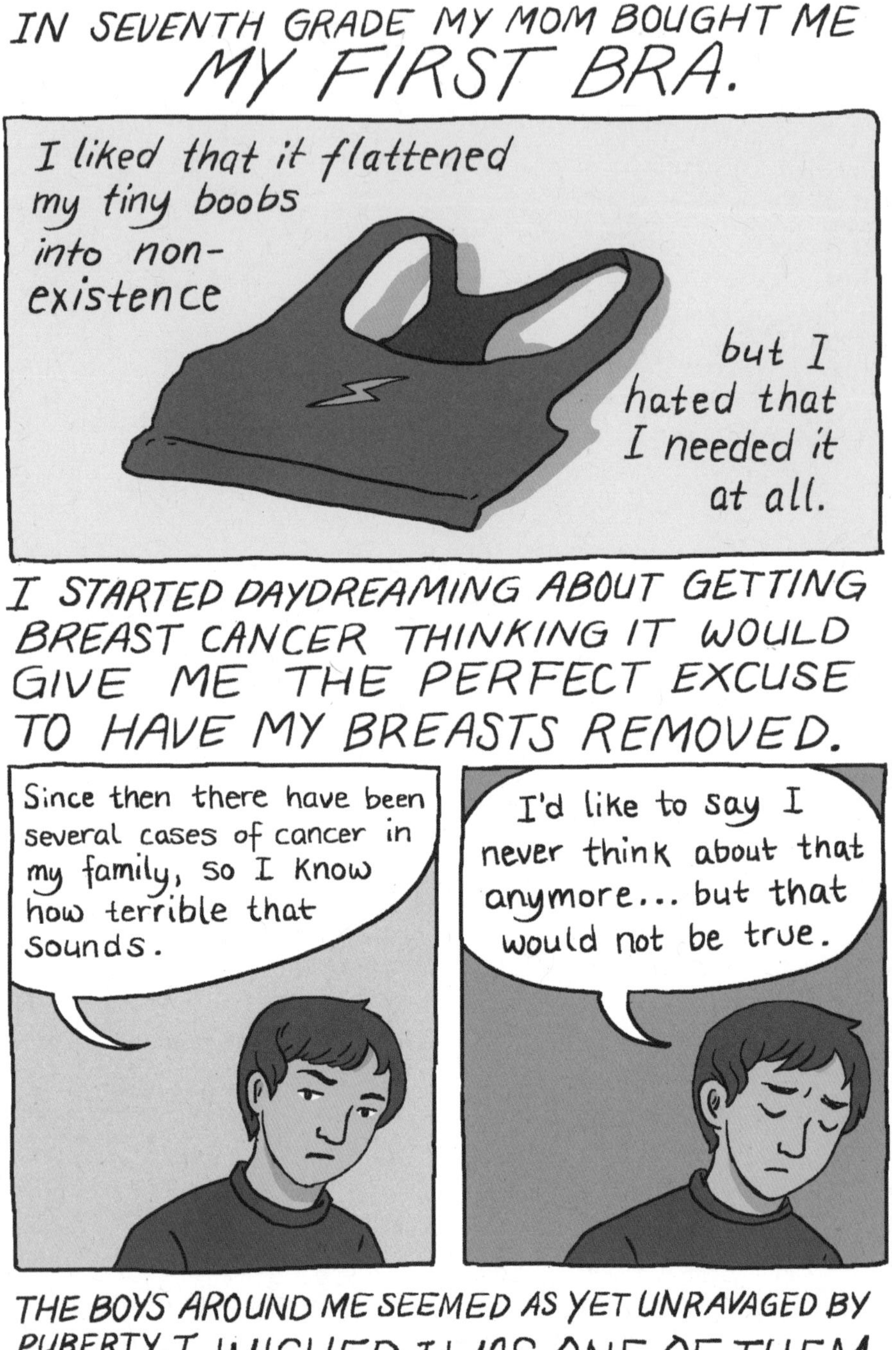
IN SEVENTH GRADE MY MOM BOUGHT ME MY FIRST BRA.
I liked that it flattened my tiny boobs into non-existence
but I hated that I needed it at all.
I STARTED DAYDREAMING ABOUT GETTING BREAST CANCER THINKING IT WOULD GIVE ME THE PERFECT EXCUSE TO HAVE MY BREASTS REMOVED.
Since then there have been several cases of cancer in my family, so I know how terrible that sounds.
I'd like to say I never think about that anymore... but that would not be true.
THE BOYS AROUND ME SEEMED AS YET UNRAVAGED BY PUBERTY. I WISHED I WAS ONE OF THEM.

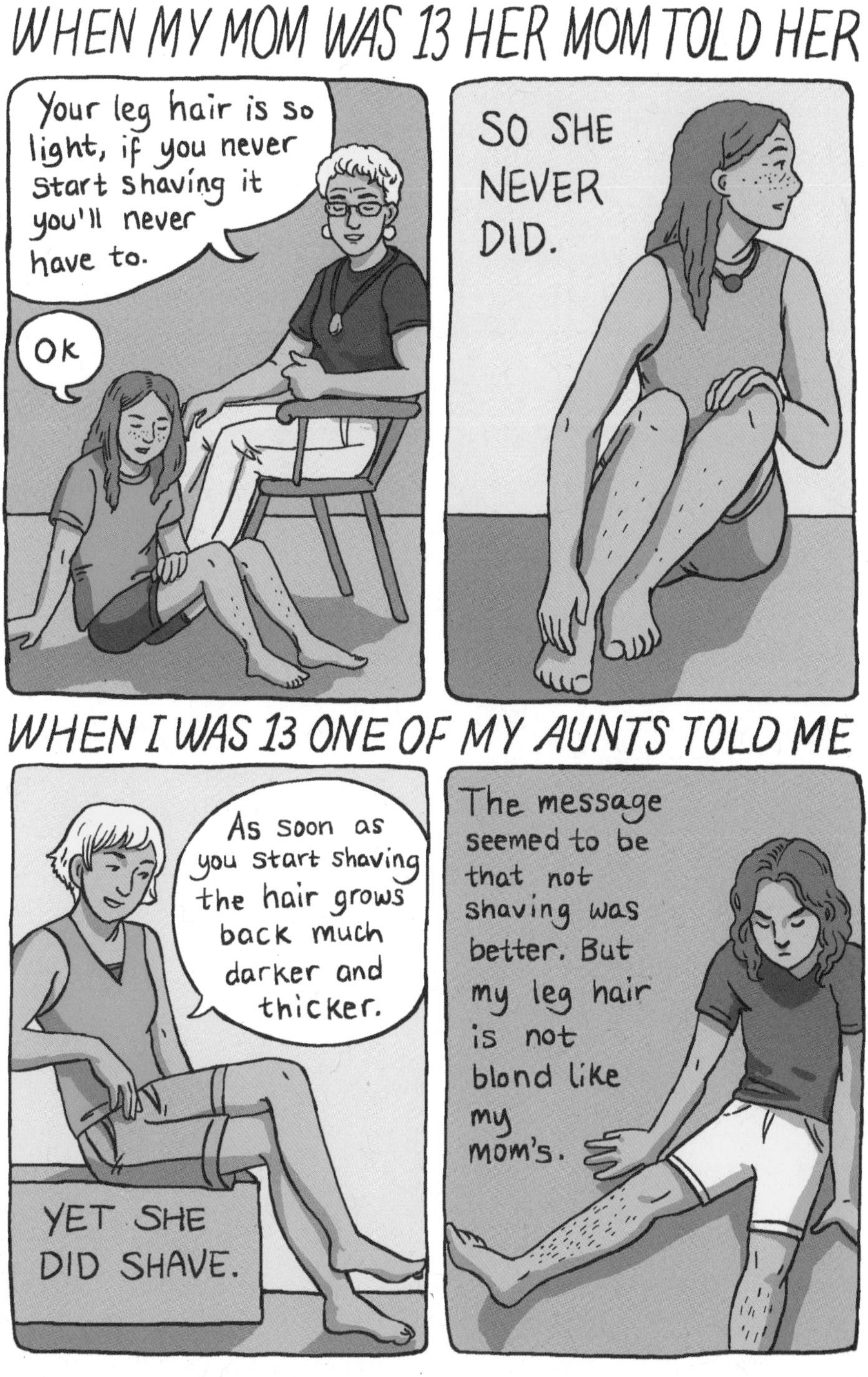
WHEN MY MOM WAS 13 HER MOM TOLD HER
Your leg hair is so light, if you never start shaving it you'll never have to.
Ok
SO SHE NEVER DID.
WHEN I WAS 13 ONE OF MY AUNTS TOLD ME
As soon as you start shaving the hair grows back much darker and thicker.
YET SHE DID SHAVE.
The message seemed to be that not shaving was better. But my leg hair is not blond like my mom's.

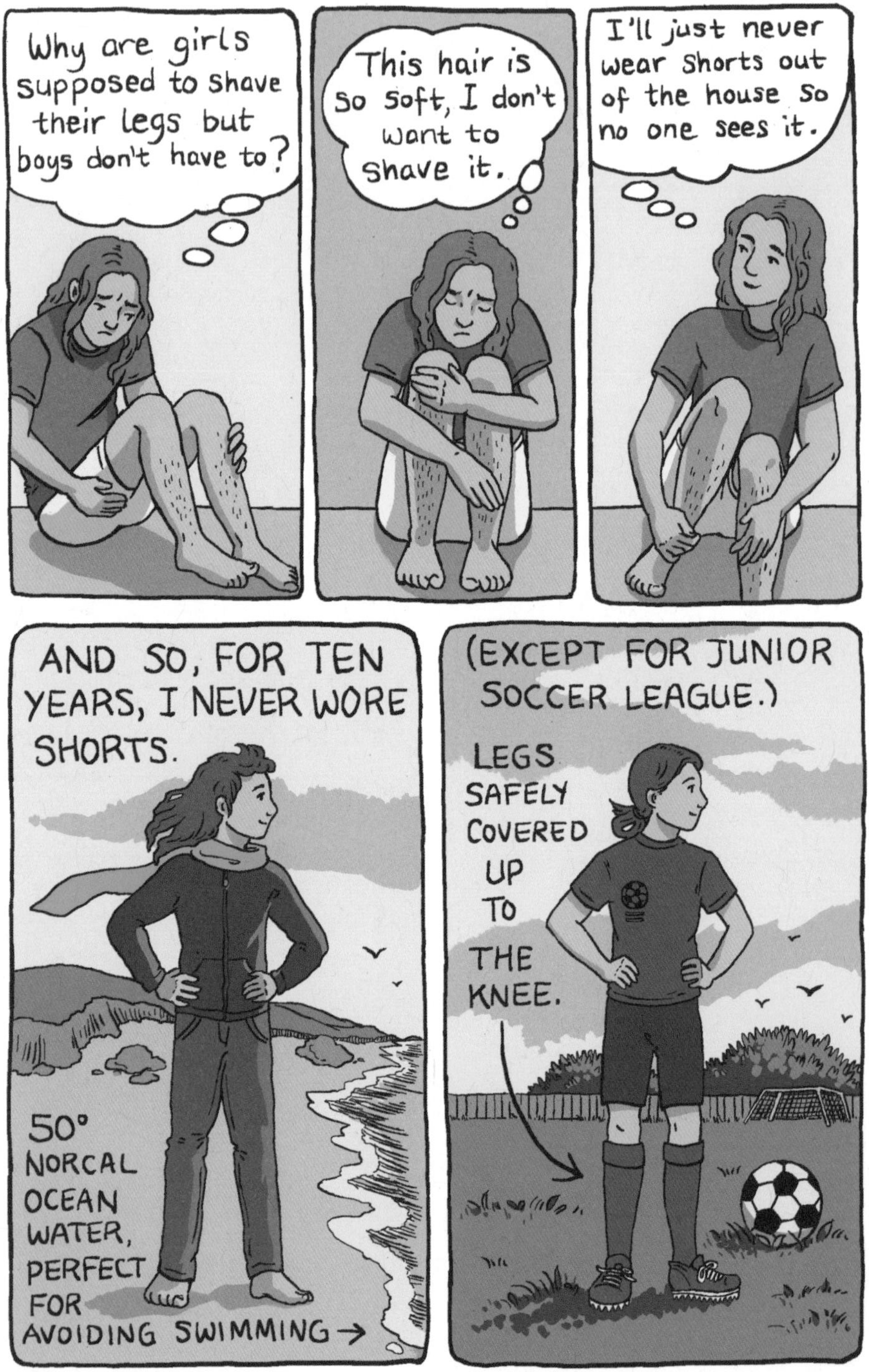
Why are girls supposed to shave their legs but boys don't have to?
This hair is so soft, I don't want to shave it.
I'll just never wear shorts out of the house so no one sees it.
AND SO, FOR TEN YEARS, I NEVER WORE SHORTS.
50° NORCAL OCEAN WATER, PERFECT FOR AVOIDING SWIMMING →
(EXCEPT FOR JUNIOR SOCCER LEAGUE.)
LEGS SAFELY COVERED UP TO THE KNEE.

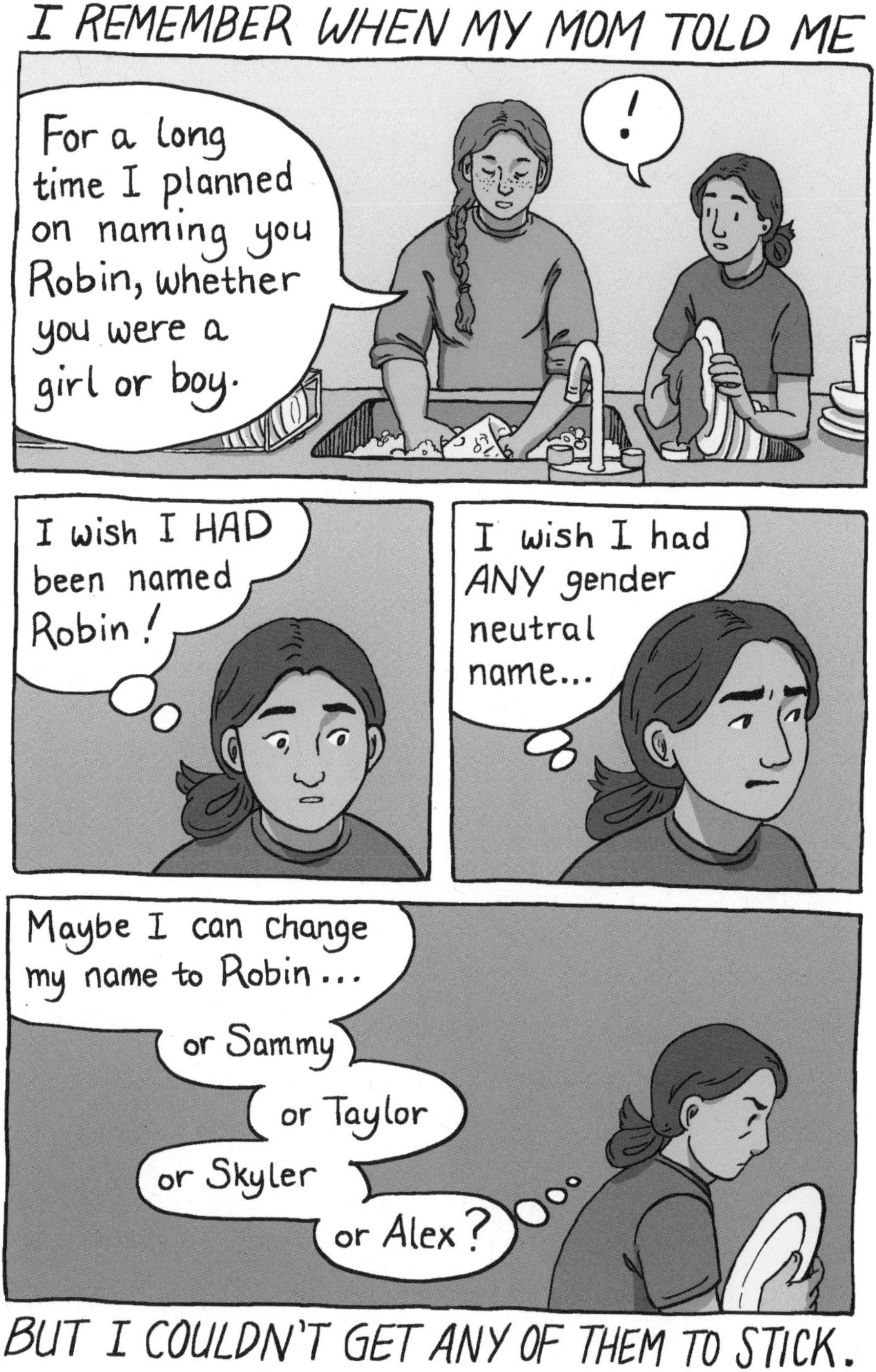
I REMEMBER WHEN MY MOM TOLD ME
For a long time I planned on naming you Robin, whether you were a girl or boy.
!
I wish I HAD been named Robin!
I wish I had ANY gender neutral name...
Maybe I can change my name to Robin...
or Sammy
or Taylor
or Skyler
or Alex?
BUT I COULDN'T GET ANY OF THEM TO STICK.

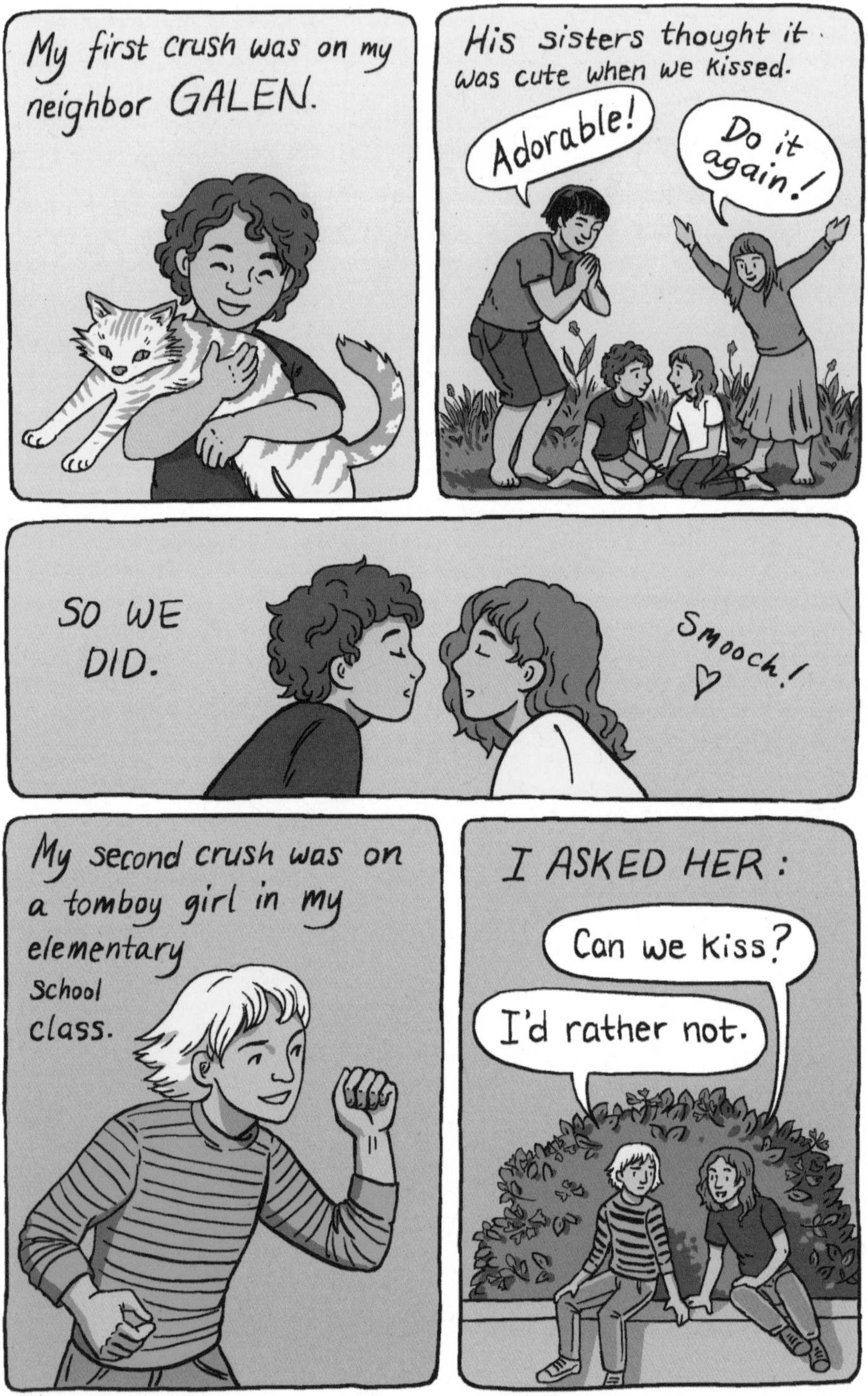
My first crush was on my neighbor GALEN.
His sisters thought it was cute when we kissed.
Adorable!
Do it again!
SO WE DID.
Smooch!
My second crush was on a tomboy girl in my elementary school class.
I ASKED HER:
Can we kiss?
I'd rather not.

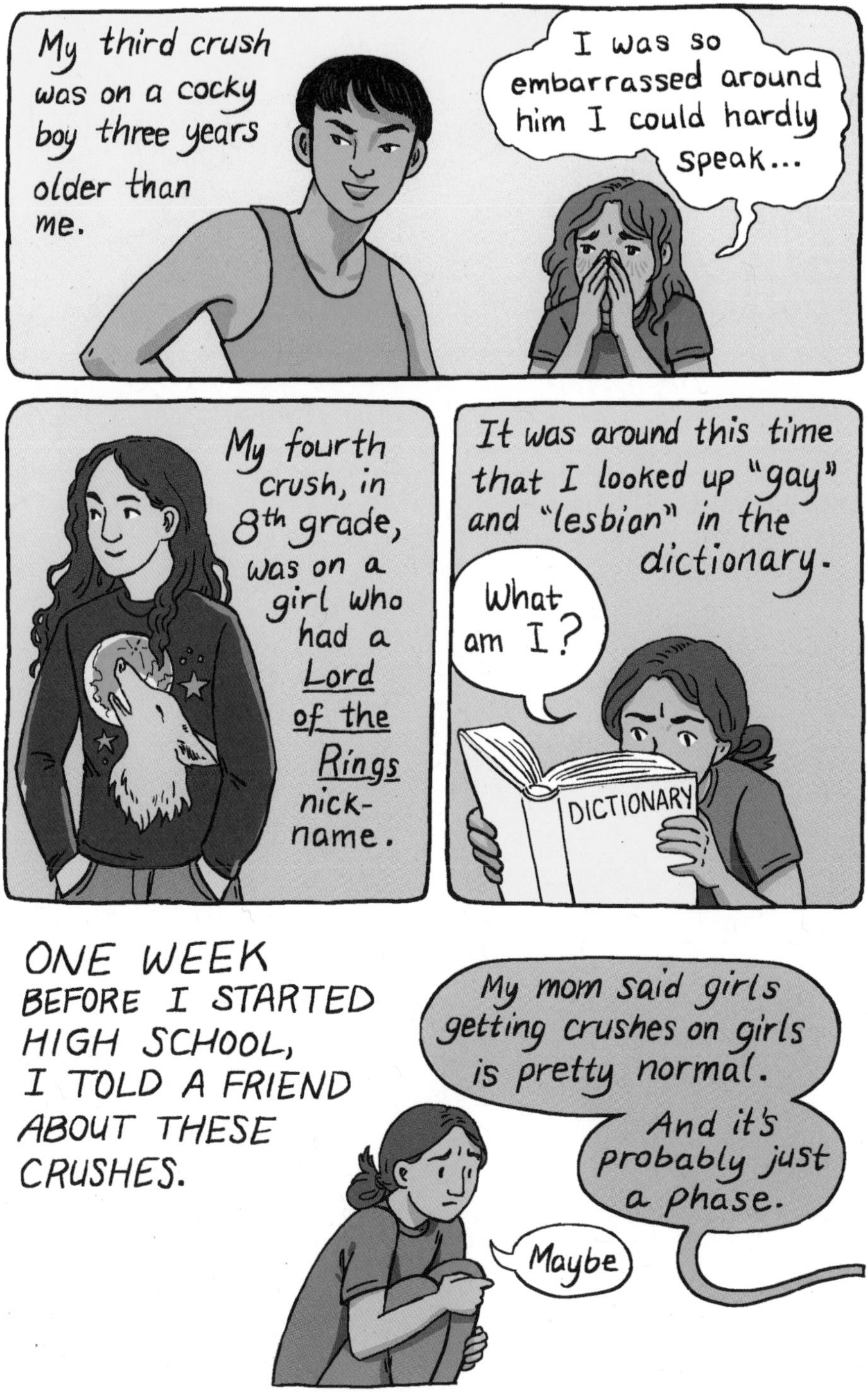
My third crush was on a cocky boy three years older than me.
I was so embarrassed around him I could hardly speak...
My fourth crush, in 8th grade, was on a girl who had a Lord of the Rings nick-name.
It was around this time that I looked up "gay" and "lesbian" in the dictionary.
What am I?
DICTIONARY
ONE WEEK BEFORE I STARTED HIGH SCHOOL, I TOLD A FRIEND ABOUT THESE CRUSHES.
My mom said girls getting crushes on girls is pretty normal.
And it's probably just a phase.
Maybe

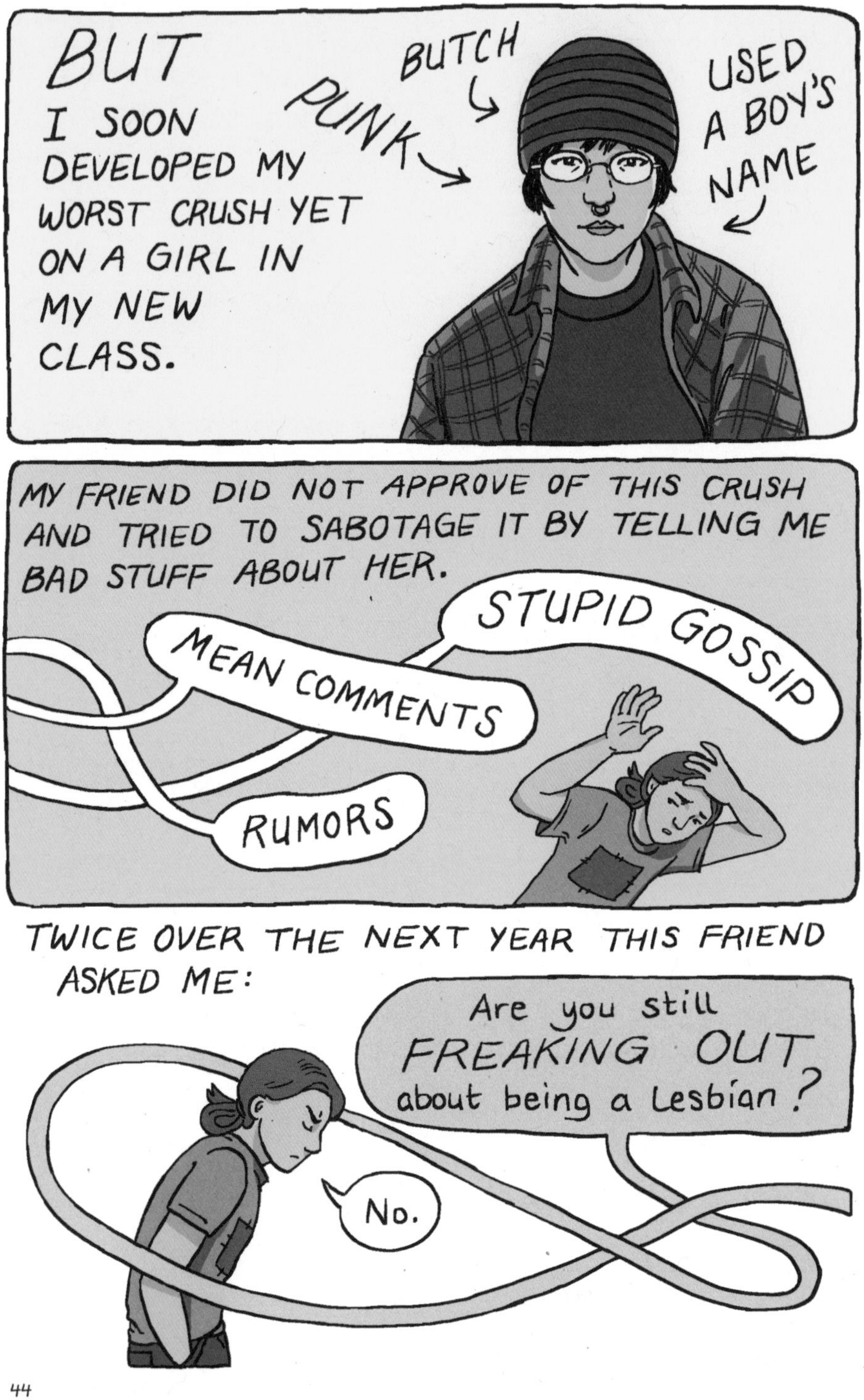
BUT I SOON DEVELOPED MY WORST CRUSH YET ON A GIRL IN MY NEW CLASS.
PUNK
BUTCH
USED A BOY'S NAME
MY FRIEND DID NOT APPROVE OF THIS CRUSH AND TRIED TO SABOTAGE IT BY TELLING ME BAD STUFF ABOUT HER.
STUPID GOSSIP
MEAN COMMENTS
RUMORS
TWICE OVER THE NEXT YEAR THIS FRIEND ASKED ME:
Are you still FREAKING OUT about being a Lesbian?
No.

AFTER SPENDING EIGHTH GRADE IN A HOMESCHOOLING PROGRAM, I WENT BACK TO WALDORF FOR HIGH SCHOOL. REQUIRED CLASSES INCLUDED:

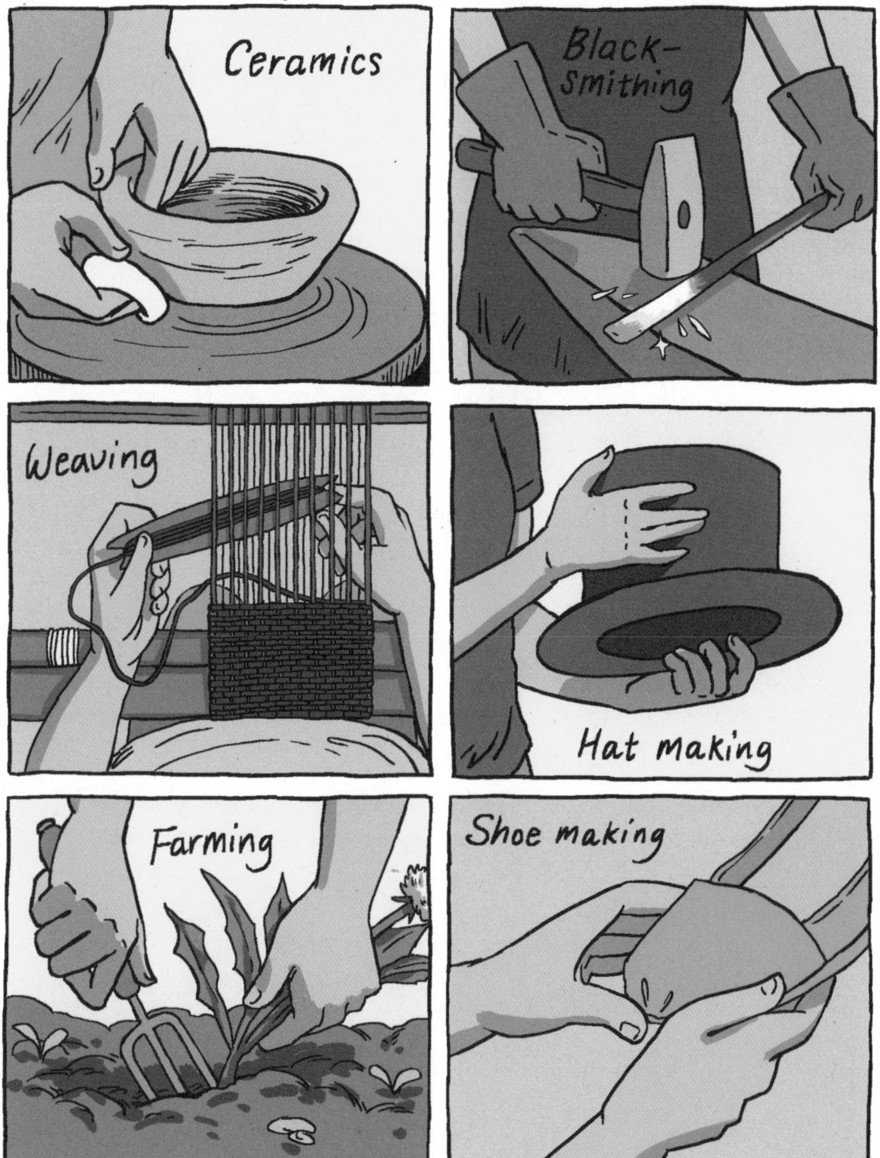

Ceramics
Black-smithing
Weaving
Hat making
Farming
Shoe making

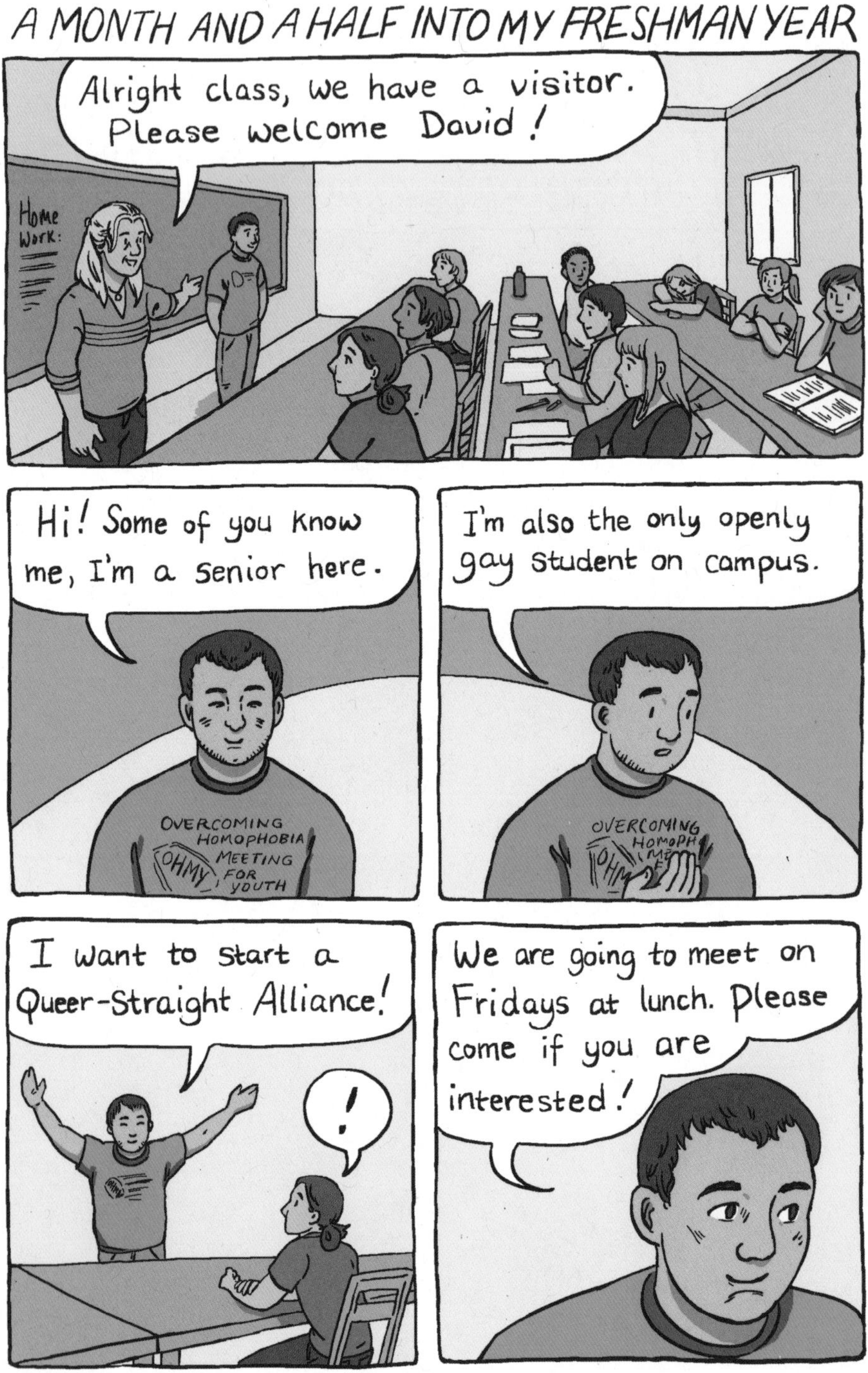
A MONTH AND A HALF INTO MY FRESHMAN YEAR
Alright class, we have a visitor. Please welcome David!
Home Work:
Hi! Some of you know me, I'm a senior here.
OVERCOMING HOMOPHOBIA MEETING FOR YOUTH
OHMY
I'm also the only openly gay student on campus.
I want to start a Queer-Straight Alliance!
!
We are going to meet on Fridays at lunch. Please come if you are interested!

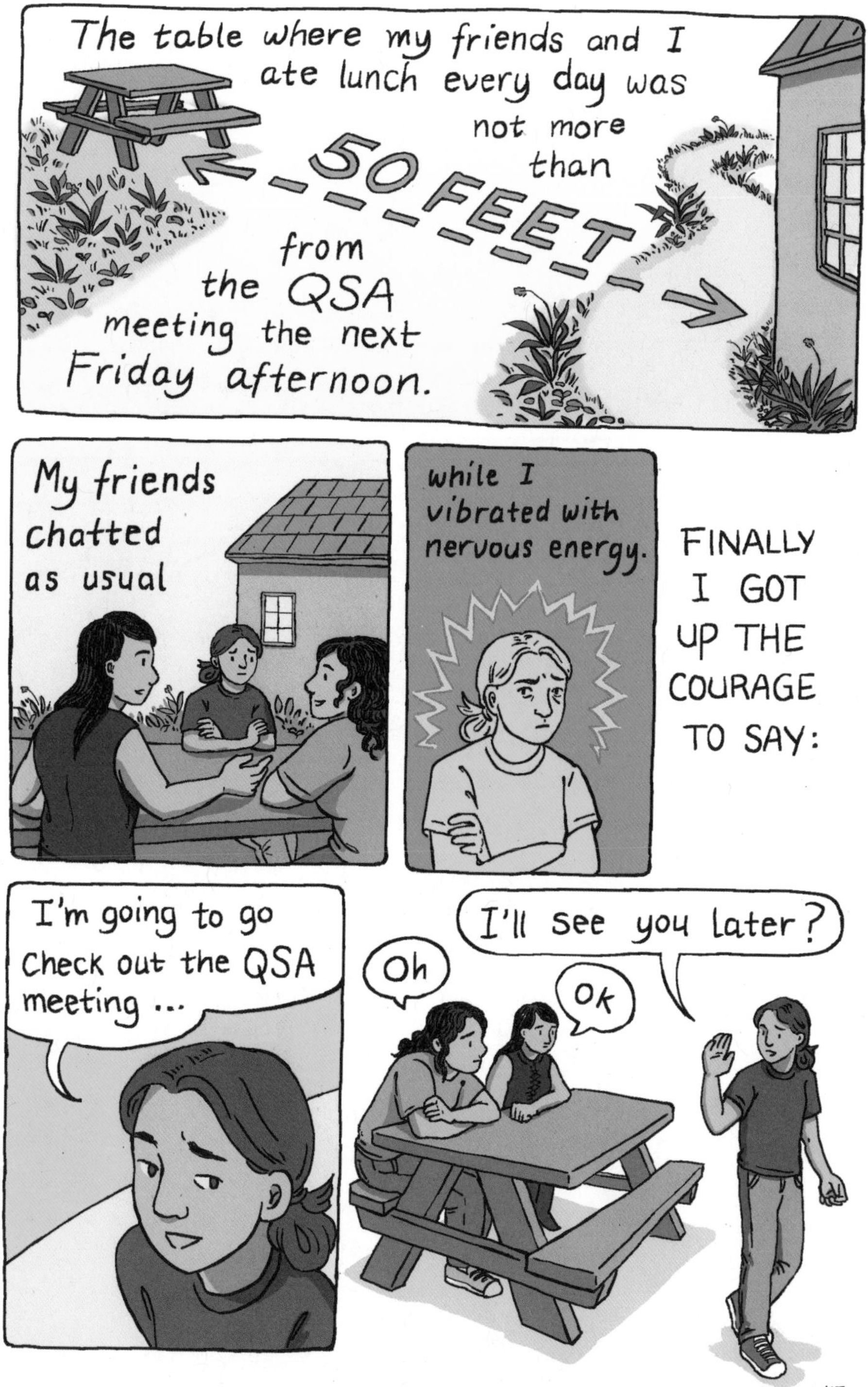
The table where my friends and I ate lunch every day was
not more than
50 FEET
from the QSA meeting the next Friday afternoon.
My friends chatted as usual
while I vibrated with nervous energy.
FINALLY I GOT UP THE COURAGE TO SAY:
I'm going to go check out the QSA meeting...
Oh
Ok
I'll see you later?

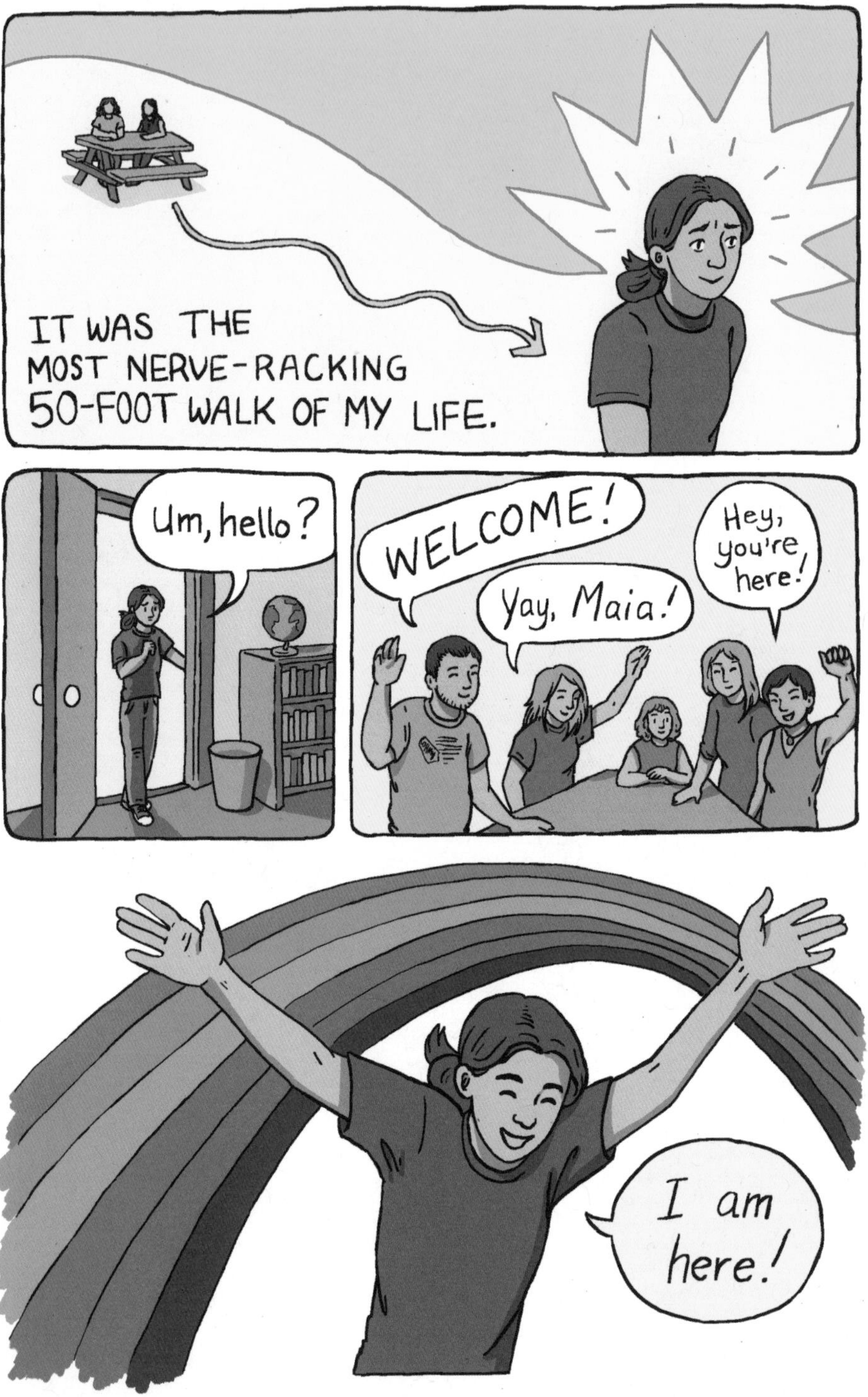
IT WAS THE MOST NERVE-RACKING 50-FOOT WALK OF MY LIFE.
Um, hello?
WELCOME!
Yay, Maia!
Hey, you're here!
I am here!

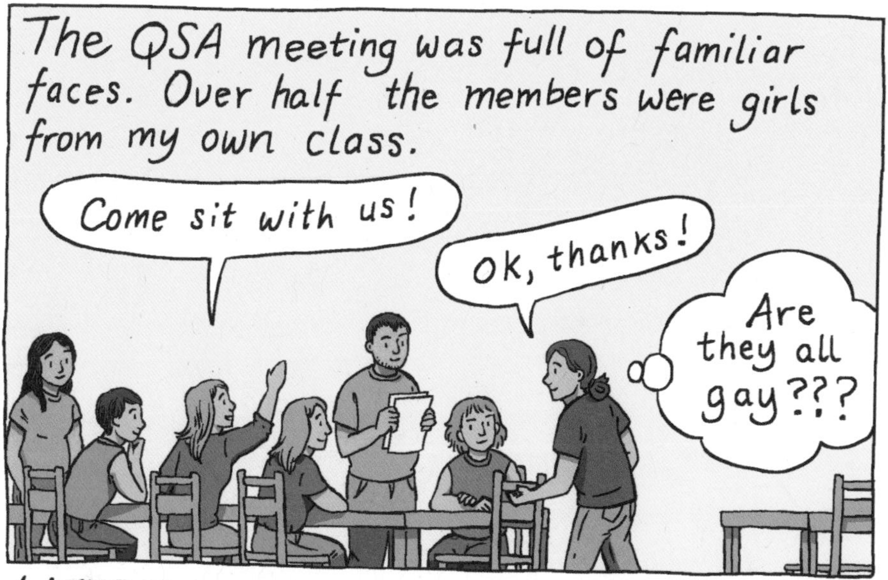
The QSA meeting was full of familiar faces. Over half the members were girls from my own class.
Come sit with us!
Ok, thanks!
Are they all gay???

LATER I WOULD LEARN THAT THREE OF THEM CAME FROM FAMILIES WITH LESBIAN MOMS; THEY AND THEIR FRIENDS CAME AS ALLIES.

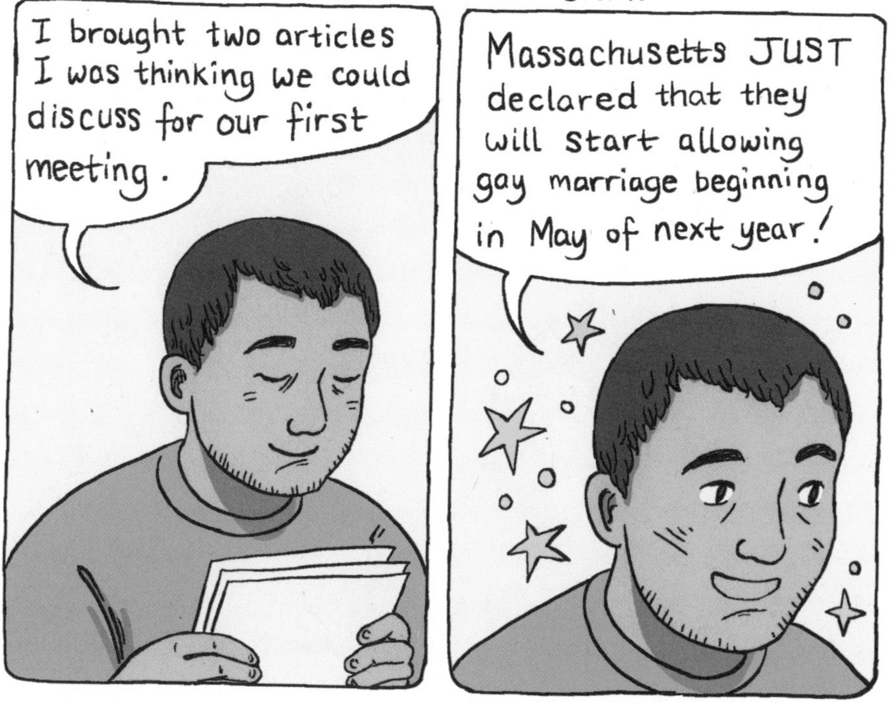
I brought two articles I was thinking we could discuss for our first meeting.
Massachusetts JUST declared that they will start allowing gay marriage beginning in May of next year!

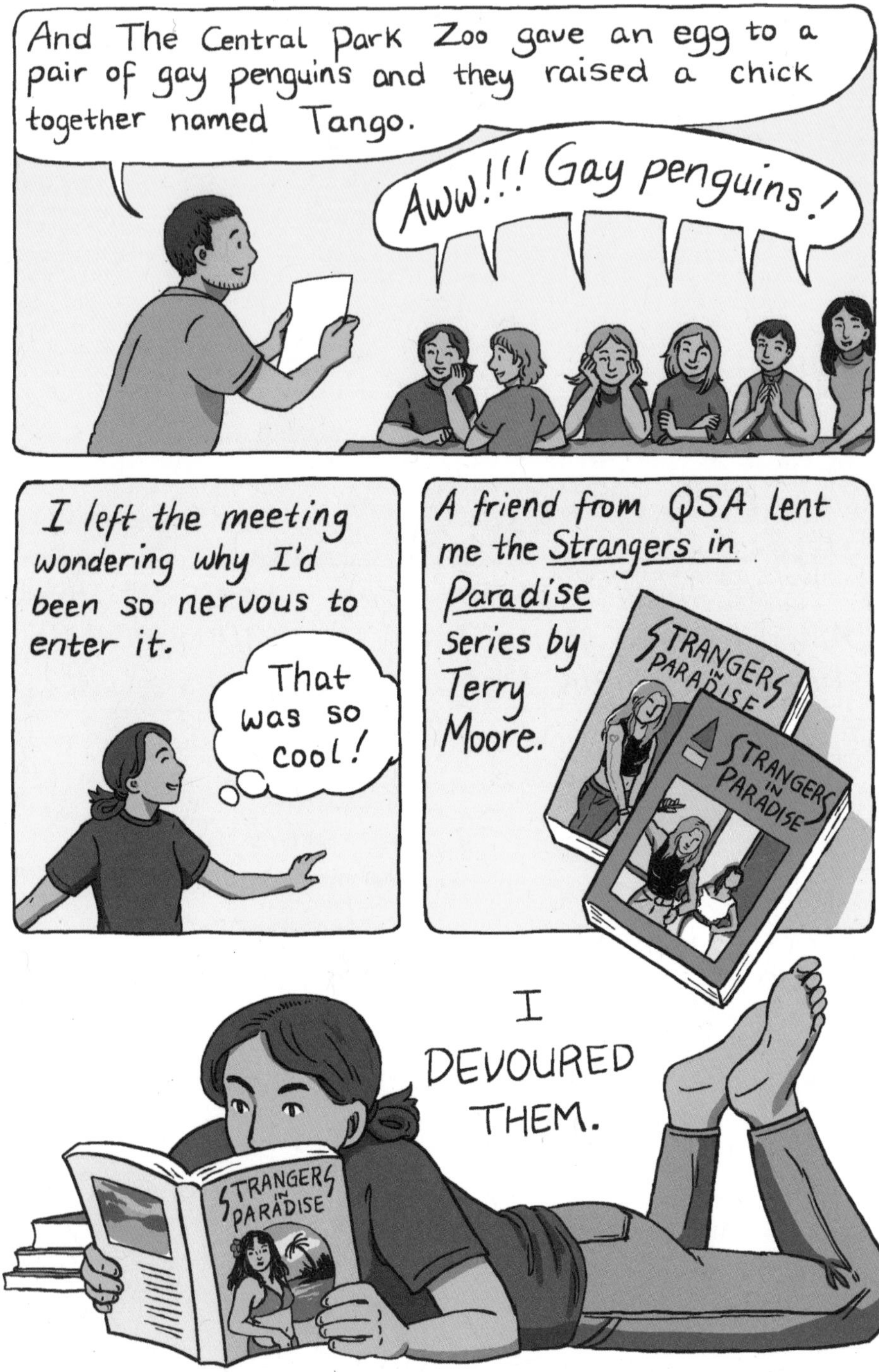
And The Central Park Zoo gave an egg to a pair of gay penguins and they raised a chick together named Tango.
Aww!!! Gay penguins!
I left the meeting wondering why I'd been so nervous to enter it.
That was so cool!
A friend from QSA lent me the Strangers in Paradise series by Terry Moore.
STRANGERS IN PARADISE
STRANGERS IN PARADISE
I DEVOURED THEM.
STRANGERS IN PARADISE

One day my best friend gave me a note:

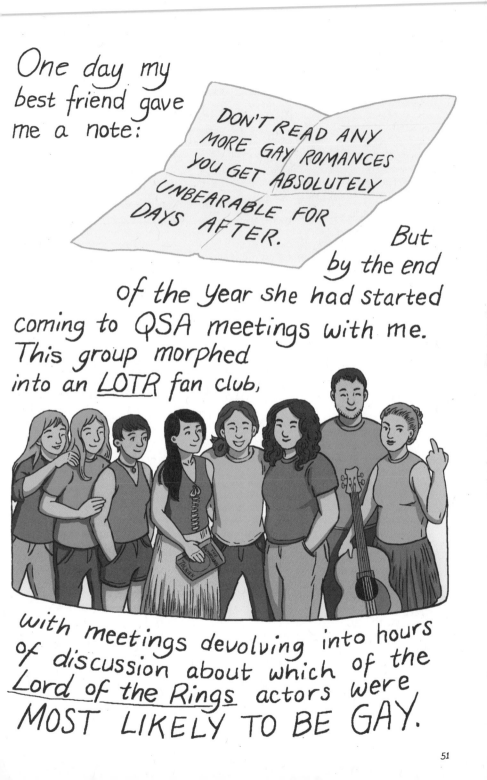

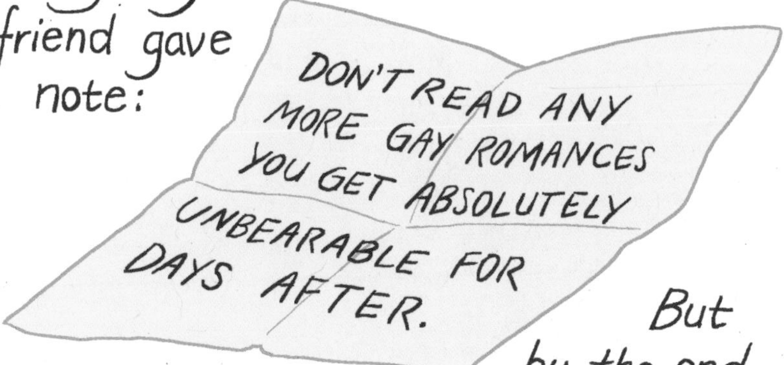
DON'T READ ANY MORE GAY ROMANCES YOU GET ABSOLUTELY UNBEARABLE FOR DAYS AFTER.

But by the end of the year she had started coming to QSA meetings with me. This group morphed into an LOTR fan club,

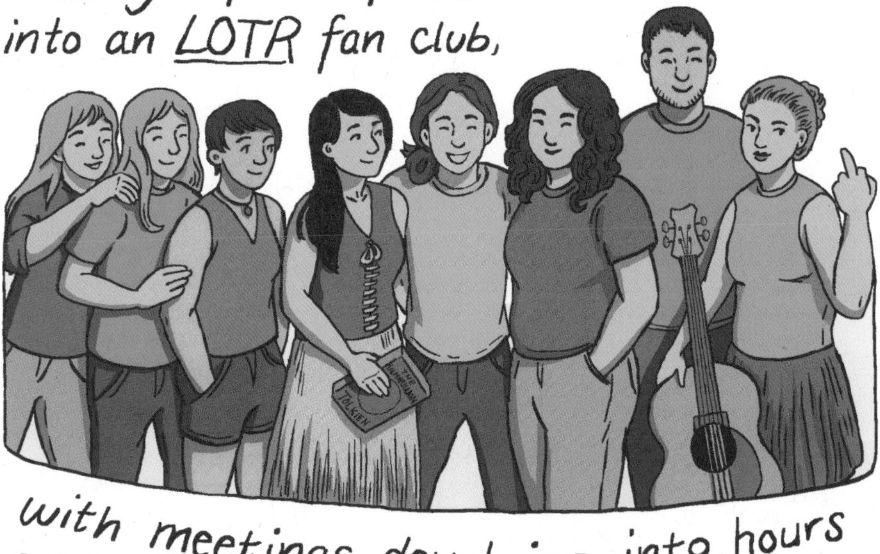
TOLKIEN

with meetings devolving into hours of discussion about which of the Lord of the Rings actors were MOST LIKELY TO BE GAY.

ONE DAY THE GUIDANCE COUNSELOR CALLED ME INTO HER OFFICE

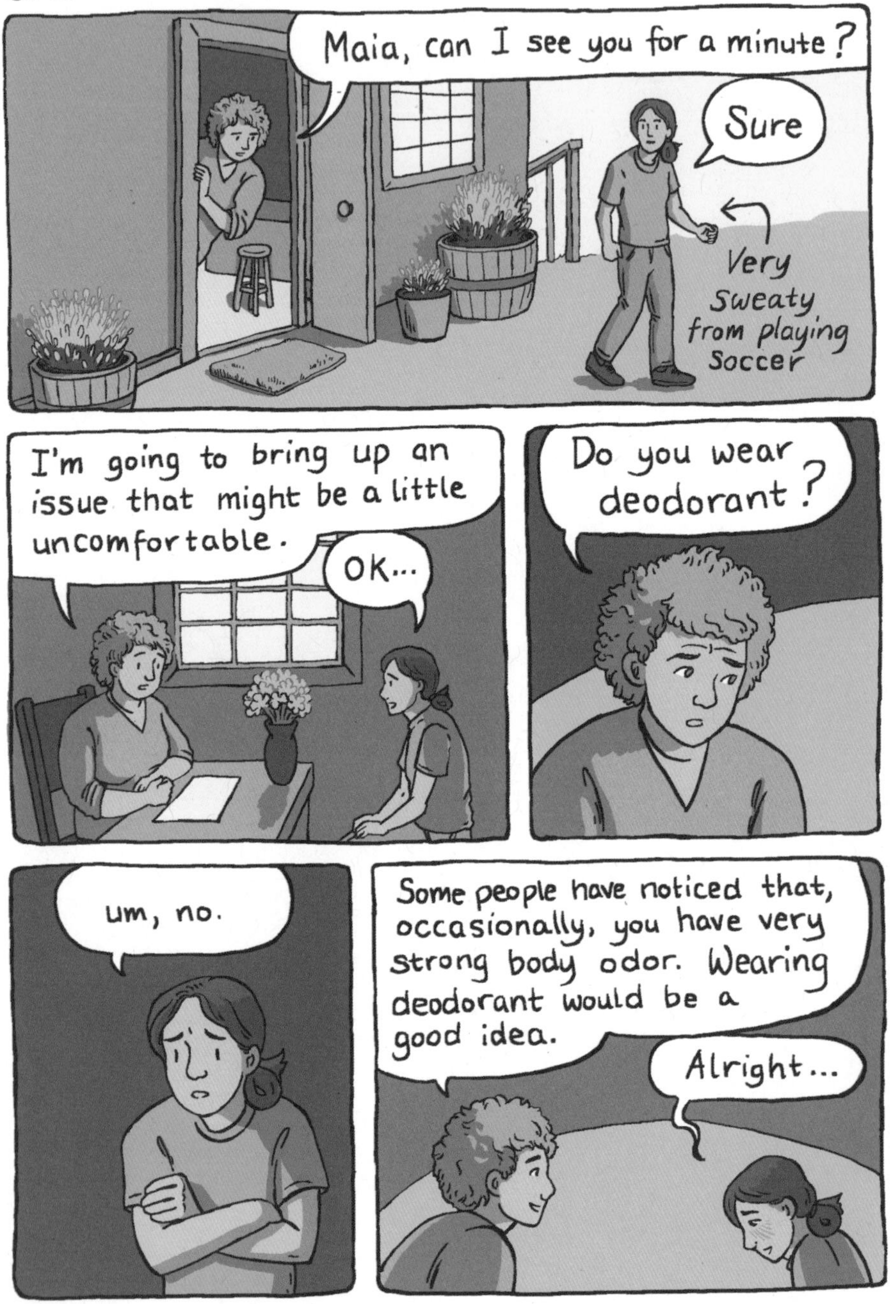
Maia, can I see you for a minute?
Sure
Very Sweaty from playing Soccer
I'm going to bring up an issue that might be a little uncomfortable.
OK...
Do you wear deodorant?
um, no.
Some people have noticed that, occasionally, you have very strong body odor. Wearing deodorant would be a good idea.
Alright...

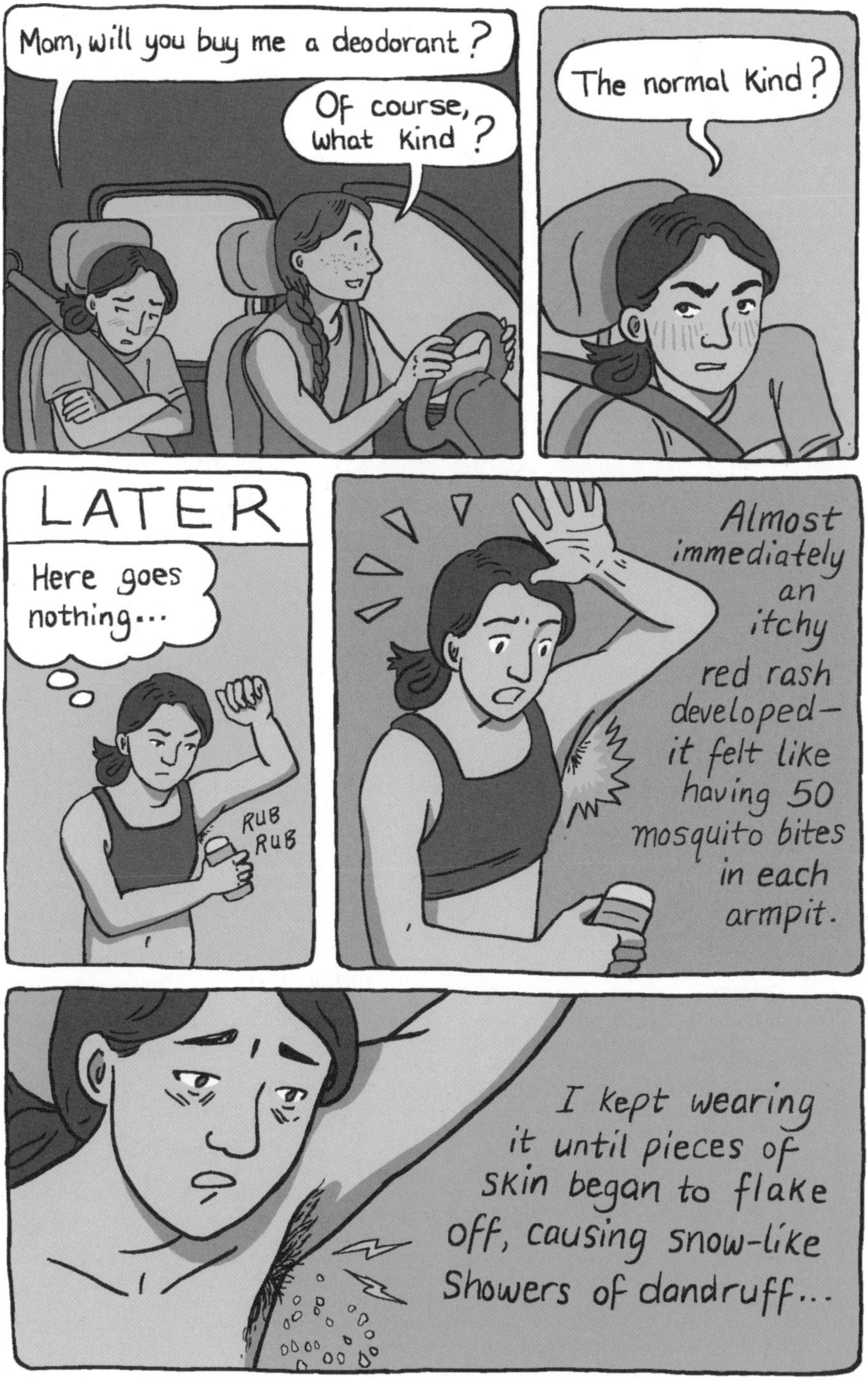
Mom, will you buy me a deodorant?
Of course, what kind?
The normal kind?
LATER
Here goes nothing...
RUB RUB
Almost immediately an itchy red rash developed—it felt like having 50 mosquito bites in each armpit.
I kept wearing it until pieces of skin began to flake off, causing snow-like showers of dandruff...

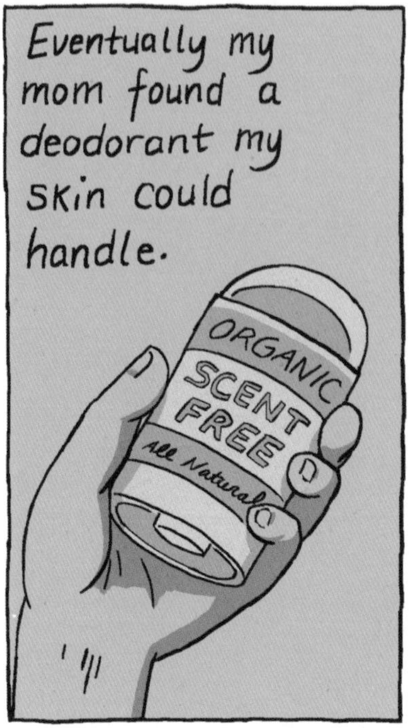
Eventually my mom found a deodorant my skin could handle.
ORGANIC
SCENT FREE
All Natural

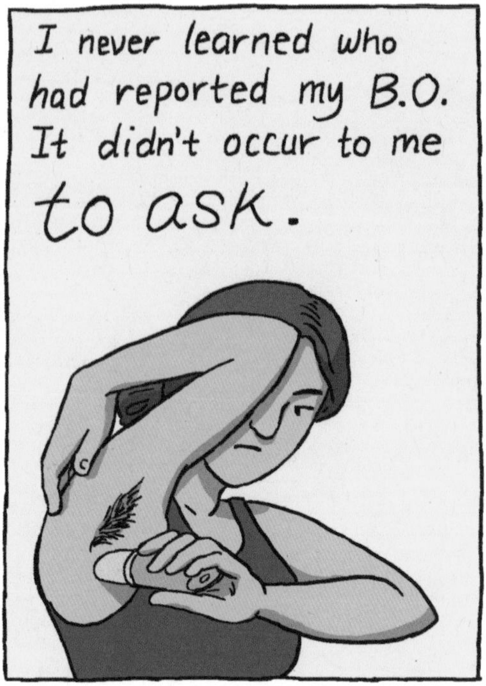
I never learned who had reported my B.O. It didn't occur to me to ask.

Probably because I didn't blame whoever it was. This was simply another example of my constant ignorance.

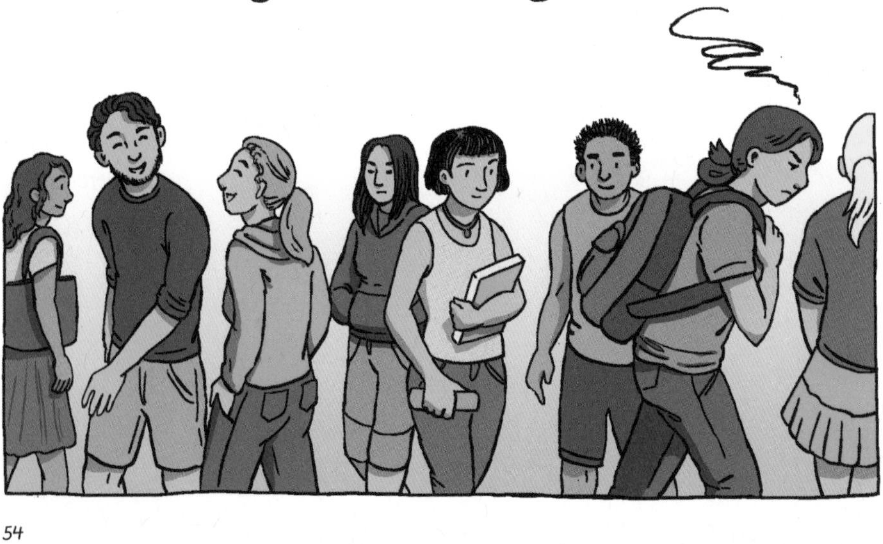

I SPENT A LOT OF TIME IN NINTH GRADE EAVESDROPPING ON MY CRUSH

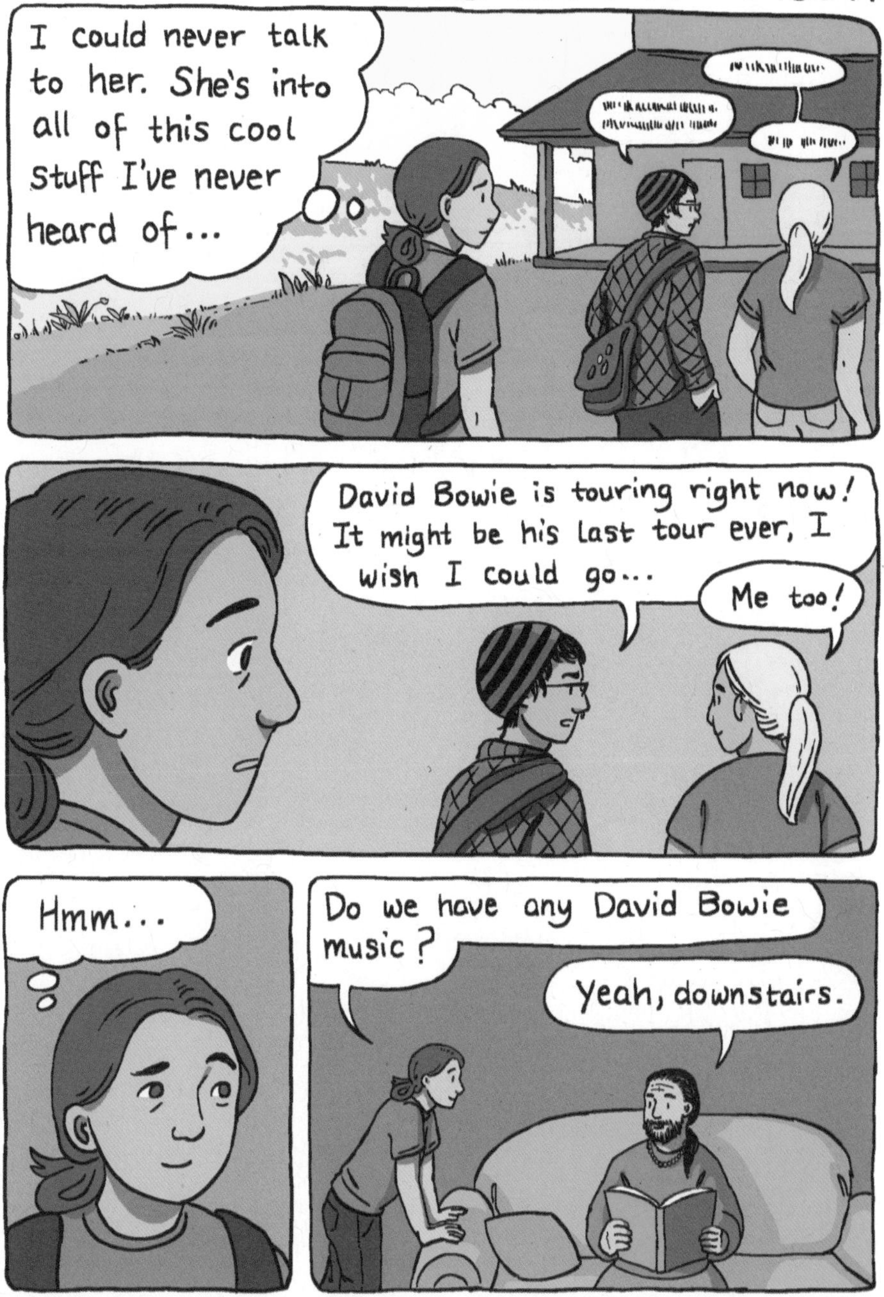
I could never talk to her. She's into all of this cool stuff I've never heard of...
David Bowie is touring right now! It might be his last tour ever, I wish I could go...
Me too!
Hmm...
Do we have any David Bowie music?
Yeah, downstairs.

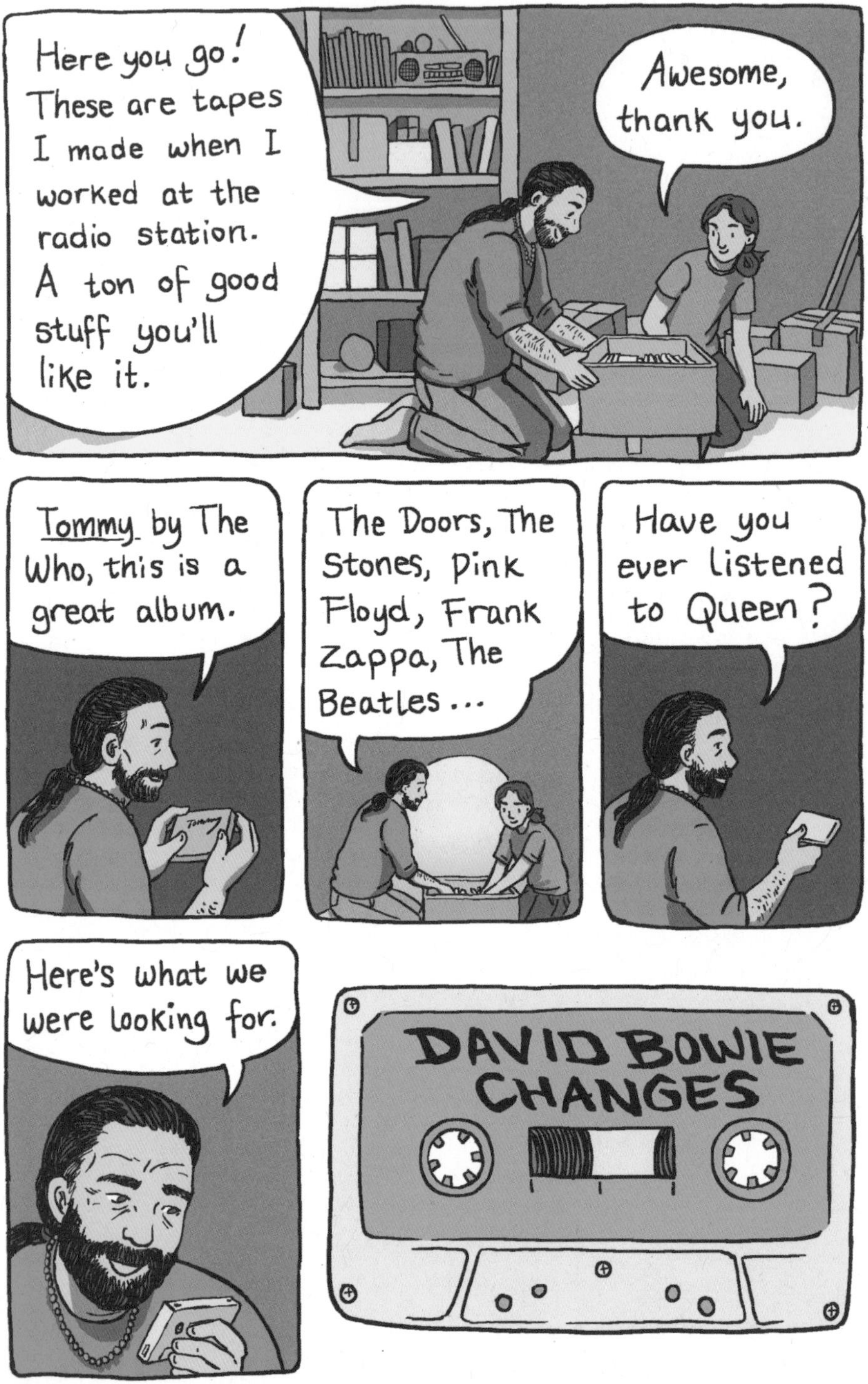

Here you go! These are tapes I made when I worked at the radio station. A ton of good stuff you'll like it.
Awesome, thank you.
Tommy by The Who, this is a great album.
The Doors, The Stones, Pink Floyd, Frank Zappa, The Beatles...
Have you ever listened to Queen?
Here's what we were looking for.
DAVID BOWIE CHANGES

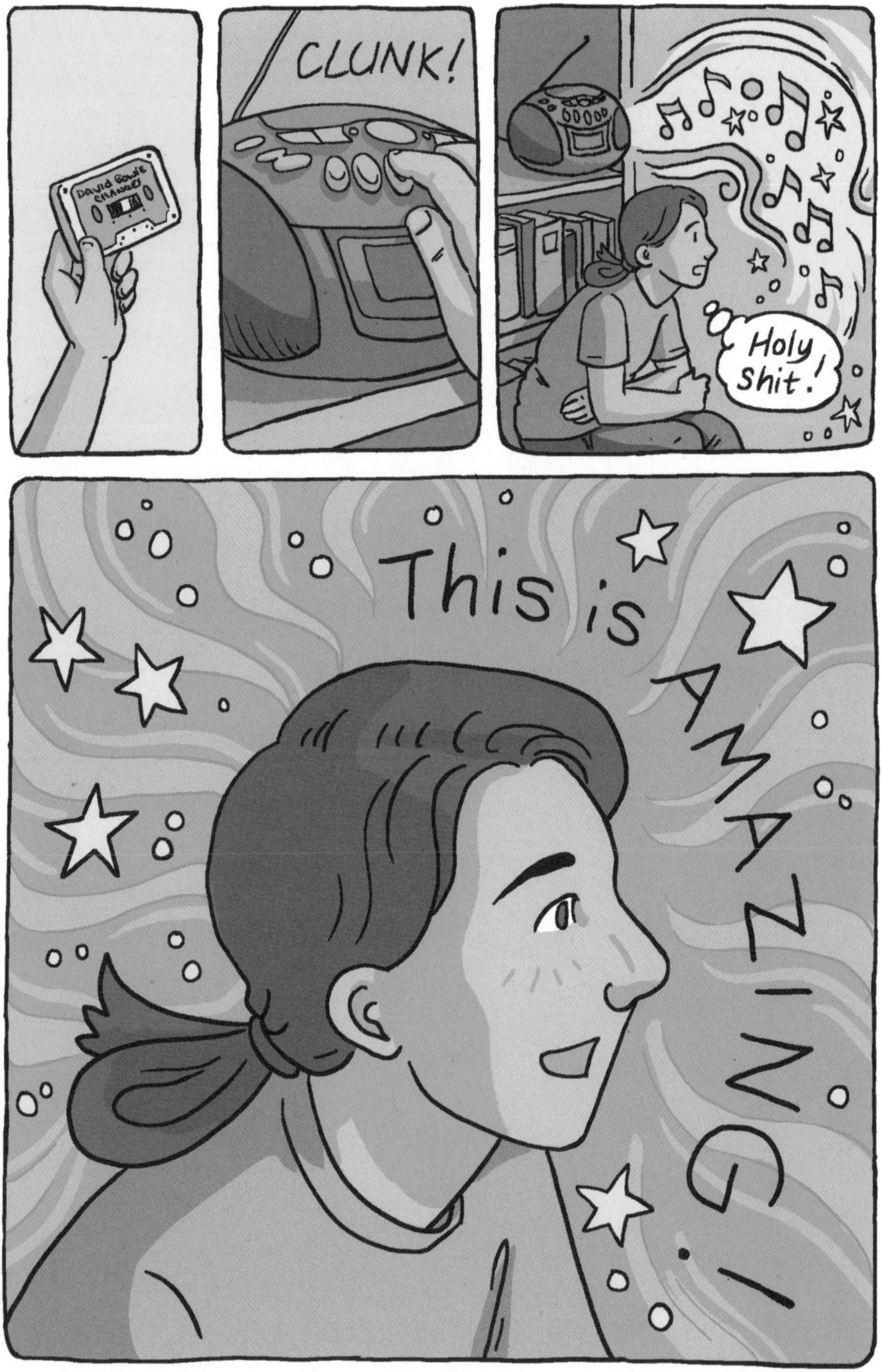
David Bowie CHANGES
CLUNK!
Holy shit!
This is AMAZING!

IT WAS THE FIRST TIME I COULD EVER REMEMBER HEARING QUEER REFERENCES IN SONG LYRICS:

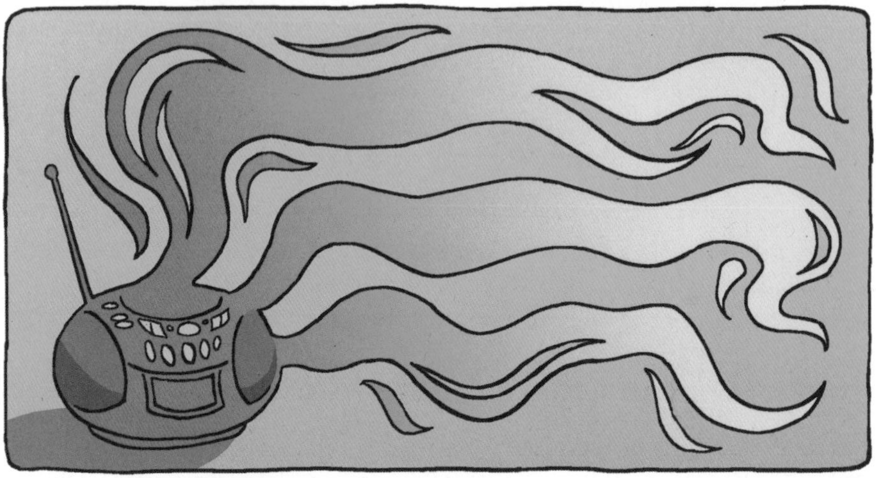

I ONLY LET MYSELF LISTEN TO THE TAPE ONCE THROUGH PER DAY

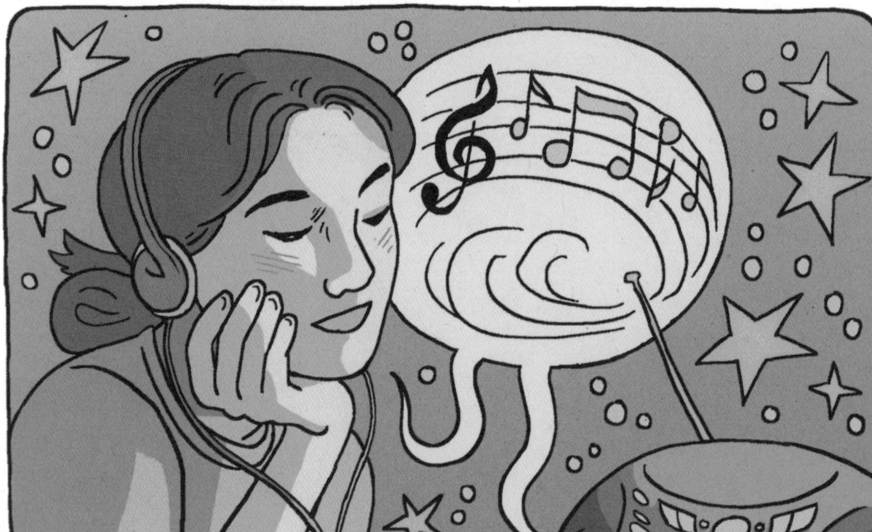

AFRAID THAT I WOULD WEAR IT OUT.

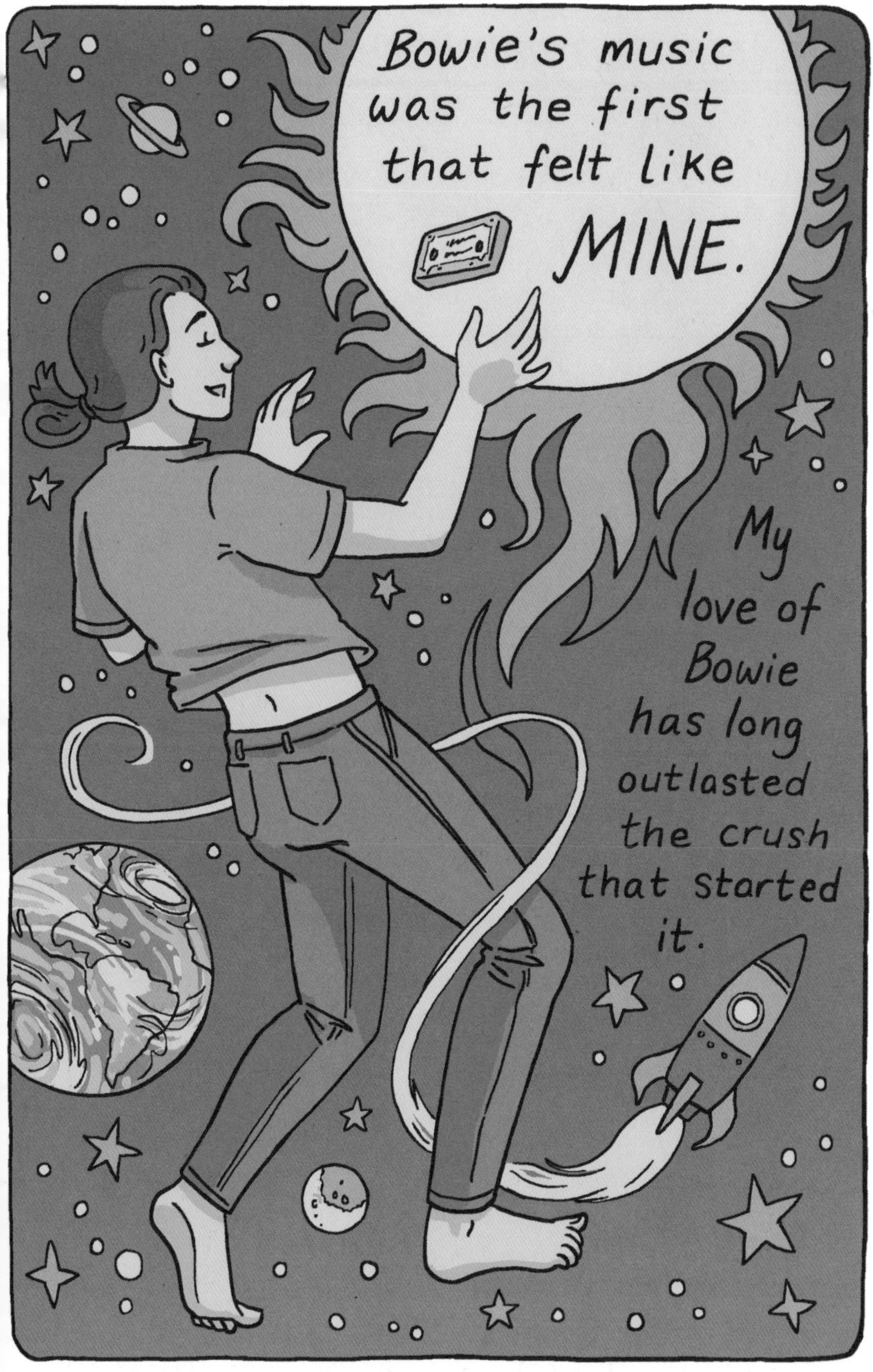
Bowie's music was the first that felt like MINE.
My love of Bowie has long outlasted the crush that started it.

I WAS 11 OR 12 YEARS OLD THE FIRST TIME I CAN REMEMBER FANTASIZING ABOUT HAVING A PENIS.

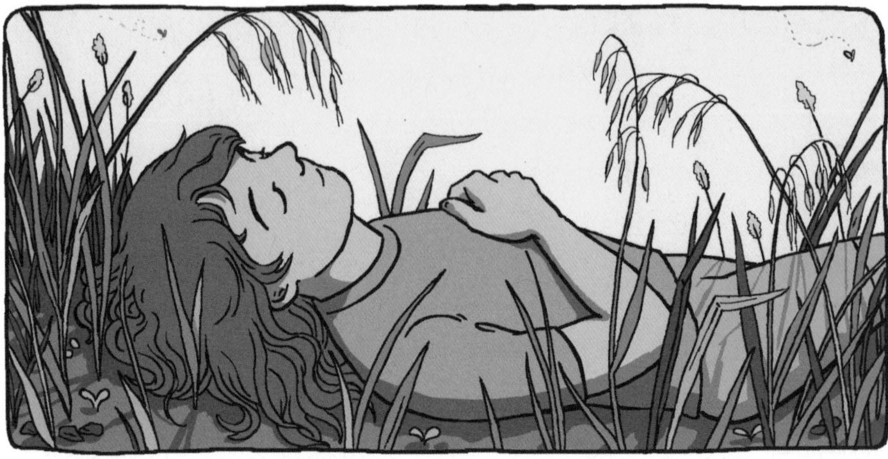

I WAS LYING, FULLY CLOTHED, ON A HILLSIDE UNDER AN OPEN SKY.

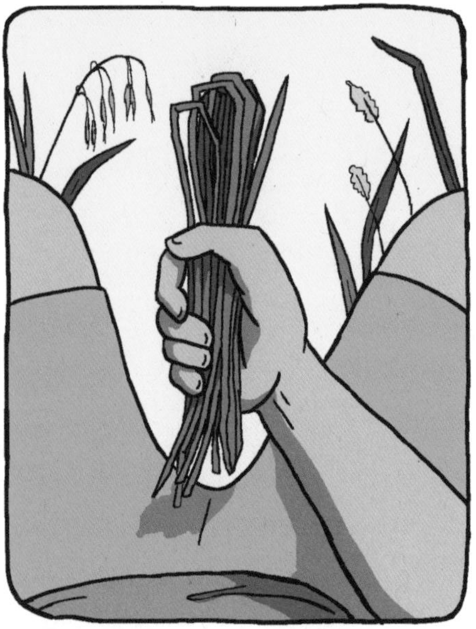

I HELD A FOLDED HANDFUL OF GRASS BETWEEN MY LEGS.

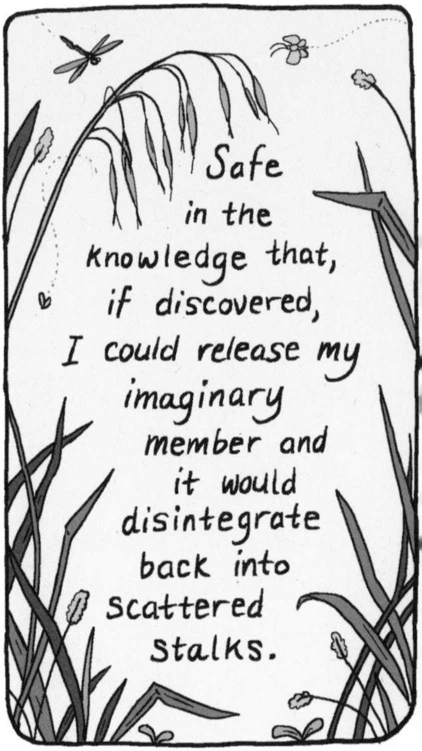
Safe in the knowledge that, if discovered, I could release my imaginary member and it would disintegrate back into scattered stalks.

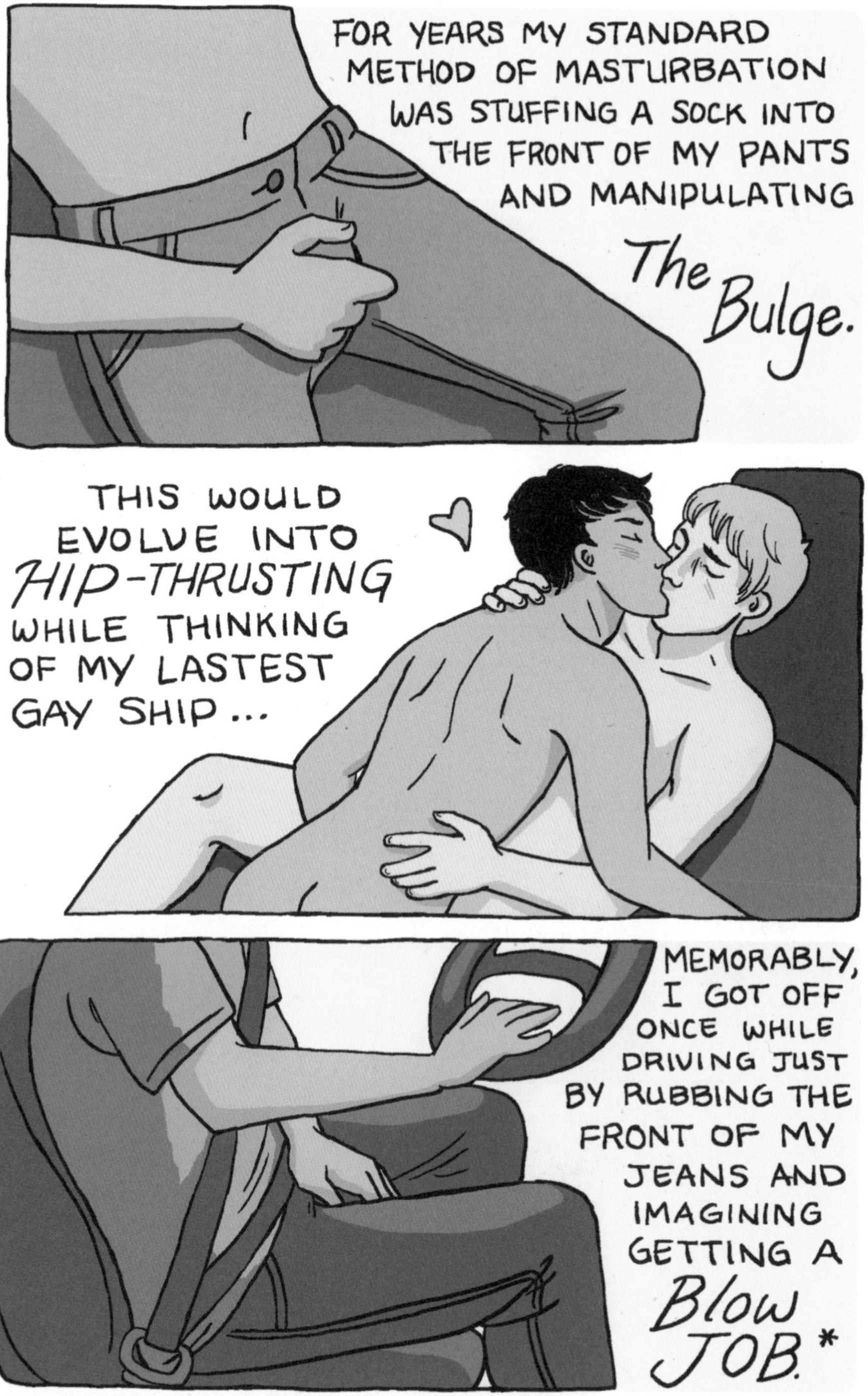
FOR YEARS MY STANDARD METHOD OF MASTURBATION WAS STUFFING A SOCK INTO THE FRONT OF MY PANTS AND MANIPULATING
The Bulge.
THIS WOULD EVOLVE INTO HIP-THRUSTING WHILE THINKING OF MY LASTEST GAY SHIP...
MEMORABLY, I GOT OFF ONCE WHILE DRIVING JUST BY RUBBING THE FRONT OF MY JEANS AND IMAGINING GETTING A
Blow JOB.*

* I PROMISE I'M A REALLY SAFE DRIVER.

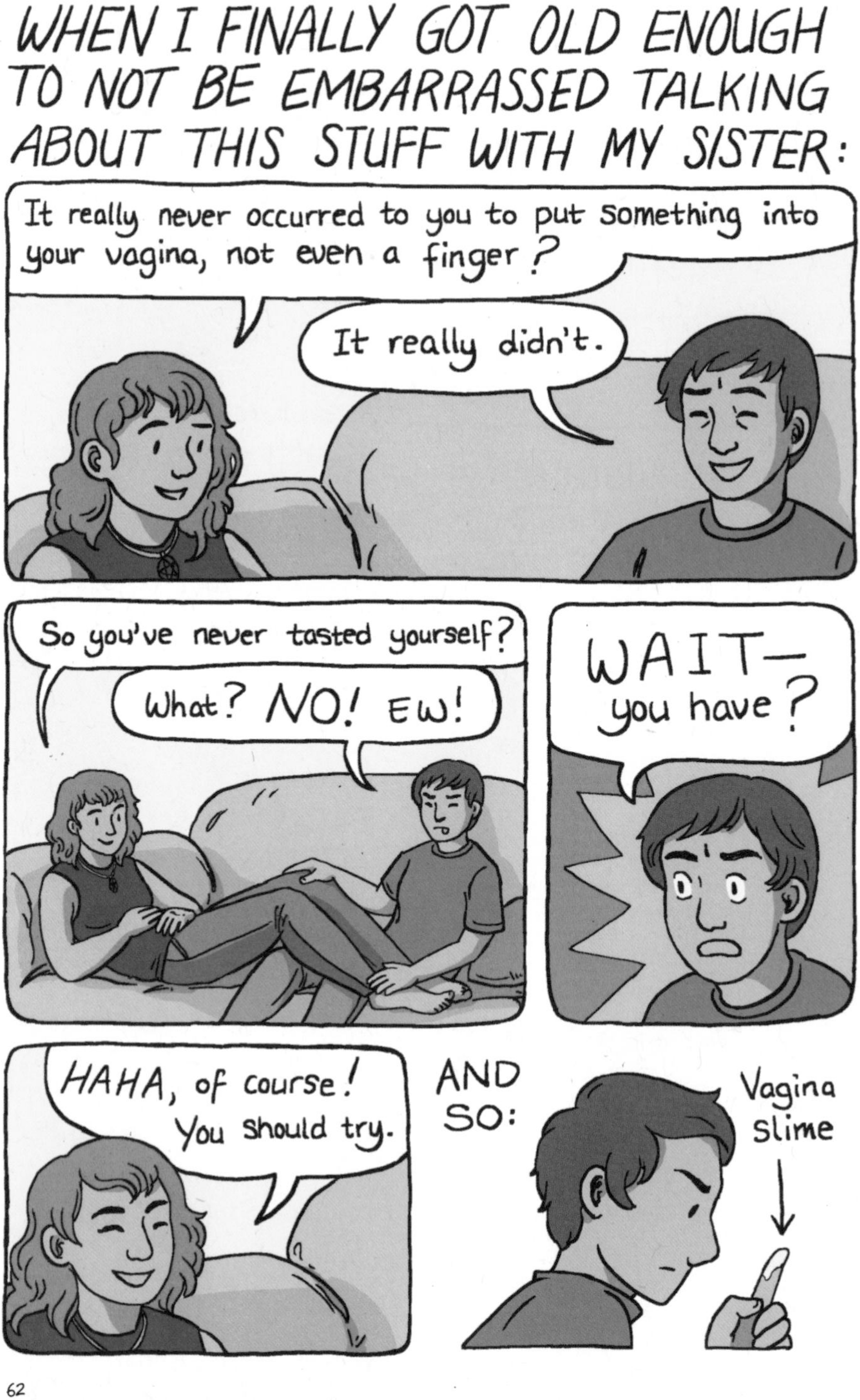
WHEN I FINALLY GOT OLD ENOUGH TO NOT BE EMBARRASSED TALKING ABOUT THIS STUFF WITH MY SISTER:
It really never occurred to you to put something into your vagina, not even a finger?
It really didn't.
So you've never tasted yourself?
What? NO! Ew!
WAIT— you have?
HAHA, of course! You should try.
AND SO:
Vagina slime

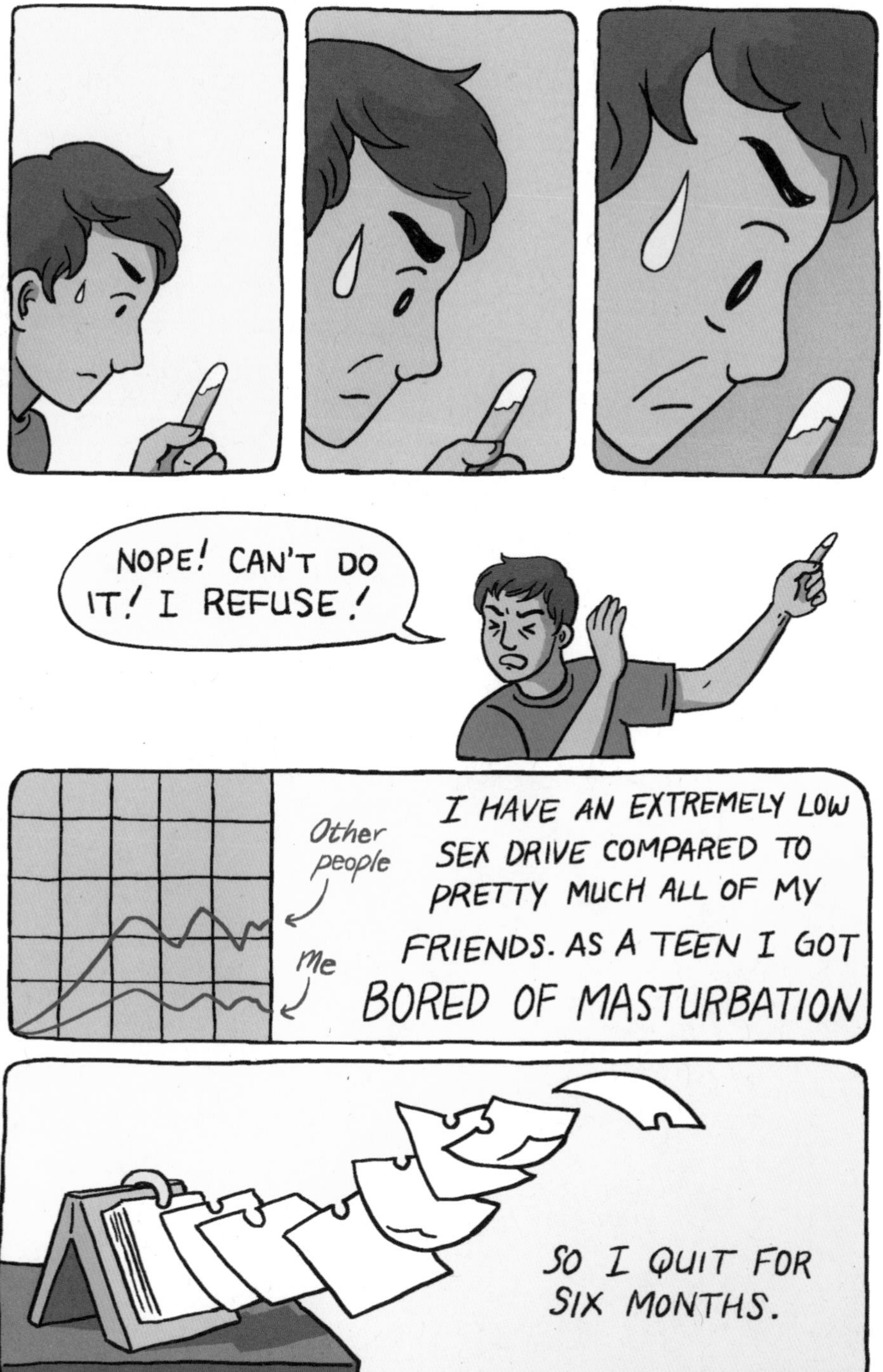
NOPE! CAN'T DO IT! I REFUSE!
Other people
Me
I HAVE AN EXTREMELY LOW SEX DRIVE COMPARED TO PRETTY MUCH ALL OF MY FRIENDS. AS A TEEN I GOT BORED OF MASTURBATION
SO I QUIT FOR SIX MONTHS.

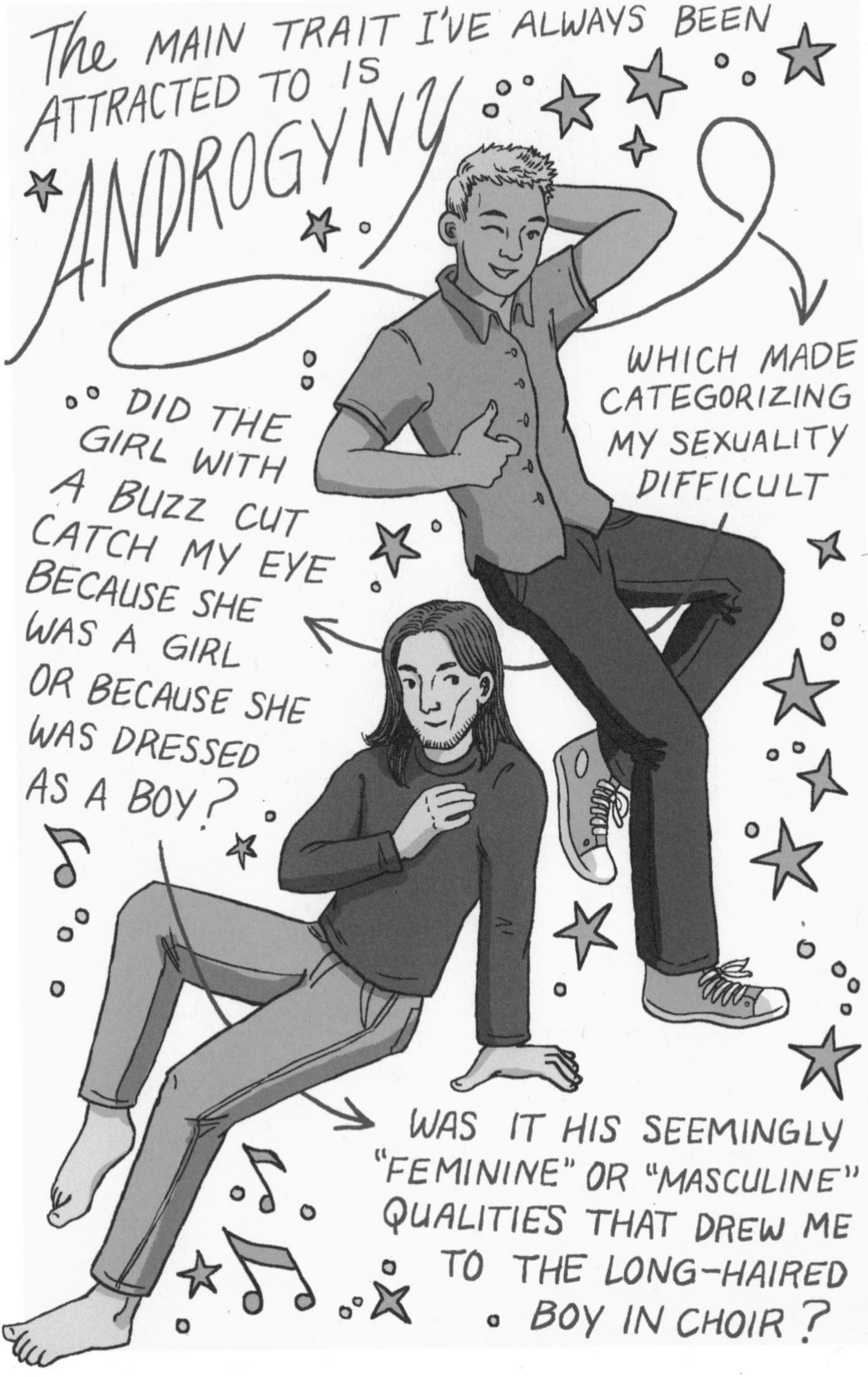
The MAIN TRAIT I'VE ALWAYS BEEN ATTRACTED TO IS
ANDROGYNY
WHICH MADE CATEGORIZING MY SEXUALITY DIFFICULT
DID THE GIRL WITH A BUZZ CUT CATCH MY EYE BECAUSE SHE WAS A GIRL OR BECAUSE SHE WAS DRESSED AS A BOY?
WAS IT HIS SEEMINGLY "FEMININE" OR "MASCULINE" QUALITIES THAT DREW ME TO THE LONG-HAIRED BOY IN CHOIR?

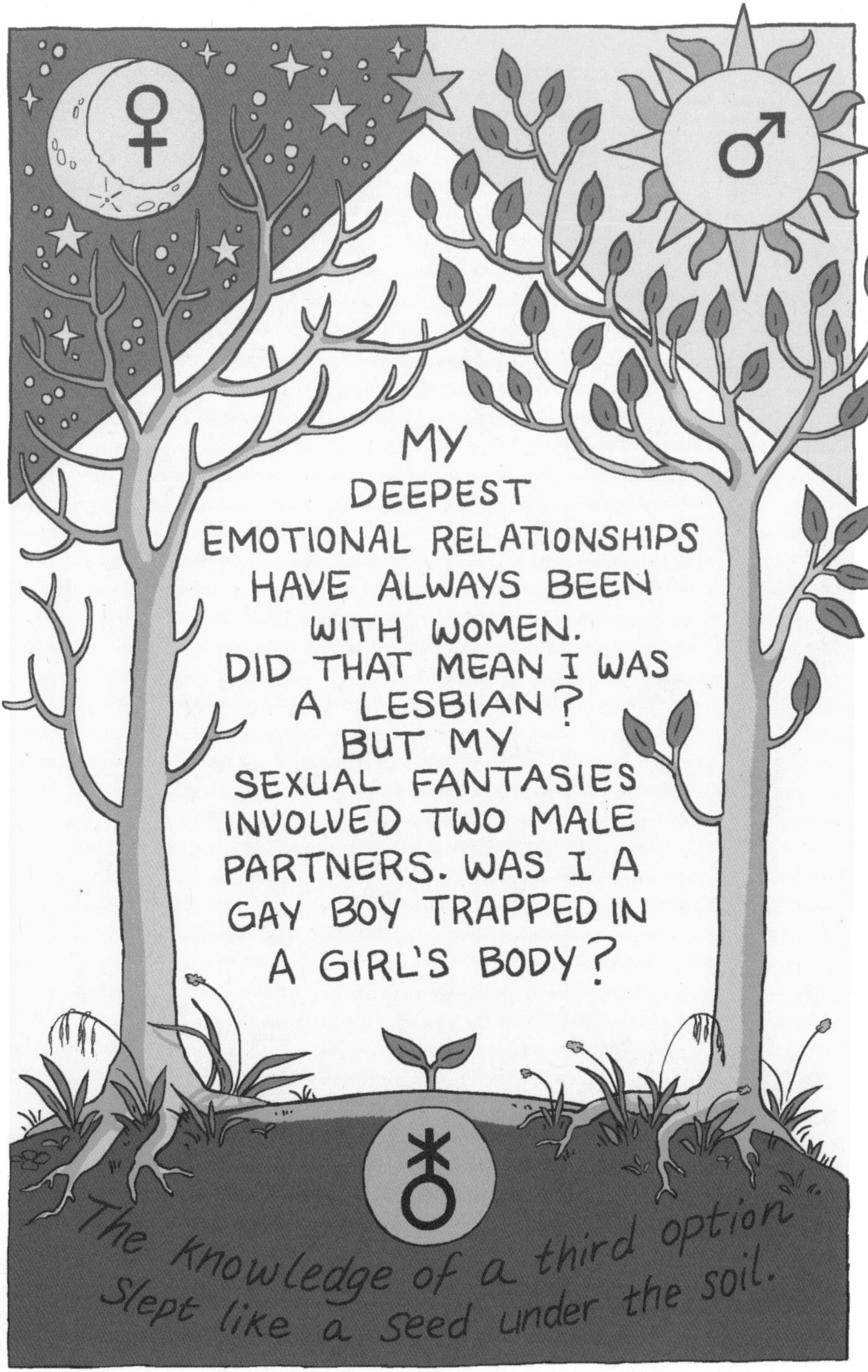
MY DEEPEST EMOTIONAL RELATIONSHIPS HAVE ALWAYS BEEN WITH WOMEN. DID THAT MEAN I WAS A LESBIAN? BUT MY SEXUAL FANTASIES INVOLVED TWO MALE PARTNERS. WAS I A GAY BOY TRAPPED IN A GIRL'S BODY?
The knowledge of a third option
Slept like a seed under the soil.

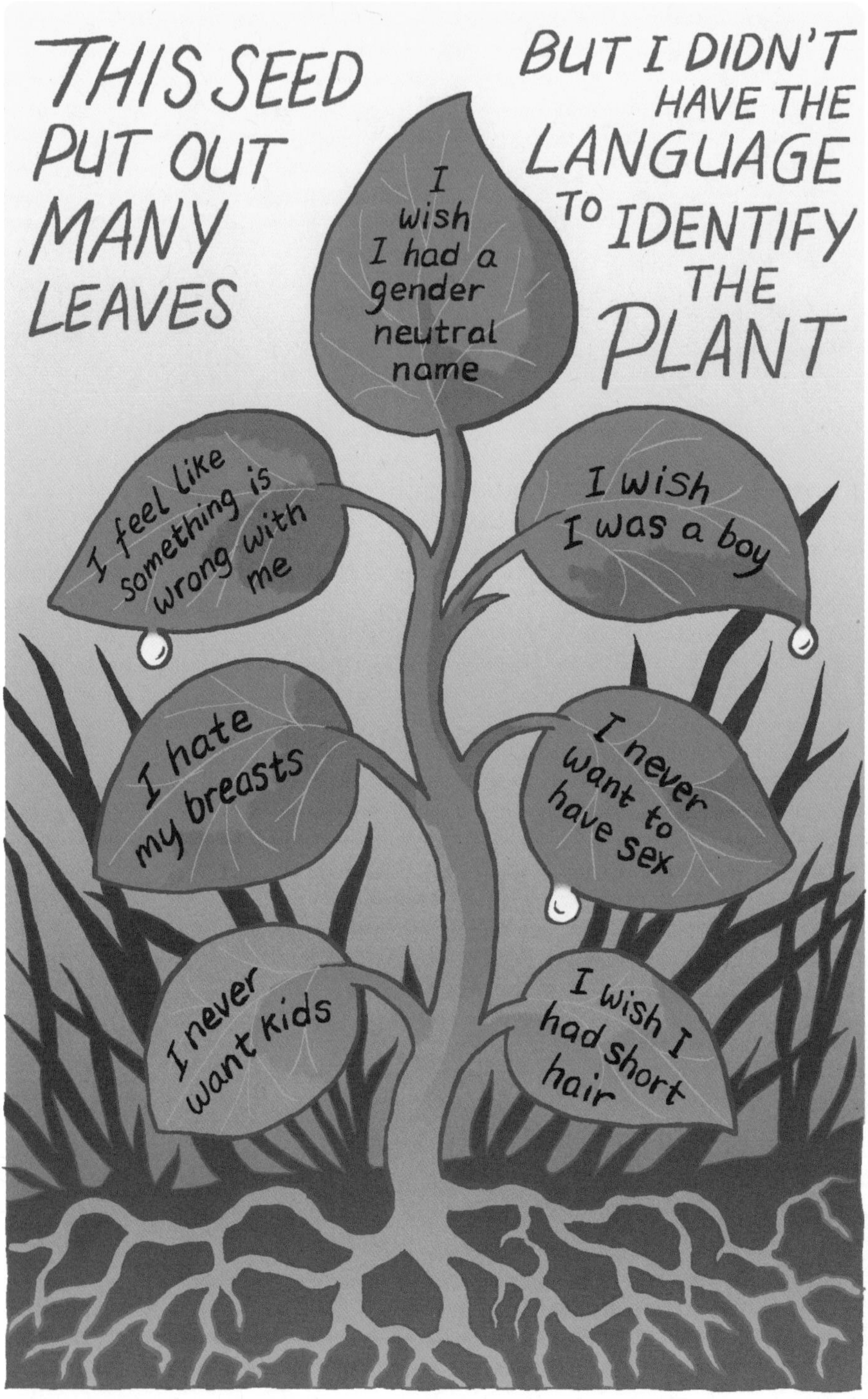
THIS SEED PUT OUT MANY LEAVES
BUT I DIDN'T HAVE THE LANGUAGE TO IDENTIFY THE PLANT
I wish I had a gender neutral name
I feel like something is wrong with me
I wish I was a boy
I hate my breasts
I never want to have sex
I never want kids
I wish I had short hair

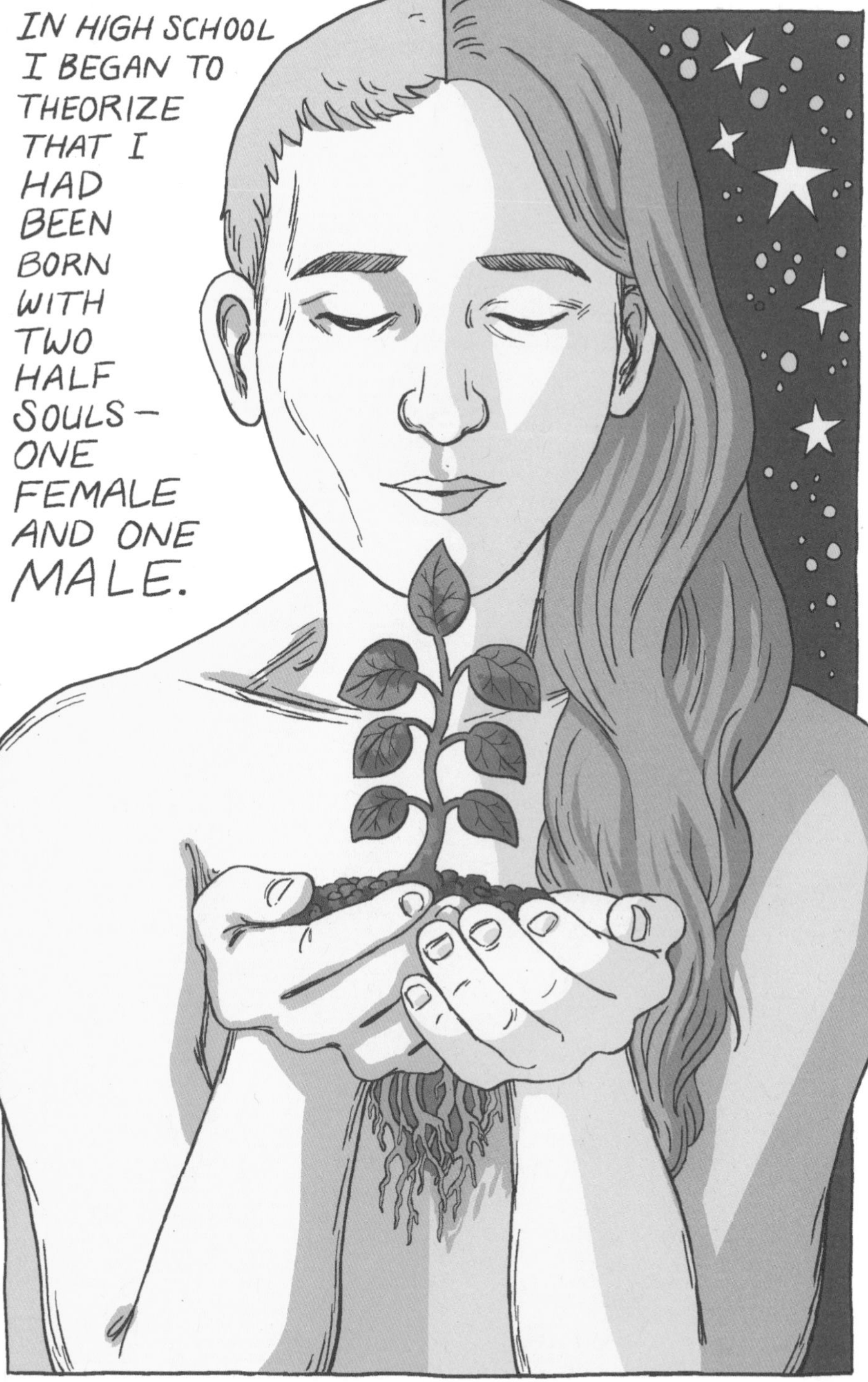
IN HIGH SCHOOL I BEGAN TO THEORIZE THAT I HAD BEEN BORN WITH TWO HALF SOULS— ONE FEMALE AND ONE MALE.

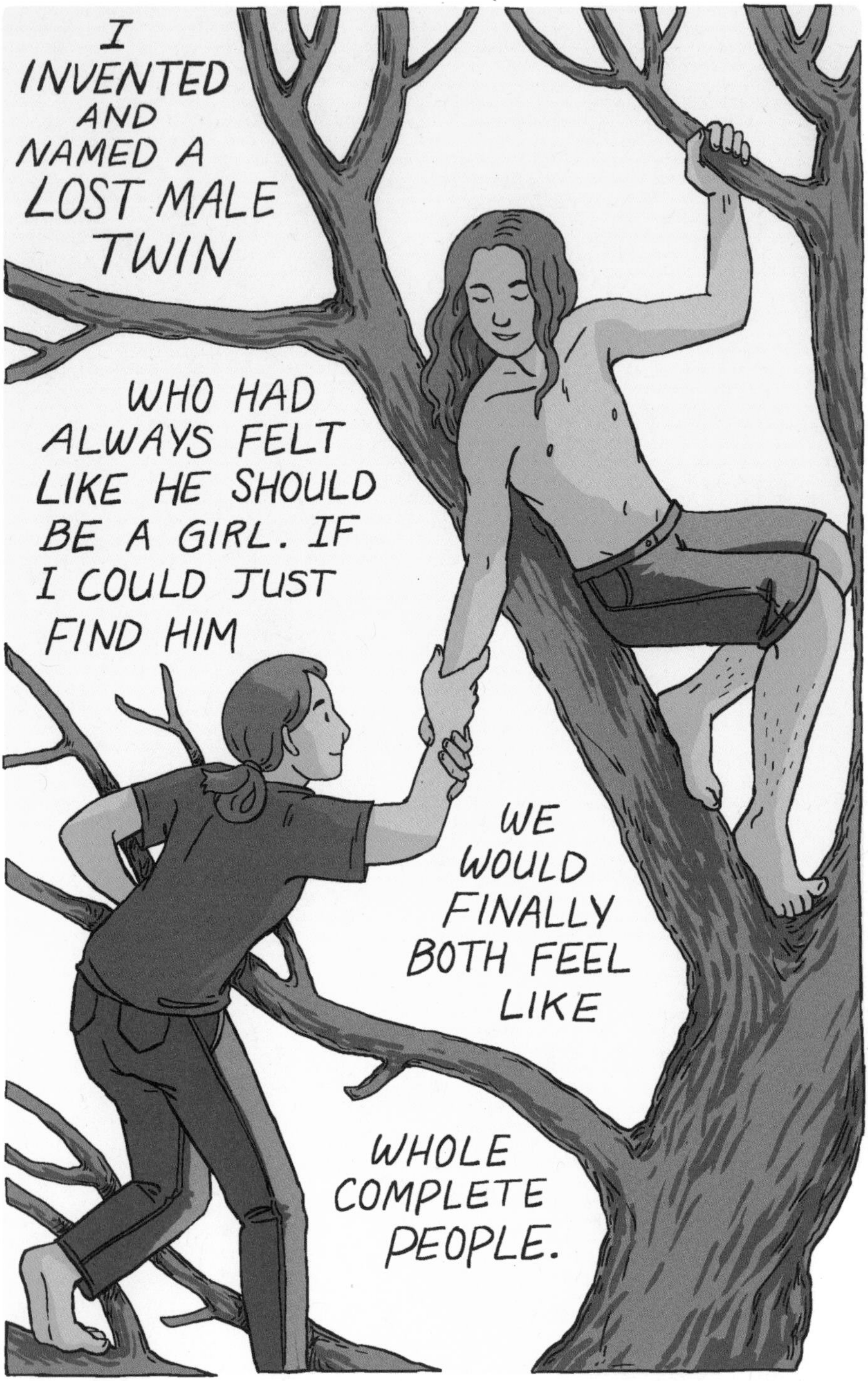
I INVENTED AND NAMED A LOST MALE TWIN
WHO HAD ALWAYS FELT LIKE HE SHOULD BE A GIRL. IF I COULD JUST FIND HIM
WE WOULD FINALLY BOTH FEEL LIKE
WHOLE COMPLETE PEOPLE.

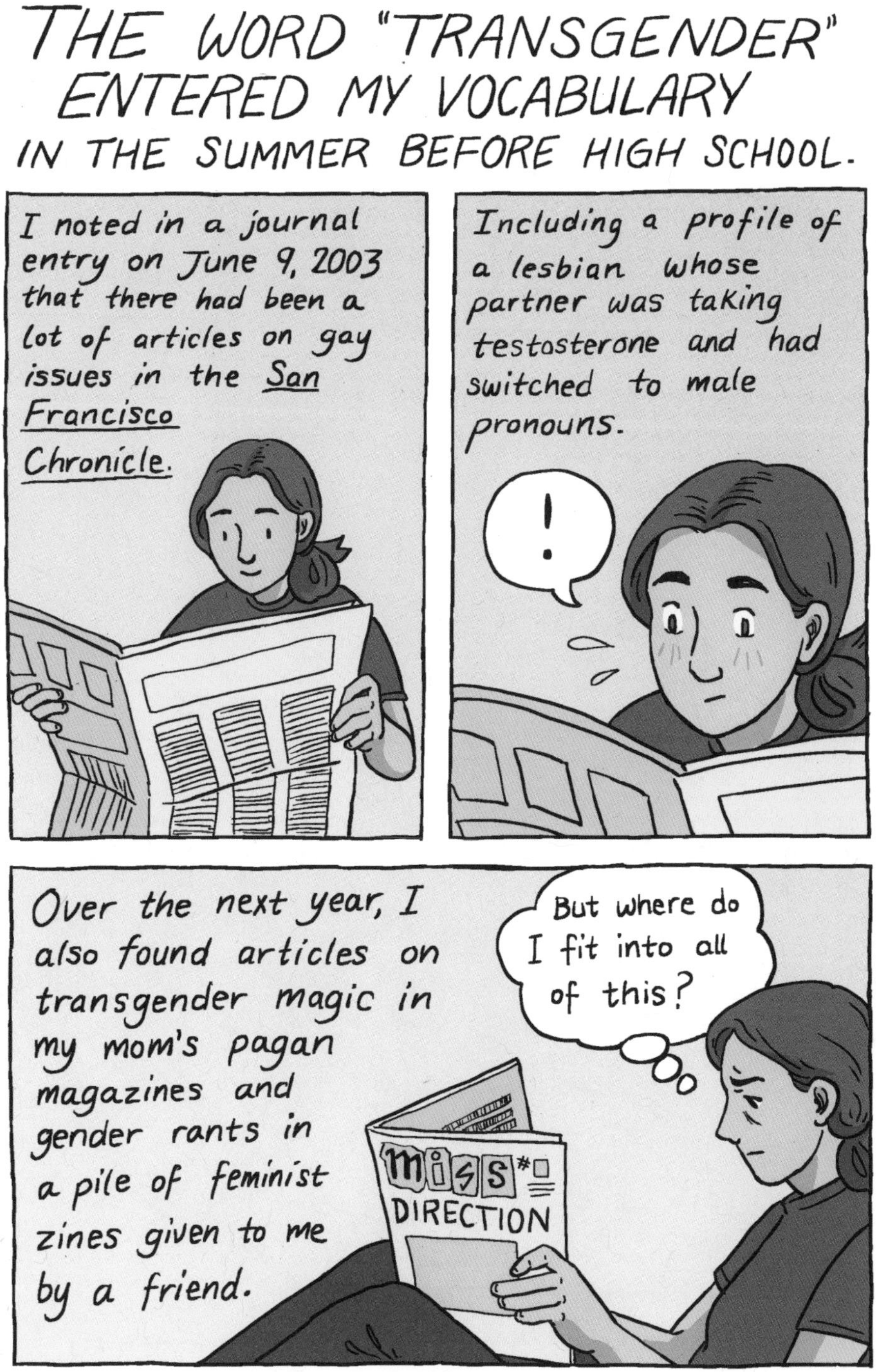
THE WORD "TRANSGENDER" ENTERED MY VOCABULARY IN THE SUMMER BEFORE HIGH SCHOOL.
I noted in a journal entry on June 9, 2003 that there had been a lot of articles on gay issues in the San Francisco Chronicle.
Including a profile of a lesbian whose partner was taking testosterone and had switched to male pronouns.
!
Over the next year, I also found articles on transgender magic in my mom's pagan magazines and gender rants in a pile of feminist zines given to me by a friend.
But where do I fit into all of this?
MISS
DIRECTION

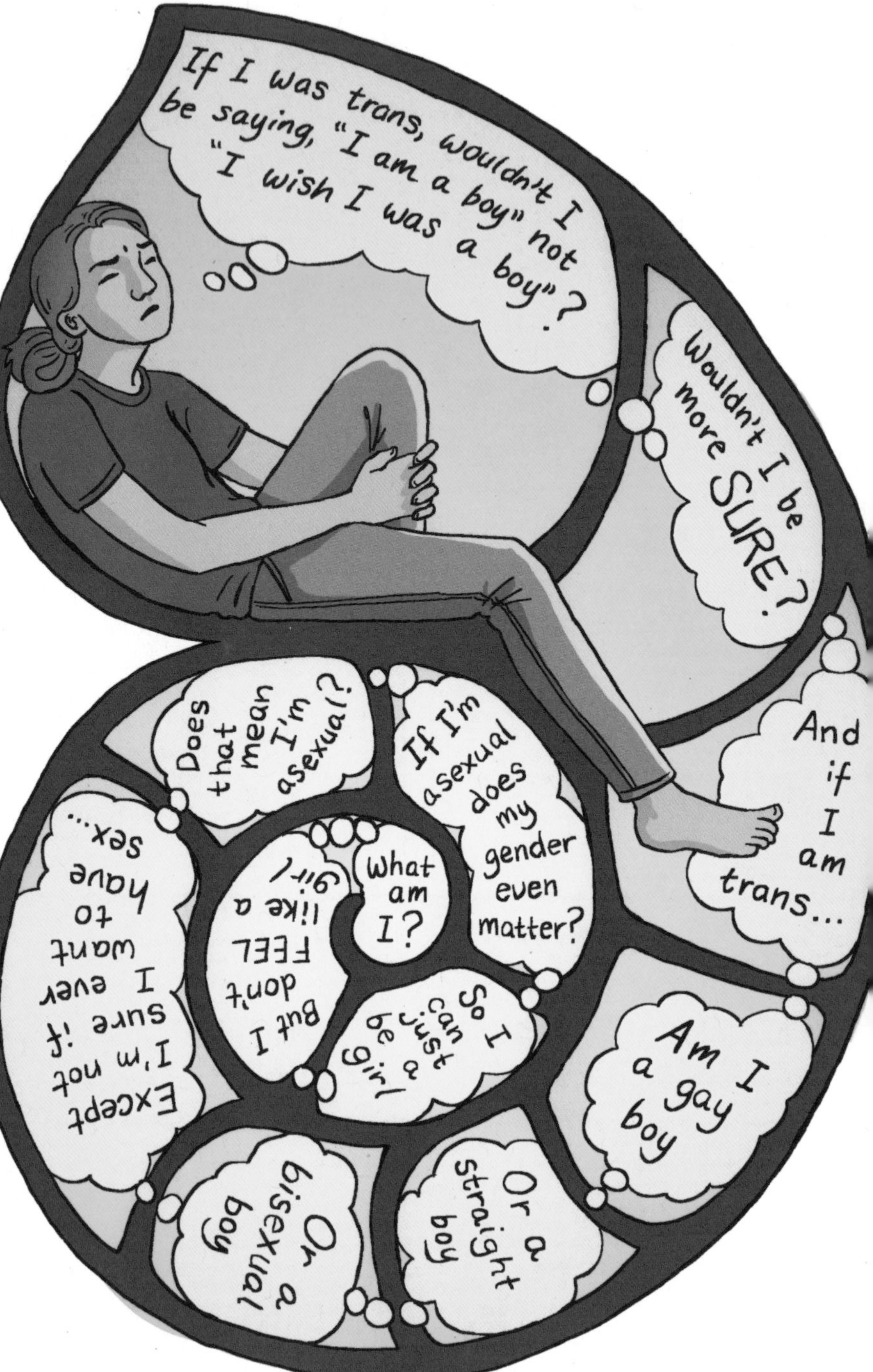
If I was trans, wouldn't I be saying, "I am a boy" not "I wish I was a boy"?
Wouldn't I be more SURE?
And if I am trans...
Am I a gay boy
Or a straight boy
Or a bisexual boy
Except I'm not sure if I ever want to have sex...
Does that mean I'm asexual?
If I'm asexual does my gender even matter?
So I can just be a girl
But I don't FEEL like a girl
What am I?

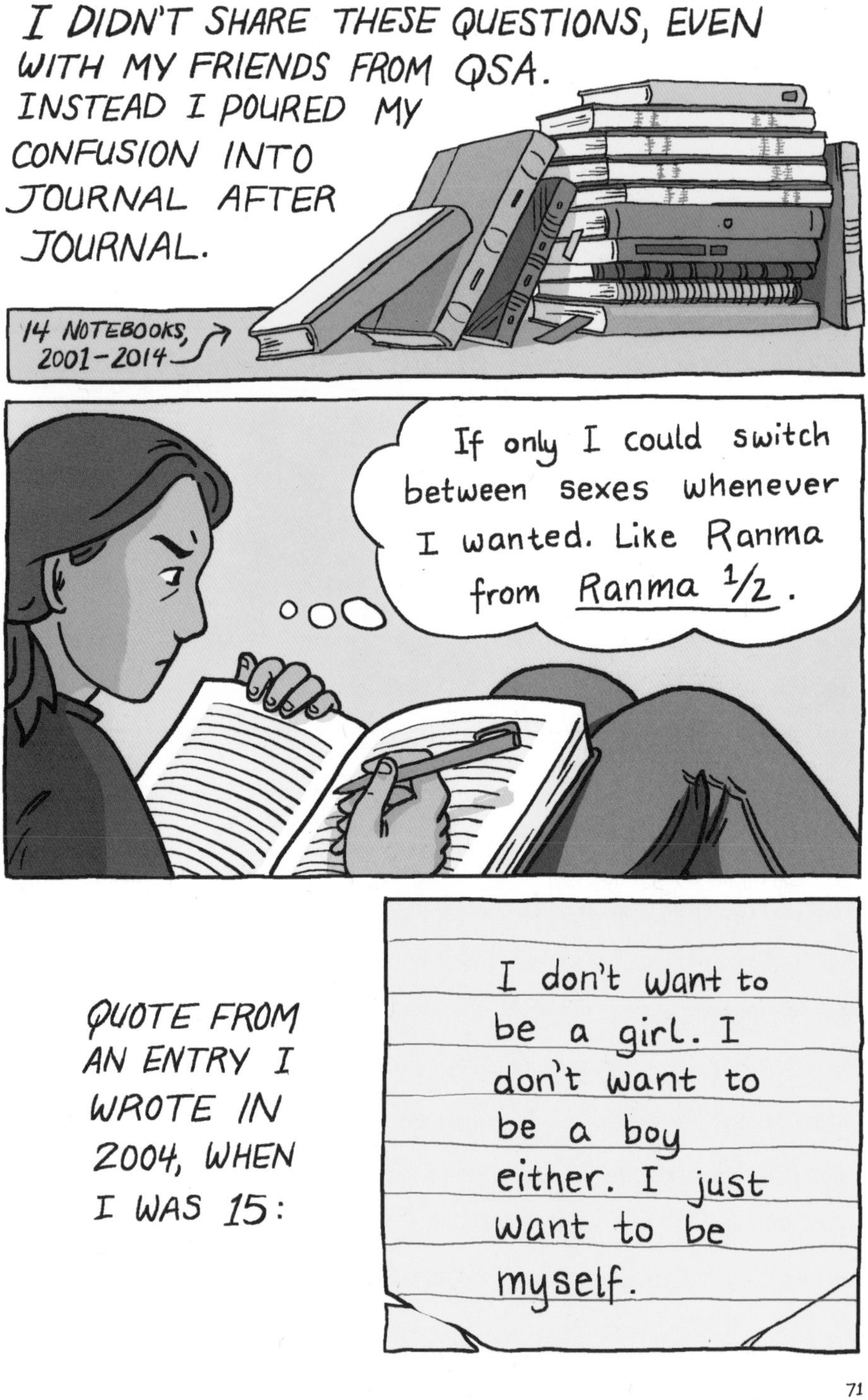
I DIDN'T SHARE THESE QUESTIONS, EVEN WITH MY FRIENDS FROM QSA. INSTEAD I POURED MY CONFUSION INTO JOURNAL AFTER JOURNAL.
14 NOTEBOOKS, 2001–2014
If only I could switch between sexes whenever I wanted. Like Ranma from Ranma 1/2.
QUOTE FROM AN ENTRY I WROTE IN 2004, WHEN I WAS 15:
I don't want to be a girl. I don't want to be a boy either. I just want to be myself.

AFTER NINTH GRADE I DECIDED TO KEEP A LIST OF ALL THE BOOKS I READ OVER THE SUMMER.

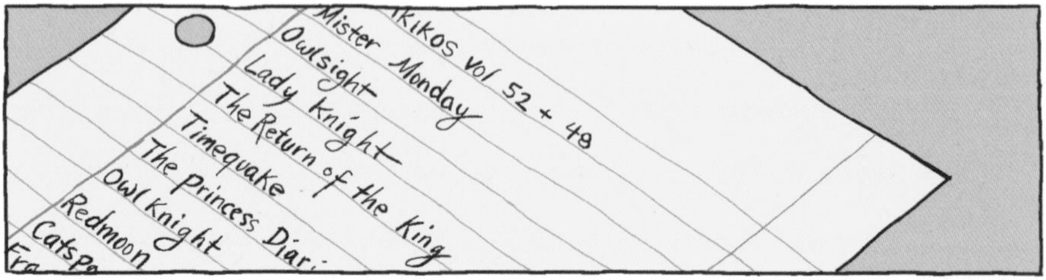
Mister Monday
Owlsight
Lady Knight
The Return of the King
Timequake
Owl Knight
Redmoon

I INCLUDED THE TWO BOOKS I READ FOR SCHOOL

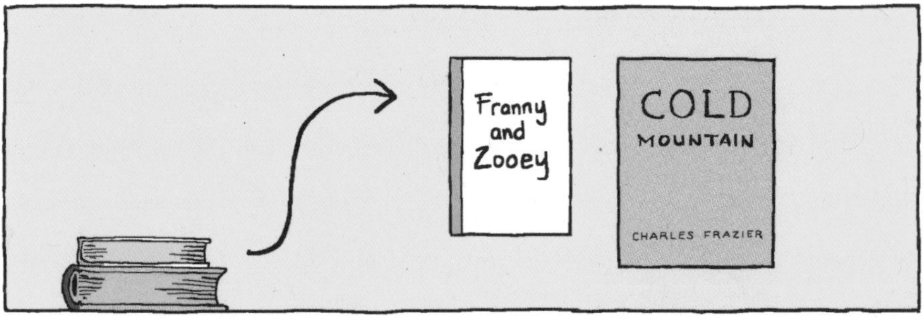
Franny and Zooey
COLD MOUNTAIN
CHARLES FRAZIER

& ALL THE ONES I READ JUST FOR MYSELF.

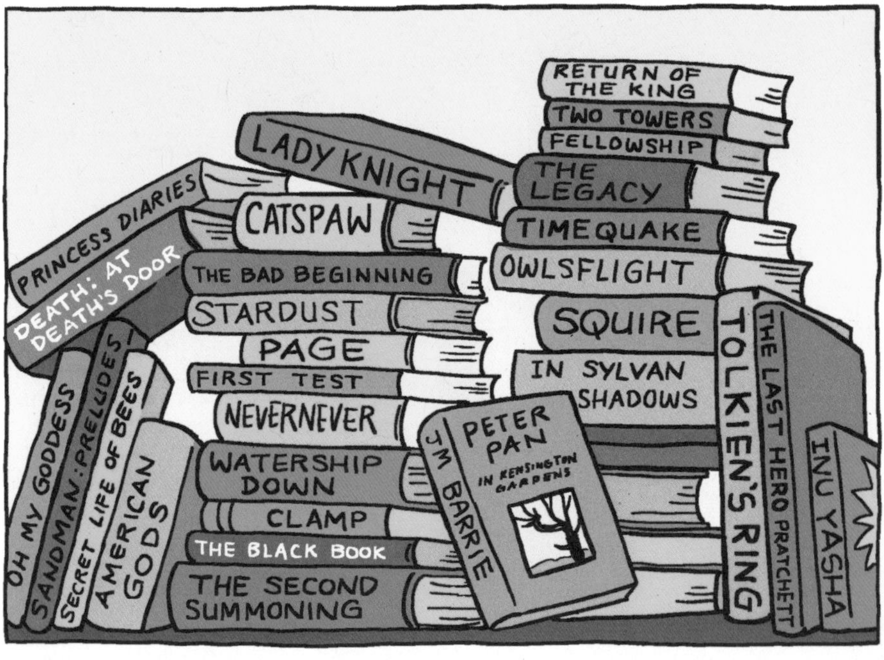
RETURN OF THE KING
TWO TOWERS
FELLOWSHIP
LADY KNIGHT
THE LEGACY
PRINCESS DIARIES
CATSPAW
TIMEQUAKE
DEATH: AT DEATH'S DOOR
THE BAD BEGINNING
OWLSFLIGHT
STARDUST
SQUIRE
PAGE
FIRST TEST
IN SYLVAN SHADOWS
NEVERNEVER
OH MY GODDESS
SANDMAN: PRELUDES
SECRET LIFE OF BEES
AMERICAN GODS
WATERSHIP DOWN
CLAMP
THE BLACK BOOK
THE SECOND SUMMONING
PETER PAN IN KENSINGTON GARDENS
JM BARRIE
TOLKIEN'S RING
THE LAST HERO PRATCHETT
INU YASHA

BY THE END OF THE SUMMER, MY LIST HAD 68 TITLES, READ IN 82 DAYS.

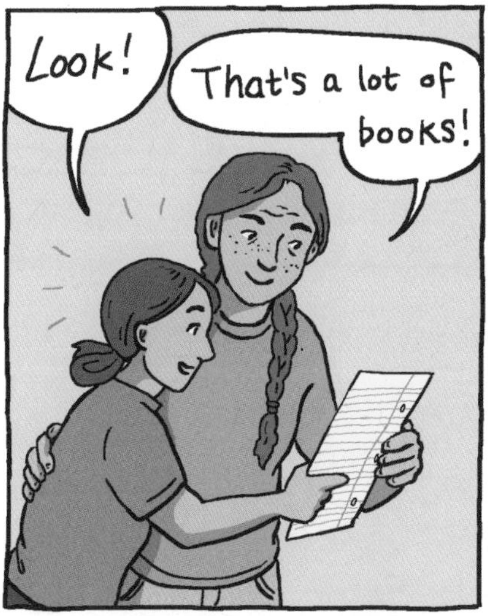
Look!
That's a lot of books!

MY PARENTS WERE DULY IMPRESSED

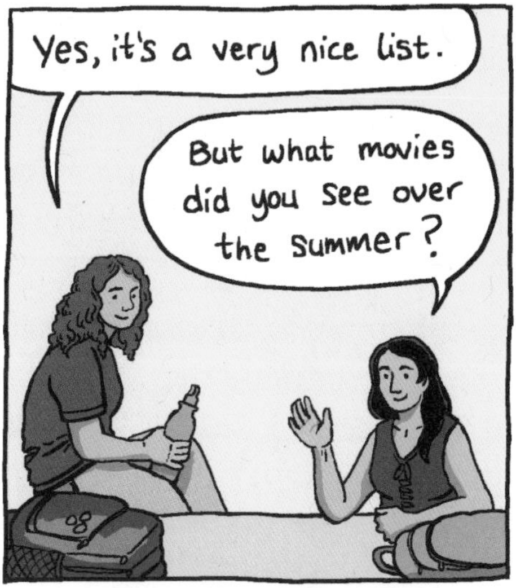
Yes, it's a very nice list.
But what movies did you see over the summer?

AND MY FRIENDS ROLLED THEIR EYES.

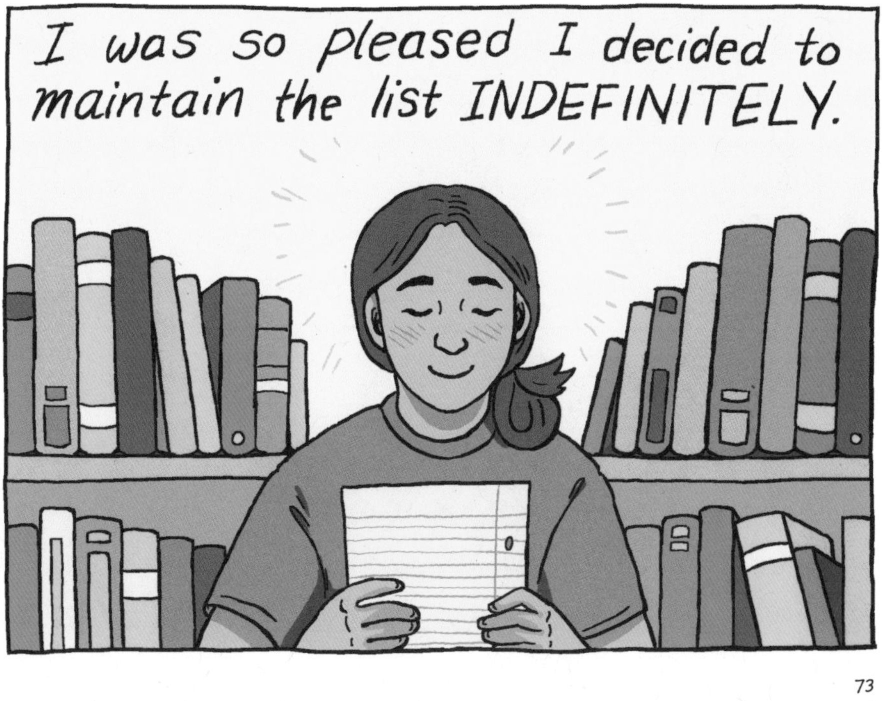
I was so pleased I decided to maintain the list INDEFINITELY.

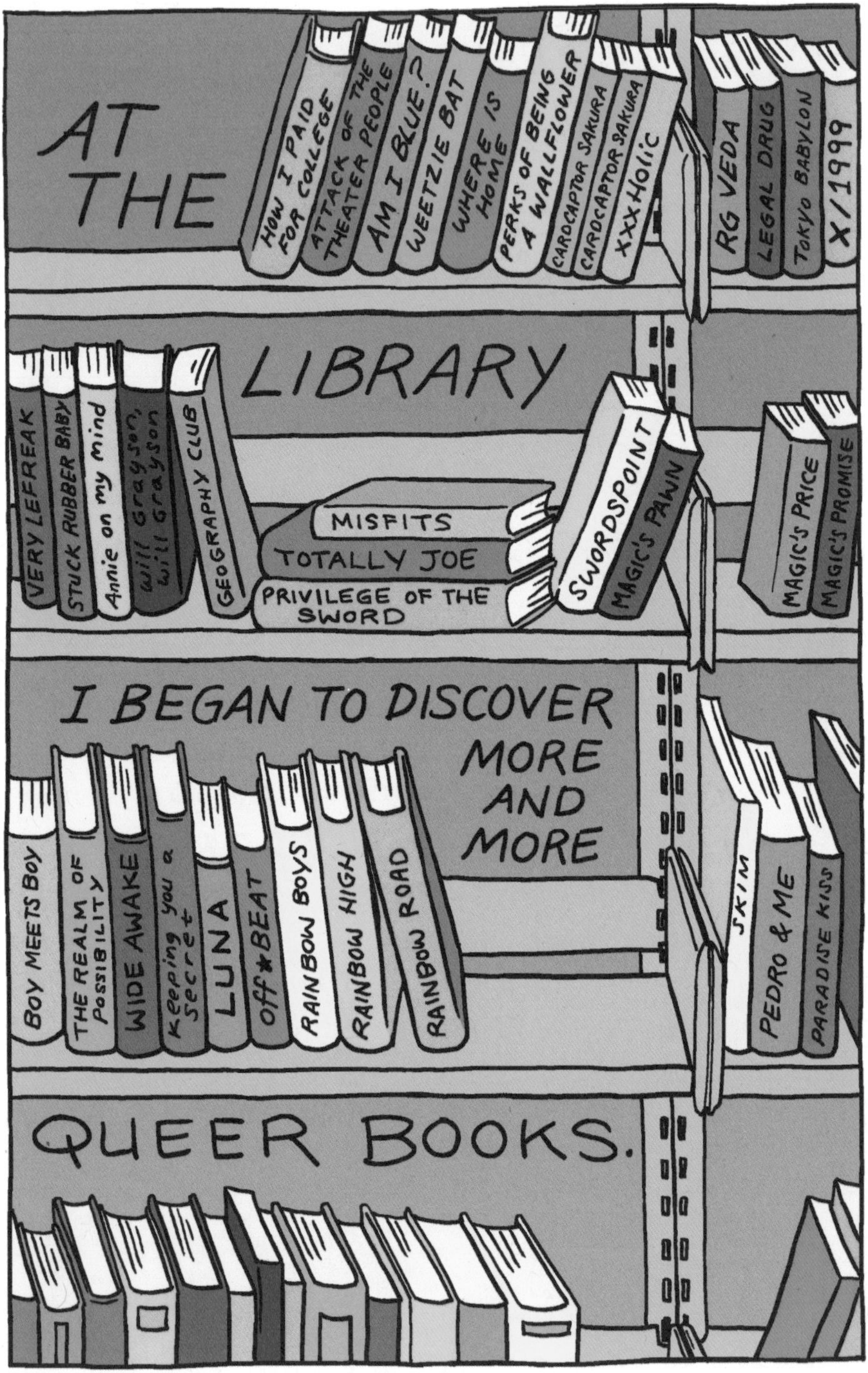
AT THE
HOW I PAID FOR COLLEGE
ATTACK OF THE THEATER PEOPLE
AM I BLUE?
WEETZIE BAT
WHERE IS HOME
PERKS OF BEING A WALLFLOWER
CARDCAPTOR SAKURA
CARDCAPTOR SAKURA
XXX HOLIC
RG VEDA
LEGAL DRUG
Tokyo BABYLON
X/1999
LIBRARY
VERY LEFREAK
STUCK RUBBER BABY
Annie on my mind
will grayson, will grayson
GEOGRAPHY CLUB
MISFITS
TOTALLY JOE
PRIVILEGE OF THE SWORD
SWORDSPOINT
MAGIC'S PAWN
MAGIC'S PRICE
MAGIC'S PROMISE
I BEGAN TO DISCOVER MORE AND MORE
BOY MEETS BOY
THE REALM OF POSSIBILITY
WIDE AWAKE
Keeping you a secret
LUNA
off*BEAT
RAINBOW BOYS
RAINBOW HIGH
RAINBOW ROAD
SKIM
PEDRO & ME
PARADISE KISS
QUEER BOOKS.

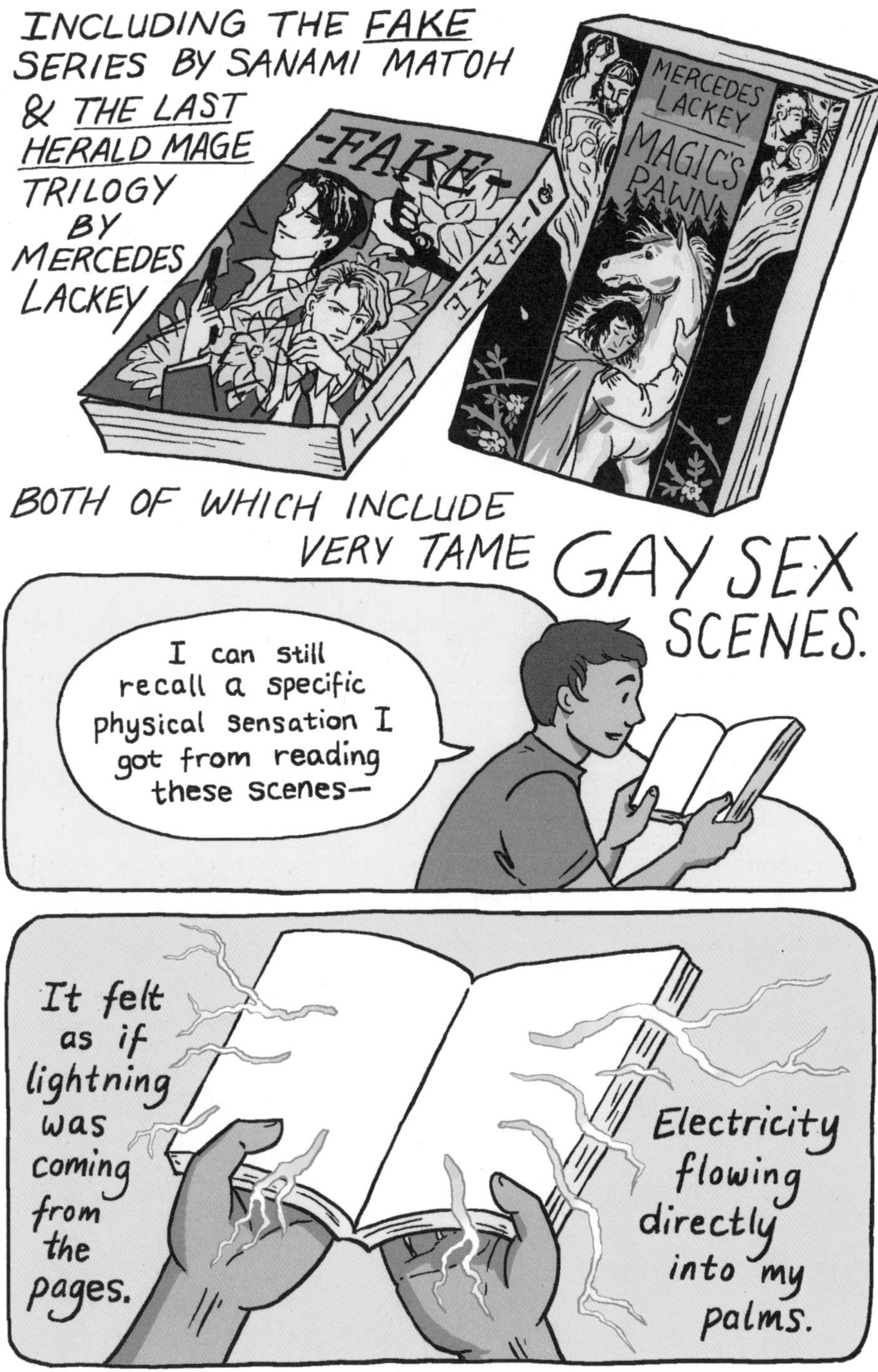
INCLUDING THE FAKE SERIES BY SANAMI MATOH & THE LAST HERALD MAGE TRILOGY BY MERCEDES LACKEY
-FAKE-
FAKE
MERCEDES LACKEY
MAGIC'S PAWN
BOTH OF WHICH INCLUDE VERY TAME GAY SEX SCENES.
I can still recall a specific physical sensation I got from reading these scenes—
It felt as if lightning was coming from the pages.
Electricity flowing directly into my palms.

THE MAIN KIND OF SEX DISCUSSED IN MY FOUR DIFFERENT SEX ED CLASSES WAS SEX INVOLVING A PENIS AND A VAGINA.

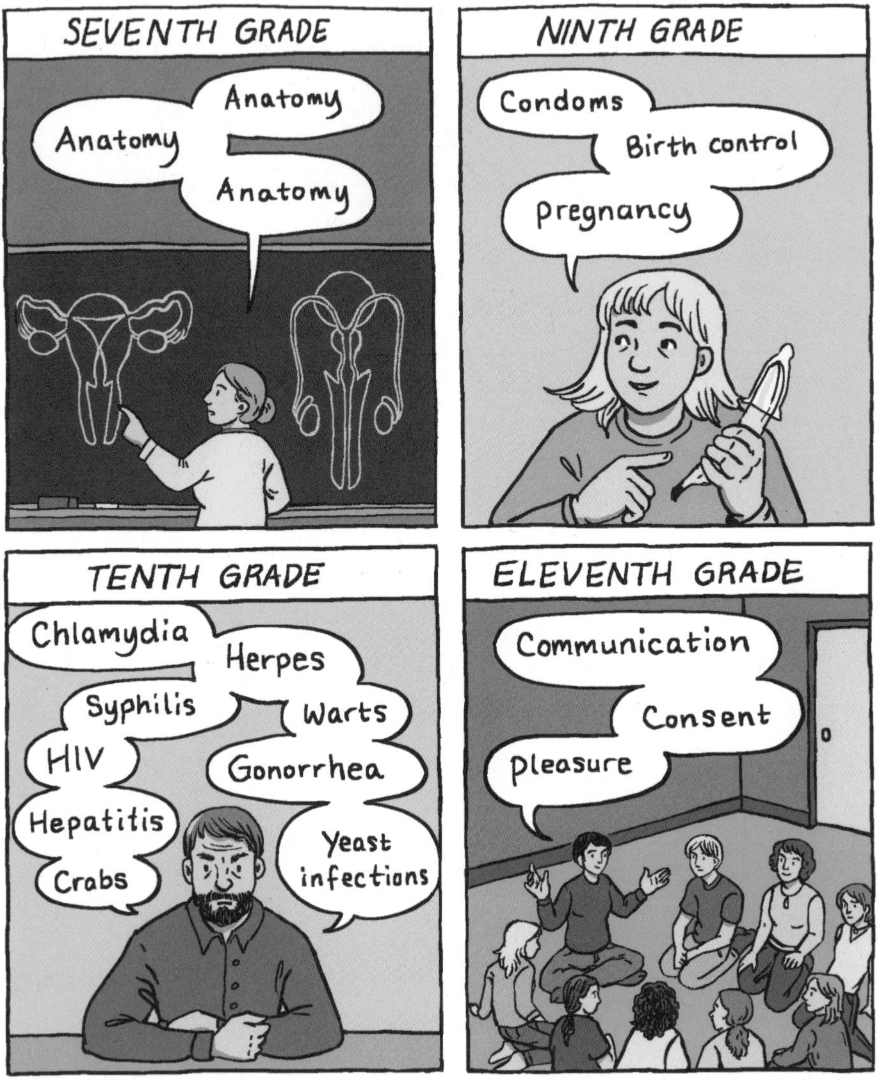
SEVENTH GRADE
Anatomy
Anatomy
Anatomy
NINTH GRADE
Condoms
Birth control
Pregnancy
TENTH GRADE
Chlamydia
Herpes
Syphilis
Warts
HIV
Gonorrhea
Hepatitis
Yeast infections
Crabs
ELEVENTH GRADE
Communication
Consent
Pleasure

THAT KIND OF SEX SOUNDED RISKY & UNAPPEALING.

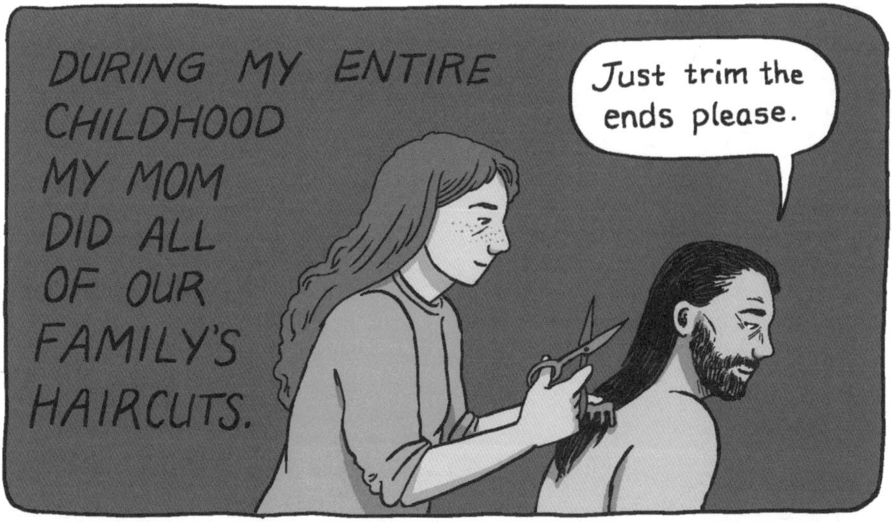
DURING MY ENTIRE CHILDHOOD MY MOM DID ALL OF OUR FAMILY'S HAIRCUTS.
Just trim the ends please.

(ASIDE FROM THE TWO MEMORABLE OCCASIONS MY SISTER CUT HER OWN.)

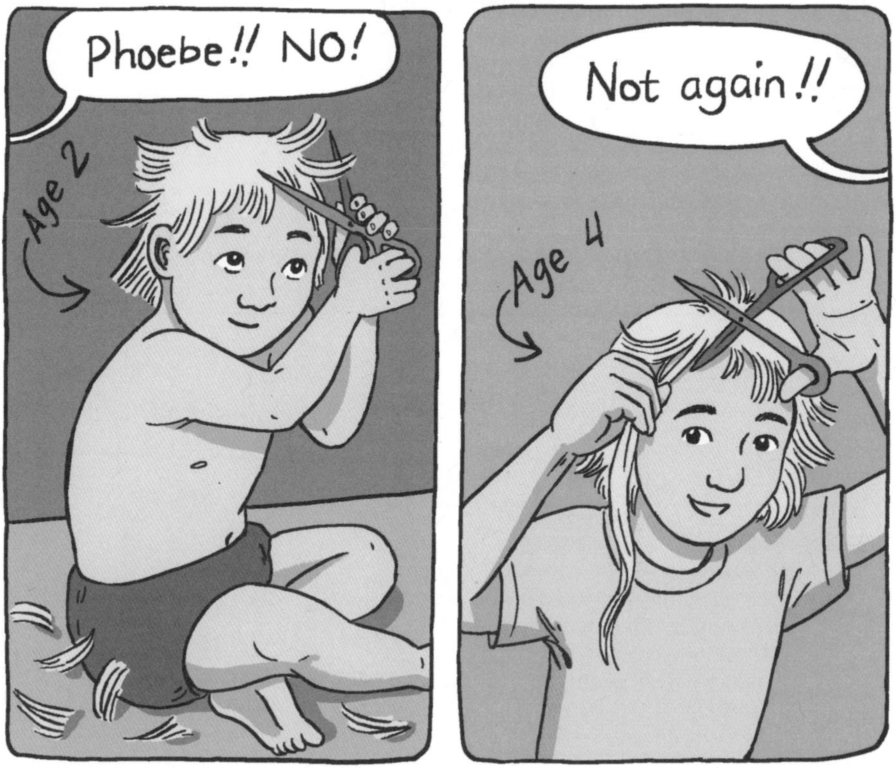
Phoebe!! NO!
Age 2
Not again!!
Age 4

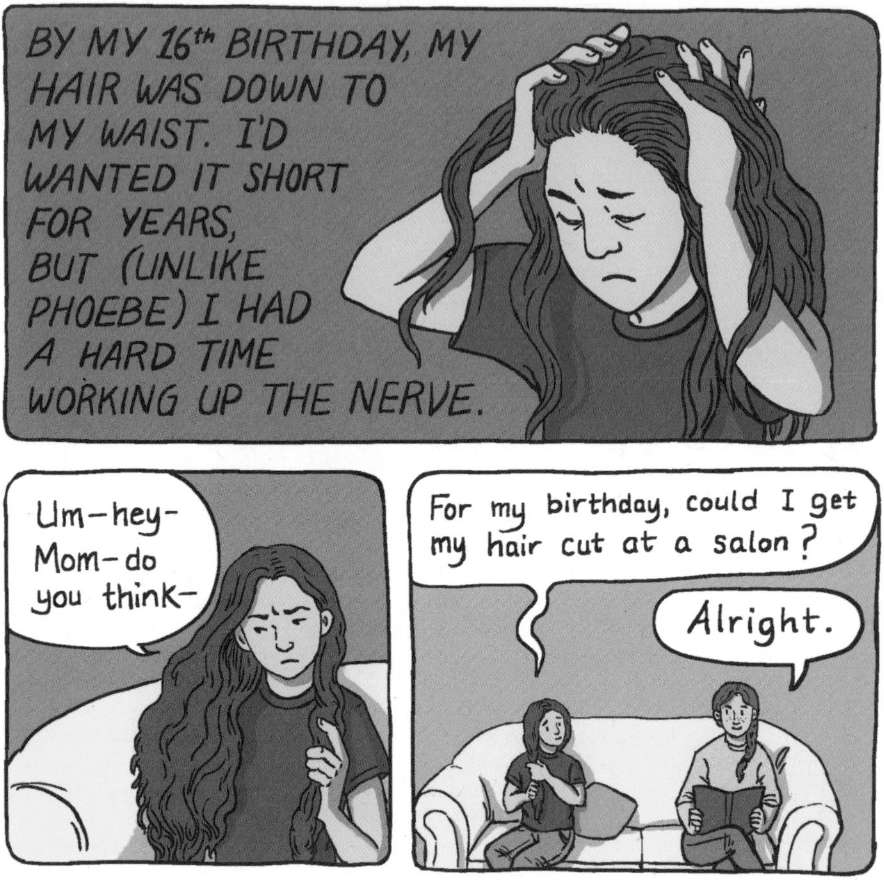
BY MY 16th BIRTHDAY, MY HAIR WAS DOWN TO MY WAIST. I'D WANTED IT SHORT FOR YEARS, BUT (UNLIKE PHOEBE) I HAD A HARD TIME WORKING UP THE NERVE.
Um–hey–Mom–do you think–
For my birthday, could I get my hair cut at a salon?
Alright.

WHEN THE DAY CAME I WAS SO NERVOUS.

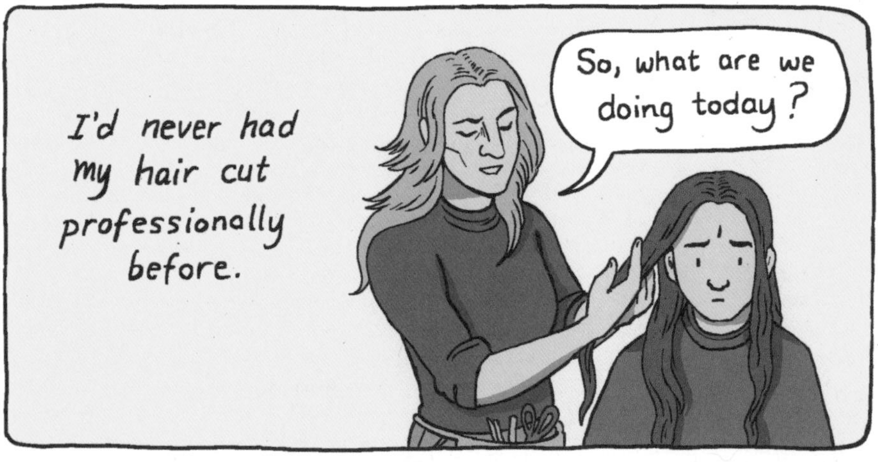
I'd never had my hair cut professionally before.
So, what are we doing today?

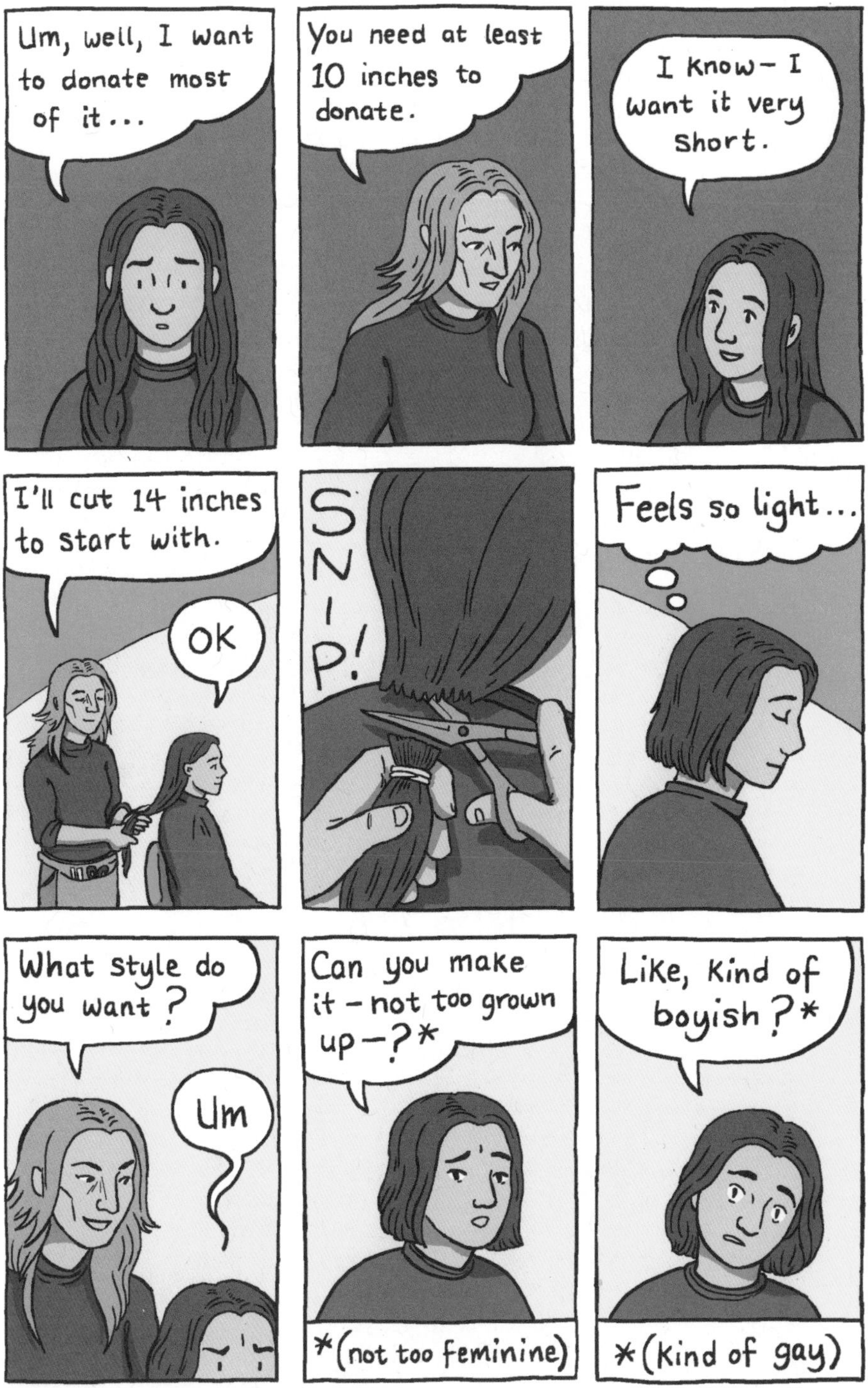
Um, well, I want to donate most of it...
You need at least 10 inches to donate.
I know- I want it very short.
I'll cut 14 inches to start with.
OK
SNIP!
Feels so light...
What style do you want?
Um
Can you make it - not too grown up-?*
*(not too feminine)
Like, Kind of boyish?*
*(Kind of gay)

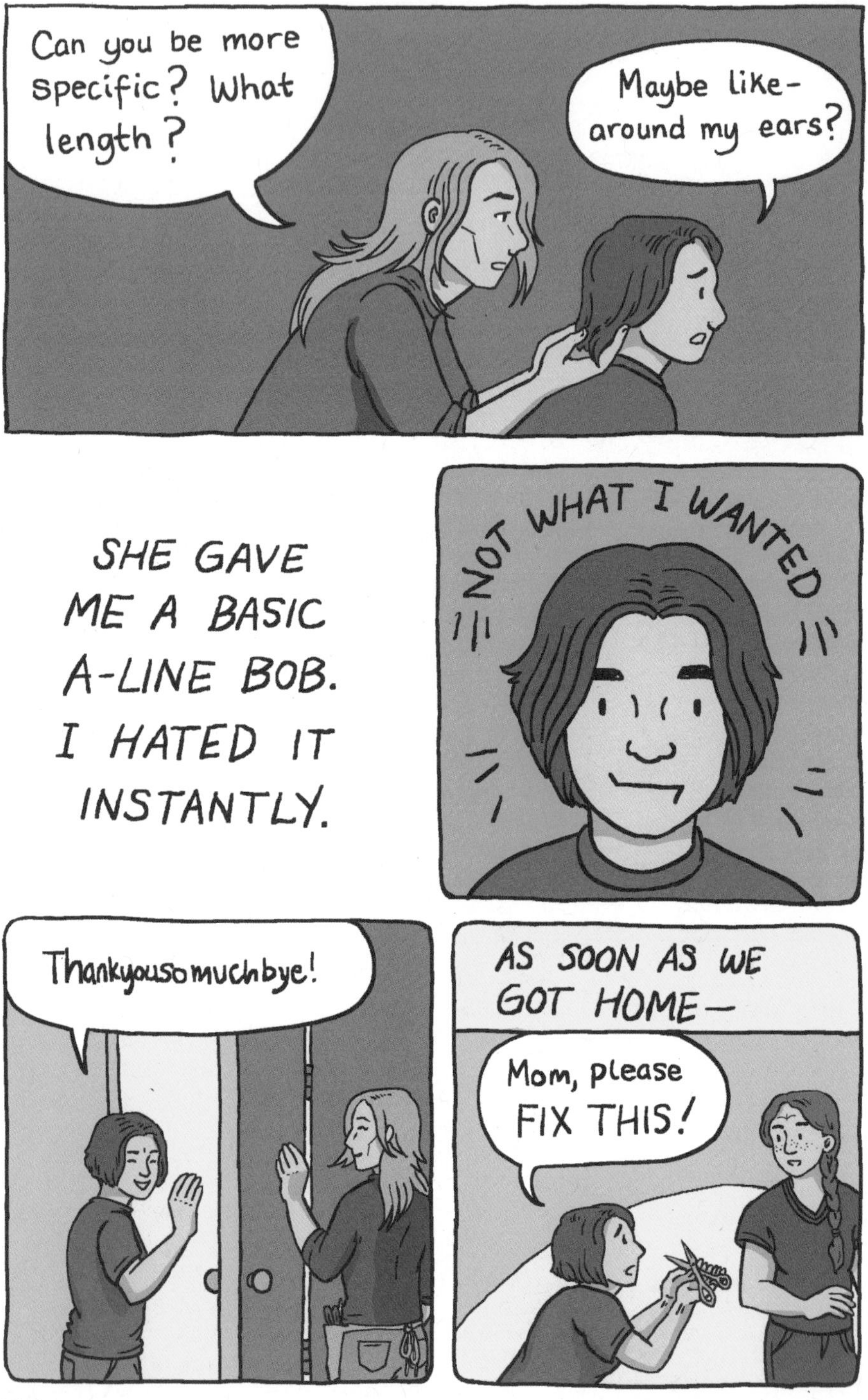
Can you be more specific? What length?
Maybe like- around my ears?
SHE GAVE ME A BASIC A-LINE BOB. I HATED IT INSTANTLY.
NOT WHAT I WANTED
Thankyousomuchbye!
AS SOON AS WE GOT HOME—
Mom, please FIX THIS!

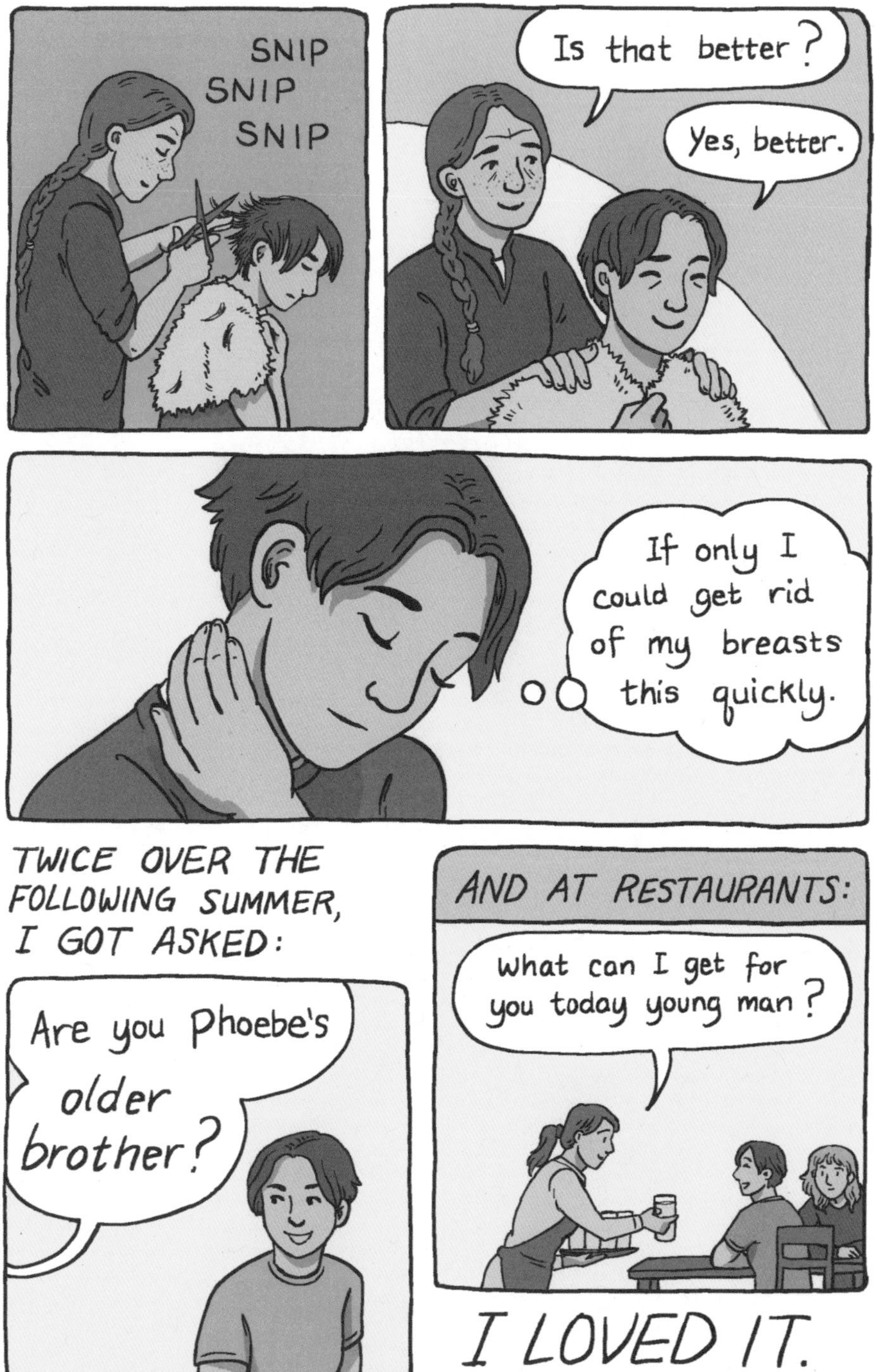
SNIP
SNIP
SNIP
Is that better?
Yes, better.
If only I could get rid of my breasts this quickly.
TWICE OVER THE FOLLOWING SUMMER, I GOT ASKED:
Are you Phoebe's older brother?
AND AT RESTAURANTS:
What can I get for you today young man?
I LOVED IT.

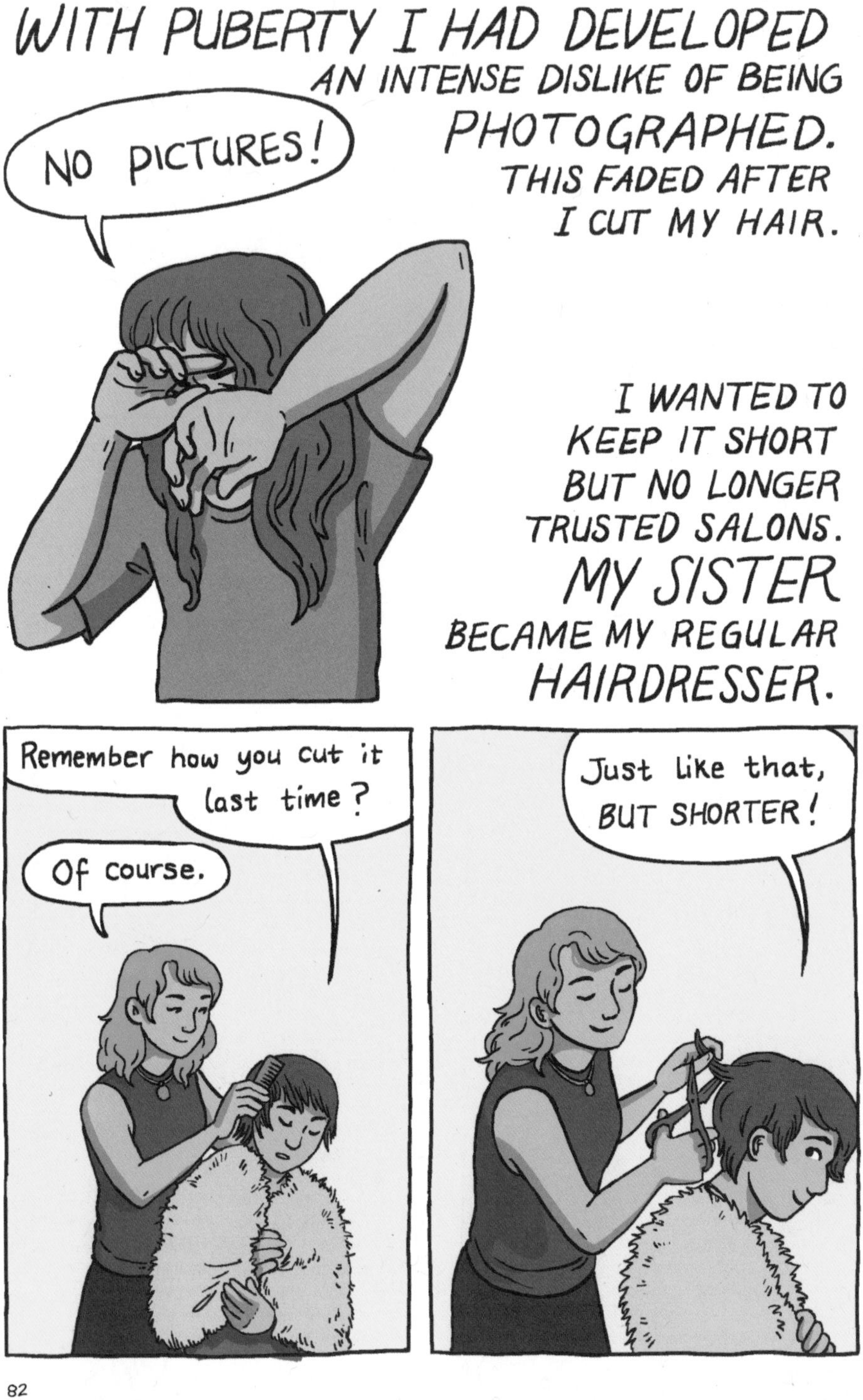
WITH PUBERTY I HAD DEVELOPED AN INTENSE DISLIKE OF BEING PHOTOGRAPHED.
NO PICTURES!
THIS FADED AFTER I CUT MY HAIR.
I WANTED TO KEEP IT SHORT BUT NO LONGER TRUSTED SALONS. MY SISTER BECAME MY REGULAR HAIRDRESSER.
Remember how you cut it last time?
Of course.
Just like that, BUT SHORTER!

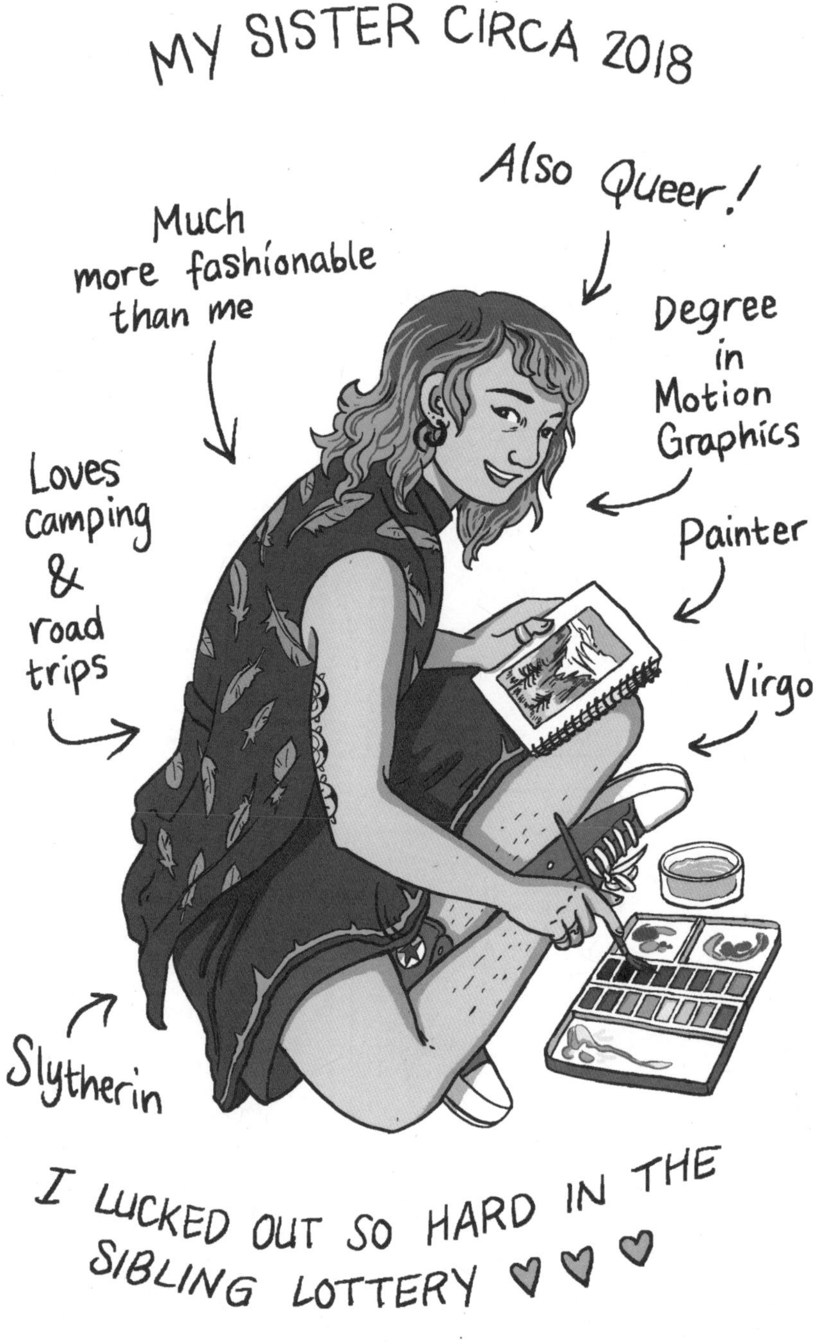
MY SISTER CIRCA 2018
Also Queer!
Much more fashionable than me
Degree in Motion Graphics
Loves camping & road trips
Painter
Virgo
Slytherin
I LUCKED OUT SO HARD IN THE SIBLING LOTTERY

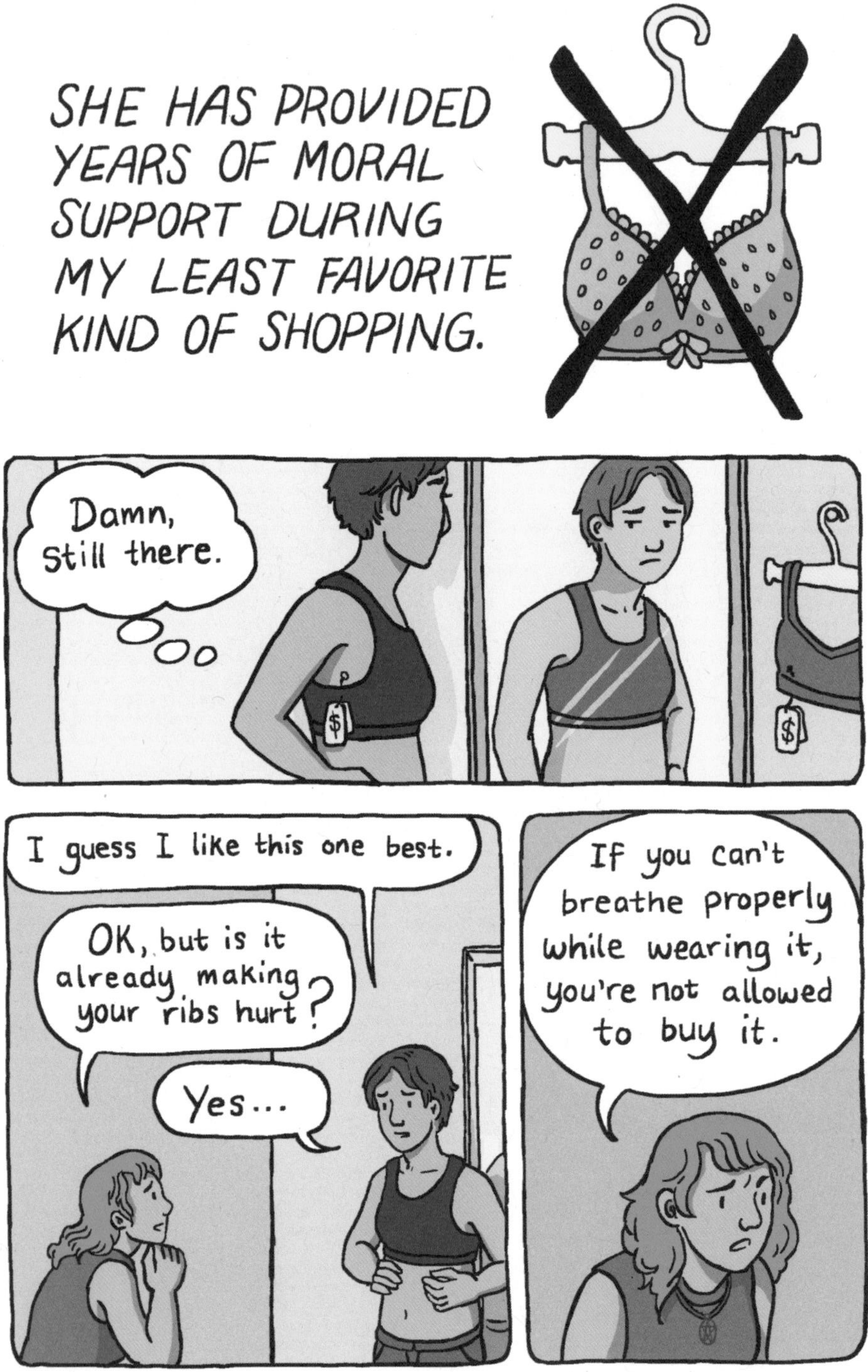
SHE HAS PROVIDED YEARS OF MORAL SUPPORT DURING MY LEAST FAVORITE KIND OF SHOPPING.
Damn, still there.
I guess I like this one best.
OK, but is it already making your ribs hurt?
Yes...
If you can't breathe properly while wearing it, you're not allowed to buy it.

WHEN I WAS CAST IN A MINOR ROLE IN A CLASS PLAY IN TENTH GRADE, PHOEBE ASKED ME:

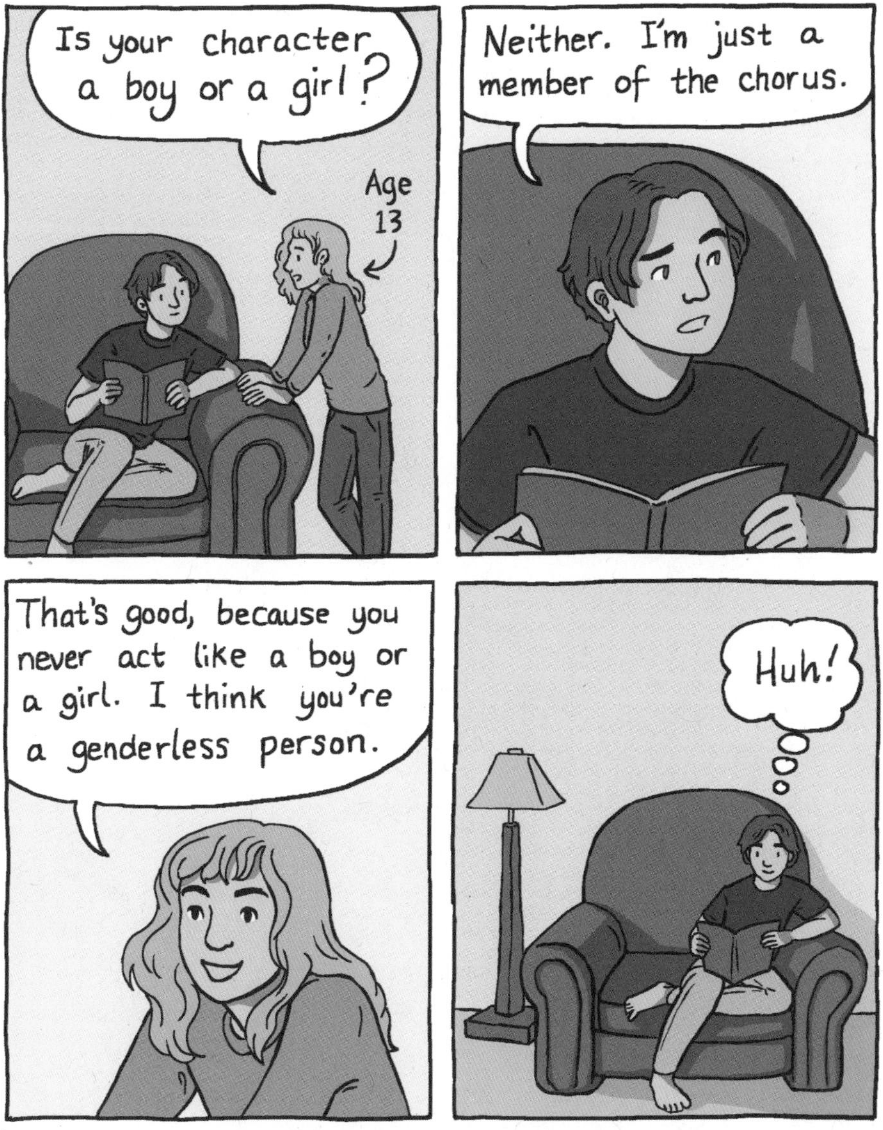
Is your character a boy or a girl?
Age 13
Neither. I'm just a member of the chorus.
That's good, because you never act like a boy or a girl. I think you're a genderless person.
Huh!

SHE KNEW BEFORE I DID.

DURING THE FOLLOWING YEAR, AN AMBITIOUS NEW DRAMA TEACHER DECIDED TO DIRECT OUR SCHOOL'S FIRST EVER MUSICAL.

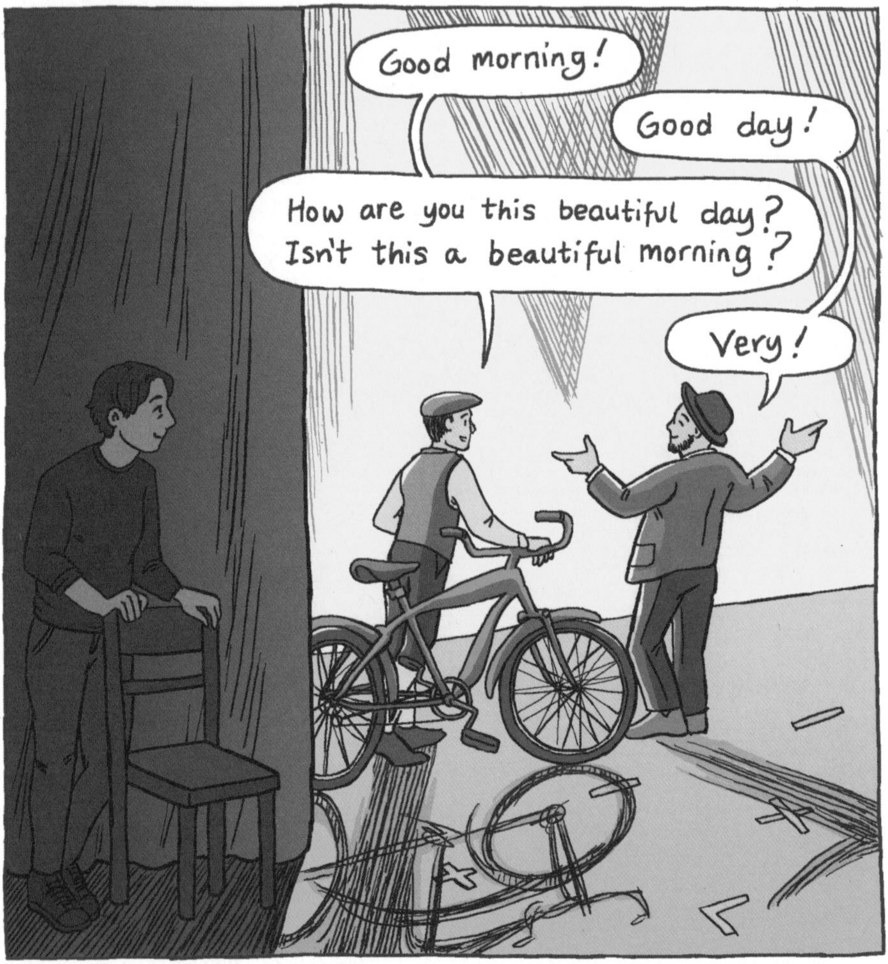
Good morning!
Good day!
How are you this beautiful day? Isn't this a beautiful morning?
Very!

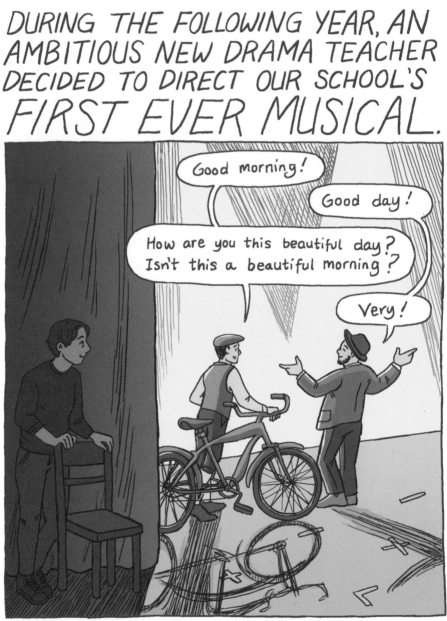

I JOINED THE BACKSTAGE CREW AND FULFILLED A STEREOTYPE BY FALLING IN LOVE WITH THEATER.

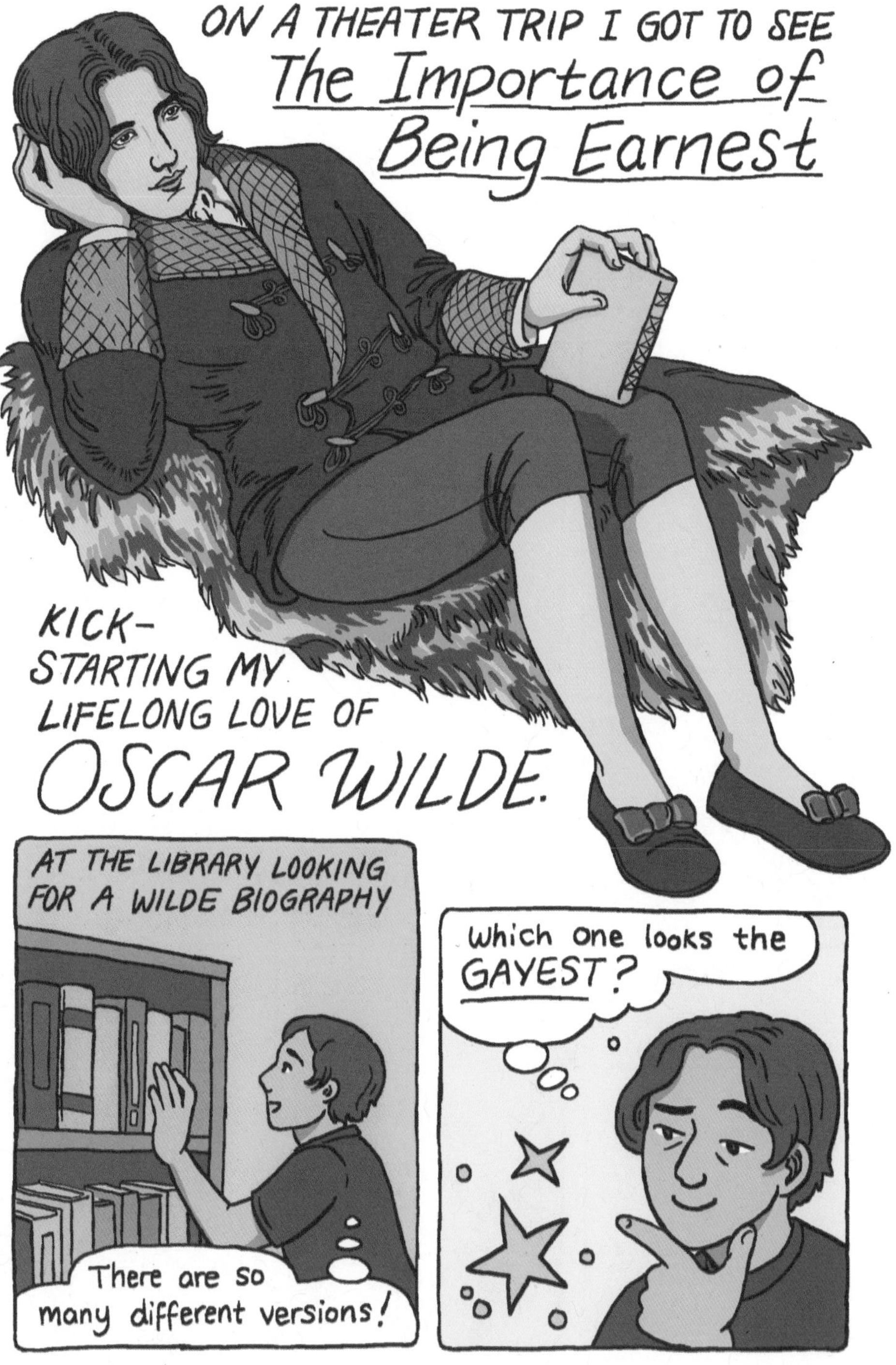
ON A THEATER TRIP I GOT TO SEE
The Importance of Being Earnest
KICK-STARTING MY LIFELONG LOVE OF
OSCAR WILDE.
AT THE LIBRARY LOOKING FOR A WILDE BIOGRAPHY
There are so many different versions!
Which one looks the GAYEST?

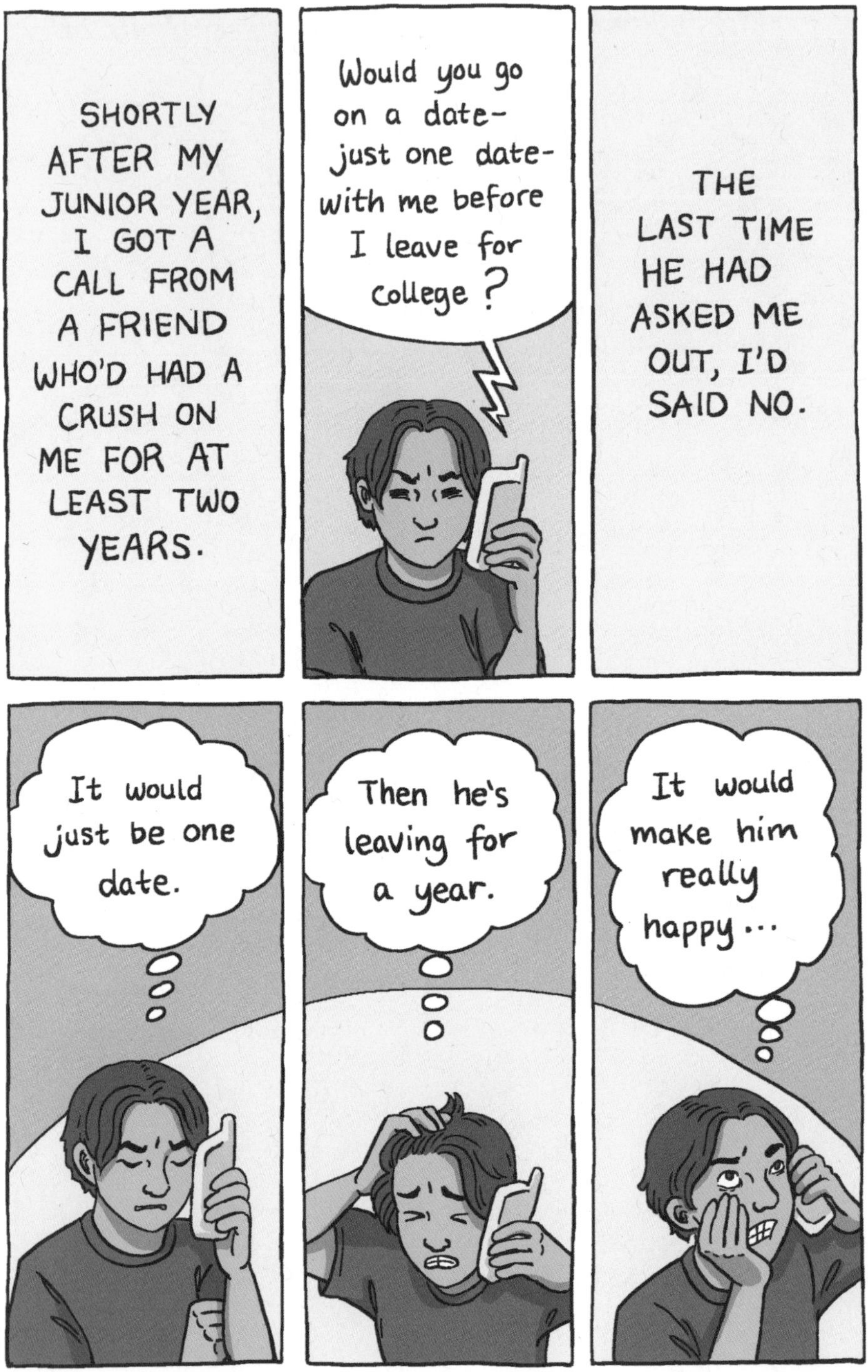
SHORTLY AFTER MY JUNIOR YEAR, I GOT A CALL FROM A FRIEND WHO'D HAD A CRUSH ON ME FOR AT LEAST TWO YEARS.
Would you go on a date- just one date- with me before I leave for college?
THE LAST TIME HE HAD ASKED ME OUT, I'D SAID NO.
It would just be one date.
Then he's leaving for a year.
It would make him really happy...

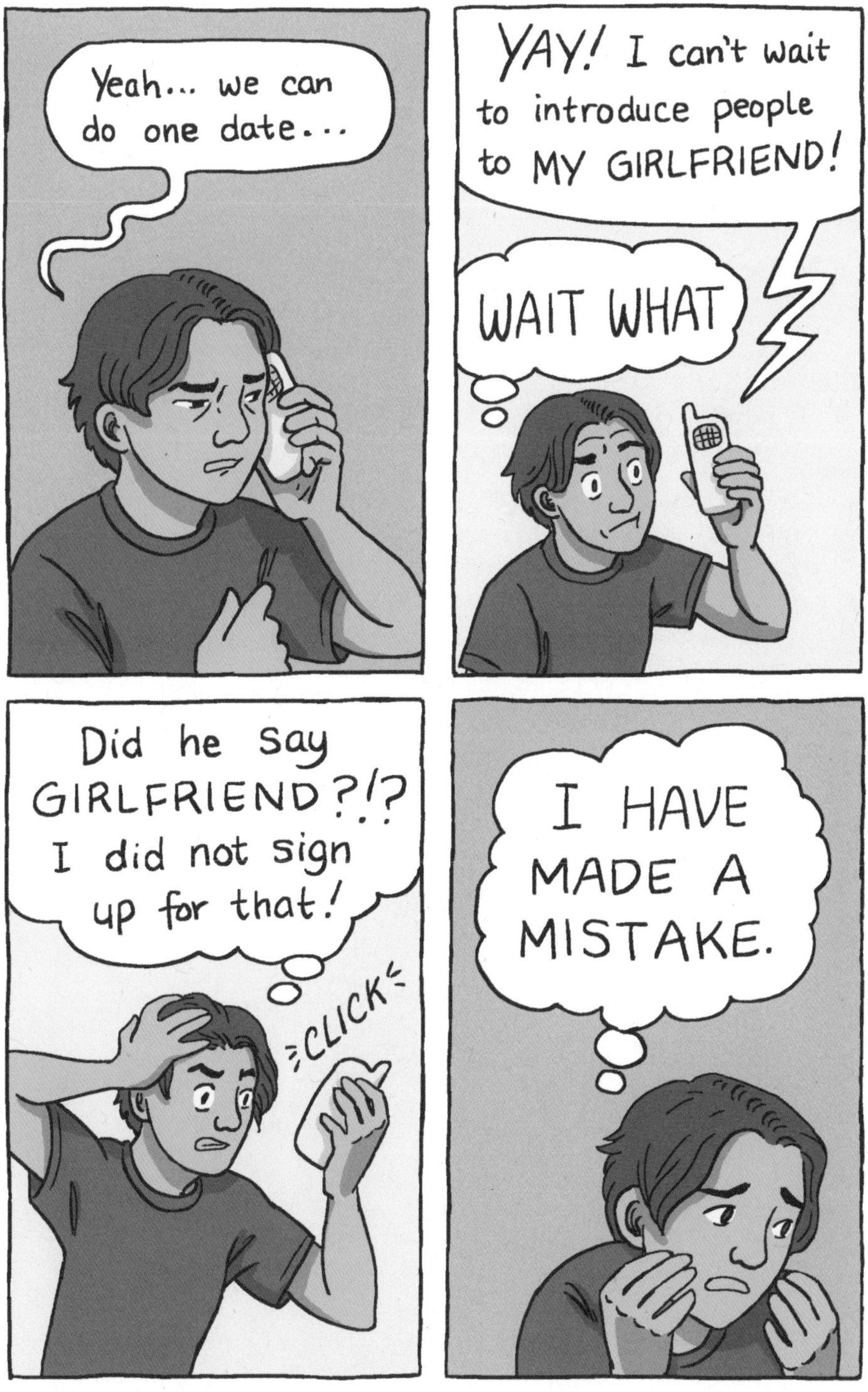
Yeah... we can do one date...
YAY! I can't wait to introduce people to MY GIRLFRIEND!
WAIT WHAT
Did he say GIRLFRIEND?!? I did not sign up for that!
CLICK
I HAVE MADE A MISTAKE.

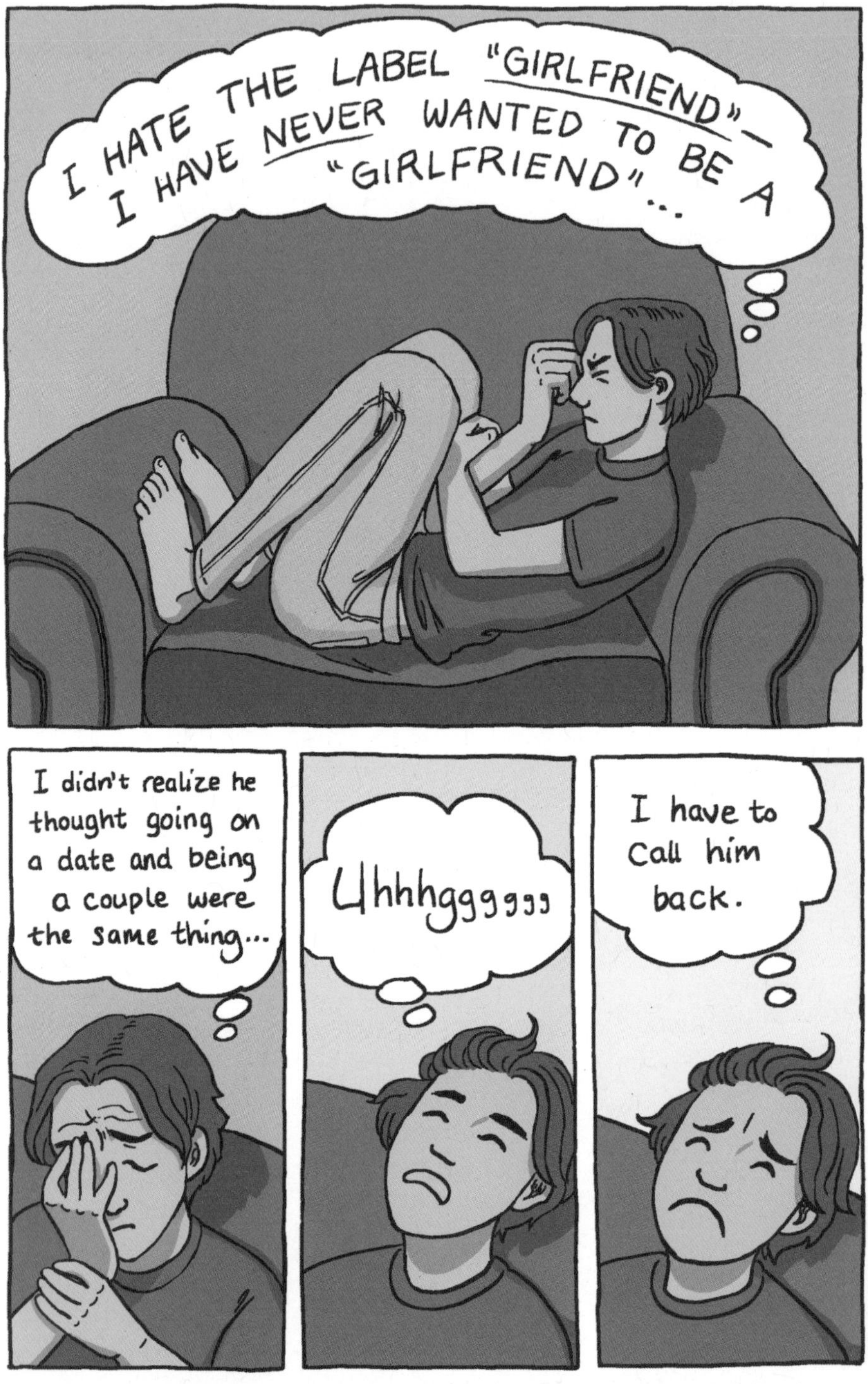
I HATE THE LABEL "GIRLFRIEND"— I HAVE NEVER WANTED TO BE A "GIRLFRIEND"...
I didn't realize he thought going on a date and being a couple were the same thing...
Uhhhggggg
I have to call him back.

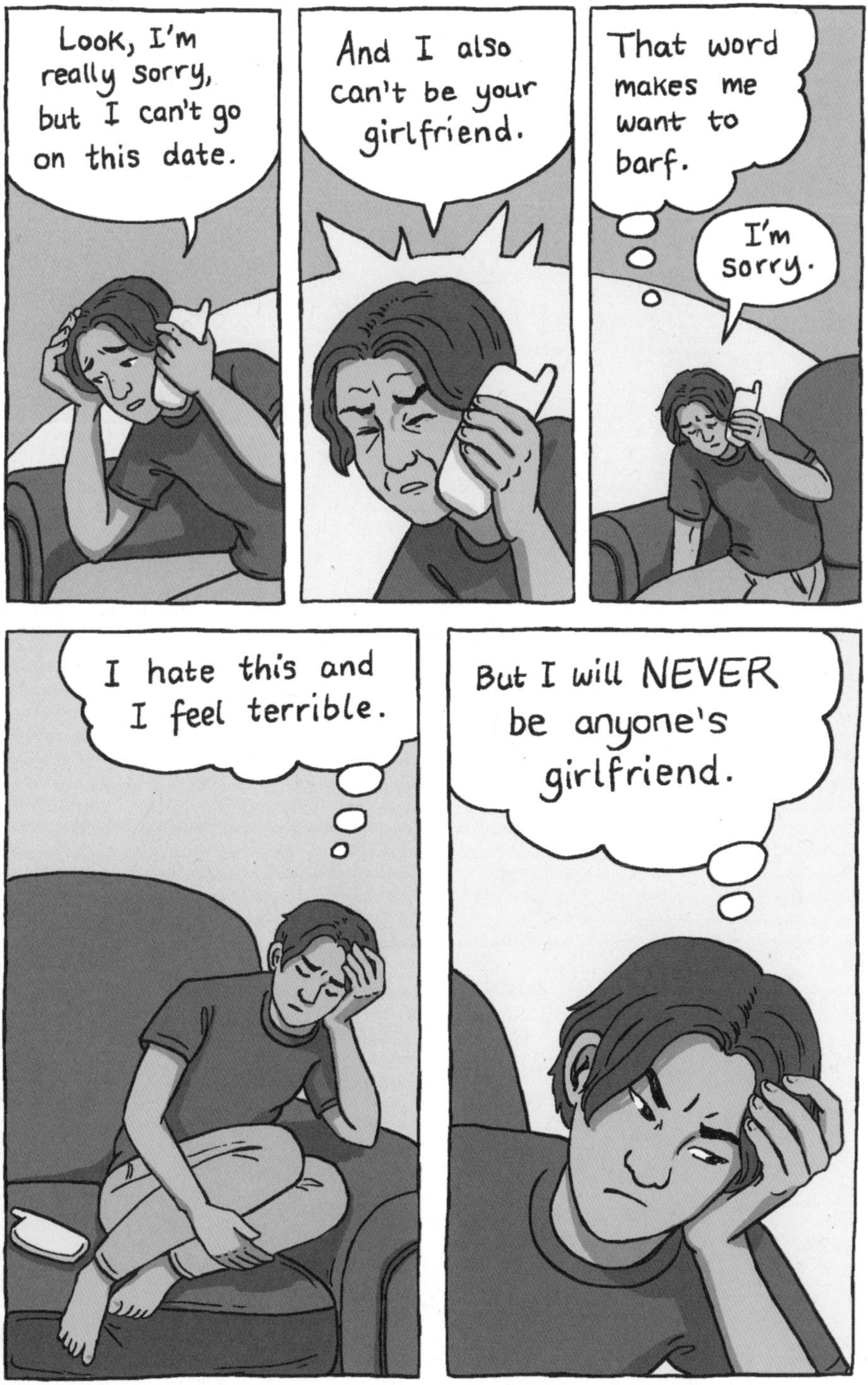
Look, I'm really sorry, but I can't go on this date.
And I also can't be your girlfriend.
That word makes me want to barf.
I'm sorry.
I hate this and I feel terrible.
But I will NEVER be anyone's girlfriend.

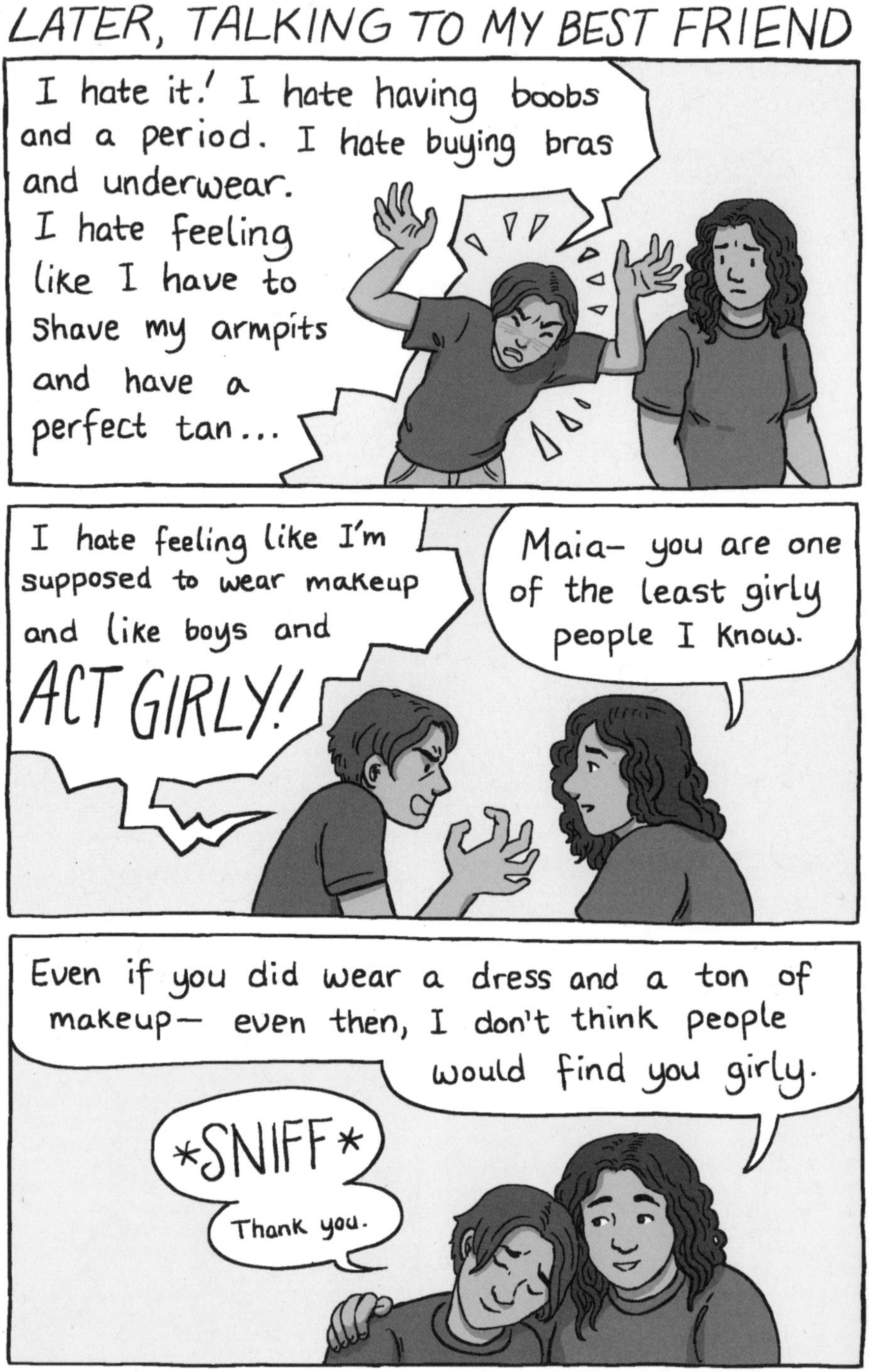
LATER, TALKING TO MY BEST FRIEND
I hate it! I hate having boobs and a period. I hate buying bras and underwear. I hate feeling like I have to shave my armpits and have a perfect tan...
I hate feeling like I'm supposed to wear makeup and like boys and ACT GIRLY!
Maia– you are one of the least girly people I know.
Even if you did wear a dress and a ton of makeup– even then, I don't think people would find you girly.
SNIFF
Thank you.

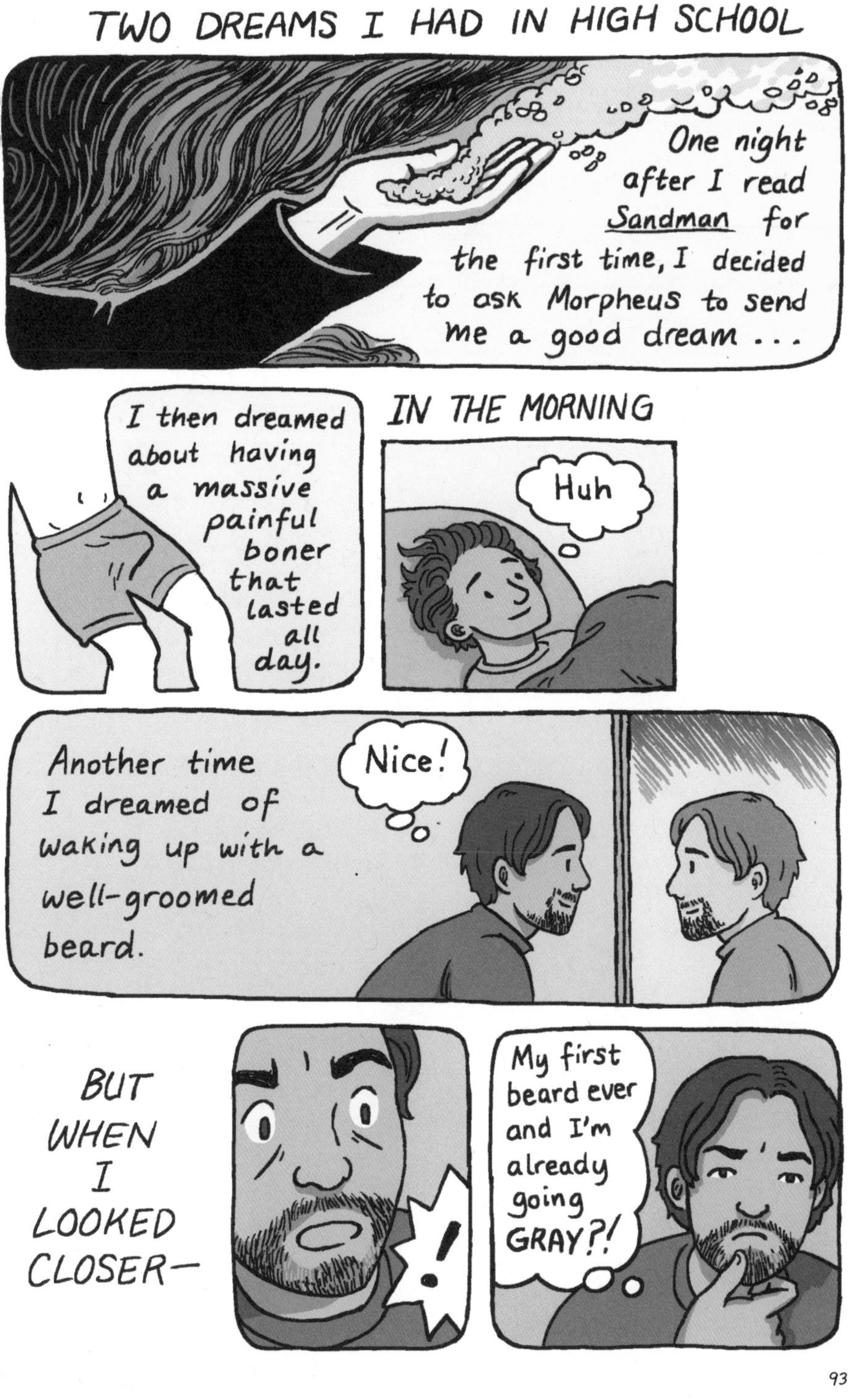
TWO DREAMS I HAD IN HIGH SCHOOL
One night after I read Sandman for the first time, I decided to ask Morpheus to send me a good dream . . .
I then dreamed about having a massive painful boner that lasted all day.
IN THE MORNING
Huh
Another time I dreamed of waking up with a well-groomed beard.
Nice!
BUT WHEN I LOOKED CLOSER—
!
My first beard ever and I'm already going GRAY?!

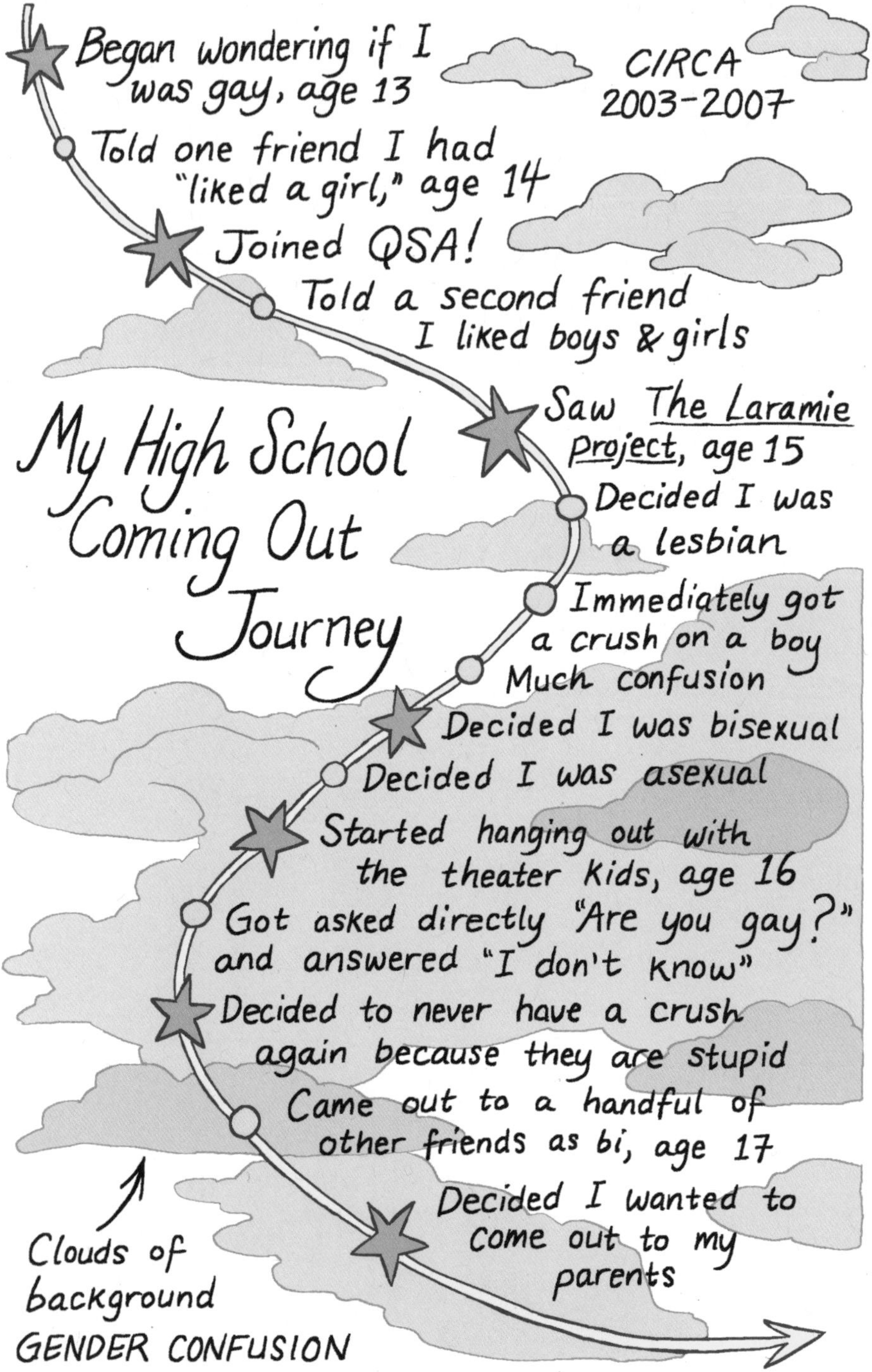
My High School Coming Out Journey
CIRCA 2003-2007
Began wondering if I was gay, age 13
Told one friend I had "liked a girl," age 14
Joined QSA!
Told a second friend I liked boys & girls
Saw The Laramie Project, age 15
Decided I was a lesbian
Immediately got a crush on a boy
Much confusion
Decided I was bisexual
Decided I was asexual
Started hanging out with the theater kids, age 16
Got asked directly "Are you gay?" and answered "I don't know"
Decided to never have a crush again because they are stupid
Came out to a handful of other friends as bi, age 17
Decided I wanted to come out to my parents
Clouds of background GENDER CONFUSION

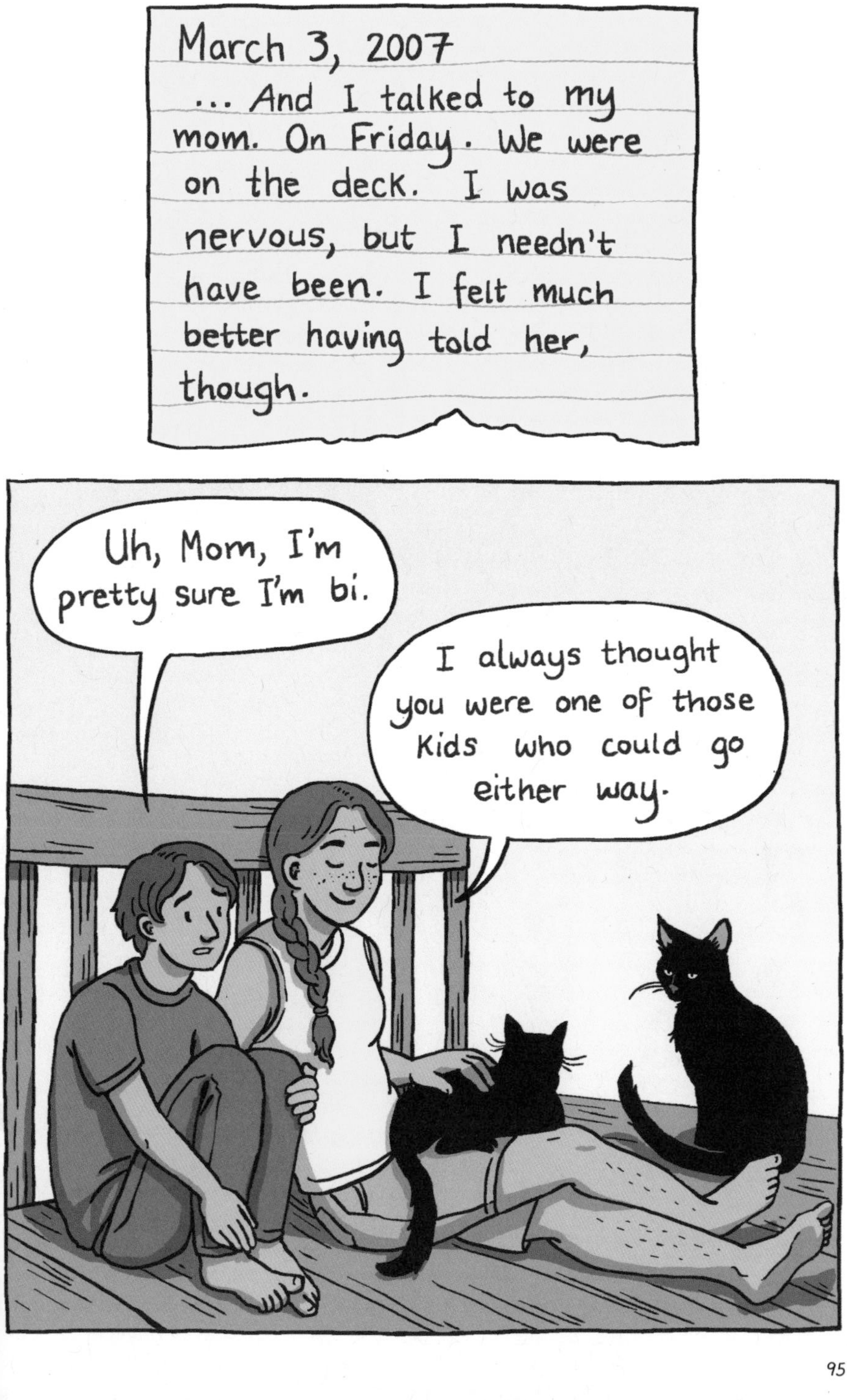
March 3, 2007
... And I talked to my mom. On Friday. We were on the deck. I was nervous, but I needn't have been. I felt much better having told her, though.
Uh, Mom, I'm pretty sure I'm bi.
I always thought you were one of those kids who could go either way.

AT MY HIGH SCHOOL GRADUATION IN 2007, I WAS THE ONLY A.F.A.B. (ASSIGNED FEMALE AT BIRTH) GRADUATE WHO WORE PANTS.

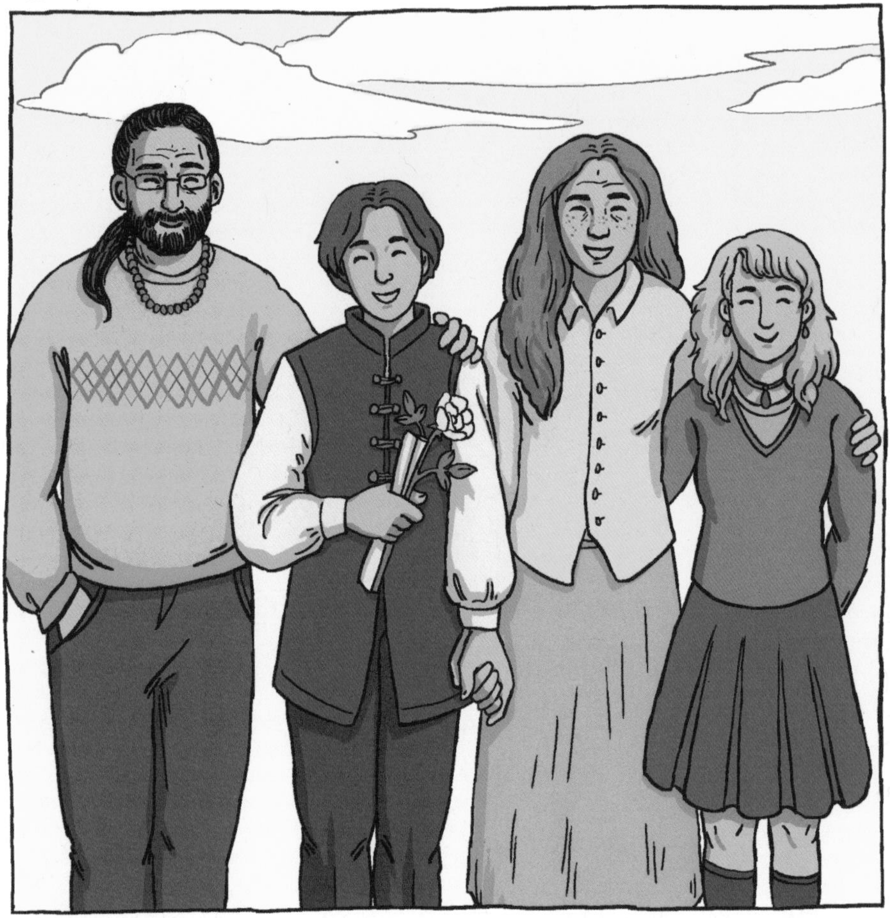

SOMETHING I LOST WHEN I CUT MY HAIR: VISUAL UNITY WITH MY LONG-HAIRED FAMILY. THINGS I GAINED: CONFIDENCE, HAPPINESS.

MY PARENTS MET WHEN THEY WERE IN COLLEGE

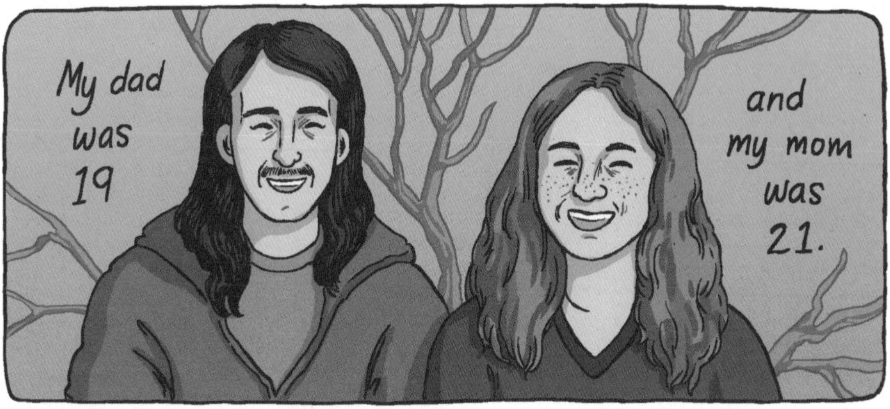
My dad was 19
and my mom was 21.

WHEN I REACHED EACH OF THESE RESPECTIVE AGES, I REMEMBER THINKING:

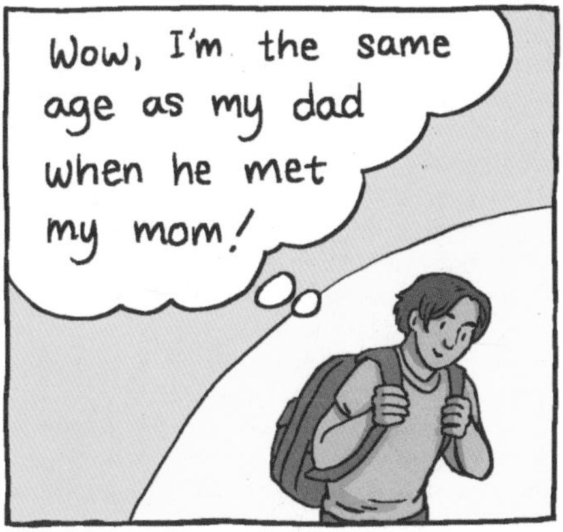
Wow, I'm the same age as my dad when he met my mom!

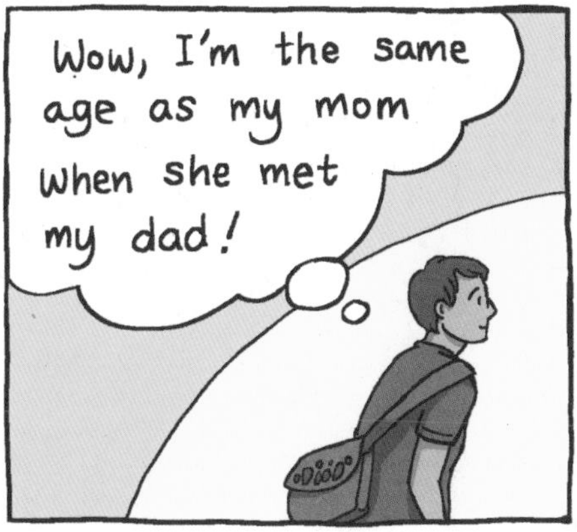
Wow, I'm the same age as my mom when she met my dad!

NOW I FIND MYSELF THINKING:

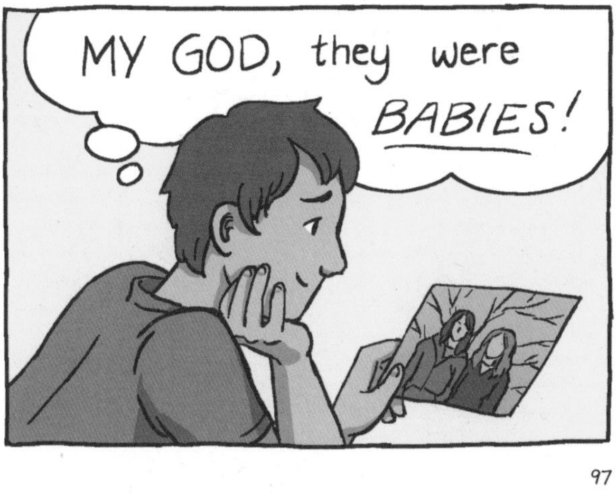
MY GOD, they were BABIES!

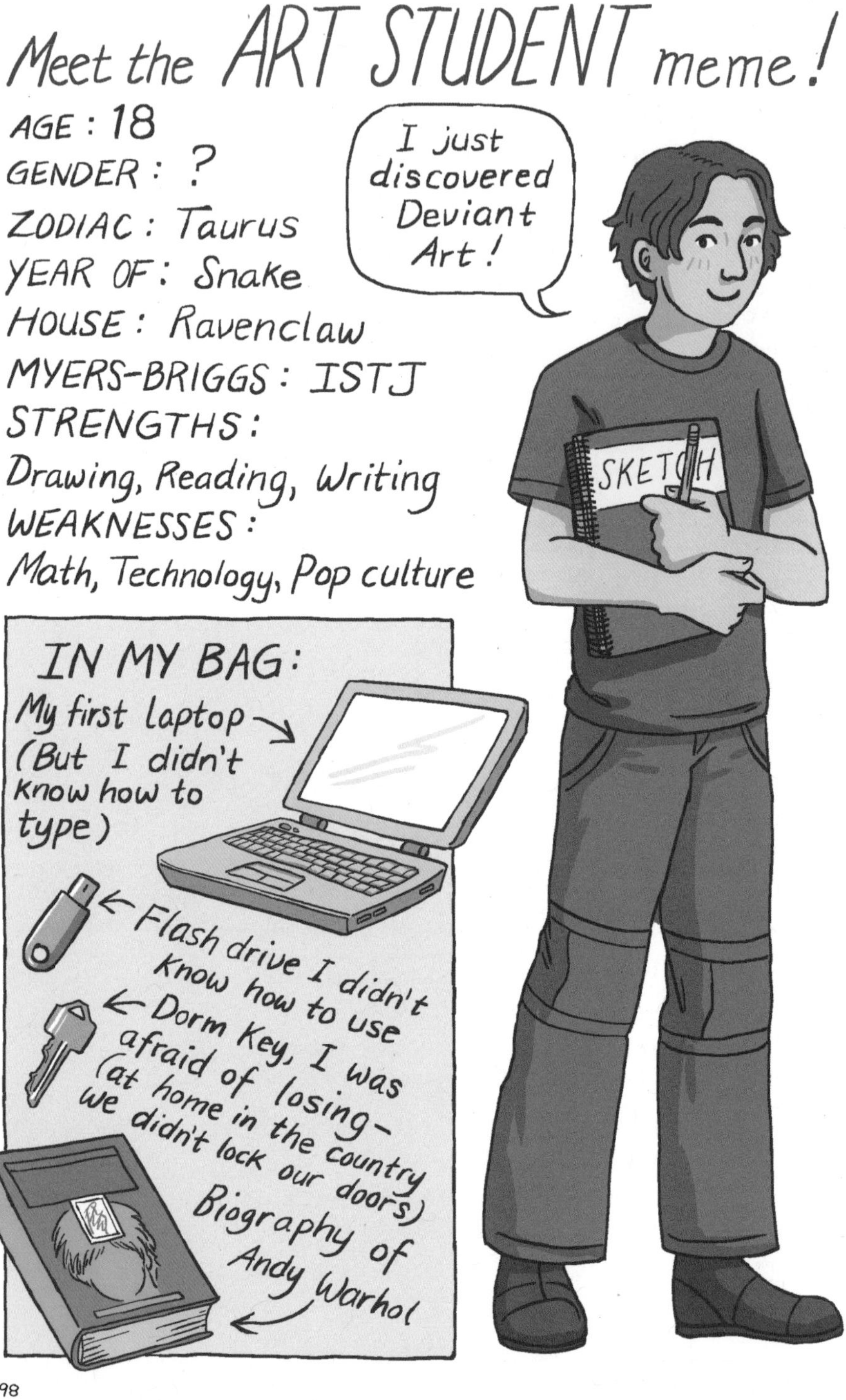
Meet the ART STUDENT meme!
AGE: 18
GENDER: ?
ZODIAC: Taurus
YEAR OF: Snake
HOUSE: Ravenclaw
MYERS-BRIGGS: ISTJ
STRENGTHS:
Drawing, Reading, Writing
WEAKNESSES:
Math, Technology, Pop culture
I just discovered Deviant Art!
SKETCH
IN MY BAG:
My first laptop (But I didn't know how to type)
Flash drive I didn't know how to use
Dorm Key, I was afraid of losing- (at home in the country we didn't lock our doors)
Biography of Andy Warhol

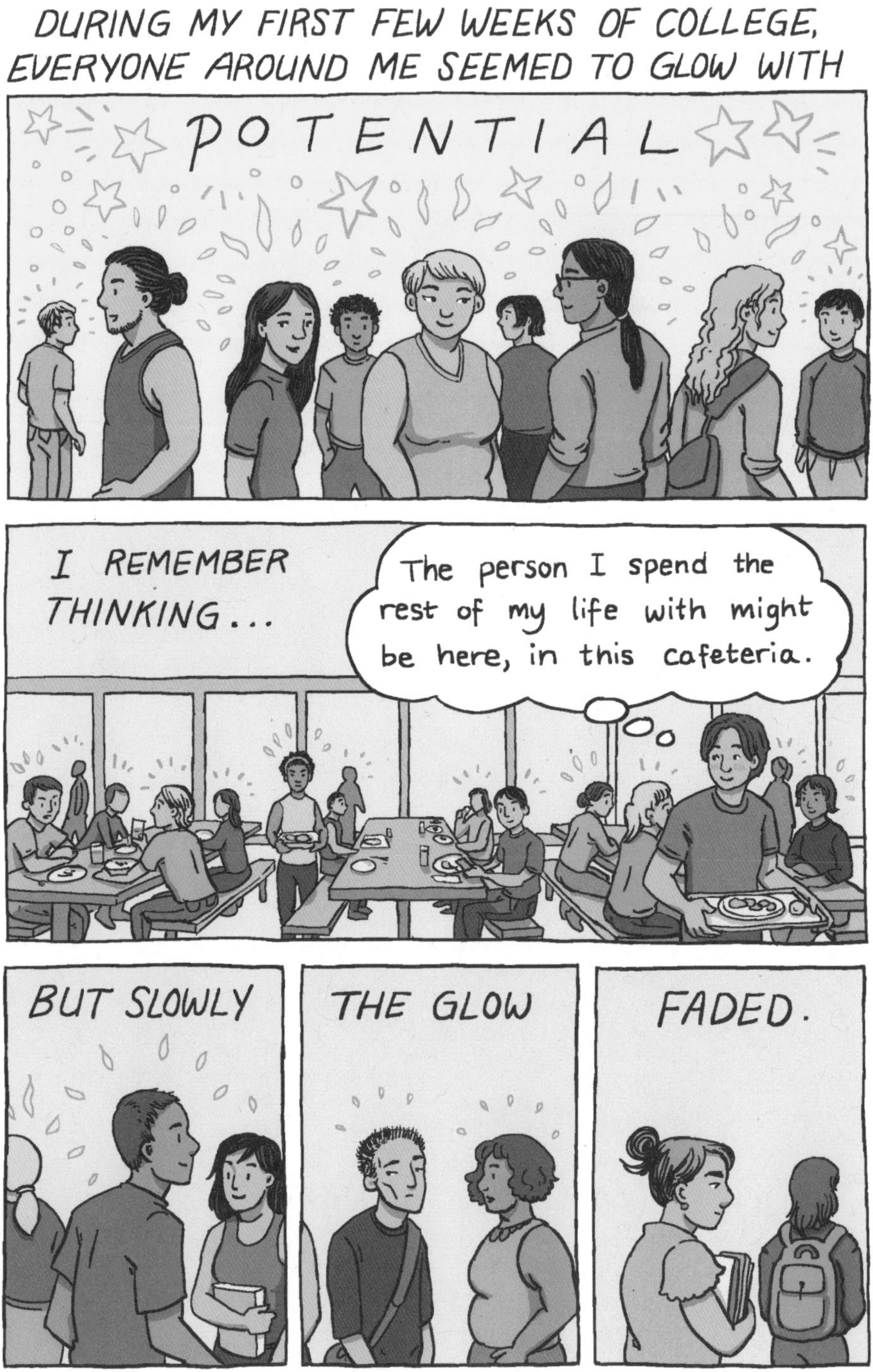
DURING MY FIRST FEW WEEKS OF COLLEGE, EVERYONE AROUND ME SEEMED TO GLOW WITH
POTENTIAL
I REMEMBER THINKING...
The person I spend the rest of my life with might be here, in this cafeteria.
BUT SLOWLY
THE GLOW
FADED.

I JOINED THE DRAMA CLUB BUT WAS DISAPPOINTED TO FIND IT SMALLER THAN THE ONE AT MY HIGH SCHOOL.

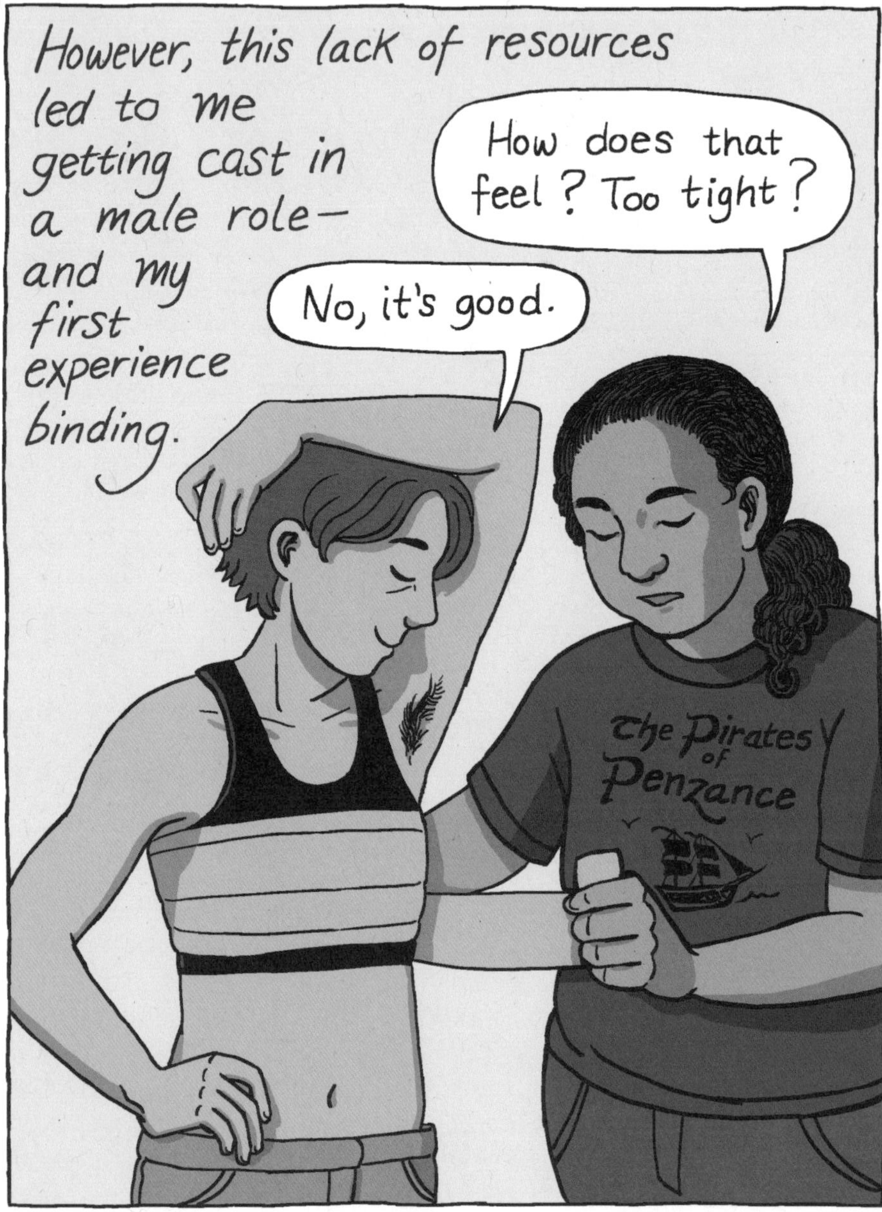

However, this lack of resources led to me getting cast in a male role— and my first experience binding.
How does that feel? Too tight?
No, it's good.
The Pirates of Penzance

AT THE TIME I DIDN'T KNOW THE DANGERS OF ACE BANDAGE BINDING— IT CAN LEAD TO CRACKED RIBS.

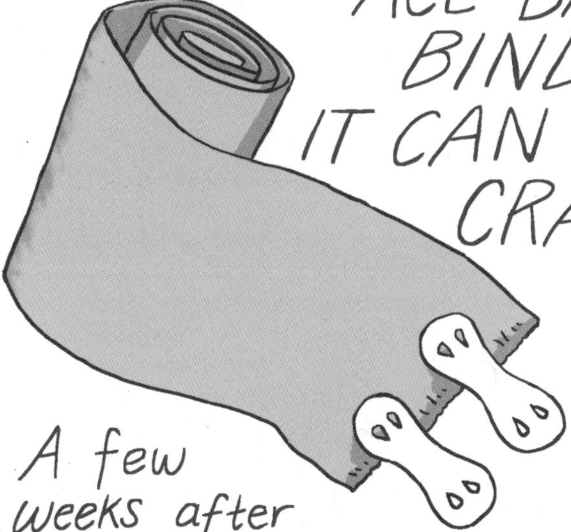

A few weeks after the show ended, I went to a formal school event wearing the ACE bandage and a too-long tie. What had felt liberating onstage felt embarrassing in public. I put the bandage away and never wore it again.

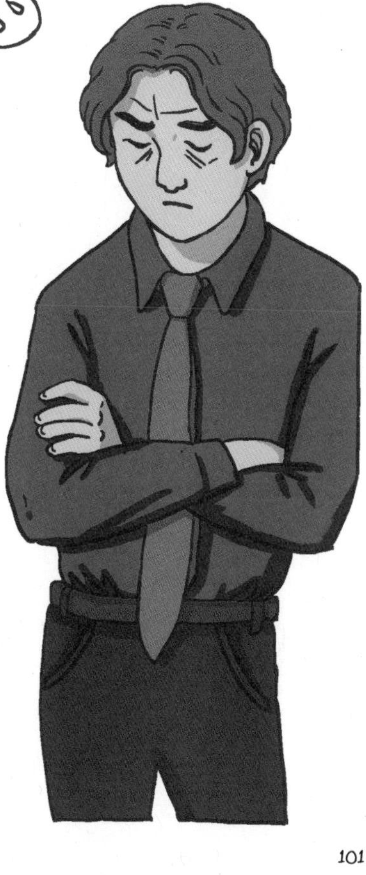

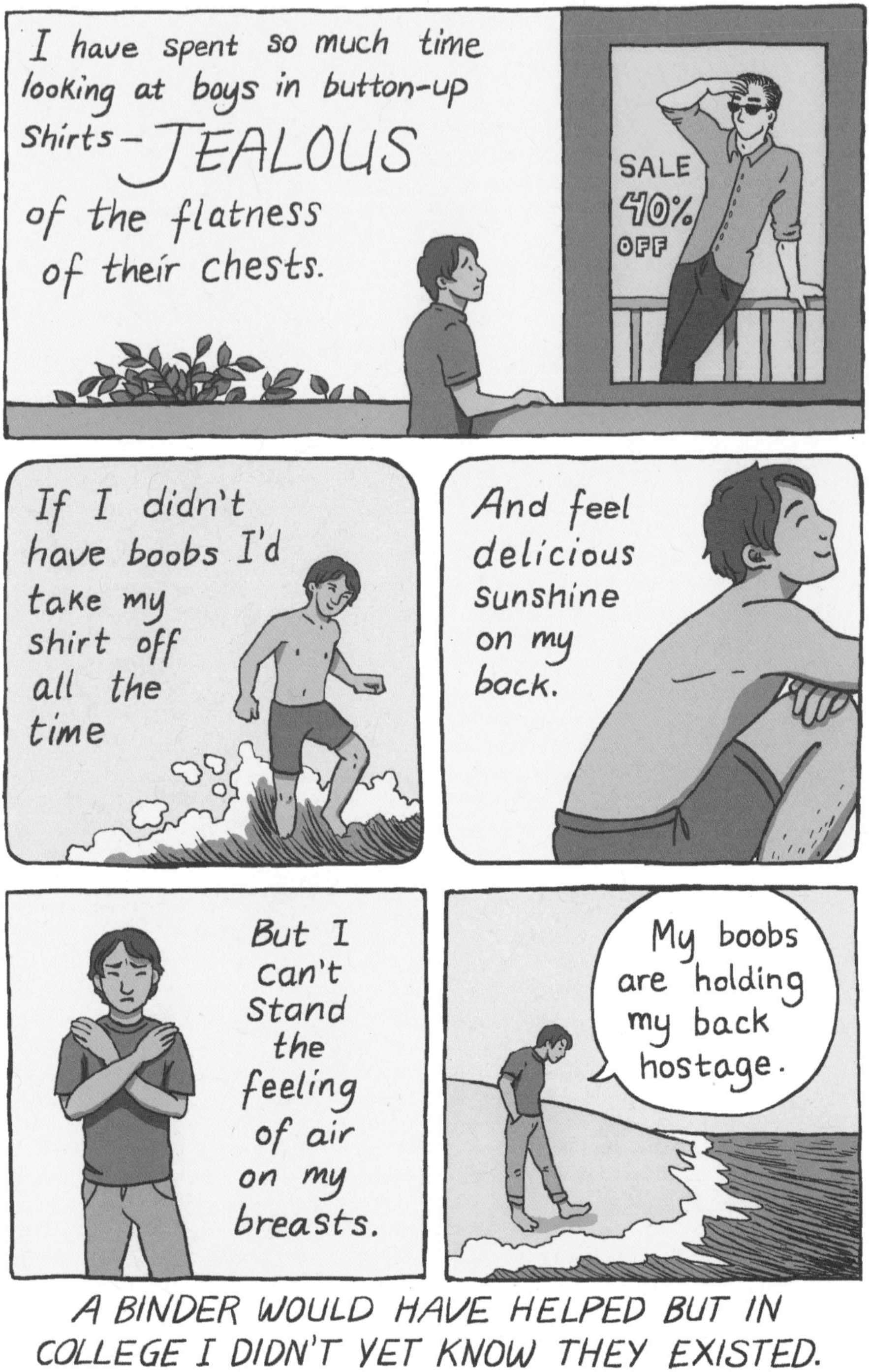
I have spent so much time looking at boys in button-up shirts– JEALOUS of the flatness of their chests.
SALE 40% OFF
If I didn't have boobs I'd take my shirt off all the time
And feel delicious sunshine on my back.
But I can't stand the feeling of air on my breasts.
My boobs are holding my back hostage.
A BINDER WOULD HAVE HELPED BUT IN COLLEGE I DIDN'T YET KNOW THEY EXISTED.

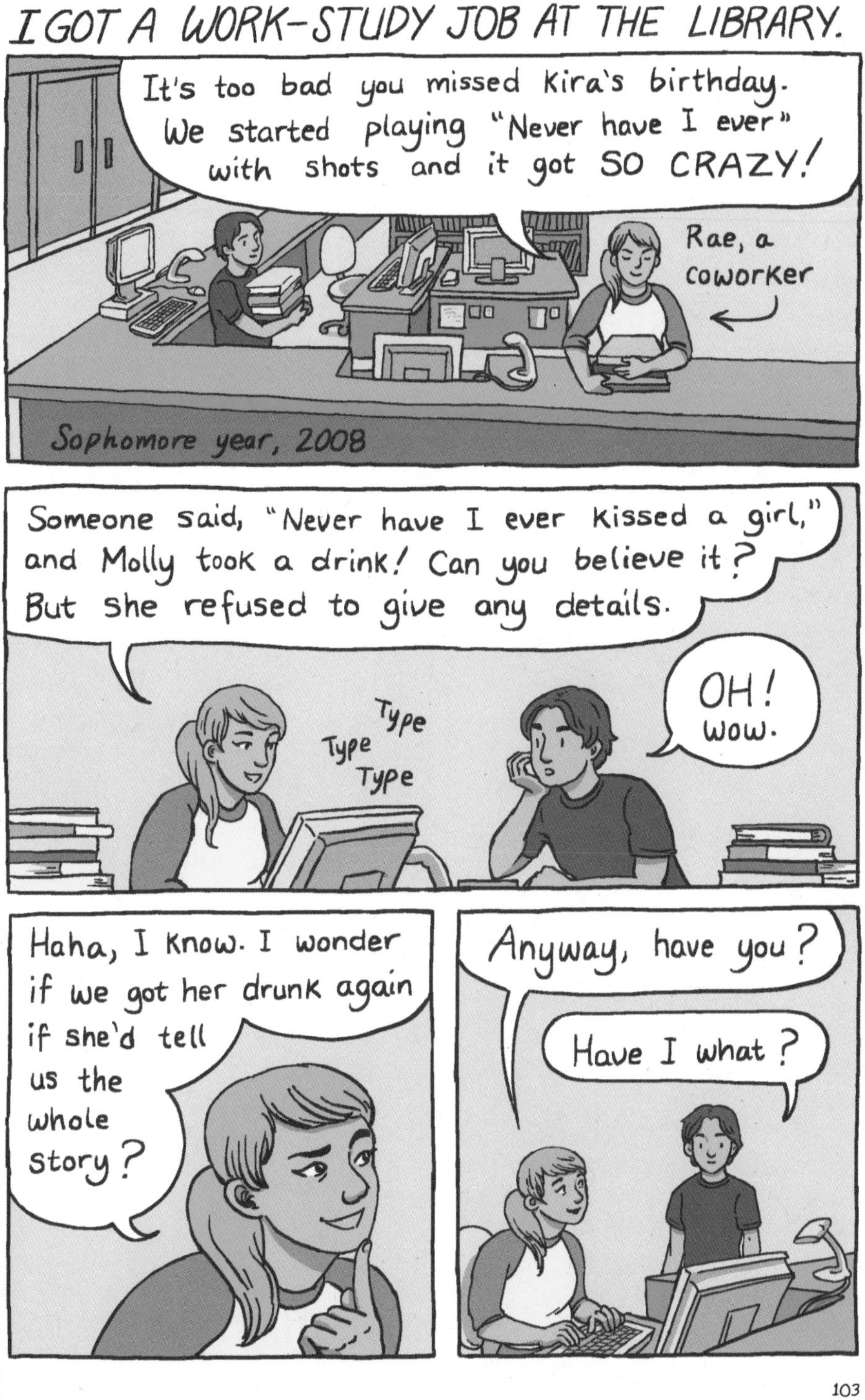
I GOT A WORK-STUDY JOB AT THE LIBRARY.
It's too bad you missed Kira's birthday. We started playing "Never have I ever" with shots and it got SO CRAZY!
Rae, a coworker
Sophomore year, 2008
Someone said, "Never have I ever kissed a girl," and Molly took a drink! Can you believe it? But she refused to give any details.
Type Type Type
OH! wow.
Haha, I know. I wonder if we got her drunk again if she'd tell us the whole story?
Anyway, have you?
Have I what?

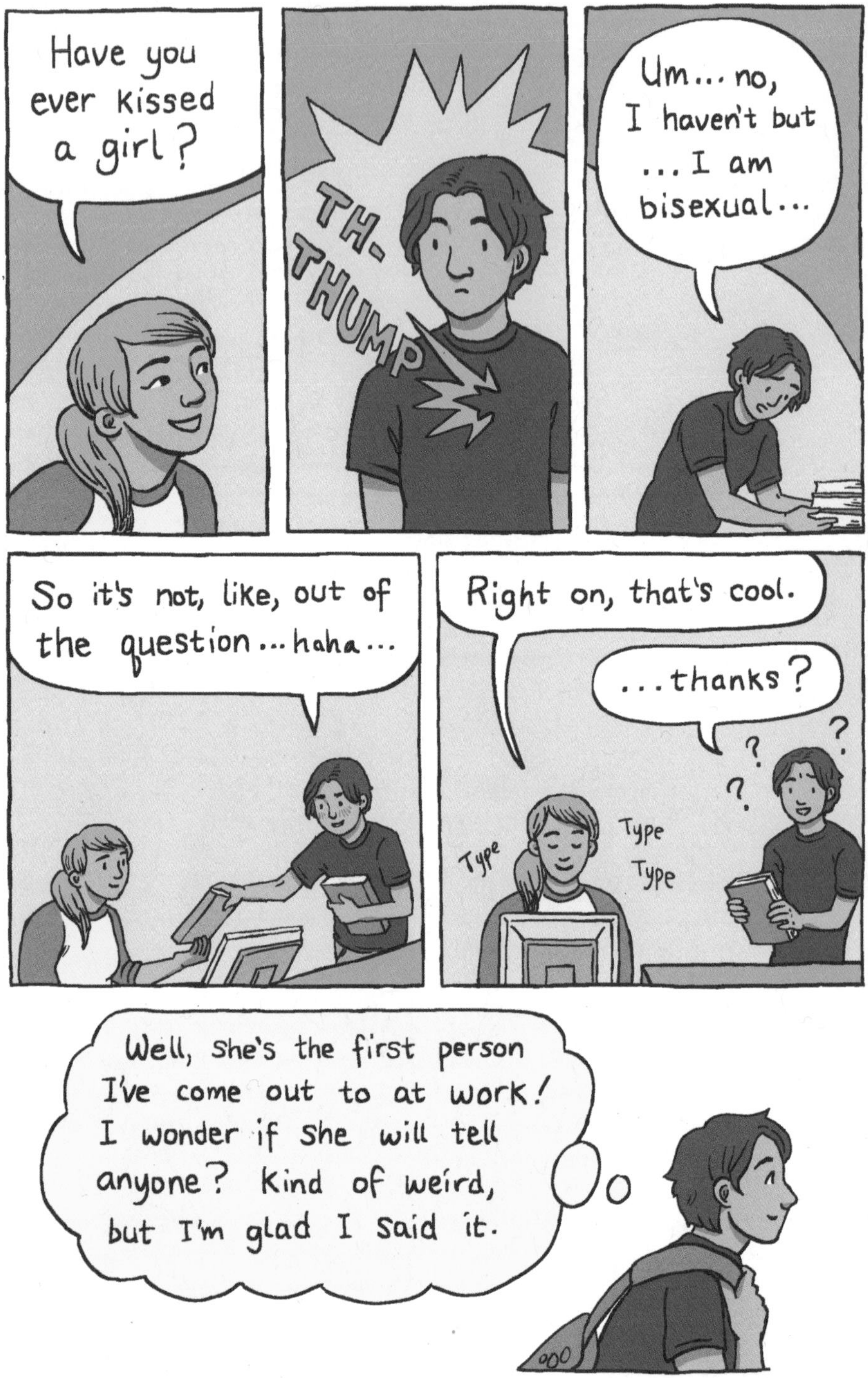
Have you ever kissed a girl?
TH-THUMP
Um... no, I haven't but ... I am bisexual...
So it's not, like, out of the question... haha...
Right on, that's cool.
...thanks?
? ? ?
Type
Type
Type
Well, she's the first person I've come out to at work! I wonder if she will tell anyone? Kind of weird, but I'm glad I said it.

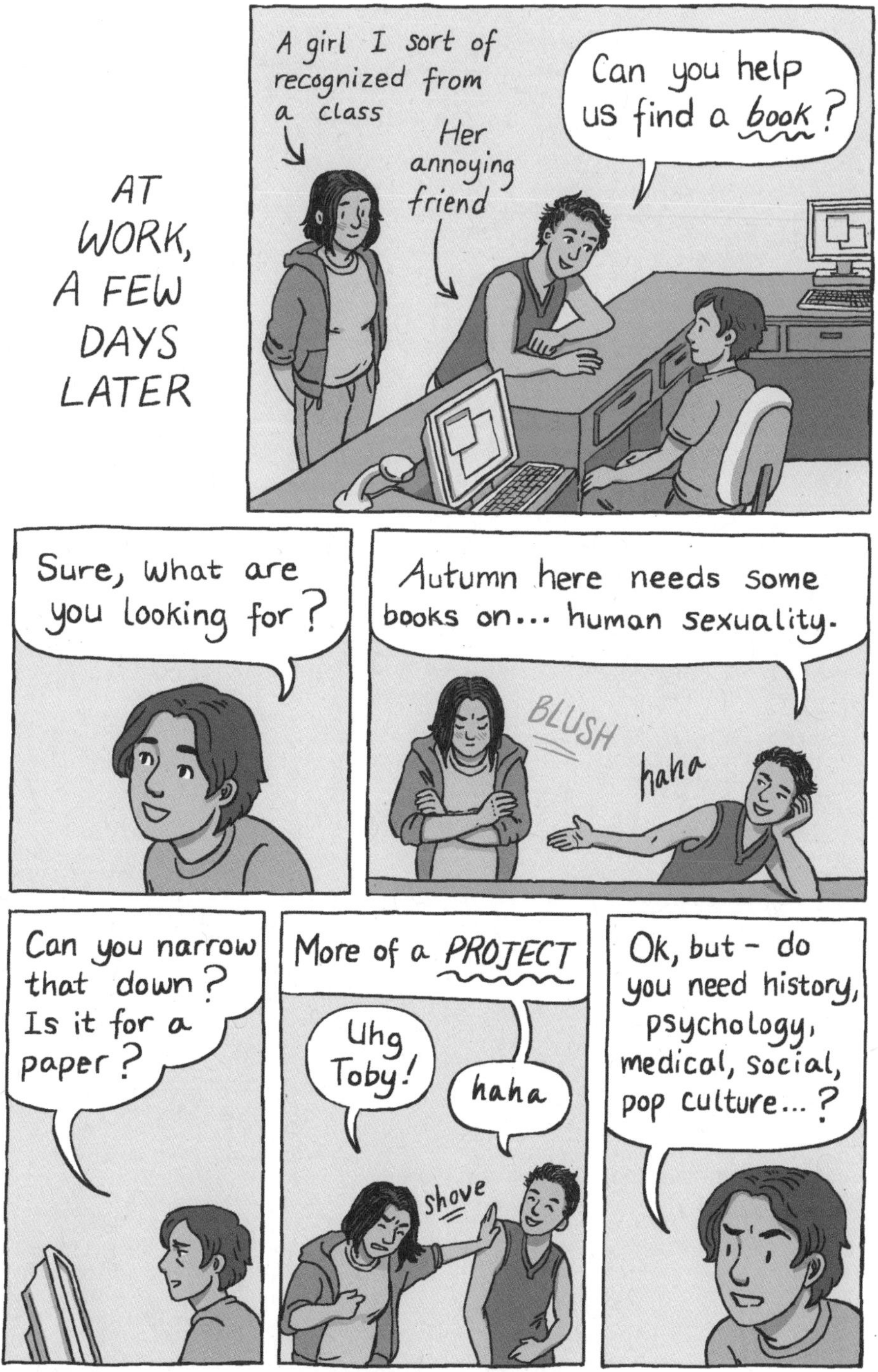
AT WORK, A FEW DAYS LATER
A girl I sort of recognized from a class
Her annoying friend
Can you help us find a book?
Sure, what are you looking for?
Autumn here needs some books on... human sexuality.
BLUSH
haha
Can you narrow that down? Is it for a paper?
More of a PROJECT
Uhg Toby!
haha
shove
Ok, but - do you need history, psychology, medical, social, pop culture...?

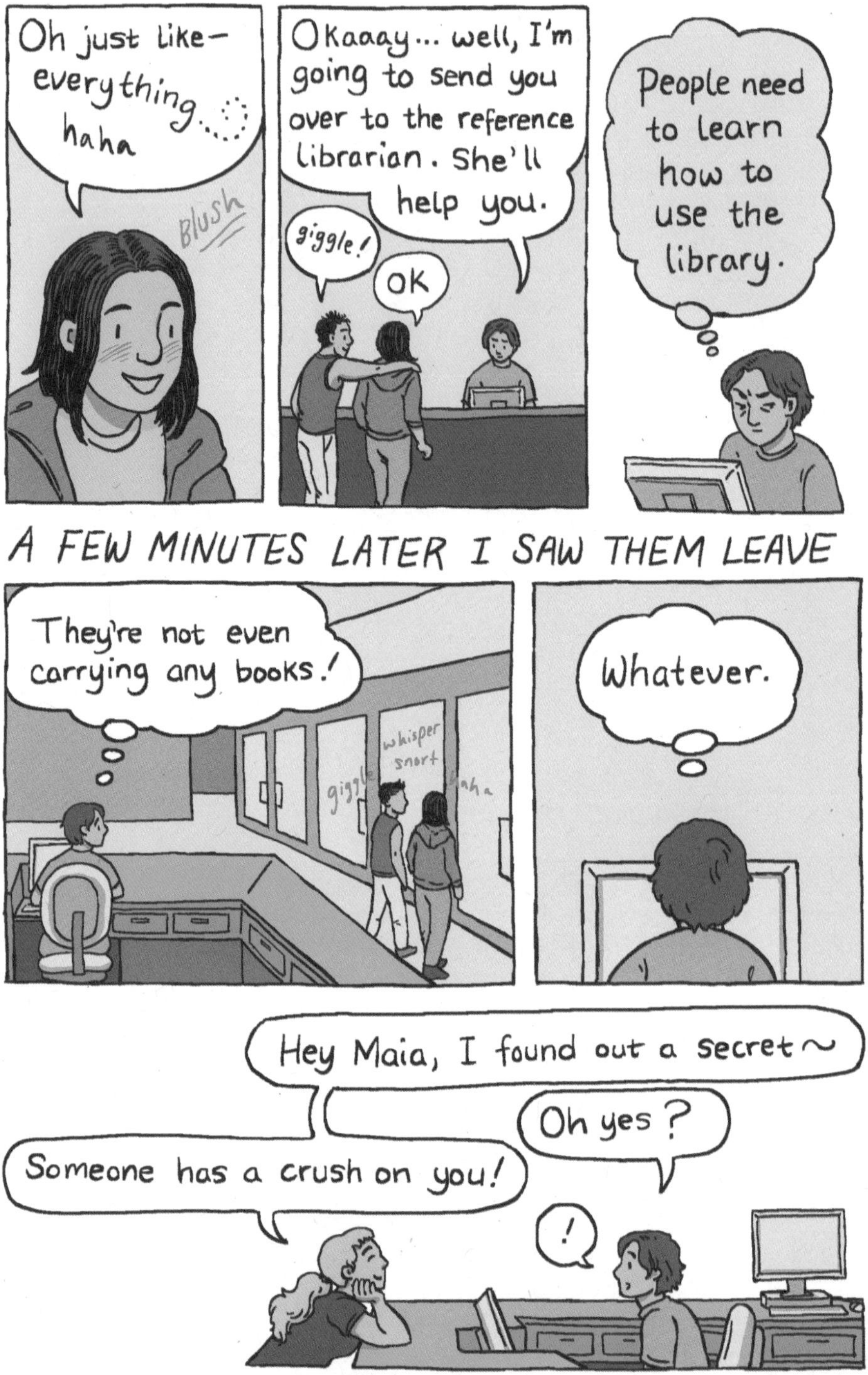

Oh just like–everything... haha
Blush
Okaaay... well, I'm going to send you over to the reference librarian. She'll help you.
giggle!
OK
People need to learn how to use the library.
A FEW MINUTES LATER I SAW THEM LEAVE
They're not even carrying any books!
whisper
snort
giggle
haha
Whatever.
Hey Maia, I found out a secret~
Oh yes?
Someone has a crush on you!
!

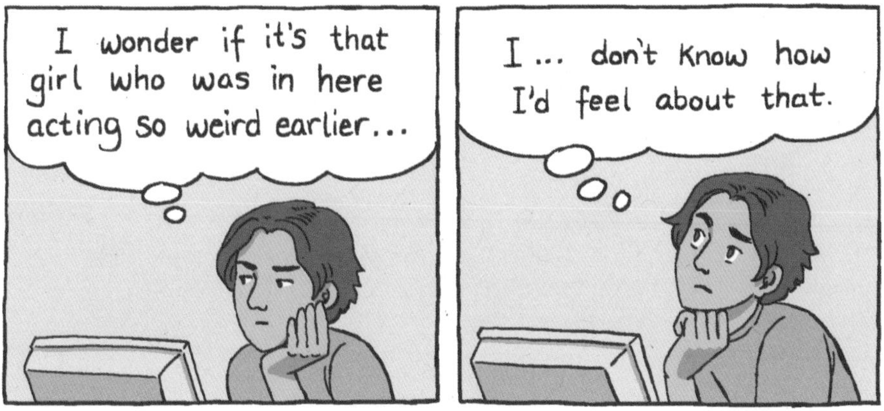
I wonder if it's that girl who was in here acting so weird earlier...
I... don't know how I'd feel about that.

THE LAST DAY BEFORE WINTER BREAK

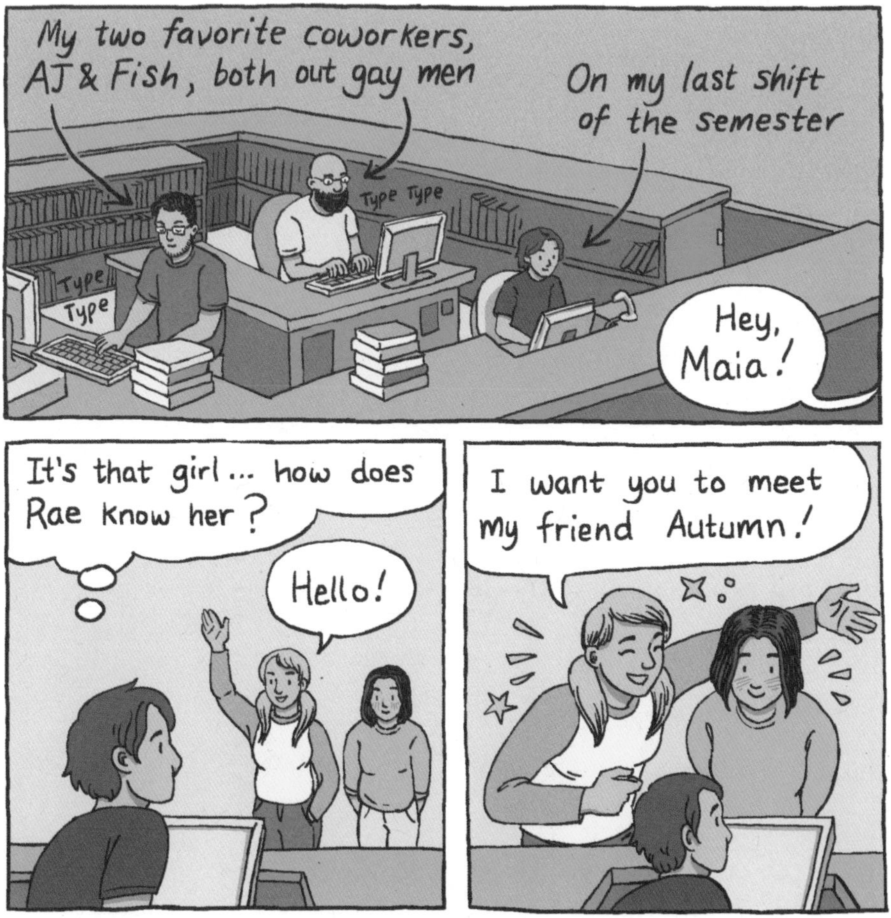
My two favorite coworkers, AJ & Fish, both out gay men
On my last shift of the semester
Type Type
Type Type
Hey, Maia!
It's that girl... how does Rae know her?
Hello!
I want you to meet my friend Autumn!

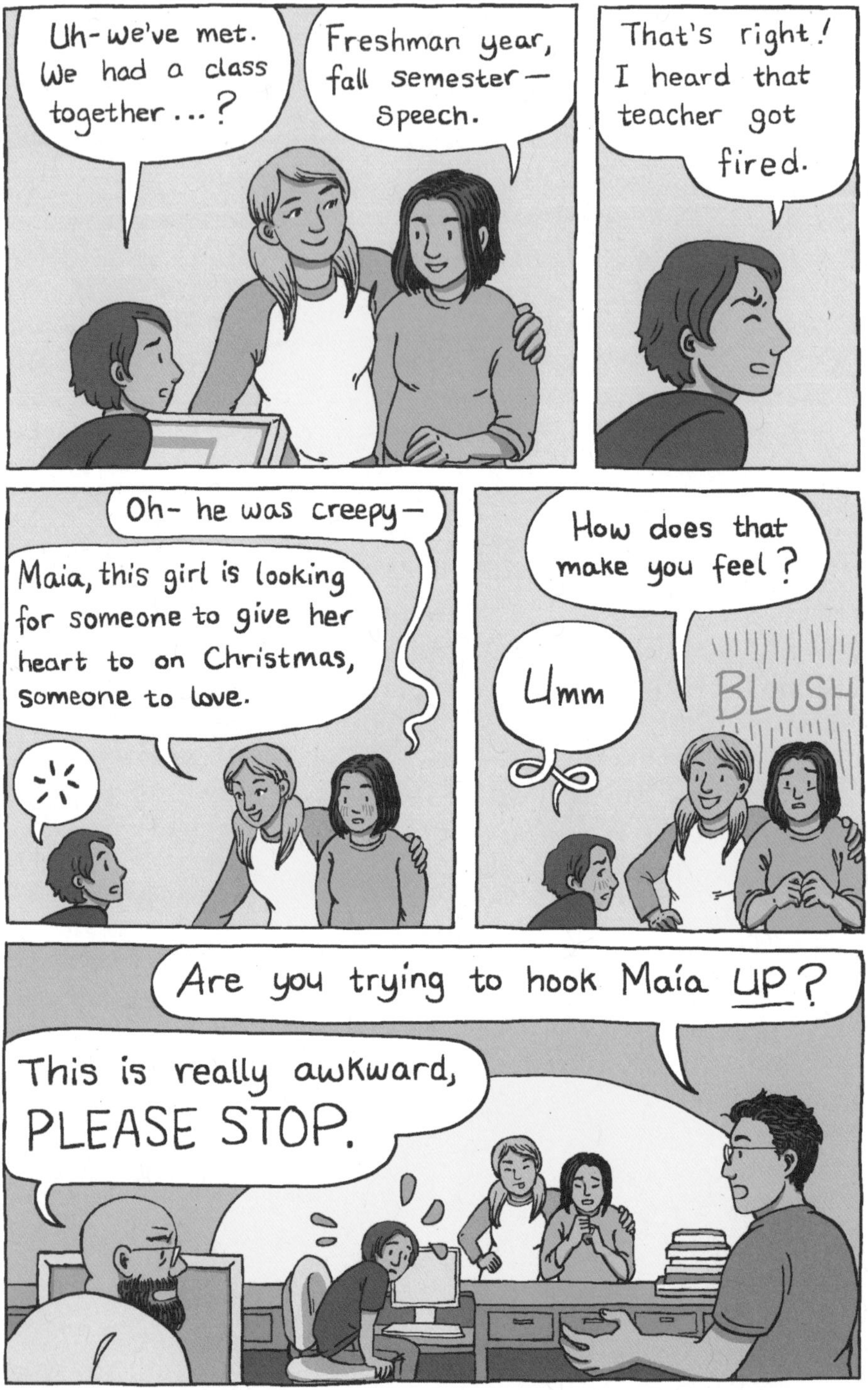
Uh-we've met. We had a class together...?
Freshman year, fall semester—Speech.
That's right! I heard that teacher got fired.
Oh- he was creepy—
Maia, this girl is looking for someone to give her heart to on Christmas, someone to love.
How does that make you feel?
Umm
BLUSH
Are you trying to hook Maía UP?
This is really awkward, PLEASE STOP.

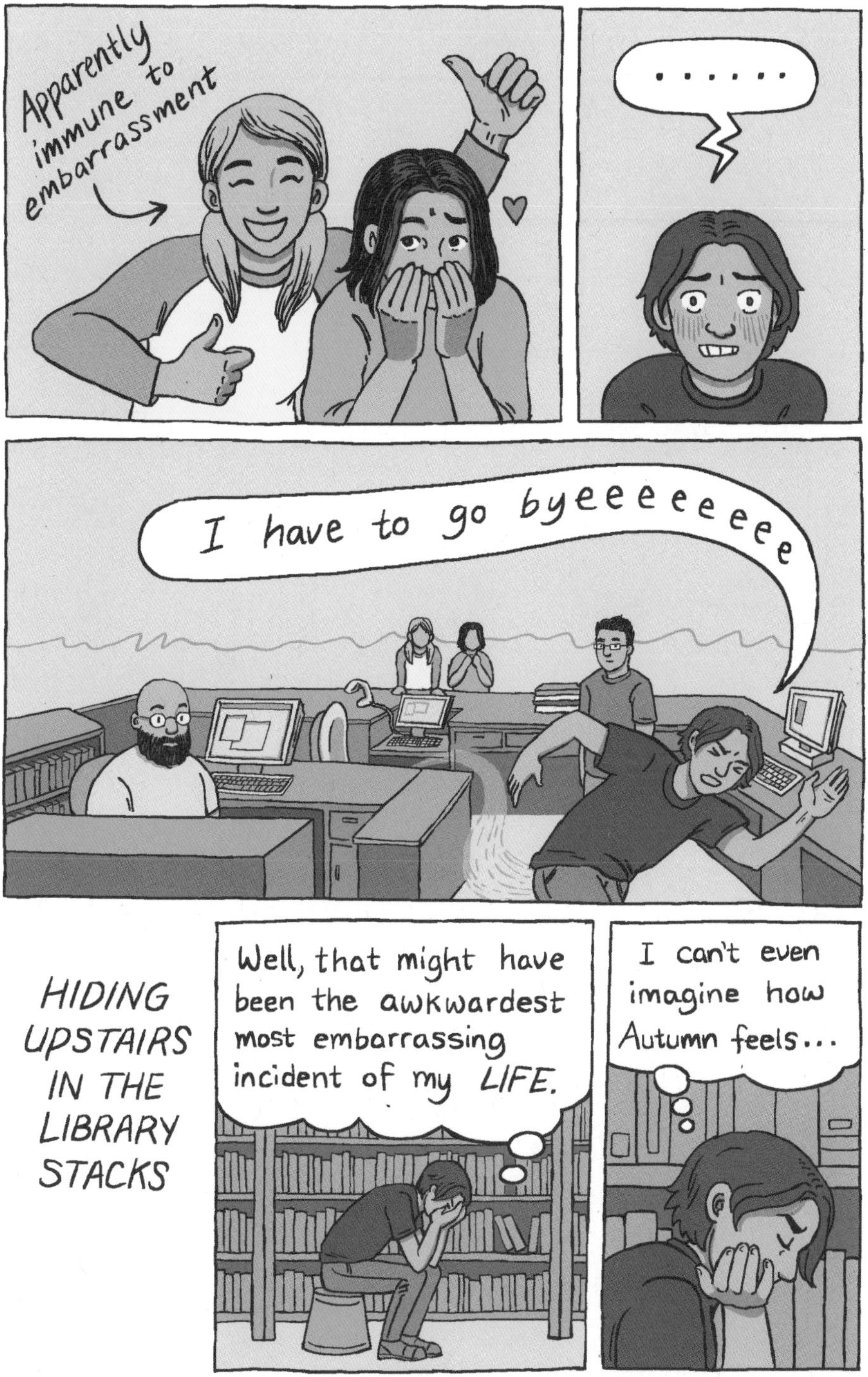
Apparently immune to embarrassment
......
I have to go byeeeeeeeee
HIDING UPSTAIRS IN THE LIBRARY STACKS
Well, that might have been the awkwardest most embarrassing incident of my LIFE.
I can't even imagine how Autumn feels...

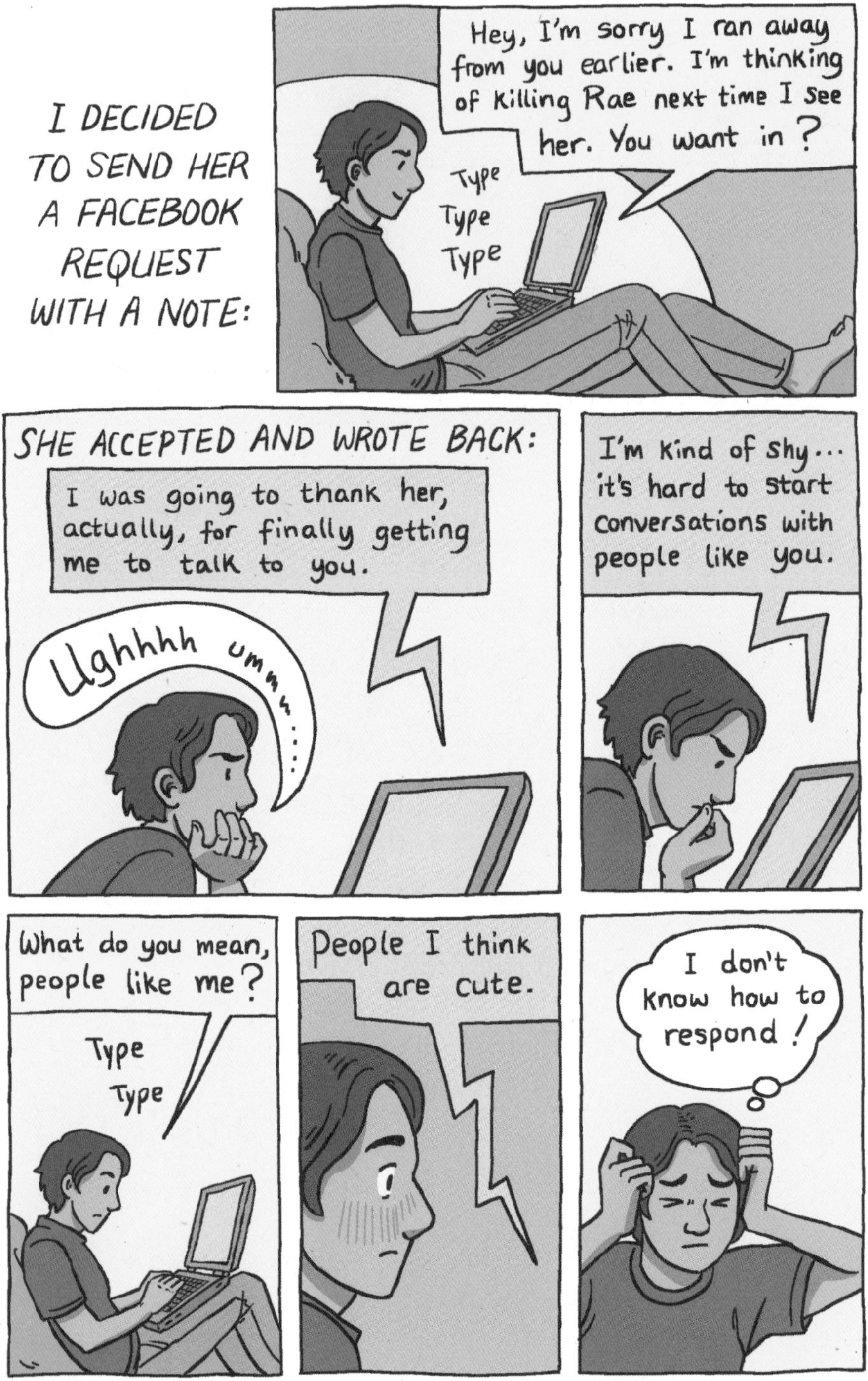
I DECIDED TO SEND HER A FACEBOOK REQUEST WITH A NOTE:
Hey, I'm sorry I ran away from you earlier. I'm thinking of killing Rae next time I see her. You want in?
Type Type Type
SHE ACCEPTED AND WROTE BACK:
I was going to thank her, actually, for finally getting me to talk to you.
Ughhhh umm...
I'm kind of shy... it's hard to start conversations with people like you.
What do you mean, people like me?
Type Type
People I think are cute.
I don't know how to respond!

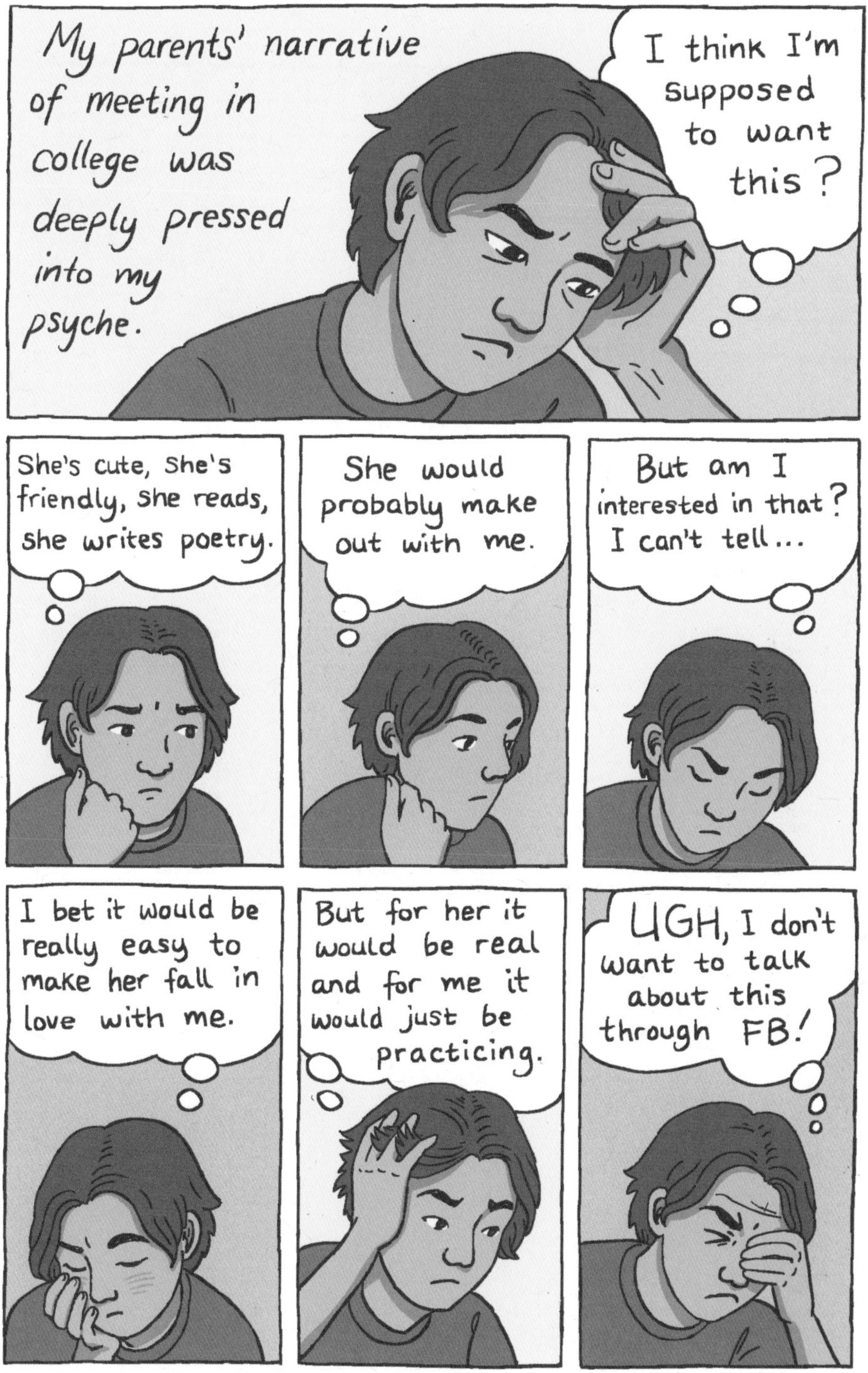
My parents' narrative of meeting in college was deeply pressed into my psyche.
I think I'm supposed to want this?
She's cute, she's friendly, she reads, she writes poetry.
She would probably make out with me.
But am I interested in that? I can't tell...
I bet it would be really easy to make her fall in love with me.
But for her it would be real and for me it would just be practicing.
UGH, I don't want to talk about this through FB!

I TOLD MY DAD ABOUT THE SITUATION.

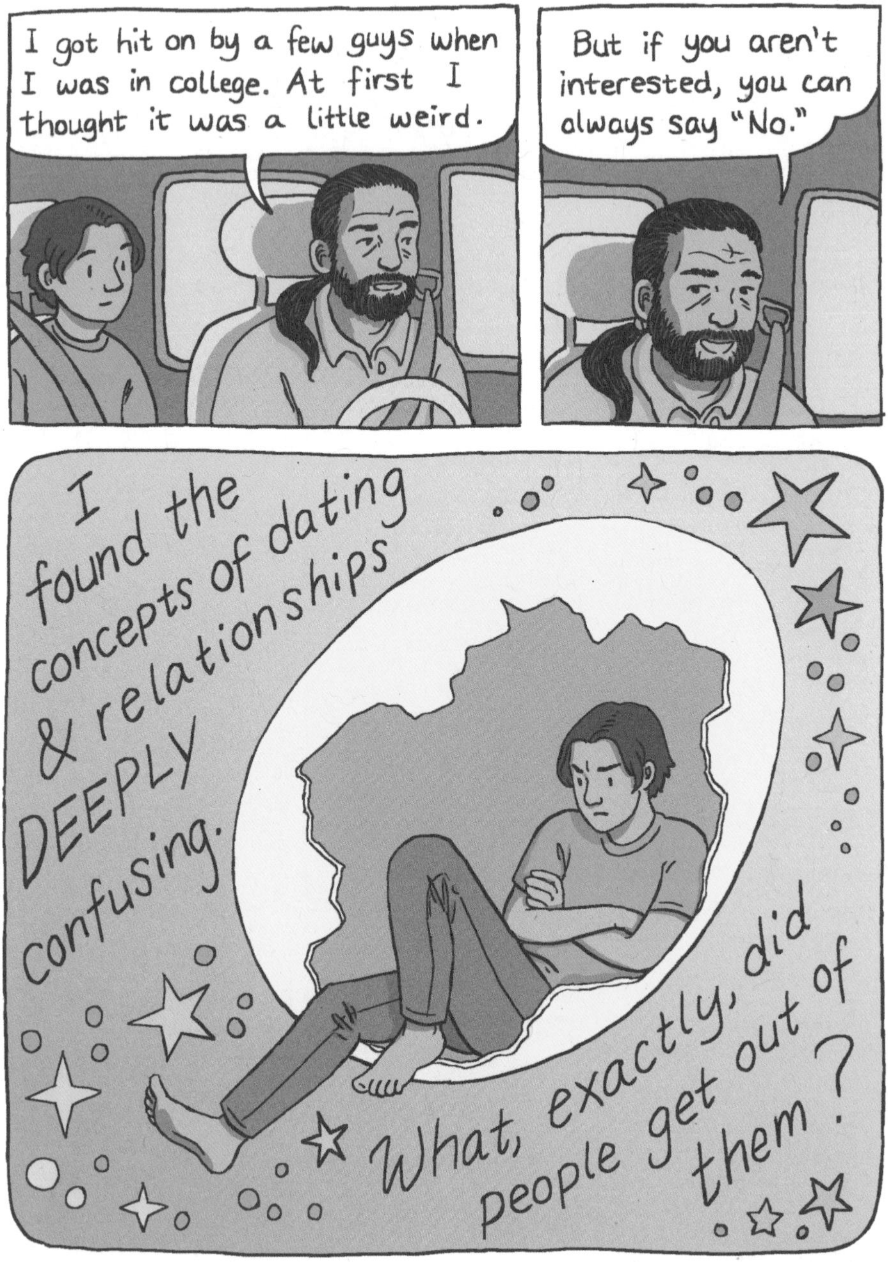
I got hit on by a few guys when I was in college. At first I thought it was a little weird.
But if you aren't interested, you can always say "No."
I found the concepts of dating & relationships DEEPLY confusing.
What, exactly, did people get out of them?

I ENDED UP CALLING HER ON THE PHONE.

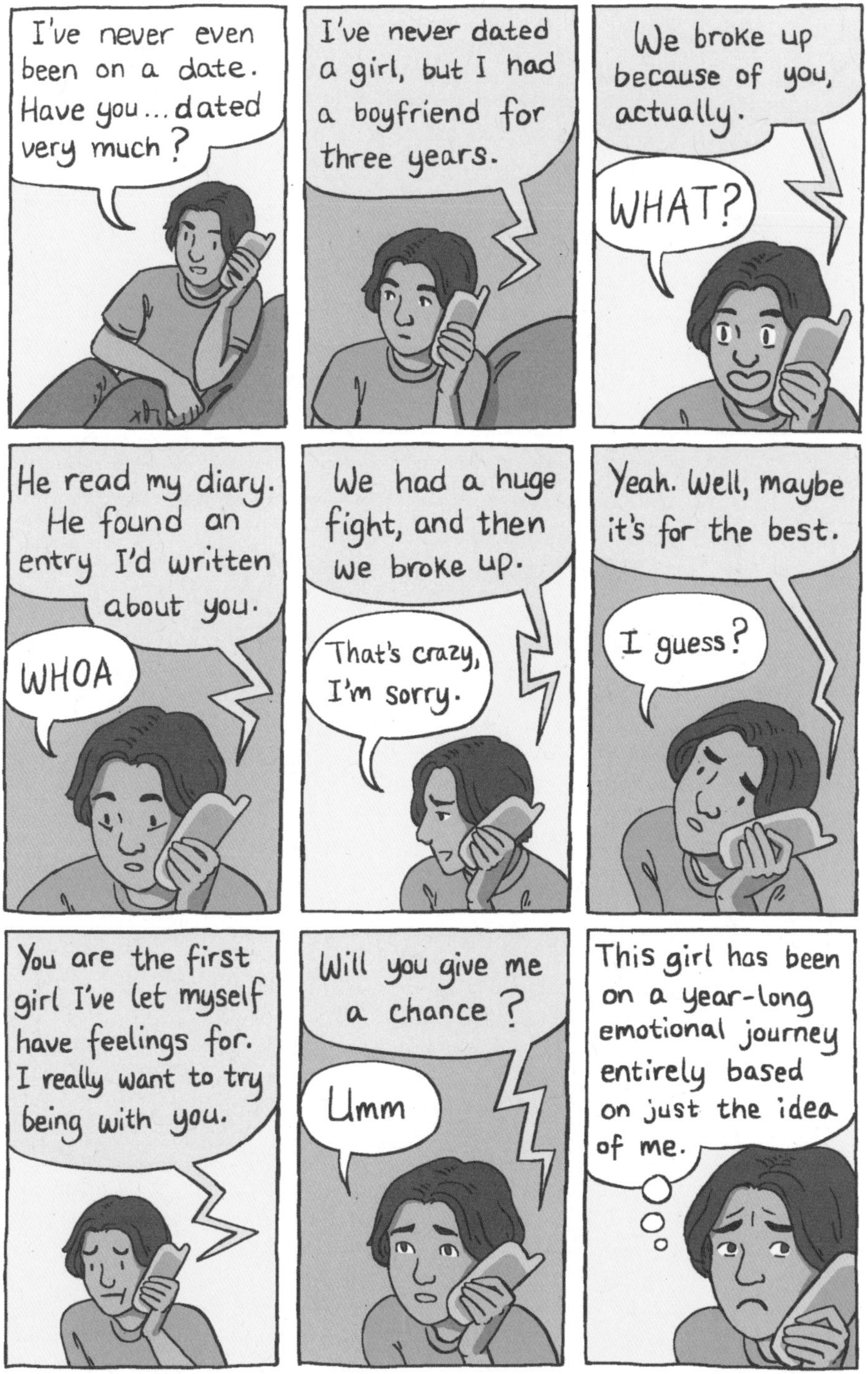
I've never even been on a date. Have you... dated very much?
I've never dated a girl, but I had a boyfriend for three years.
We broke up because of you, actually.
WHAT?
He read my diary. He found an entry I'd written about you.
WHOA
We had a huge fight, and then we broke up.
That's crazy, I'm sorry.
Yeah. Well, maybe it's for the best.
I guess?
You are the first girl I've let myself have feelings for. I really want to try being with you.
Will you give me a chance?
Umm
This girl has been on a year-long emotional journey entirely based on just the idea of me.

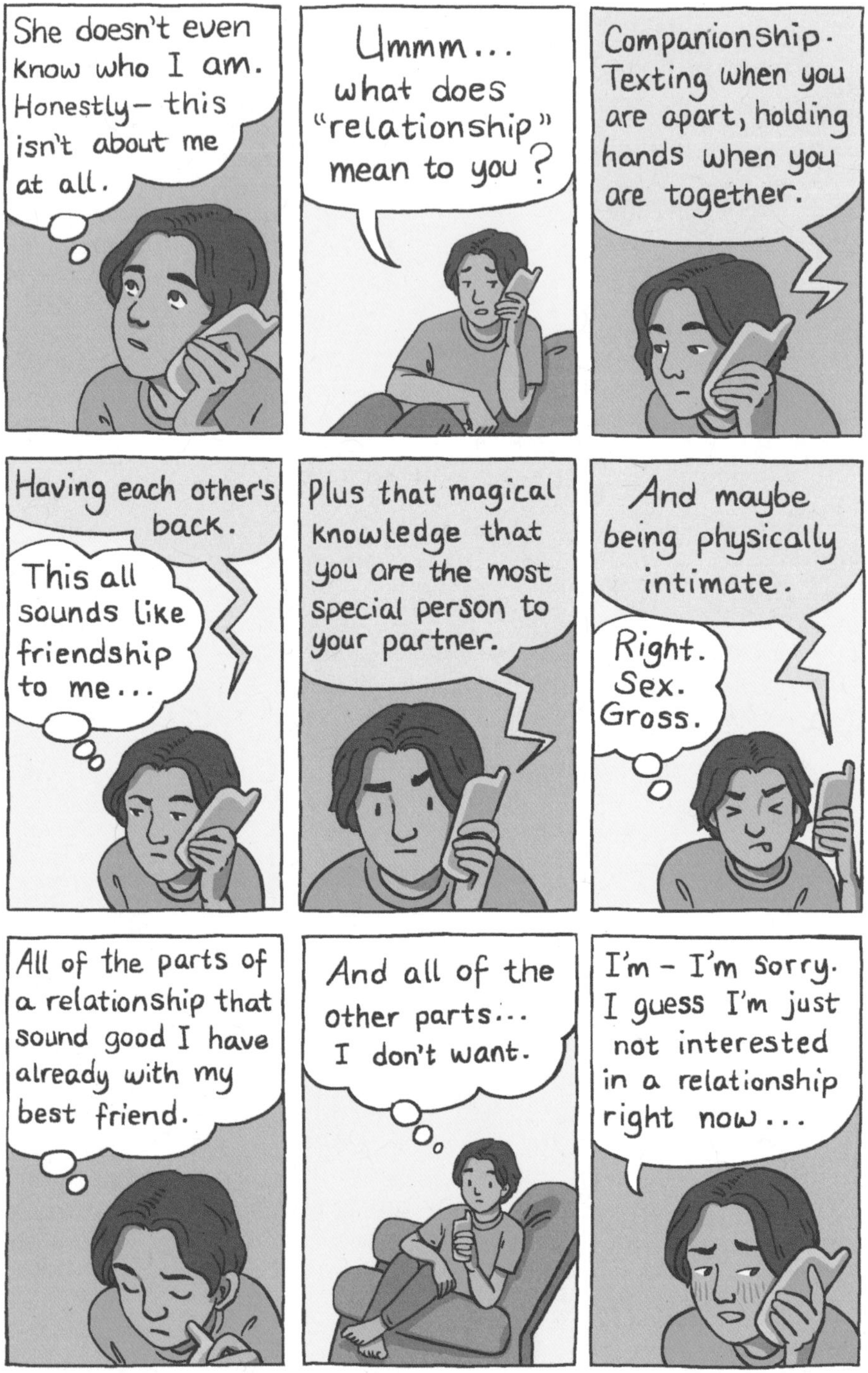
She doesn't even know who I am. Honestly— this isn't about me at all.
Ummm... what does "relationship" mean to you?
Companionship. Texting when you are apart, holding hands when you are together.
Having each other's back.
This all sounds like friendship to me...
Plus that magical knowledge that you are the most special person to your partner.
And maybe being physically intimate.
Right. Sex. Gross.
All of the parts of a relationship that sound good I have already with my best friend.
And all of the other parts... I don't want.
I'm – I'm sorry. I guess I'm just not interested in a relationship right now...

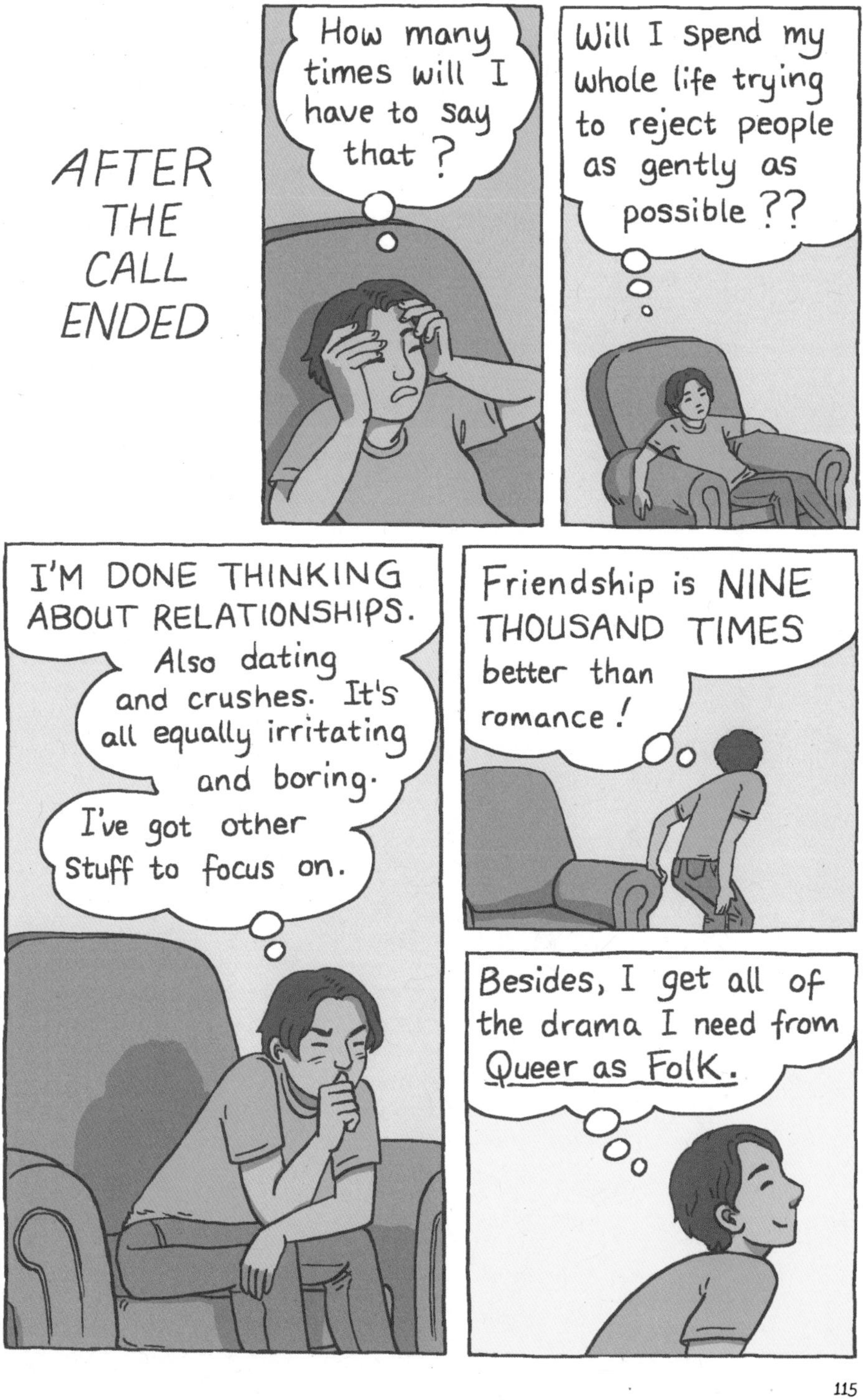
AFTER THE CALL ENDED
How many times will I have to say that ?
Will I spend my whole life trying to reject people as gently as possible ??
I'M DONE THINKING ABOUT RELATIONSHIPS.
Also dating and crushes. It's all equally irritating and boring.
I've got other stuff to focus on.
Friendship is NINE THOUSAND TIMES better than romance!
Besides, I get all of the drama I need from Queer as Folk.

INTEREST IN EROTIC GAY FICTION HAS BEEN SO PREVALENT IN MY FRIENDSHIPS, ONE COULD MISTAKE IT FOR A PREREQUISITE.

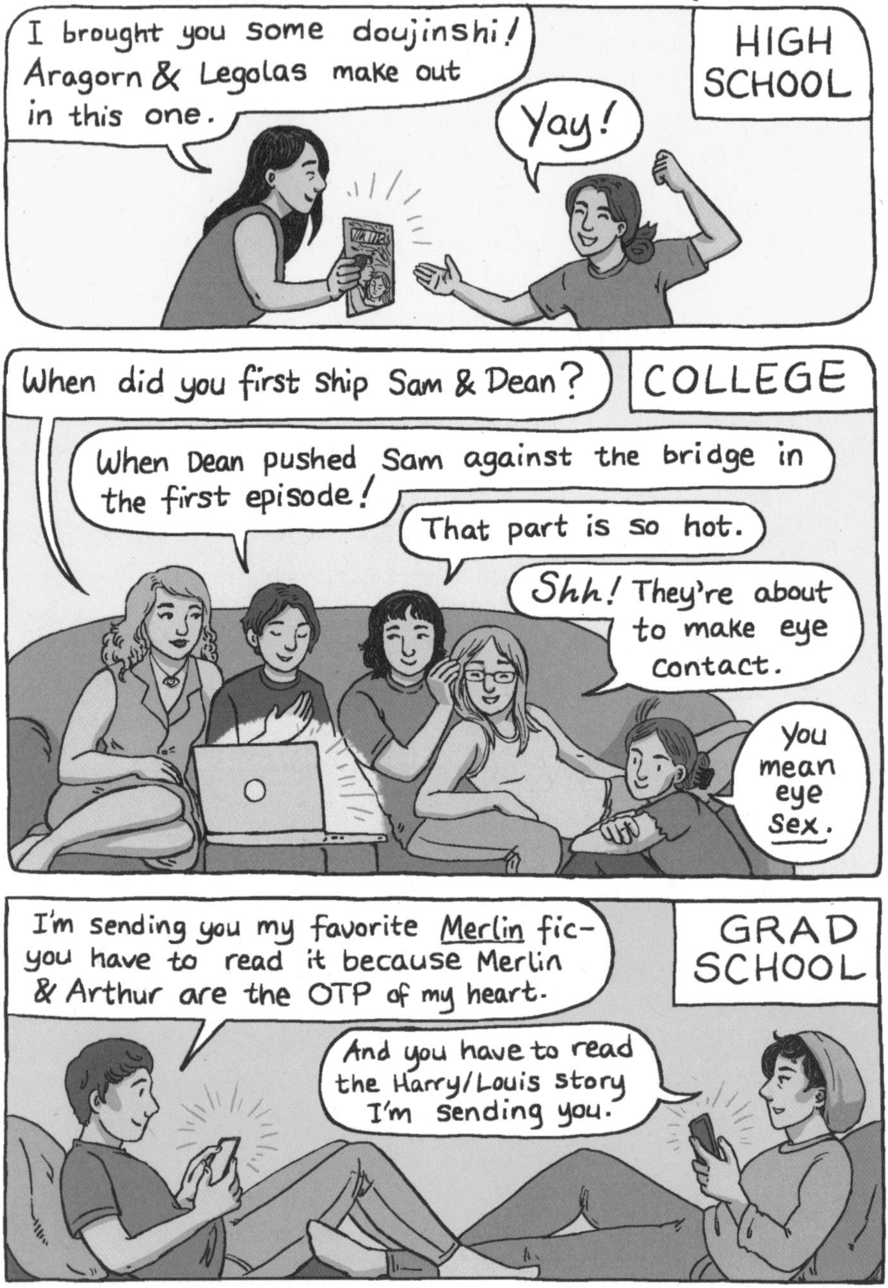

I brought you some doujinshi! Aragorn & Legolas make out in this one.
HIGH SCHOOL
Yay!
When did you first ship Sam & Dean?
COLLEGE
When Dean pushed Sam against the bridge in the first episode!
That part is so hot.
Shh! They're about to make eye contact.
You mean eye sex.
I'm sending you my favorite Merlin fic– you have to read it because Merlin & Arthur are the OTP of my heart.
GRAD SCHOOL
And you have to read the Harry/Louis story I'm sending you.

IN FACT, I'M SHOCKED WHEN A FRIEND SAYS:

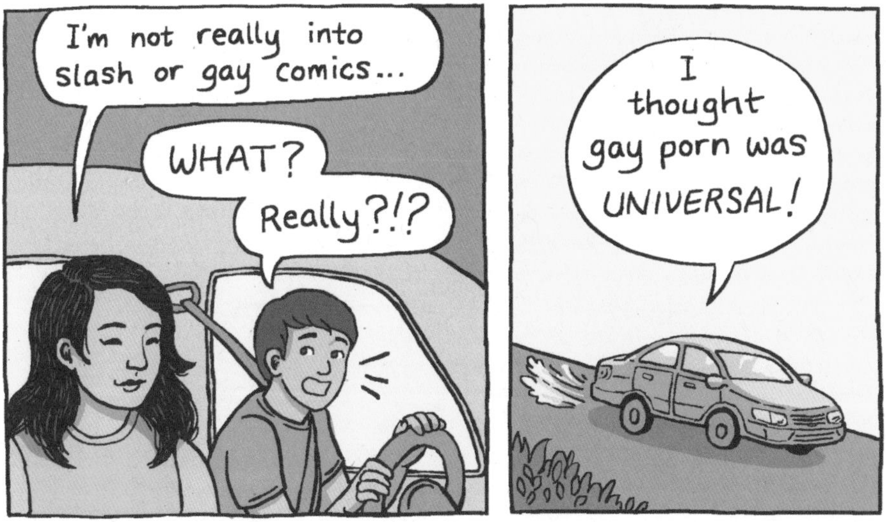
I'm not really into slash or gay comics...
WHAT?
Really?!?
I thought gay porn was UNIVERSAL!

LATER SHE DESCRIBED HERSELF AS HETERO-FLEXIBLE AND TRIED TO EXPLAIN WHY SHE LIKED LESBIAN PORN MORE THAN GAY PORN.

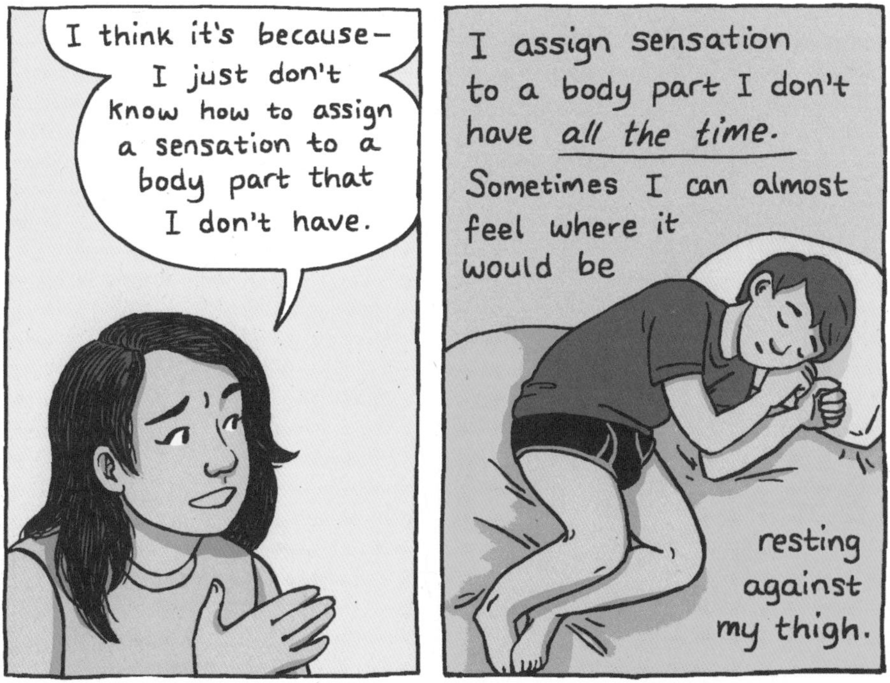
I think it's because- I just don't know how to assign a sensation to a body part that I don't have.
I assign sensation to a body part I don't have all the time.
Sometimes I can almost feel where it would be
resting against my thigh.

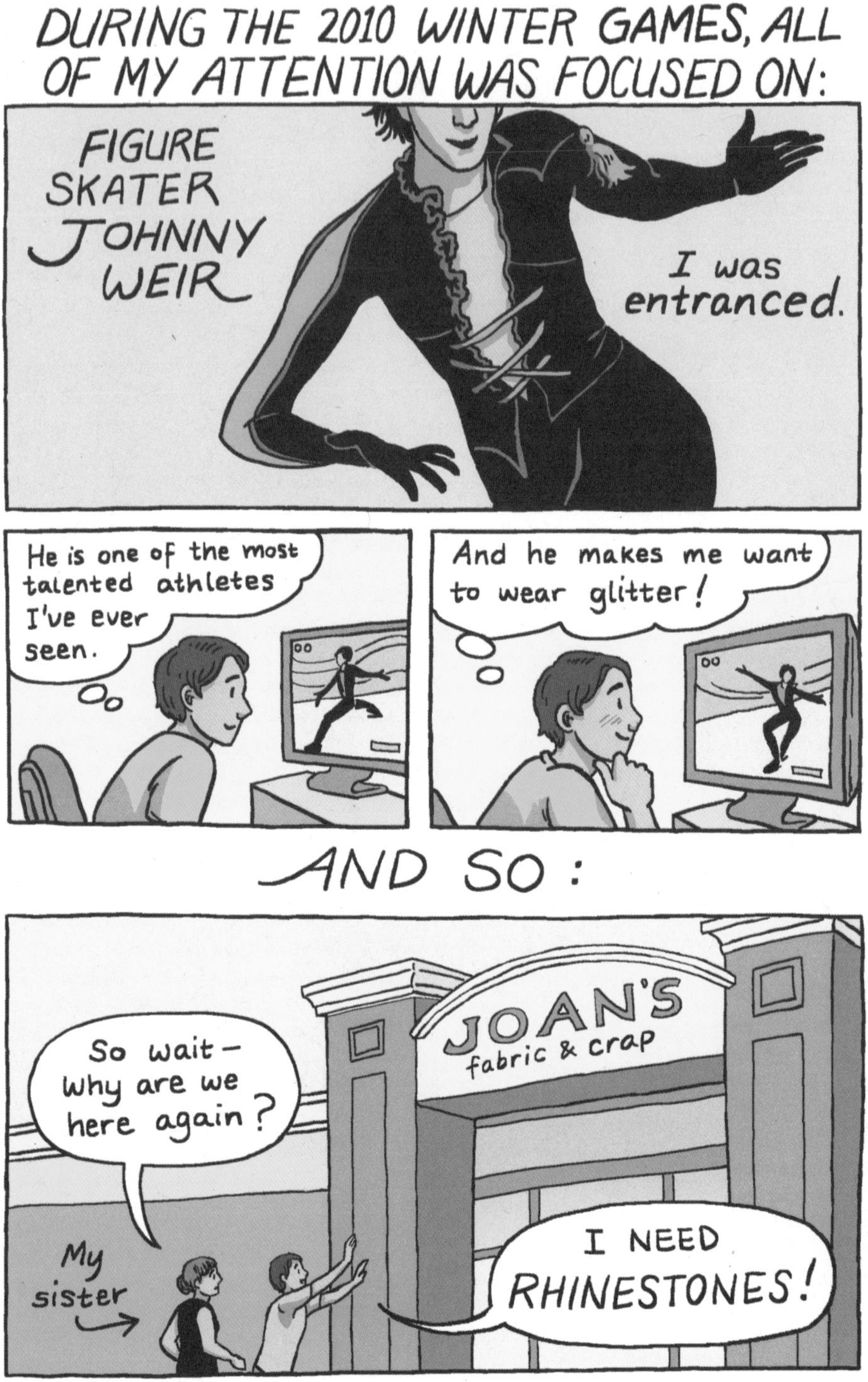
DURING THE 2010 WINTER GAMES, ALL OF MY ATTENTION WAS FOCUSED ON:
FIGURE SKATER JOHNNY WEIR
I was entranced.
He is one of the most talented athletes I've ever seen.
And he makes me want to wear glitter!
AND SO:
JOAN'S fabric & crap
So wait- Why are we here again?
My sister
I NEED RHINESTONES!

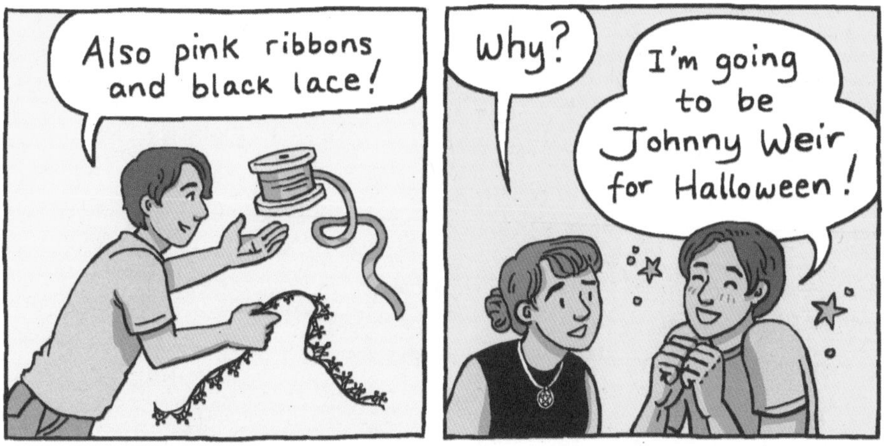
Also pink ribbons and black lace!
Why?
I'm going to be Johnny Weir for Halloween!

I WENT ALL OUT FOR MY COSTUME.

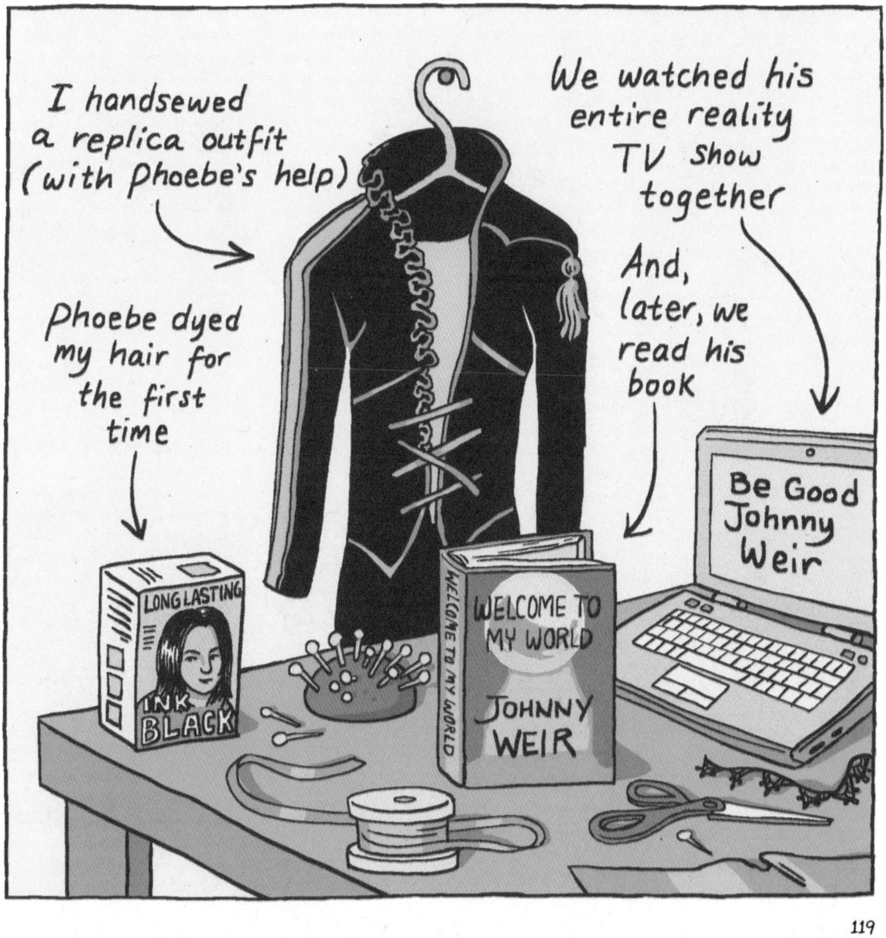
I handsewed a replica outfit (with Phoebe's help)
We watched his entire reality TV show together
And, later, we read his book
Phoebe dyed my hair for the first time
Be Good Johnny Weir
LONG LASTING
INK BLACK
WELCOME TO MY WORLD
JOHNNY WEIR
WELCOME TO MY WORLD

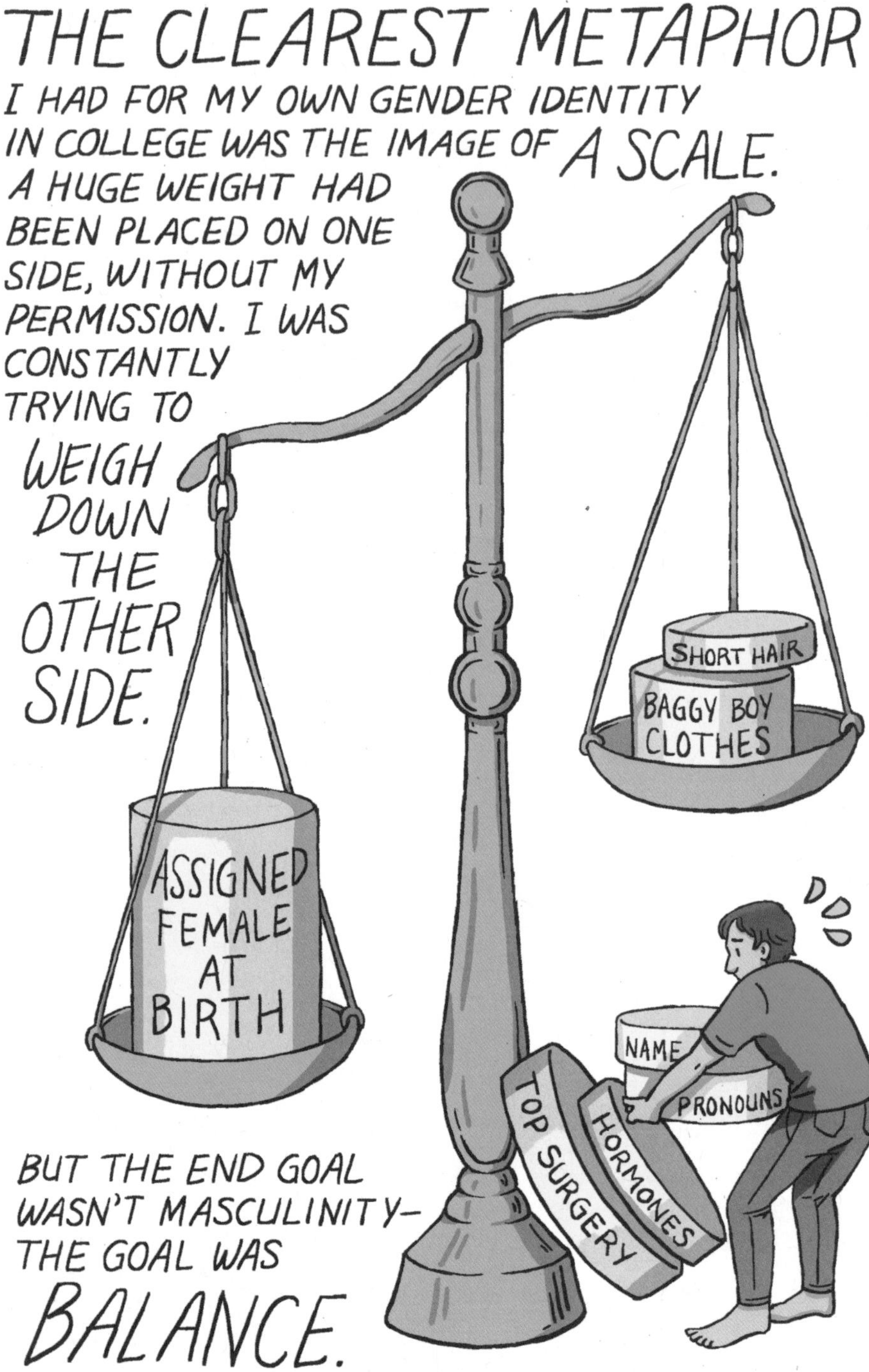
THE CLEAREST METAPHOR
I HAD FOR MY OWN GENDER IDENTITY IN COLLEGE WAS THE IMAGE OF A SCALE.
A HUGE WEIGHT HAD BEEN PLACED ON ONE SIDE, WITHOUT MY PERMISSION. I WAS CONSTANTLY TRYING TO
WEIGH DOWN THE OTHER SIDE.
SHORT HAIR
BAGGY BOY CLOTHES
ASSIGNED FEMALE AT BIRTH
NAME
PRONOUNS
TOP SURGERY
HORMONES
BUT THE END GOAL WASN'T MASCULINITY— THE GOAL WAS
BALANCE.

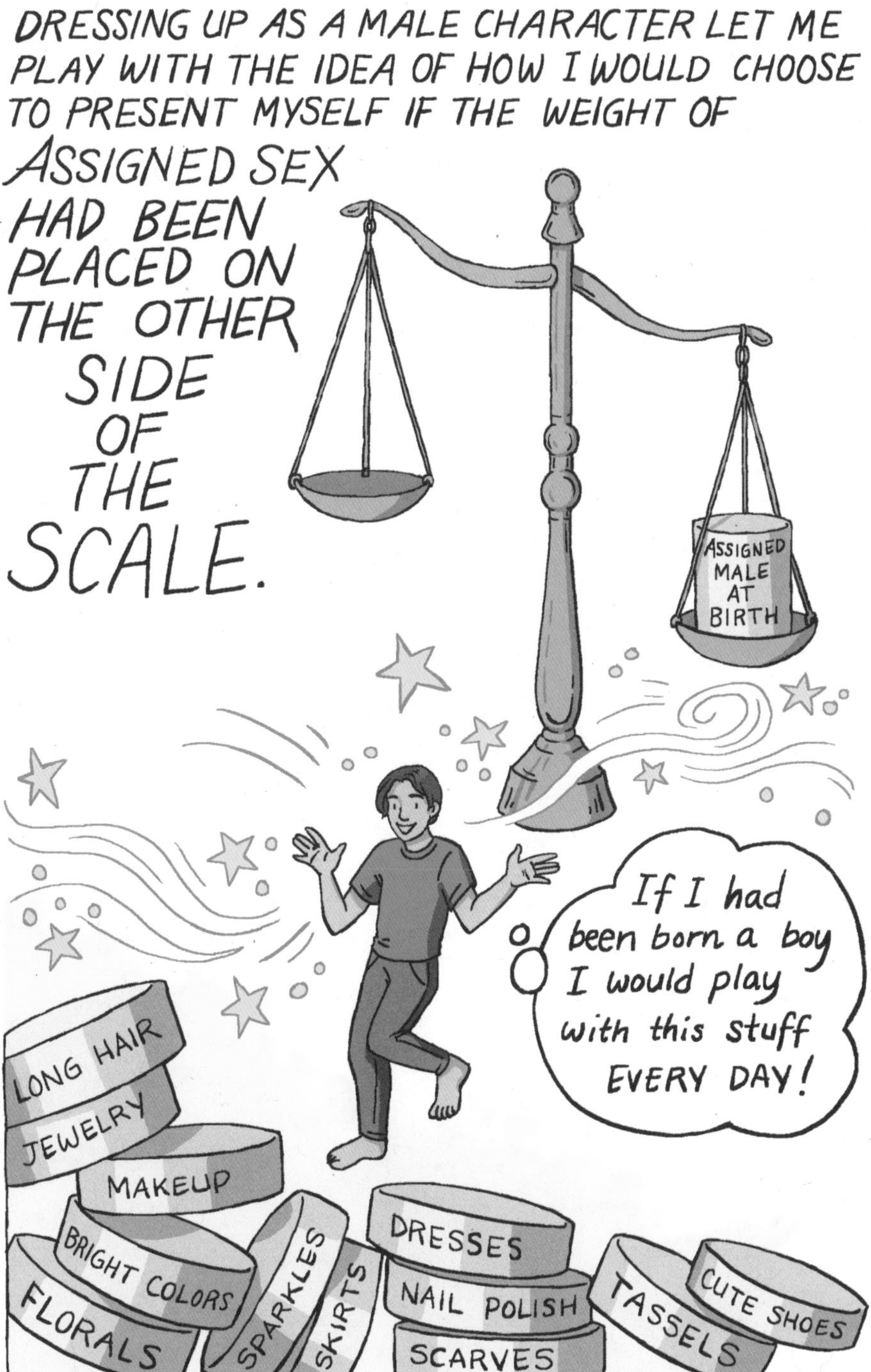
DRESSING UP AS A MALE CHARACTER LET ME PLAY WITH THE IDEA OF HOW I WOULD CHOOSE TO PRESENT MYSELF IF THE WEIGHT OF ASSIGNED SEX HAD BEEN PLACED ON THE OTHER SIDE OF THE SCALE.
ASSIGNED MALE AT BIRTH
If I had been born a boy I would play with this stuff EVERY DAY!
LONG HAIR
JEWELRY
MAKEUP
BRIGHT COLORS
FLORALS
SPARKLES
SKIRTS
DRESSES
NAIL POLISH
SCARVES
TASSELS
CUTE SHOES

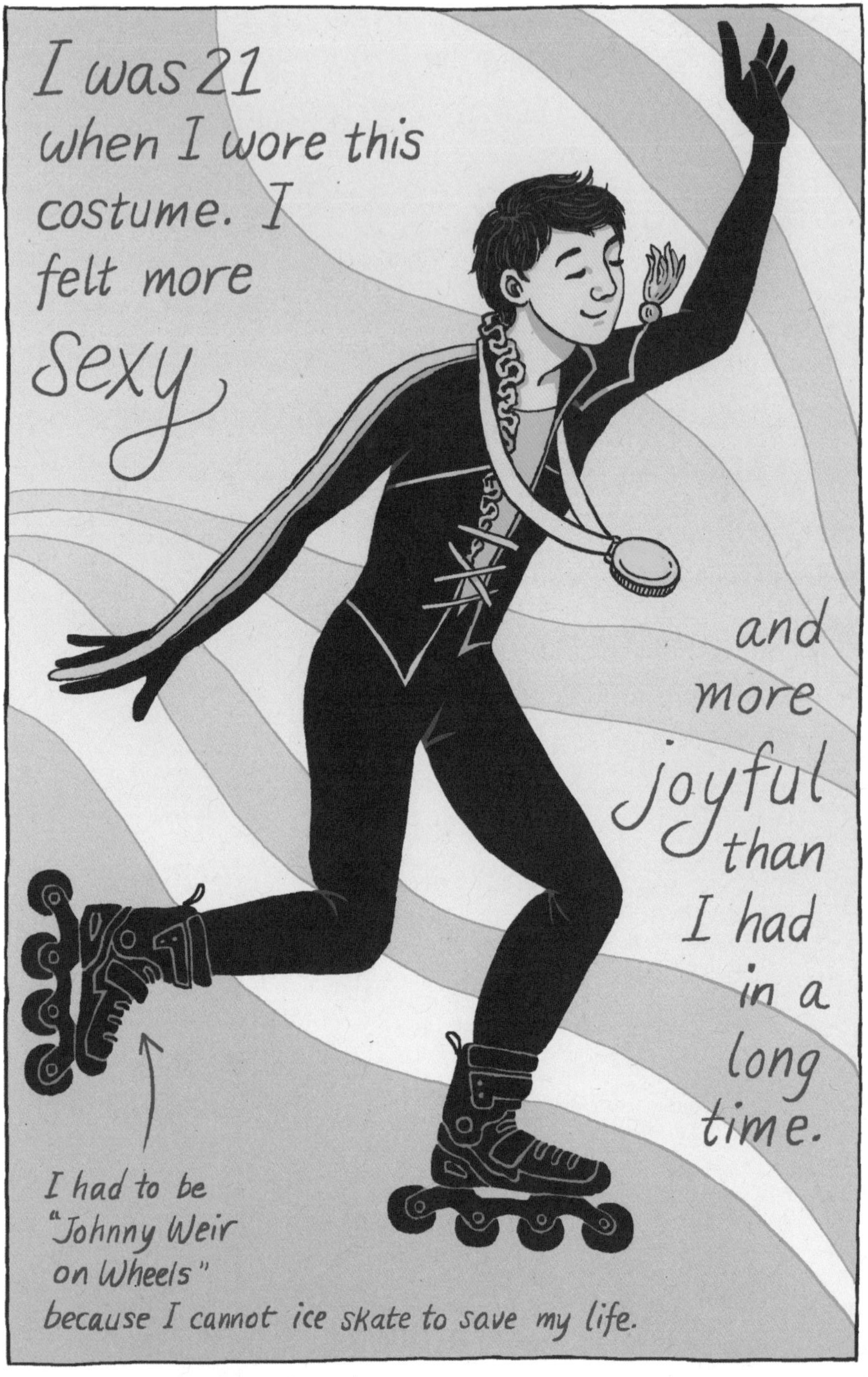
I was 21 when I wore this costume. I felt more Sexy
and more joyful than I had in a long time.
I had to be "Johnny Weir on Wheels" because I cannot ice skate to save my life.

REALITY REINSERTED ITSELF.

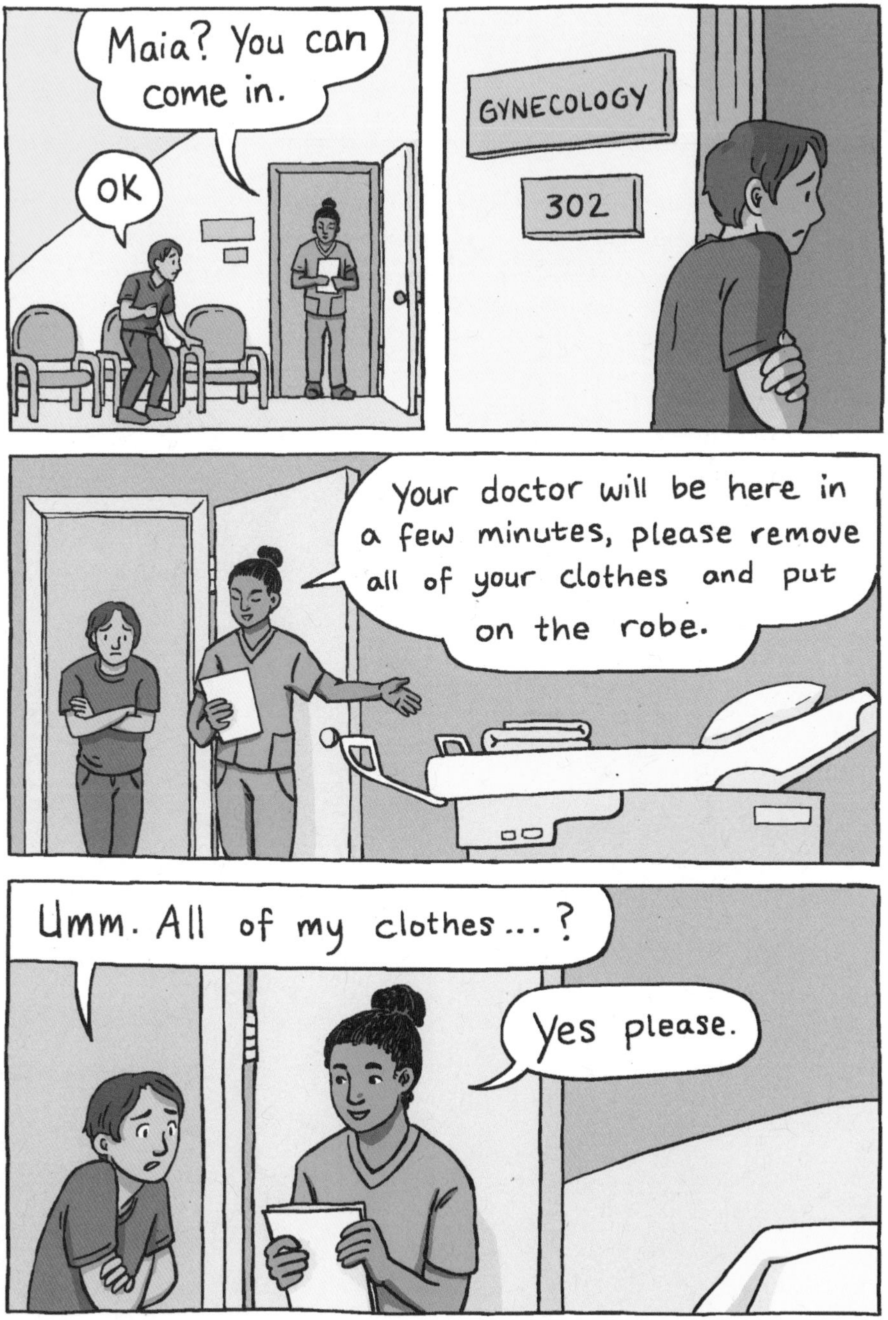
Maia? You can come in.
OK
GYNECOLOGY
302
Your doctor will be here in a few minutes, please remove all of your clothes and put on the robe.
Umm. All of my clothes...?
Yes please.

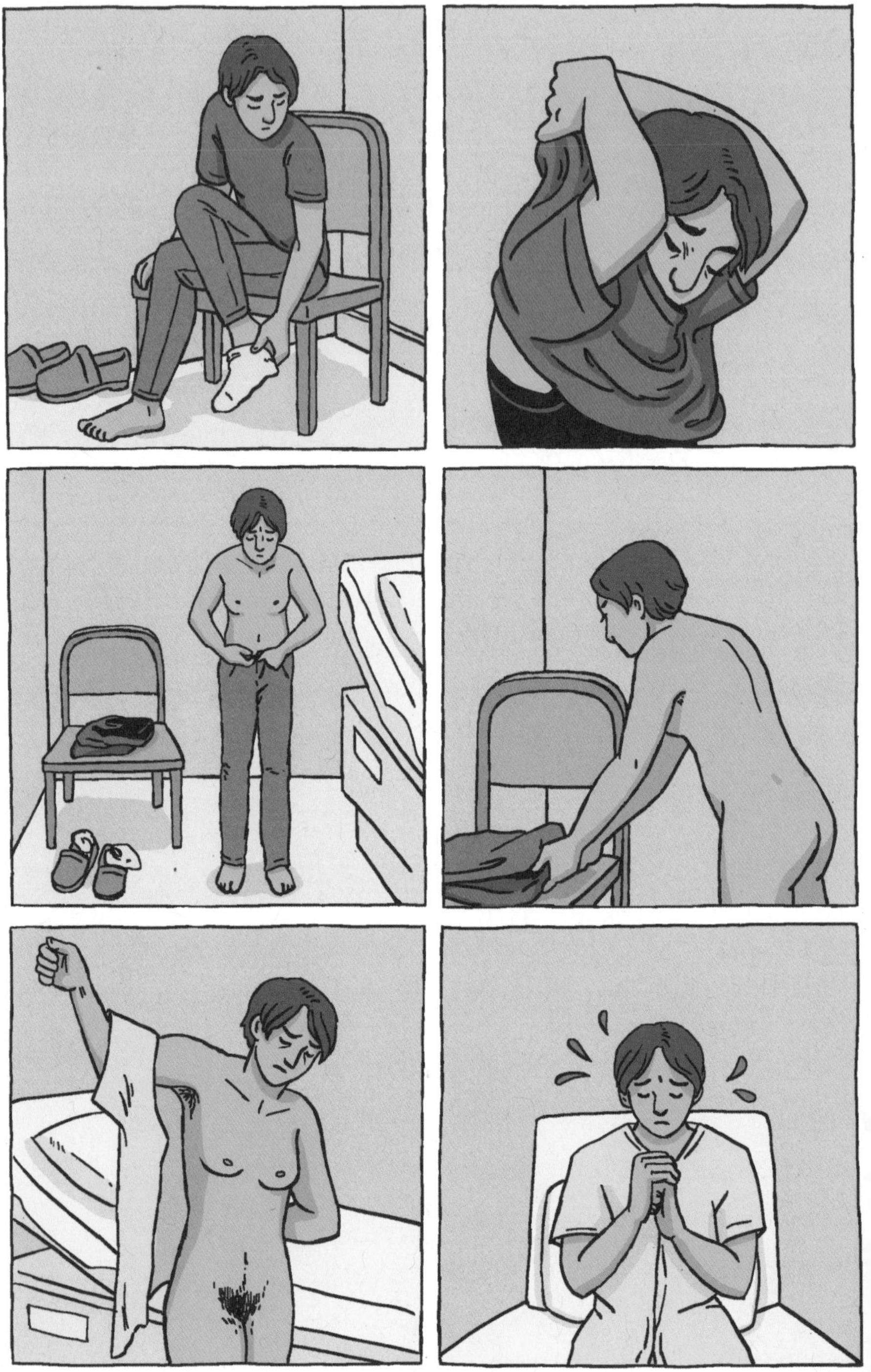

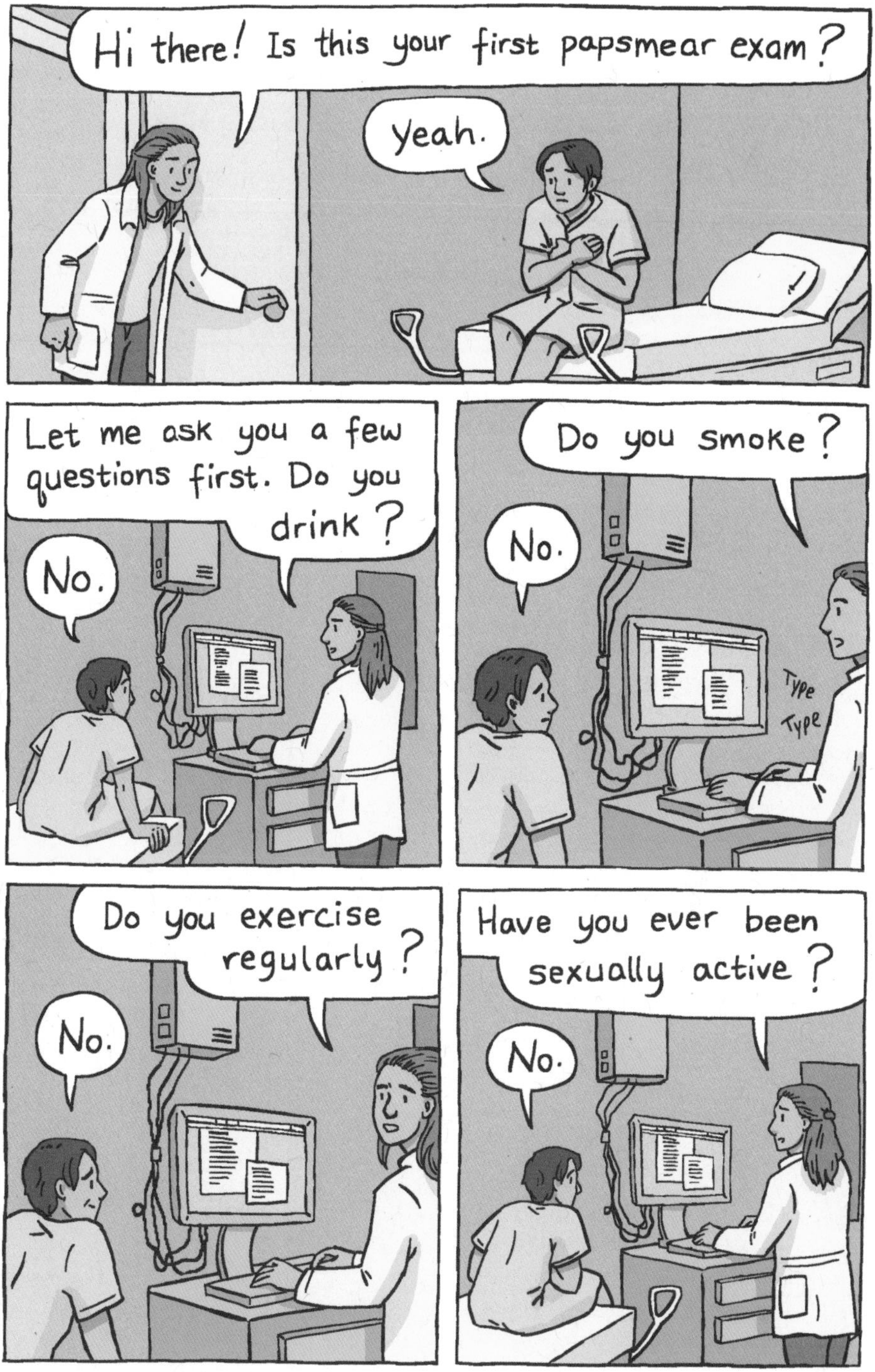
Hi there! Is this your first papsmear exam?
yeah.
Let me ask you a few questions first. Do you drink?
No.
Do you smoke?
No.
Type
Type
Do you exercise regularly?
No.
Have you ever been sexually active?
No.

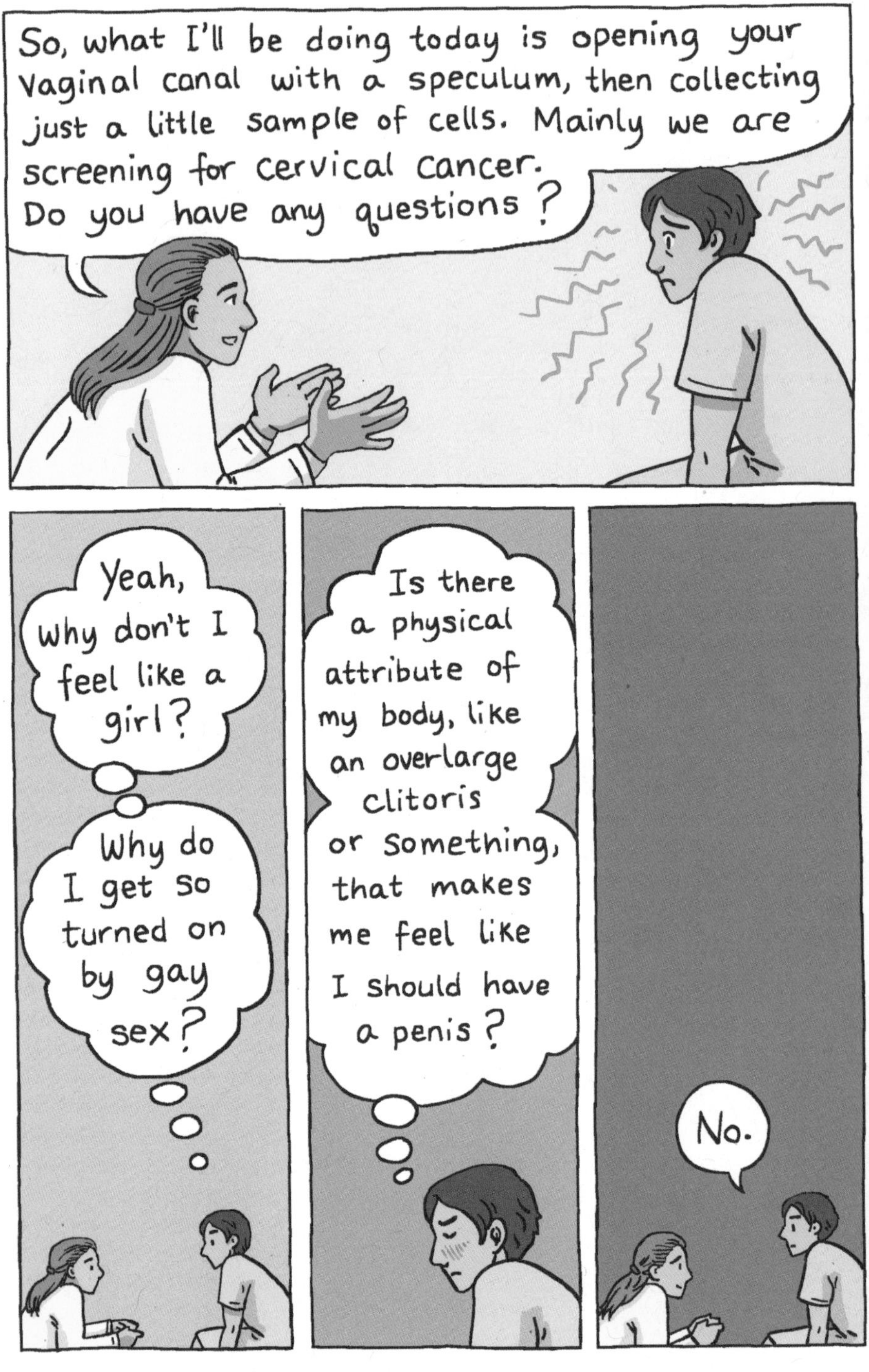
So, what I'll be doing today is opening your vaginal canal with a speculum, then collecting just a little sample of cells. Mainly we are screening for cervical cancer. Do you have any questions?
Yeah, why don't I feel like a girl?
Why do I get so turned on by gay sex?
Is there a physical attribute of my body, like an overlarge clitoris or something, that makes me feel like I should have a penis?
No.

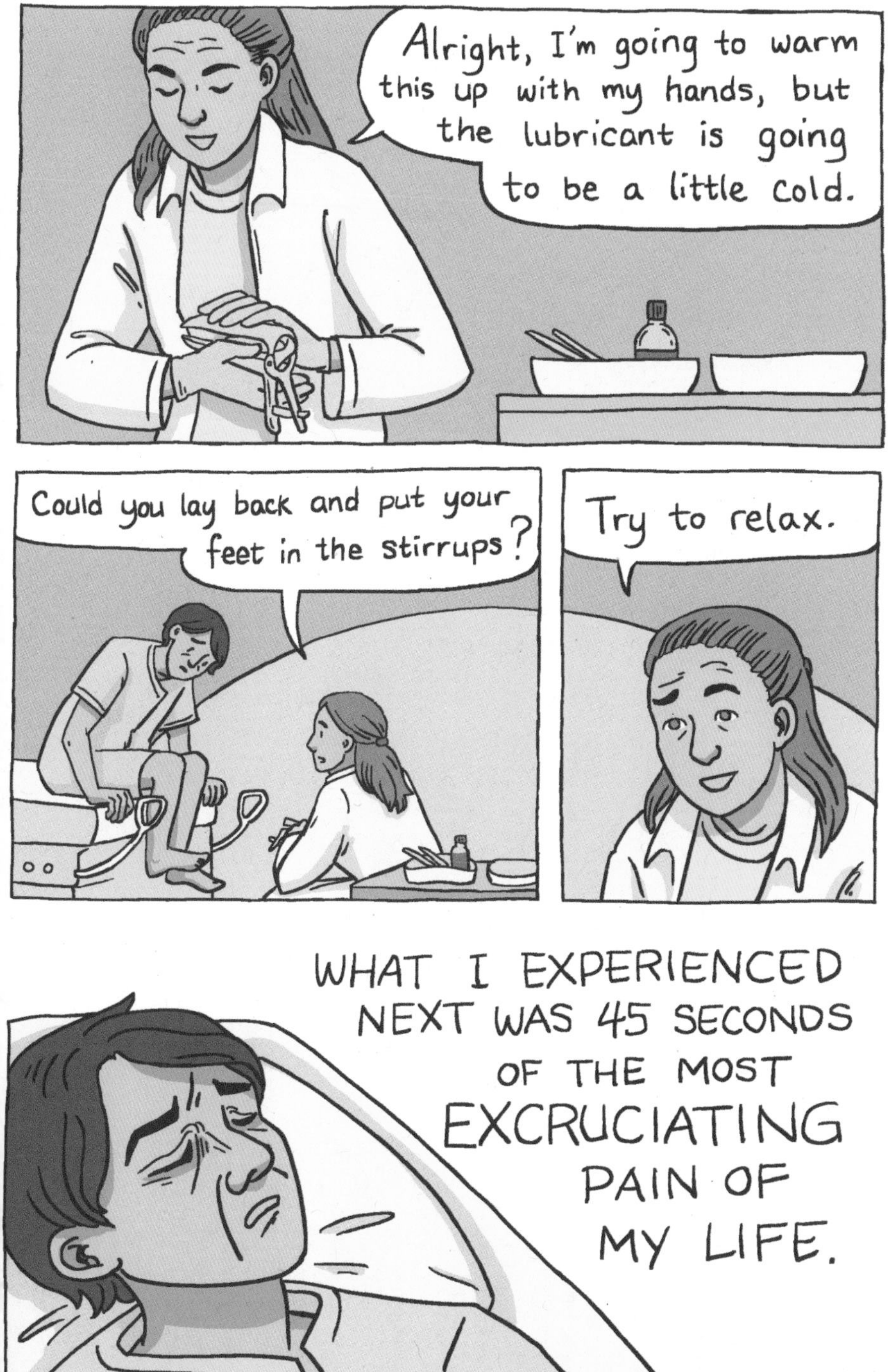
Alright, I'm going to warm this up with my hands, but the lubricant is going to be a little cold.
Could you lay back and put your feet in the stirrups?
Try to relax.
WHAT I EXPERIENCED NEXT WAS 45 SECONDS OF THE MOST EXCRUCIATING PAIN OF MY LIFE.

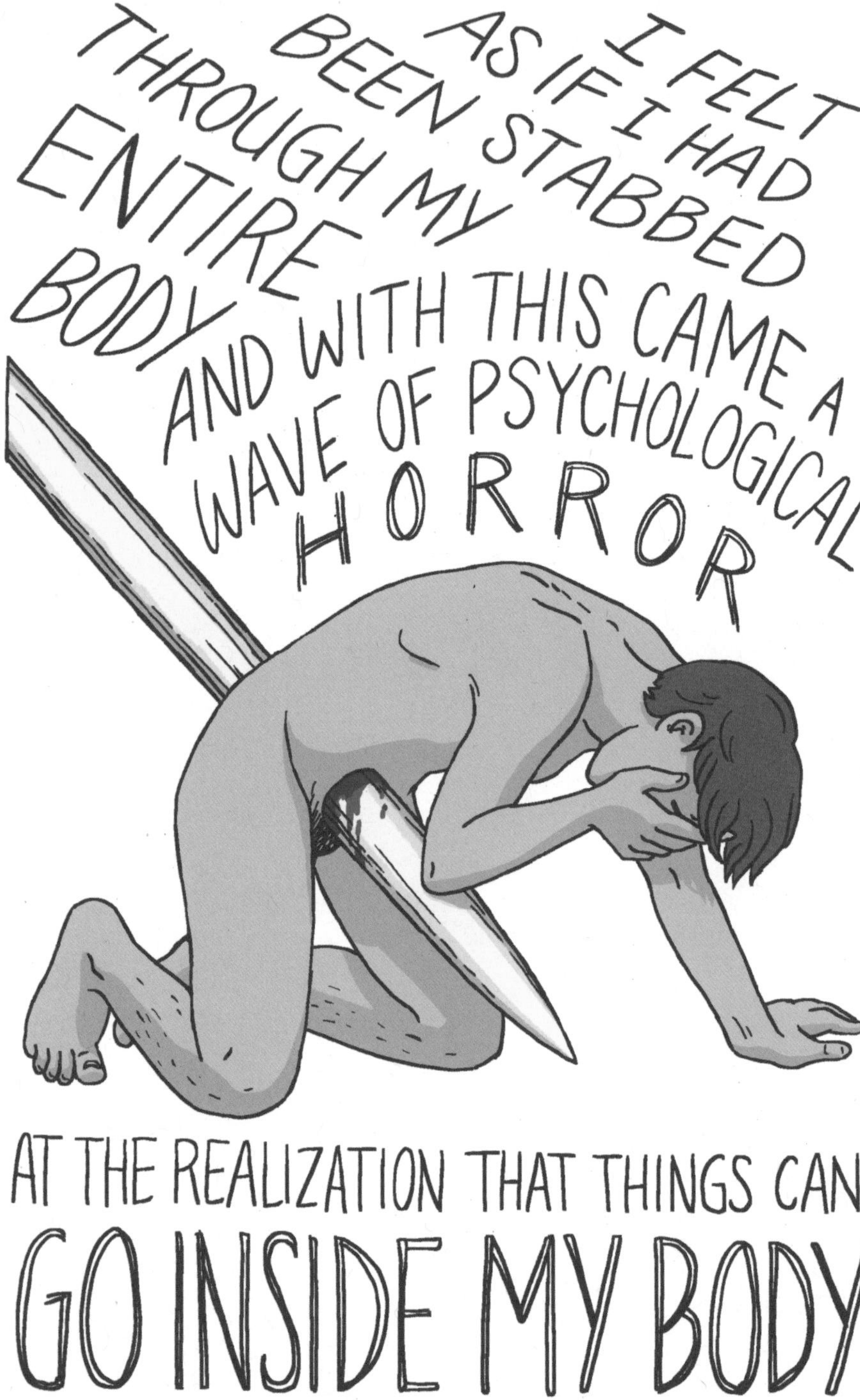
I FELT AS IF I HAD BEEN STABBED THROUGH MY ENTIRE BODY
AND WITH THIS CAME A WAVE OF PSYCHOLOGICAL HORROR
AT THE REALIZATION THAT THINGS CAN
GO INSIDE MY BODY

OF COURSE I ALREADY
KNEW THIS FACT INTELLECTUALLY;

embodied

KNOWLEDGE IS
AN ENTIRELY
DIFFERENT
MATTER.

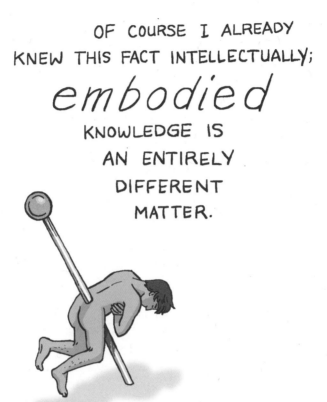

WHAT MY BODY
TOLD ME WAS THAT THIS
INTRUSION OF THE OUTSIDE
WORLD INTO MY INTERNAL PHYSICAL
BEING WAS WRONG ON A LEVEL
TOO DEEP FOR WORDS.

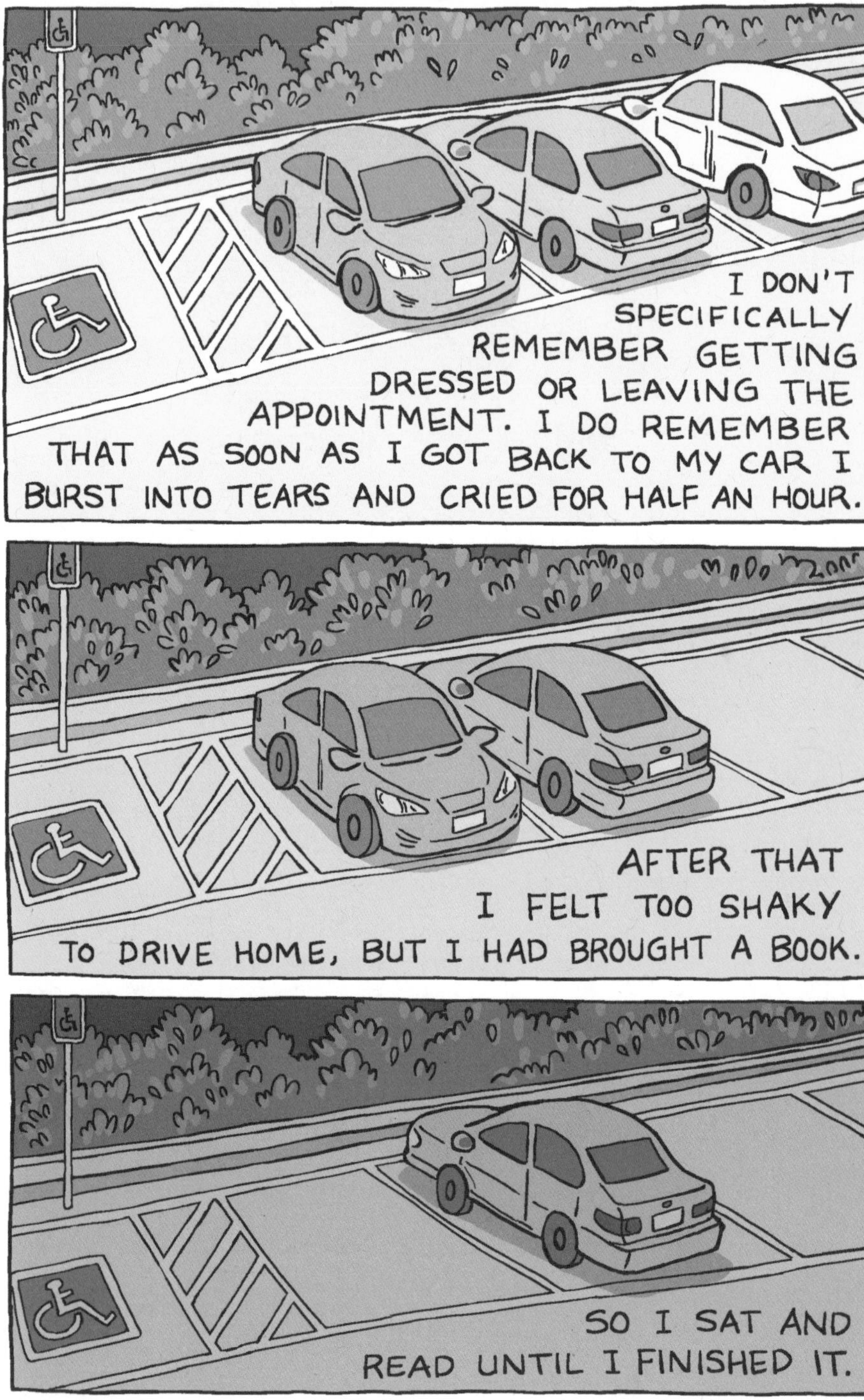
I DON'T SPECIFICALLY REMEMBER GETTING DRESSED OR LEAVING THE APPOINTMENT. I DO REMEMBER THAT AS SOON AS I GOT BACK TO MY CAR I BURST INTO TEARS AND CRIED FOR HALF AN HOUR.
AFTER THAT I FELT TOO SHAKY TO DRIVE HOME, BUT I HAD BROUGHT A BOOK.
SO I SAT AND READ UNTIL I FINISHED IT.

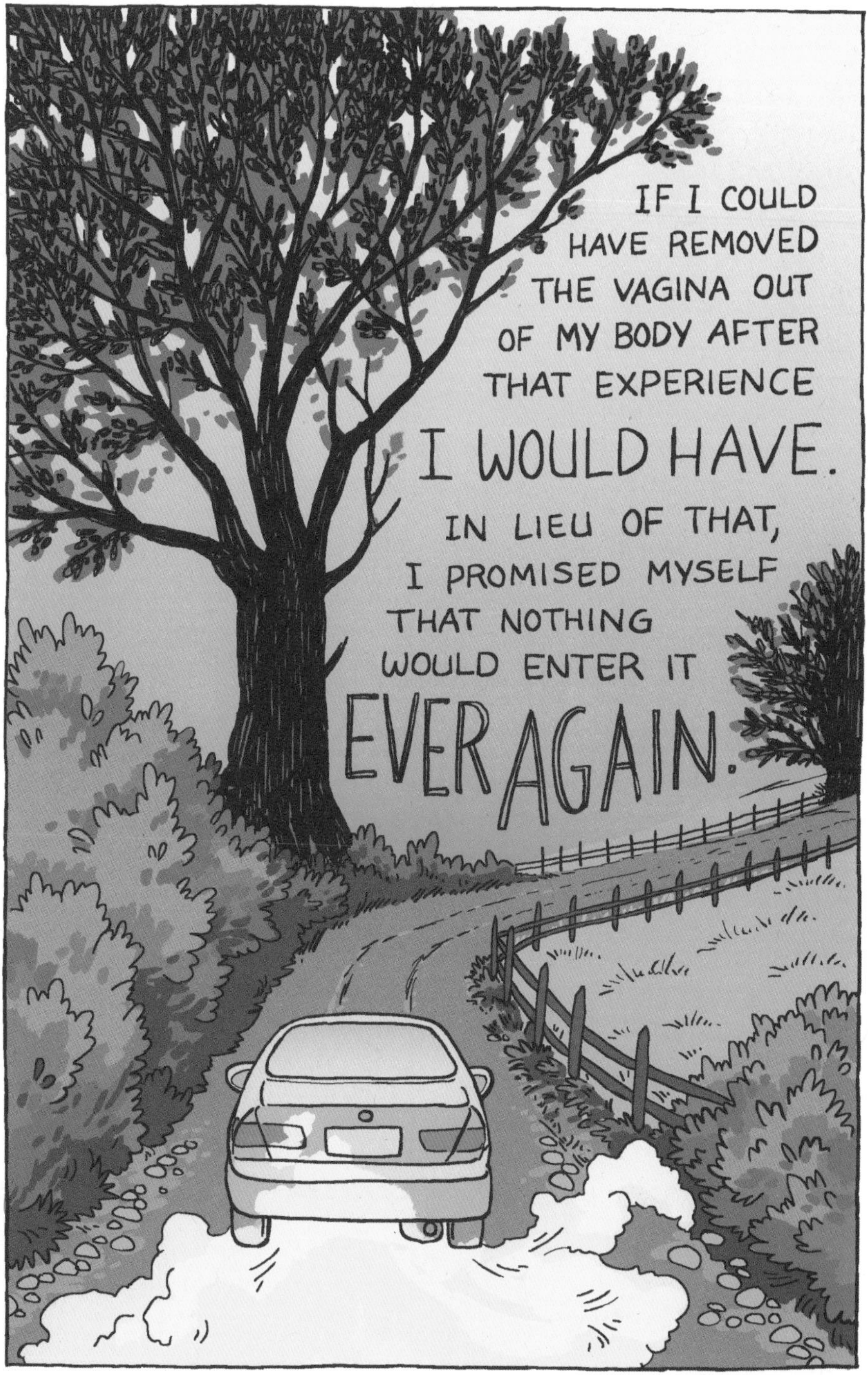
IF I COULD HAVE REMOVED THE VAGINA OUT OF MY BODY AFTER THAT EXPERIENCE
I WOULD HAVE.
IN LIEU OF THAT, I PROMISED MYSELF THAT NOTHING WOULD ENTER IT
EVER AGAIN.

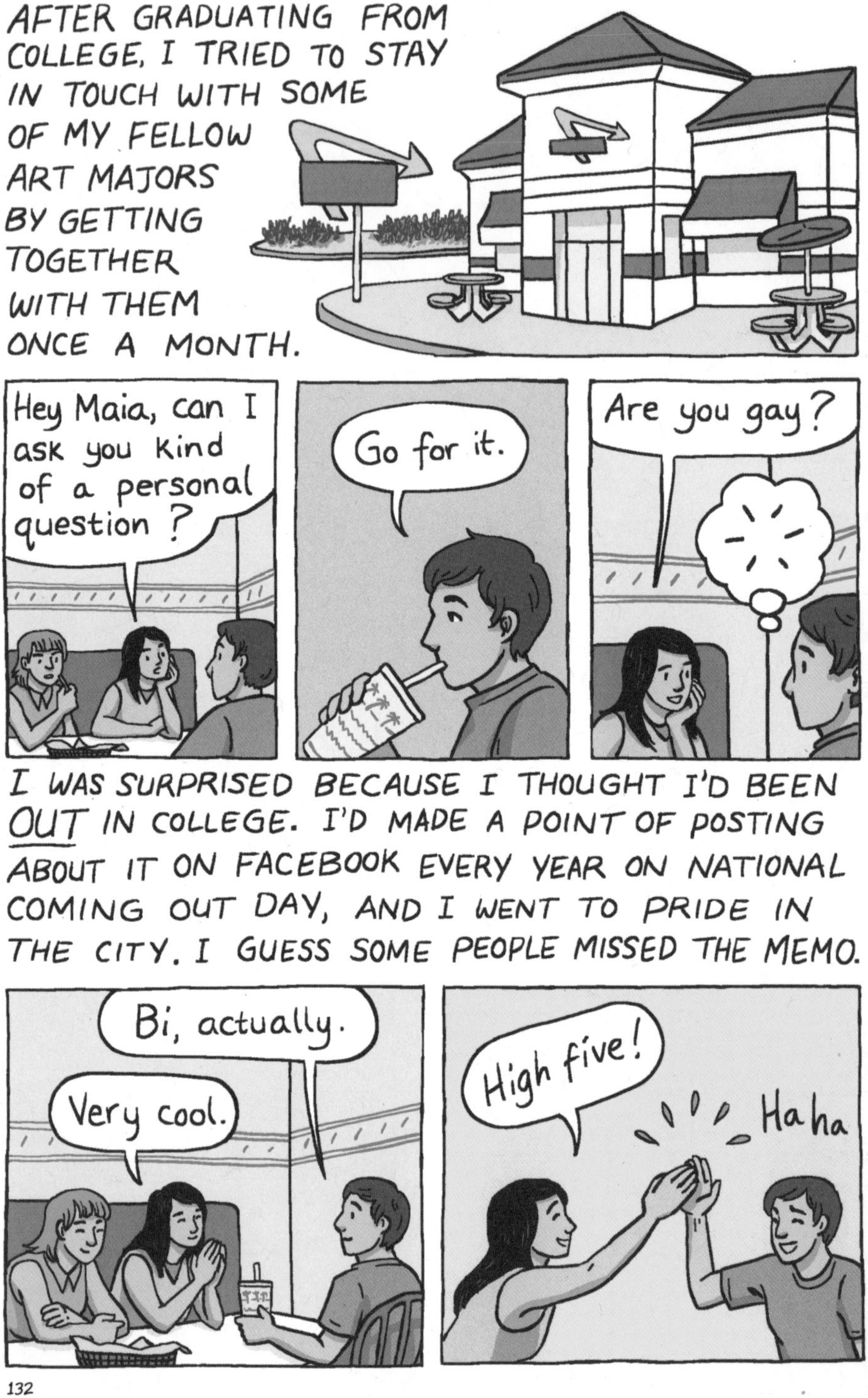
AFTER GRADUATING FROM COLLEGE, I TRIED TO STAY IN TOUCH WITH SOME OF MY FELLOW ART MAJORS BY GETTING TOGETHER WITH THEM ONCE A MONTH.
Hey Maia, can I ask you kind of a personal question?
Go for it.
Are you gay?
I WAS SURPRISED BECAUSE I THOUGHT I'D BEEN OUT IN COLLEGE. I'D MADE A POINT OF POSTING ABOUT IT ON FACEBOOK EVERY YEAR ON NATIONAL COMING OUT DAY, AND I WENT TO PRIDE IN THE CITY. I GUESS SOME PEOPLE MISSED THE MEMO.
Bi, actually.
Very cool.
High five!
Haha

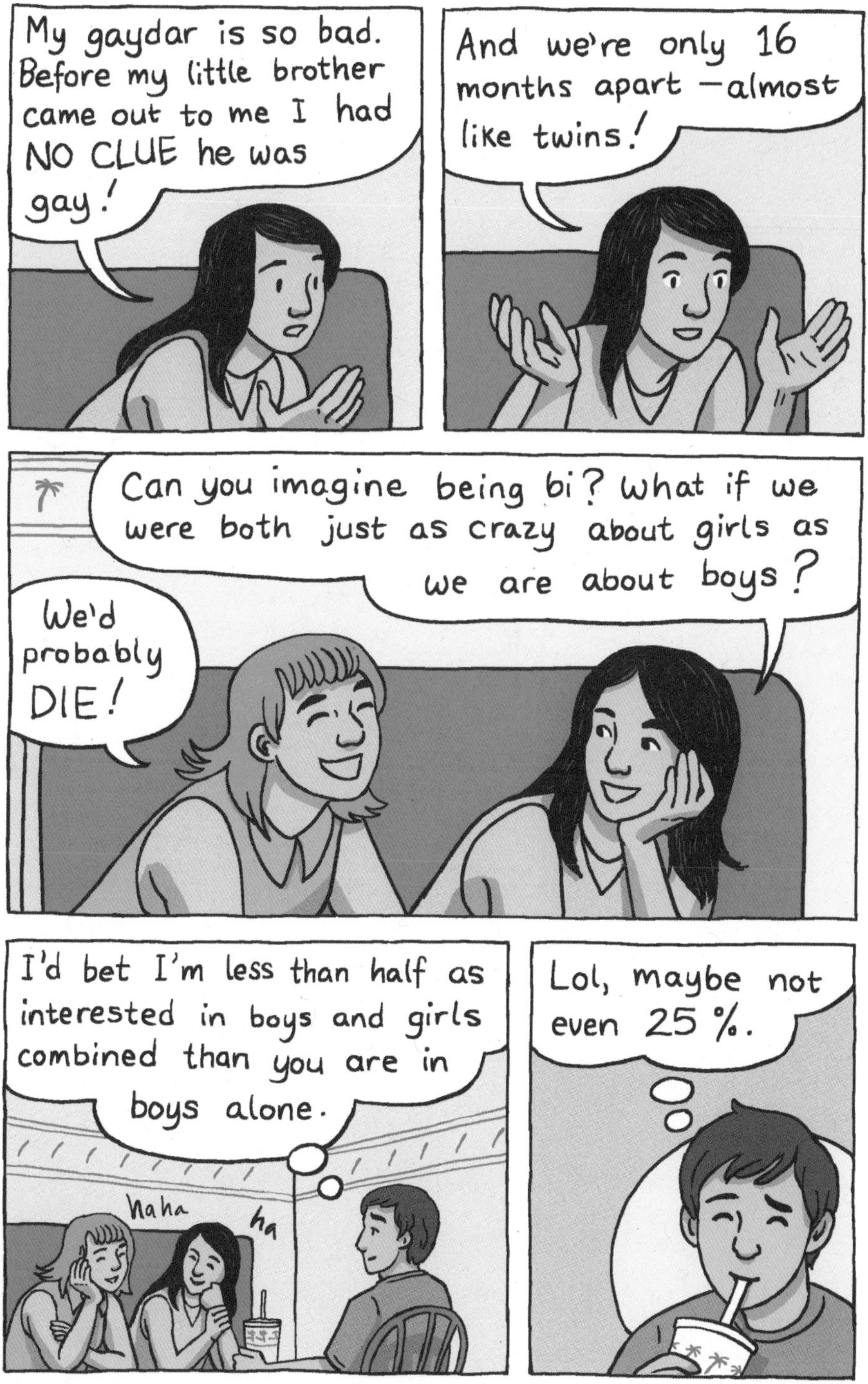
My gaydar is so bad. Before my little brother came out to me I had NO CLUE he was gay!
And we're only 16 months apart—almost like twins!
Can you imagine being bi? What if we were both just as crazy about girls as we are about boys?
We'd probably DIE!
I'd bet I'm less than half as interested in boys and girls combined than you are in boys alone.
haha
ha
Lol, maybe not even 25%.

WHEN I WAS 14 OR SO I TOLD A CLOSE FRIEND

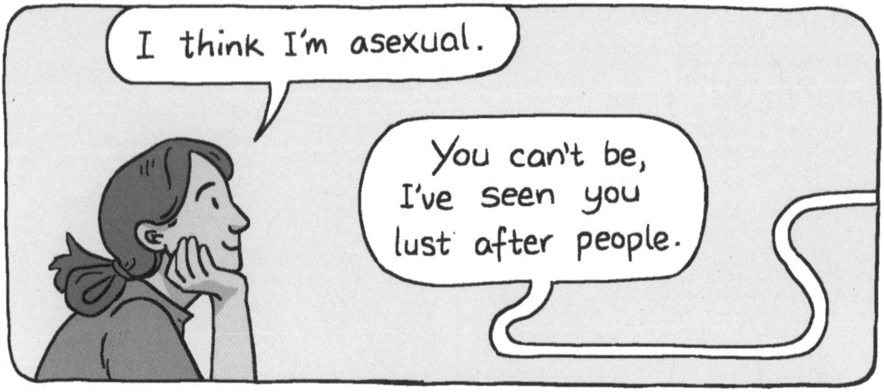
I think I'm asexual.
You can't be, I've seen you lust after people.

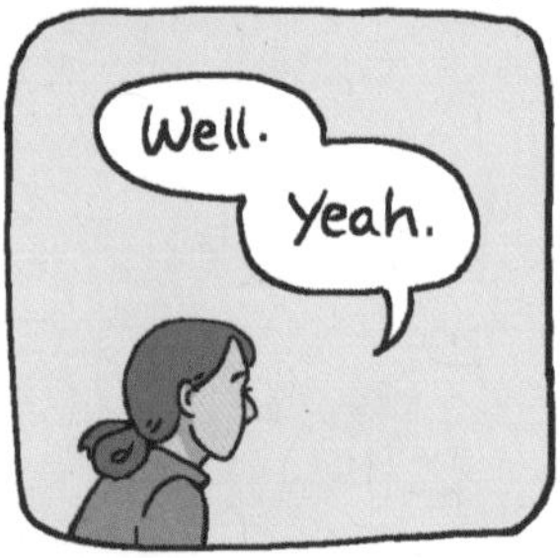
Well.
Yeah.

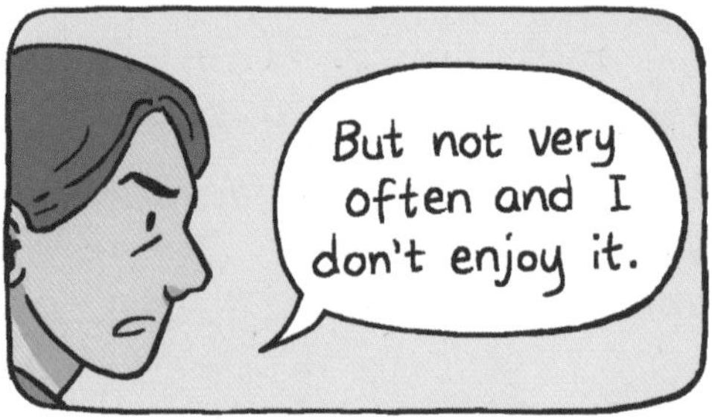
But not very often and I don't enjoy it.

I REMEMBER MY FIRST YEAR AT S.F. PRIDE THINKING THAT THE ASEXUAL GROUP HAD

THE BEST SIGNS.

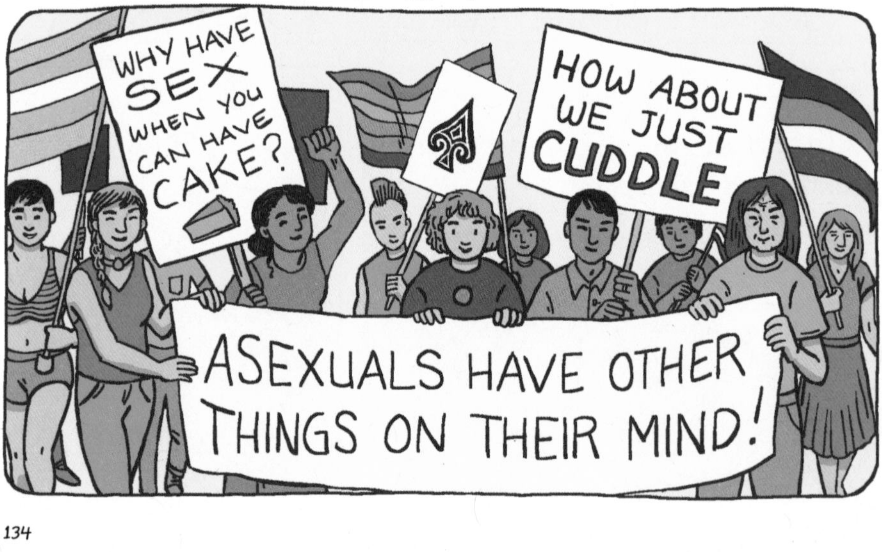
WHY HAVE SEX WHEN YOU CAN HAVE CAKE?
HOW ABOUT WE JUST CUDDLE
ASEXUALS HAVE OTHER THINGS ON THEIR MIND!

ALISON BECHDEL WRITES IN FUN HOME ABOUT DISCOVERING MASTURBATION SOON AFTER HER FIRST PERIOD (PAGE 170).

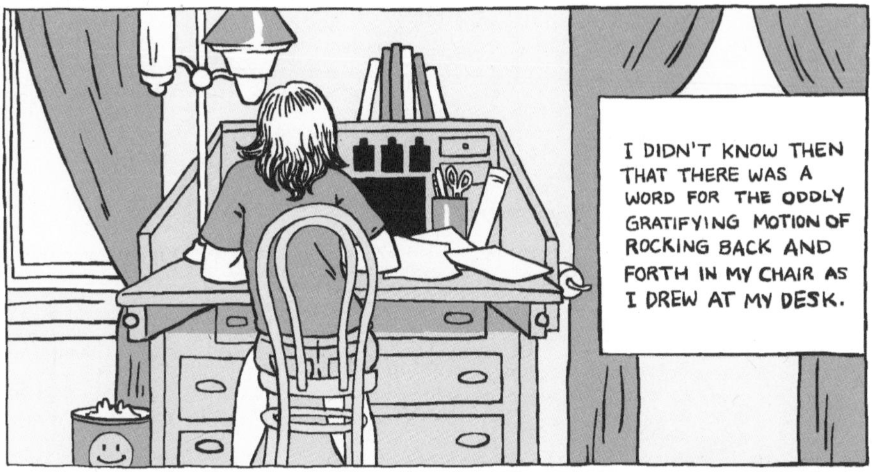
I DIDN'T KNOW THEN THAT THERE WAS A WORD FOR THE ODDLY GRATIFYING MOTION OF ROCKING BACK AND FORTH IN MY CHAIR AS I DREW AT MY DESK.

I DISCOVERED IT AT AROUND THE SAME AGE, FOLLOWED BY THE FURTHER REALIZATION THAT MY ABILITY TO BECOME AROUSED WAS GOVERNED BY A STRICT LAW OF DIMINISHING RETURNS.

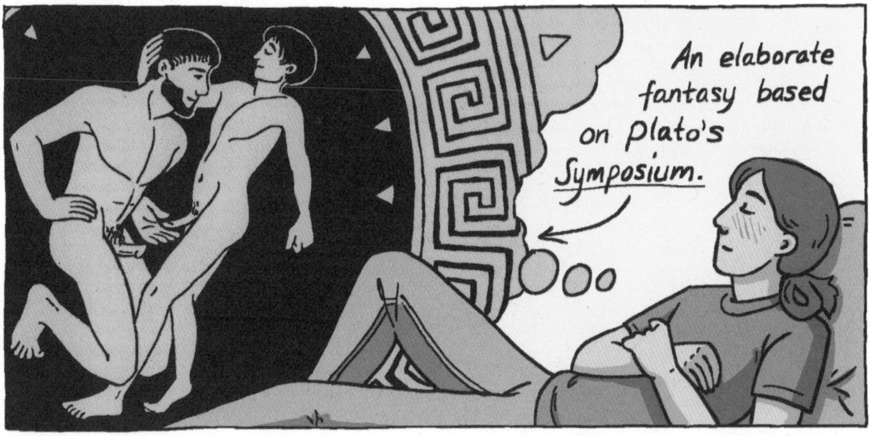
An elaborate fantasy based on Plato's Symposium.

THE MORE I HAD TO INTERACT WITH MY GENITALS THE LESS LIKELY I WAS TO REACH A POINT OF ANY SATISFACTION. THE BEST FANTASY WAS ONE THAT DIDN'T REQUIRE ANY PHYSICAL TOUCH AT ALL.

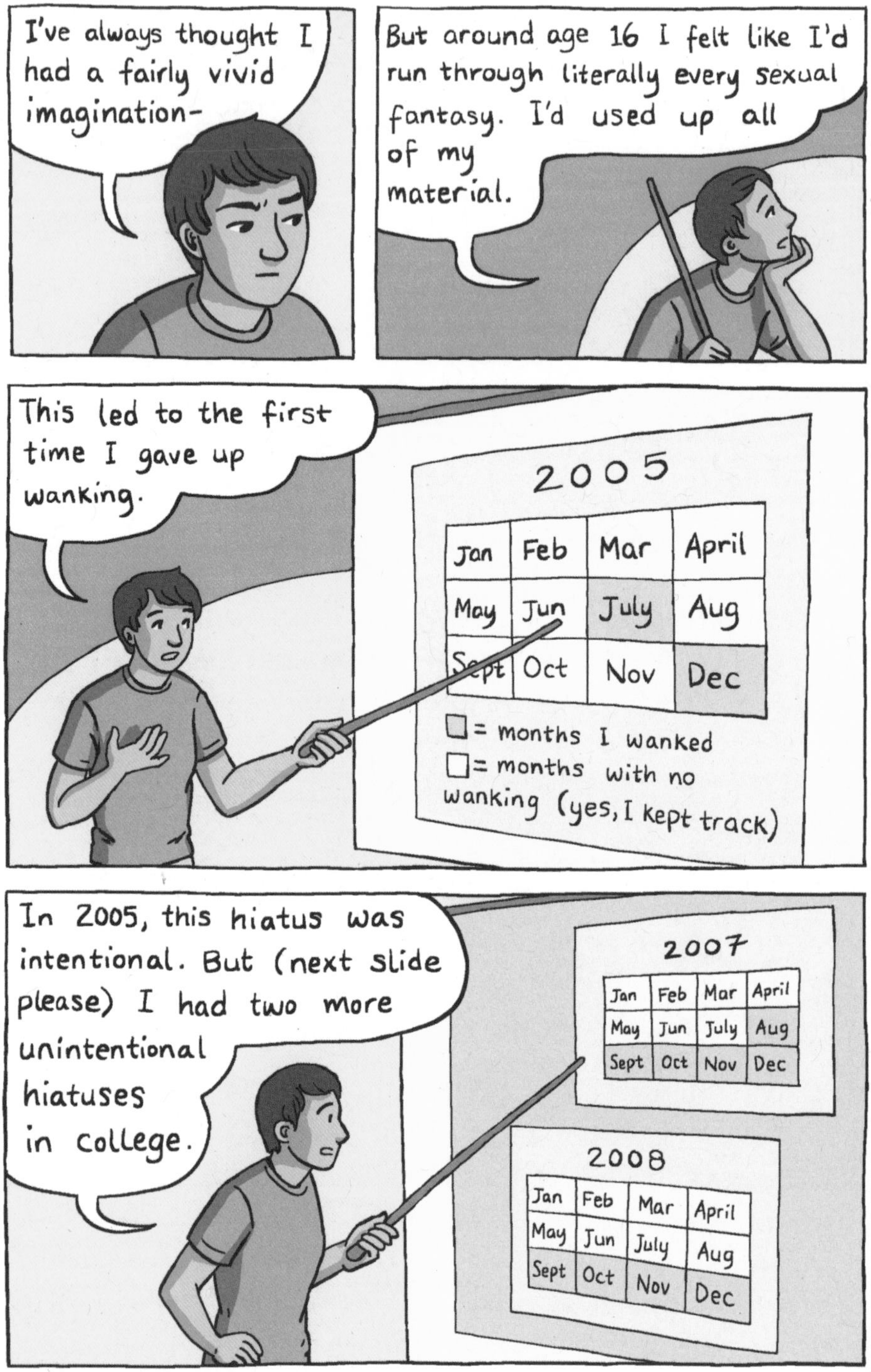
I've always thought I had a fairly vivid imagination-
But around age 16 I felt like I'd run through literally every sexual fantasy. I'd used up all of my material.
This led to the first time I gave up wanking.
2005
Jan Feb Mar April
May Jun July Aug
Sept Oct Nov Dec
= months I wanked
= months with no wanking (yes, I kept track)
In 2005, this hiatus was intentional. But (next slide please) I had two more unintentional hiatuses in college.
2007
Jan Feb Mar April
May Jun July Aug
Sept Oct Nov Dec
2008
Jan Feb Mar April
May Jun July Aug
Sept Oct Nov Dec

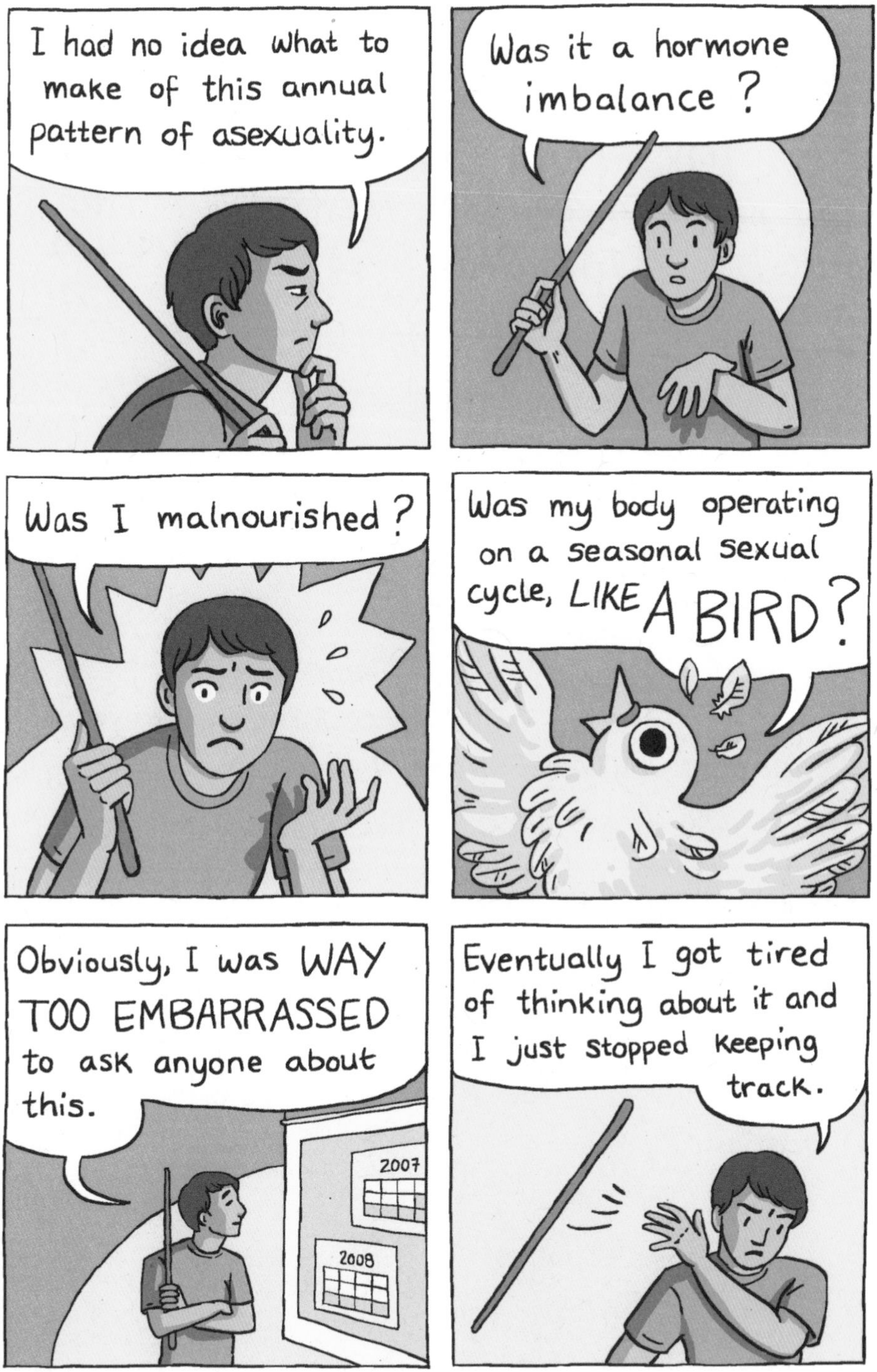
I had no idea what to make of this annual pattern of asexuality.
Was it a hormone imbalance?
Was I malnourished?
Was my body operating on a seasonal sexual cycle, LIKE A BIRD?
Obviously, I was WAY TOO EMBARRASSED to ask anyone about this.
2007
2008
Eventually I got tired of thinking about it and I just stopped keeping track.

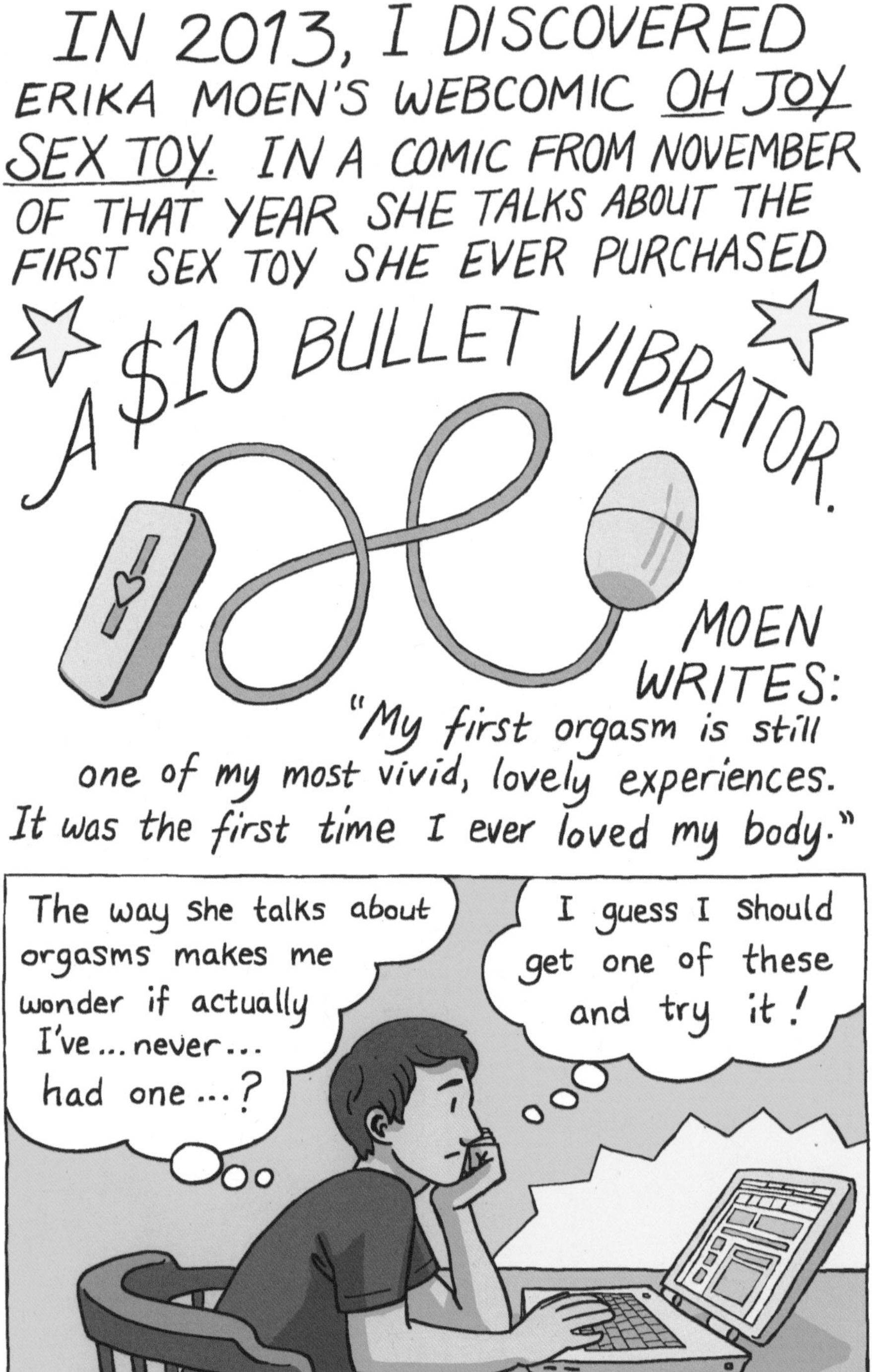
IN 2013, I DISCOVERED ERIKA MOEN'S WEBCOMIC OH JOY SEX TOY. IN A COMIC FROM NOVEMBER OF THAT YEAR SHE TALKS ABOUT THE FIRST SEX TOY SHE EVER PURCHASED
A $10 BULLET VIBRATOR.
MOEN WRITES:
"My first orgasm is still one of my most vivid, lovely experiences. It was the first time I ever loved my body."
The way she talks about orgasms makes me wonder if actually I've... never... had one...?
I guess I should get one of these and try it!

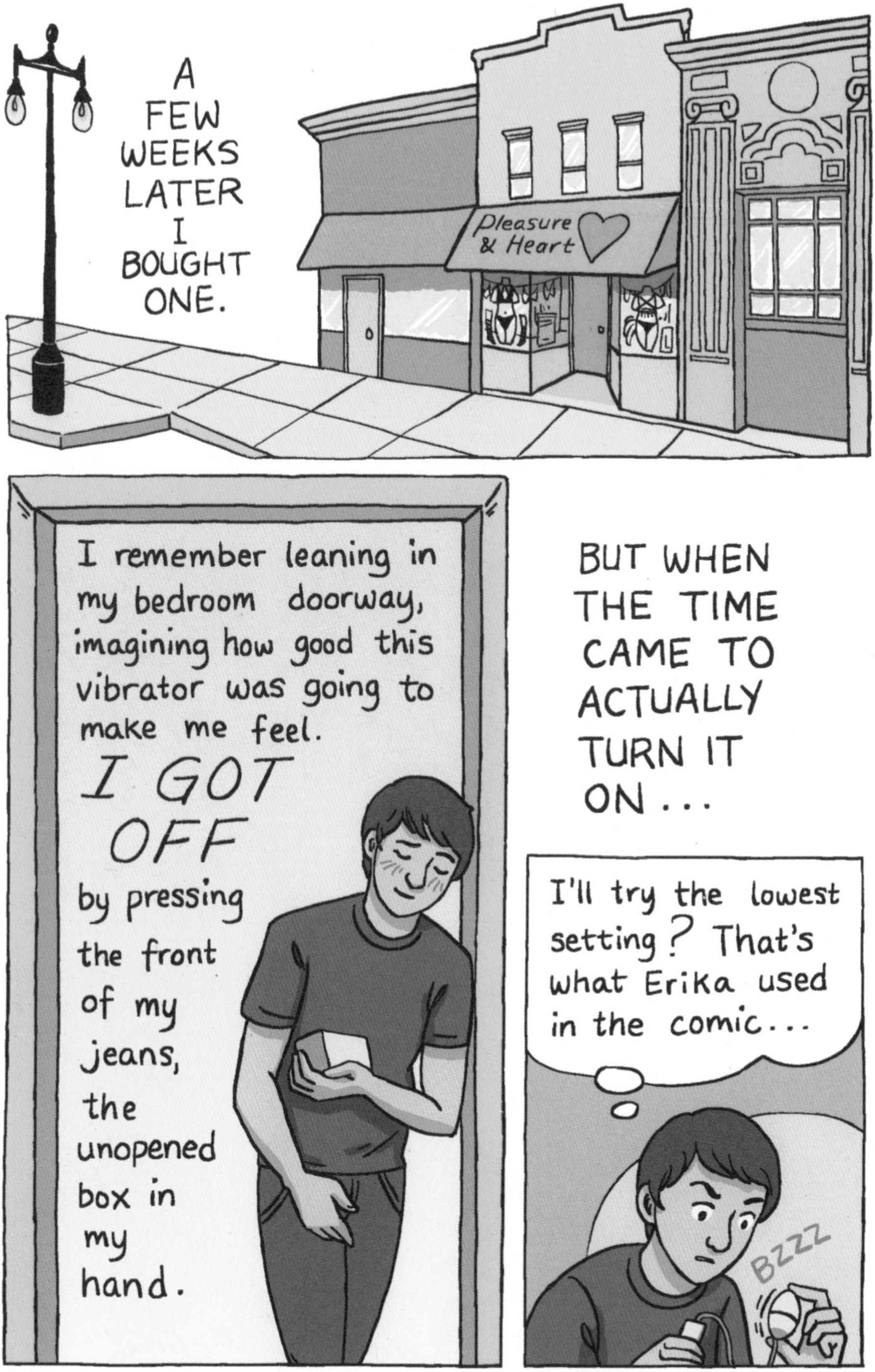
A FEW WEEKS LATER I BOUGHT ONE.
Pleasure & Heart
I remember leaning in my bedroom doorway, imagining how good this vibrator was going to make me feel.
I GOT OFF
by pressing the front of my jeans, the unopened box in my hand.
BUT WHEN THE TIME CAME TO ACTUALLY TURN IT ON...
I'll try the lowest setting? That's what Erika used in the comic...
BZZZ

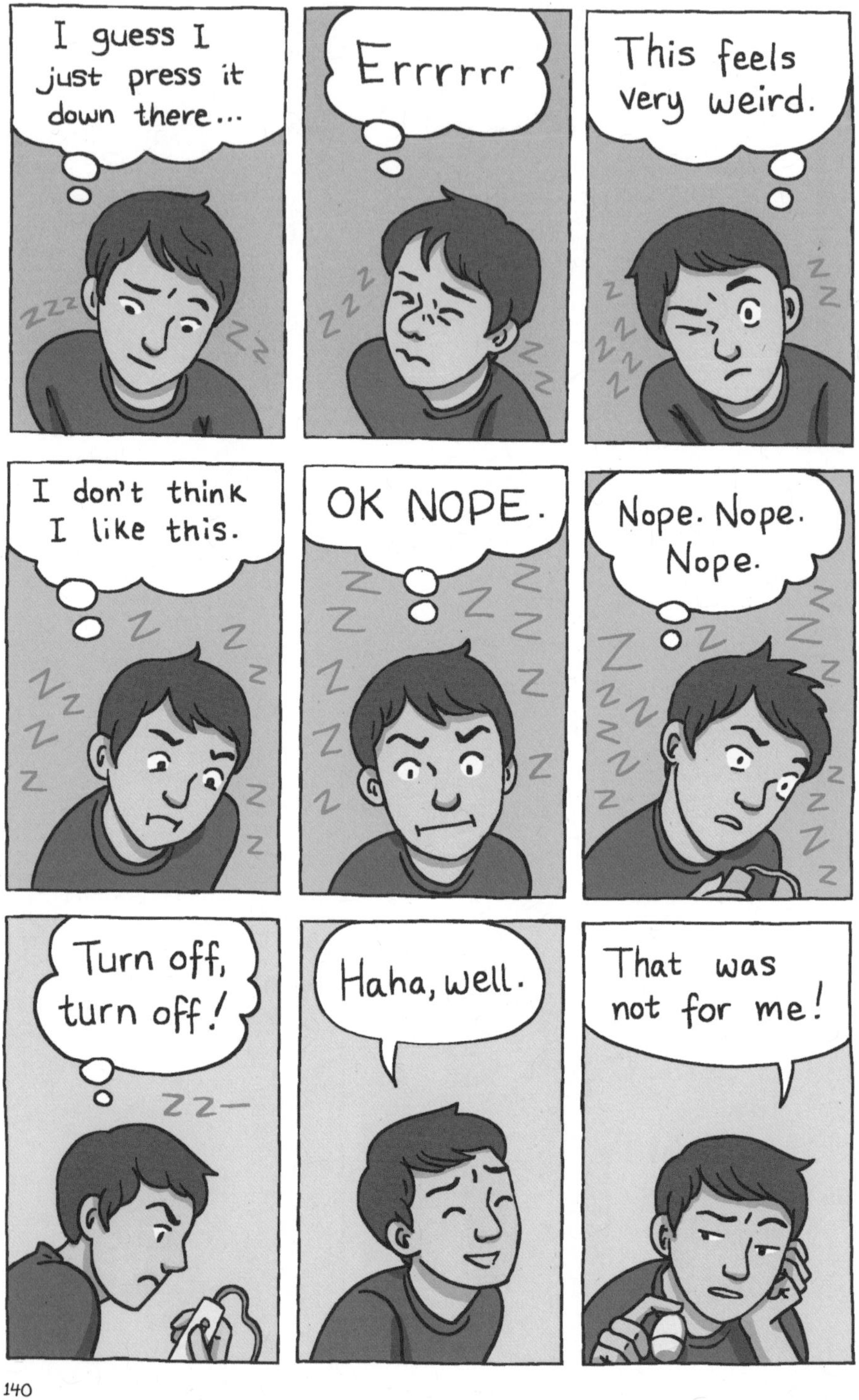
I guess I just press it down there...
Errrrrr
This feels very weird.
I don't think I like this.
OK NOPE.
Nope. Nope. Nope.
Turn off, turn off!
Haha, well.
That was not for me!

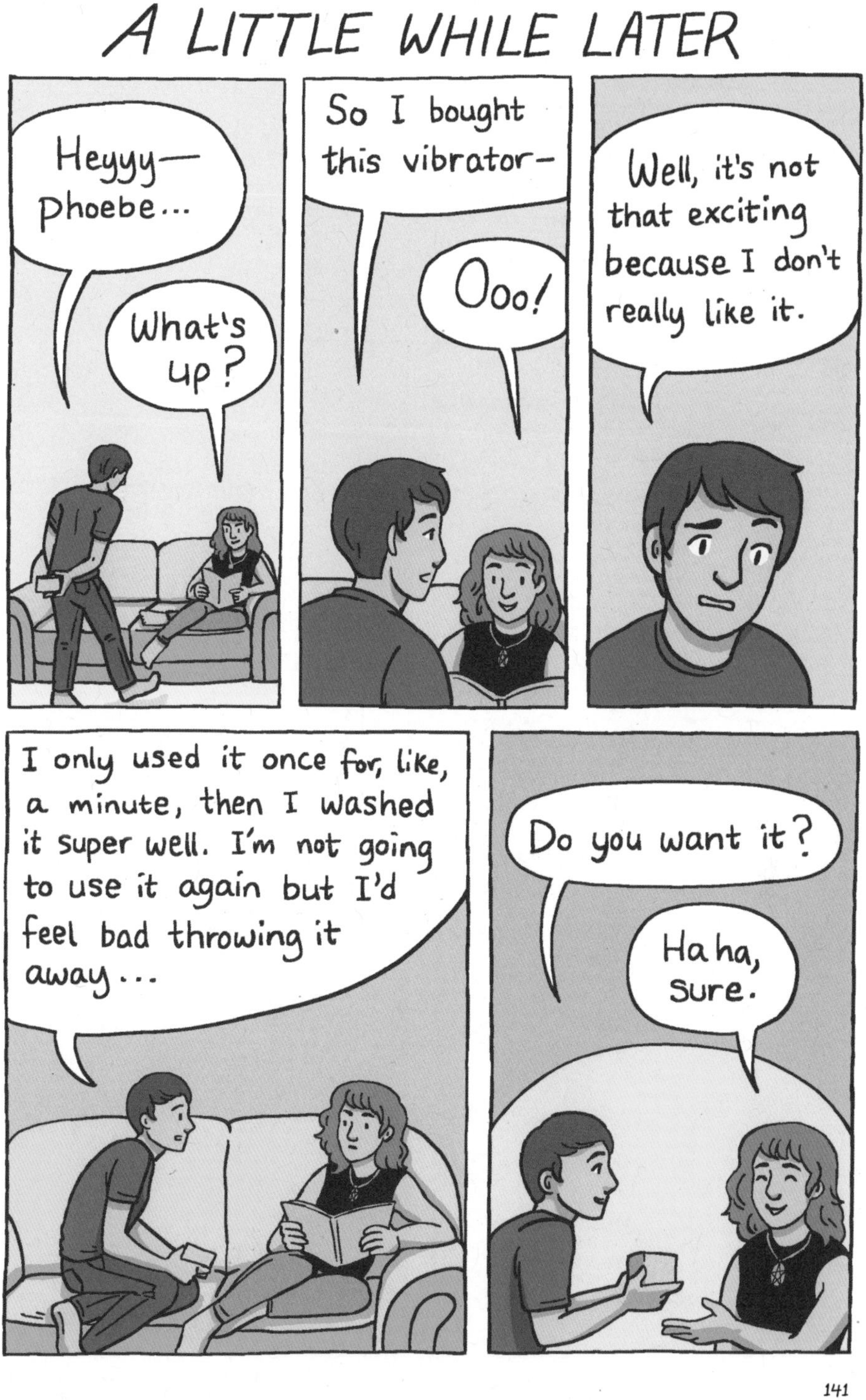
A LITTLE WHILE LATER
Heyyy— phoebe...
What's up?
So I bought this vibrator–
Ooo!
Well, it's not that exciting because I don't really like it.
I only used it once for, like, a minute, then I washed it super well. I'm not going to use it again but I'd feel bad throwing it away...
Do you want it?
Ha ha, sure.

BACK WHEN FB FIRST ADDED MORE GENDER OPTIONS

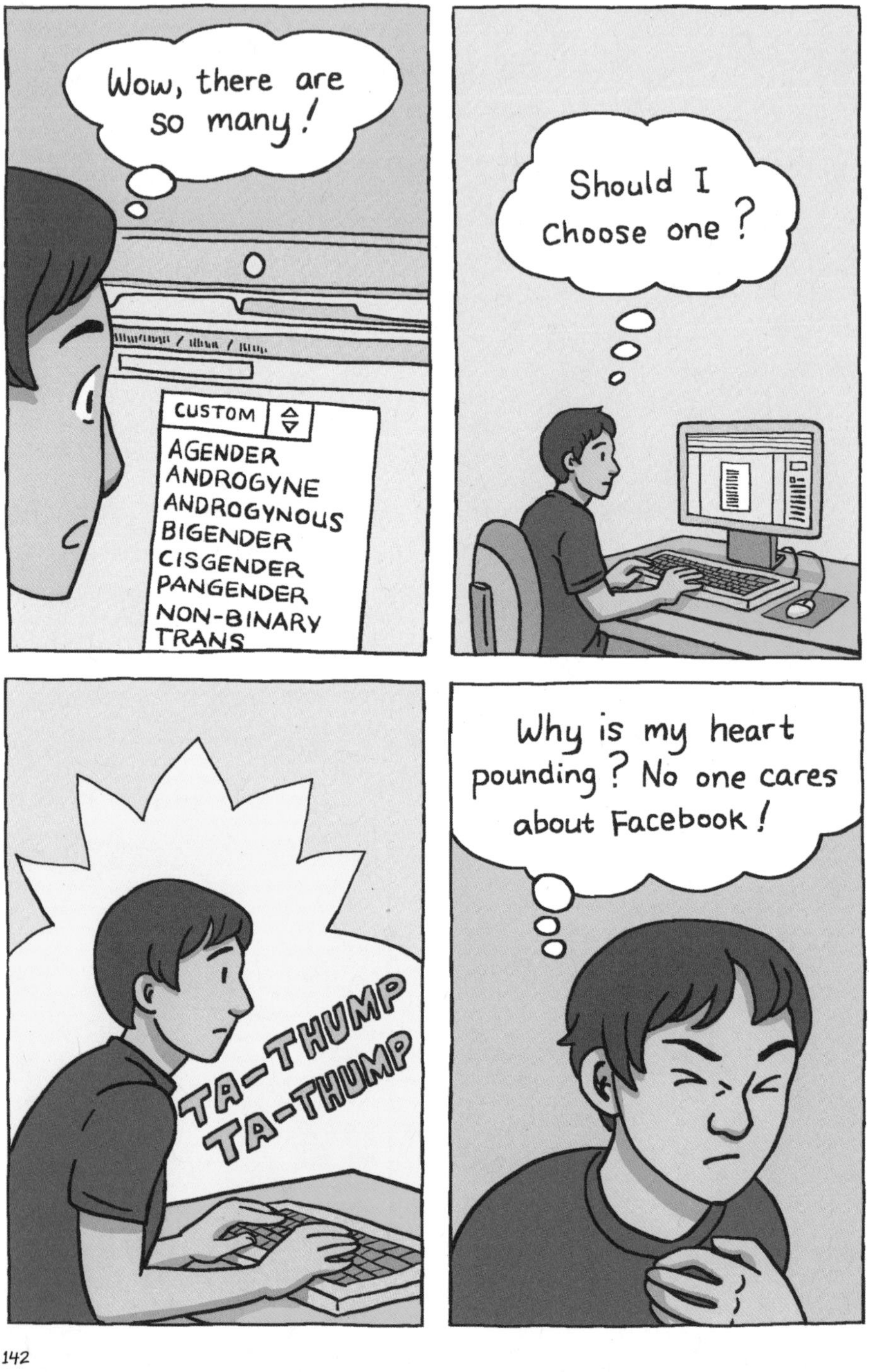
Wow, there are so many!
CUSTOM
AGENDER
ANDROGYNE
ANDROGYNOUS
BIGENDER
CISGENDER
PANGENDER
NON-BINARY
TRANS
Should I choose one?
TA-THUMP
TA-THUMP
Why is my heart pounding? No one cares about Facebook!

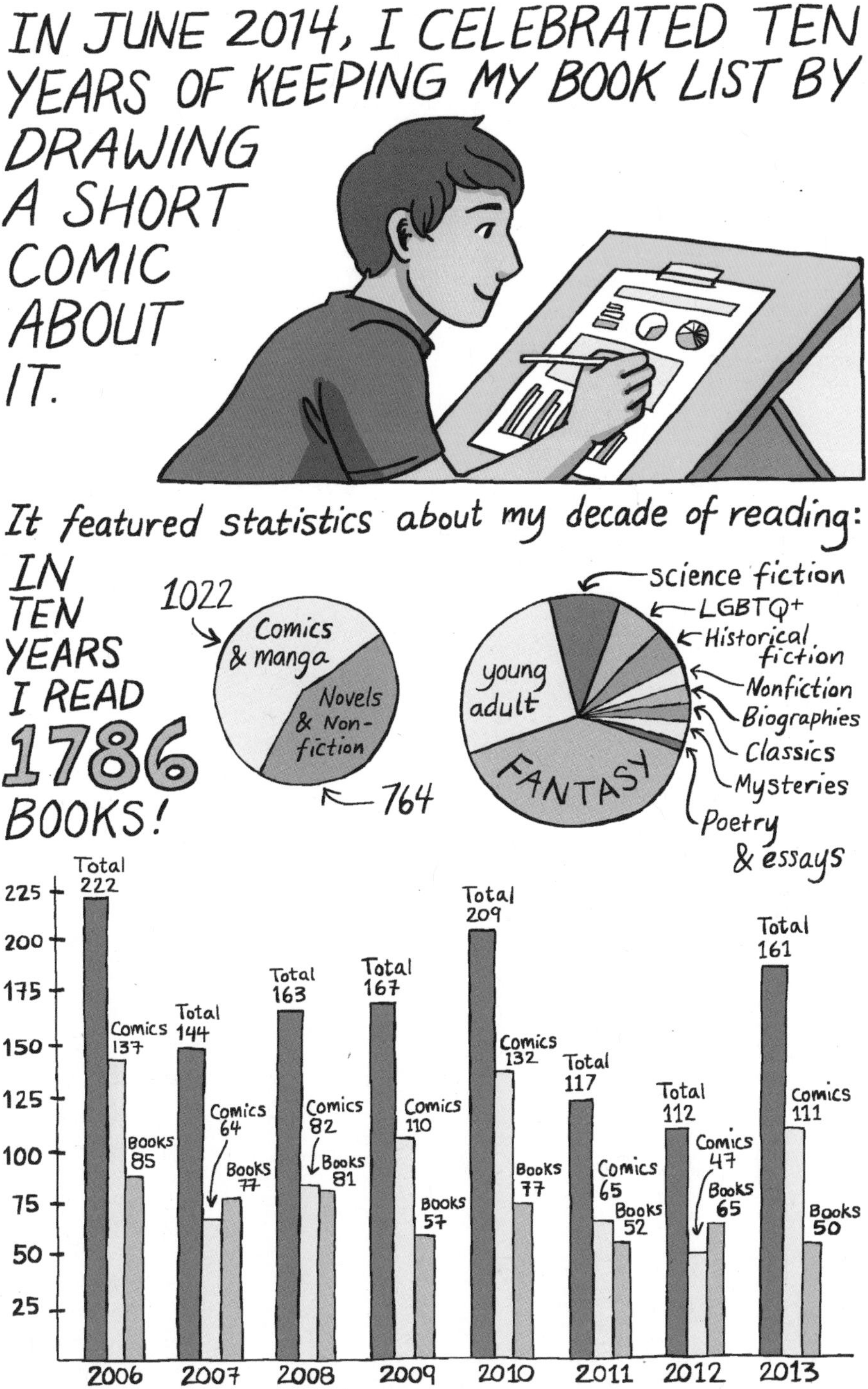

IN JUNE 2014, I CELEBRATED TEN YEARS OF KEEPING MY BOOK LIST BY DRAWING A SHORT COMIC ABOUT IT.
It featured statistics about my decade of reading:
IN TEN YEARS I READ 1786 BOOKS!
1022
Comics & manga
Novels & Non-fiction
764
science fiction
LGBTQ+
Historical fiction
Nonfiction
Biographies
Classics
Mysteries
Poetry & essays
young adult
FANTASY
225
200
175
150
125
100
75
50
25
Total 222
Comics 137
Books 85
Total 144
Comics 64
Books 77
Total 163
Comics 82
Books 81
Total 167
Comics 110
Books 57
Total 209
Comics 132
Books 77
Total 117
Comics 65
Books 52
Total 112
Comics 47
Books 65
Total 161
Comics 111
Books 50
2006
2007
2008
2009
2010
2011
2012
2013

MOST READ WESTERN AUTHORS*

Author	
Neil Gaiman, 37 books read	
Terry Pratchett, 36 books	
Tamora Pierce, 28	
Lois McMaster Bujold, 26	
Mercedes Lackey, 18	
J.K. Rowling, 17	
Holly Black, 16	
J.R.R. Tolkien, 14	
Roger Zelazny, 13	
U.K. Le Guin, 12	

* These numbers include re-reads

← Between 2004–2014 I read most of the Harry Potter series twice & books 6 & 7 four times each

← The Hobbit & the LOTR Trilogy read three times each

MOST READ MANGA & MANHWA AUTHORS

Author	Works
CLAMP (a collective of four people) — 77 books	
Kosuke Fujishima, 24	– Oh My Goddess!
Rumiko Takahashi, 22	– Ranma ½, Inuyasha
Masashi Kishimoto	15 – Naruto
Hiromu Arakawa	14 – Fullmetal Alchemist
Emura	14 – W. Juliet
Maki Murakami	12 – Gravitation
Higuchi Tachibana	12 – Gakuen Alice
Choi Kyung-Ah	12 – Snow Drop
Kiyohiko Azuma	12 – Yotsuba&!, Azumanga Daioh

THIS COMIC WAS VERY WARMLY RECIEVED BY BOOK LOVERS, TEACHERS, AND LIBRARIANS, BUT I REMEMBER THINKING:

This is definitely the last autobiographical comic I will ever write.

The only thing I feel comfortable with strangers knowing about me is what I read!

NOT LONG AFTER THIS, I HAD A CONVERSATION ABOUT THE WORD "CISGENDER" WITH A CIS, STRAIGHT, MALE FRIEND FROM HIGH SCHOOL.

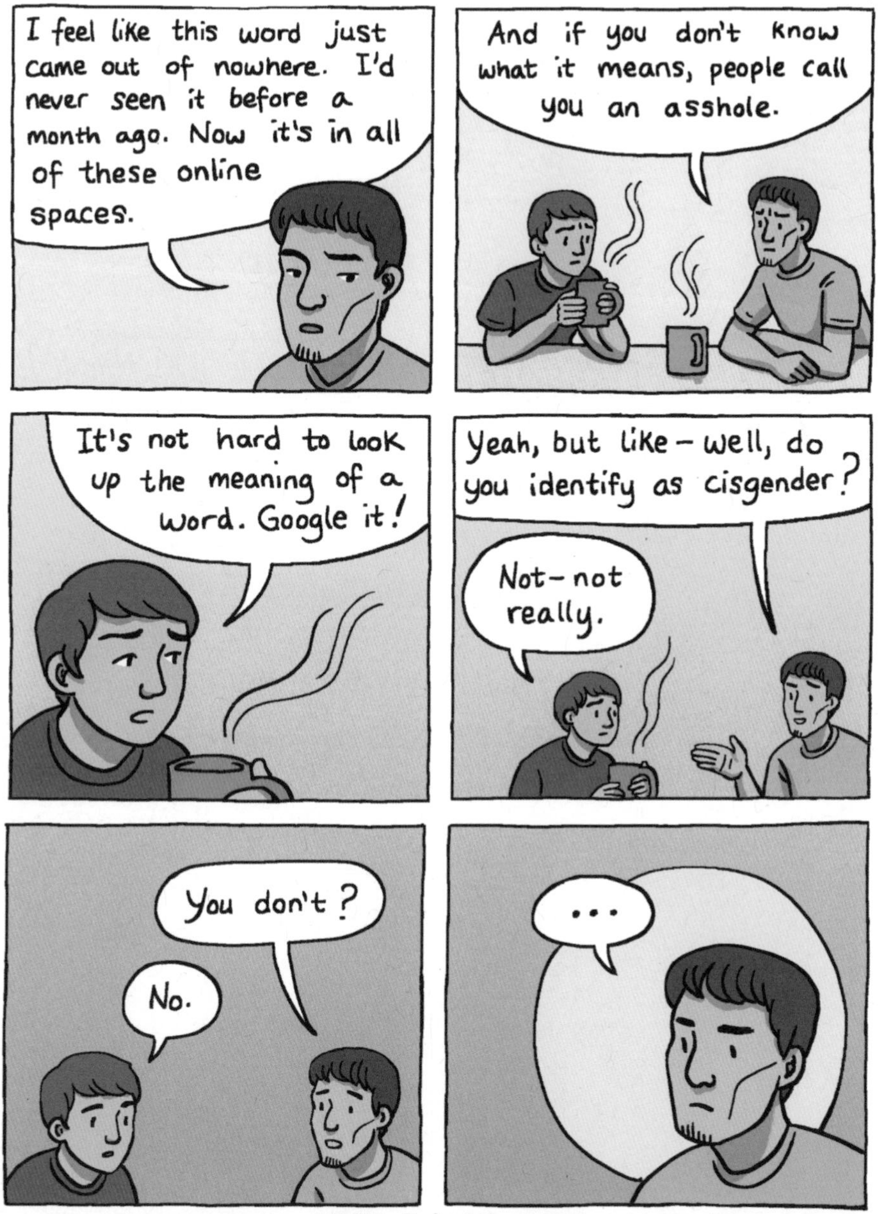
I feel like this word just came out of nowhere. I'd never seen it before a month ago. Now it's in all of these online spaces.
And if you don't know what it means, people call you an asshole.
It's not hard to look up the meaning of a word. Google it!
Yeah, but like—well, do you identify as cisgender?
Not—not really.
You don't?
No.
...

IT WAS THE FIRST TIME I HAD SAID THAT OUT LOUD.

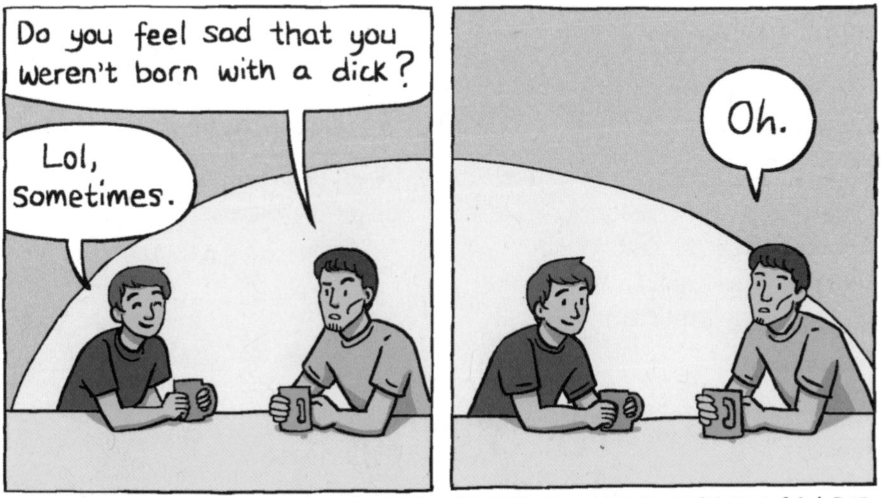
Do you feel sad that you weren't born with a dick?
Lol, Sometimes.
Oh.

NATURALLY, I RELAYED THIS WHOLE EXCHANGE TO ANOTHER (QUEER, FEMALE) FRIEND.

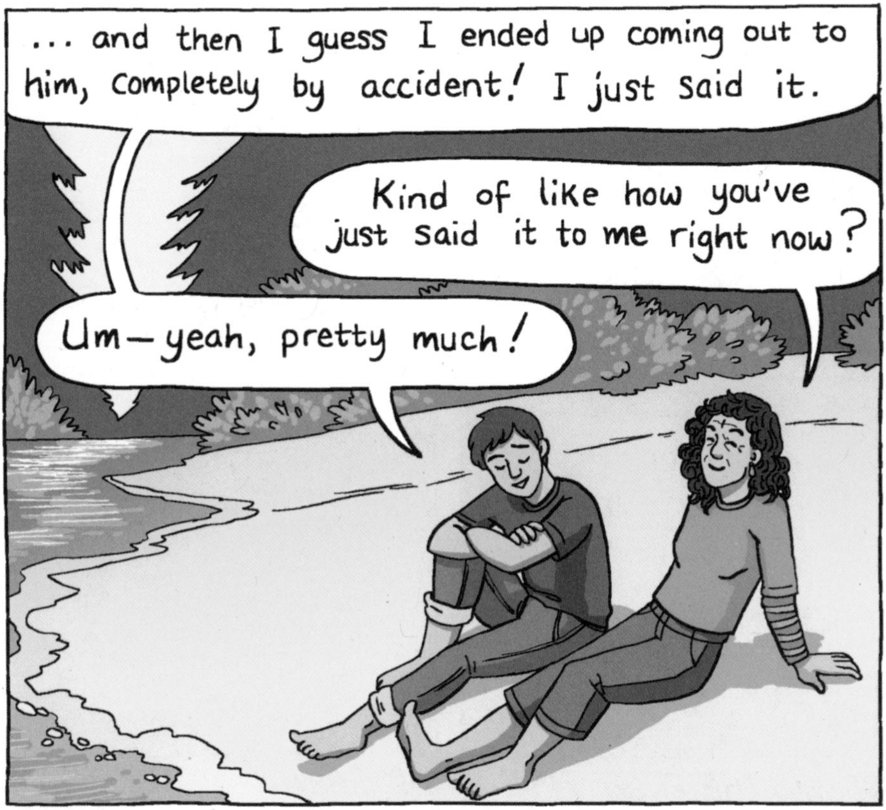
... and then I guess I ended up coming out to him, completely by accident! I just said it.
Kind of like how you've just said it to me right now?
Um—yeah, pretty much!

I DECIDED TO TALK TO MY MOM ABOUT IT.

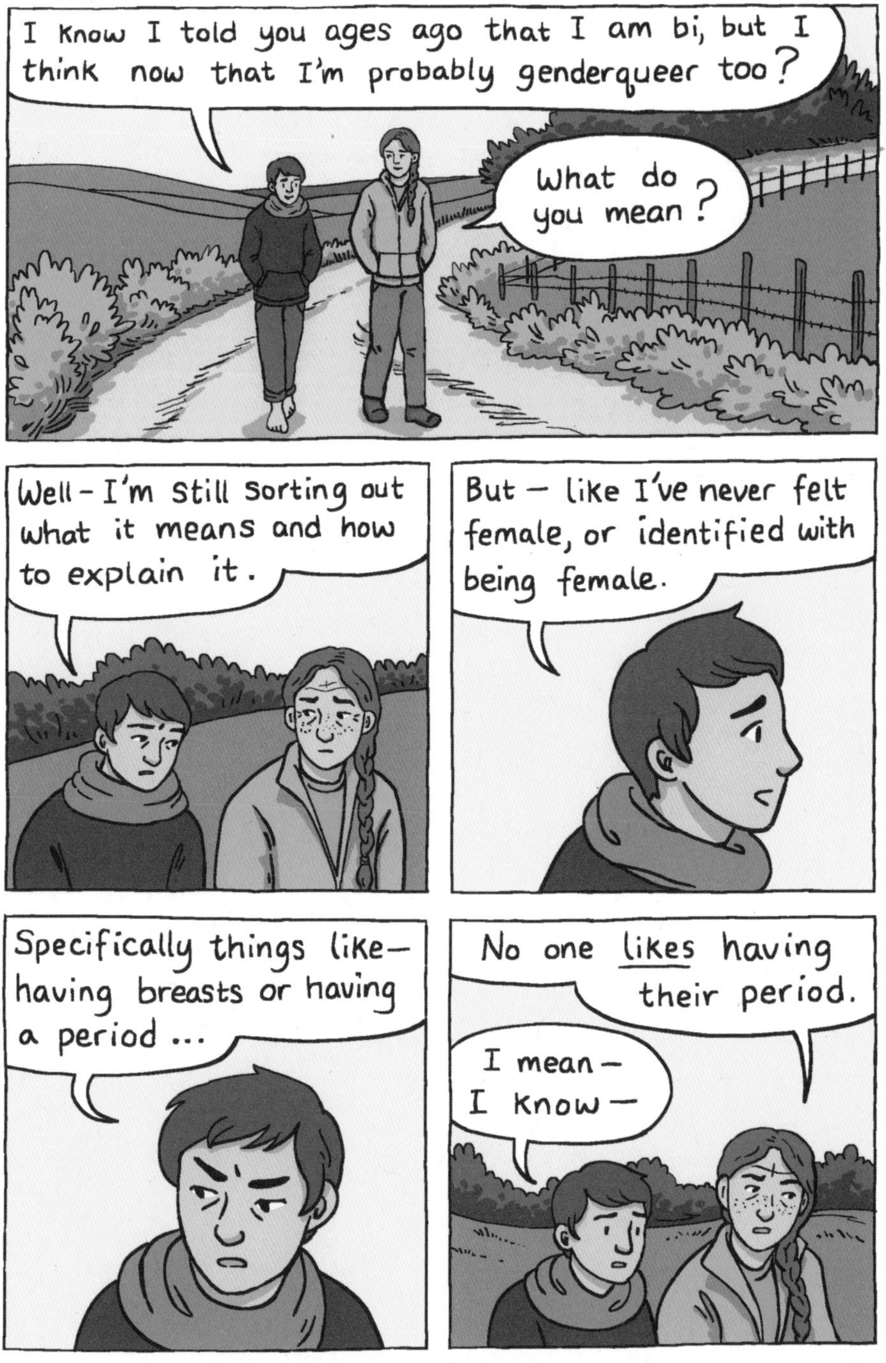
I know I told you ages ago that I am bi, but I think now that I'm probably genderqueer too?
What do you mean?
Well - I'm still sorting out what it means and how to explain it.
But - like I've never felt female, or identified with being female.
Specifically things like - having breasts or having a period...
No one likes having their period.
I mean -
I know -

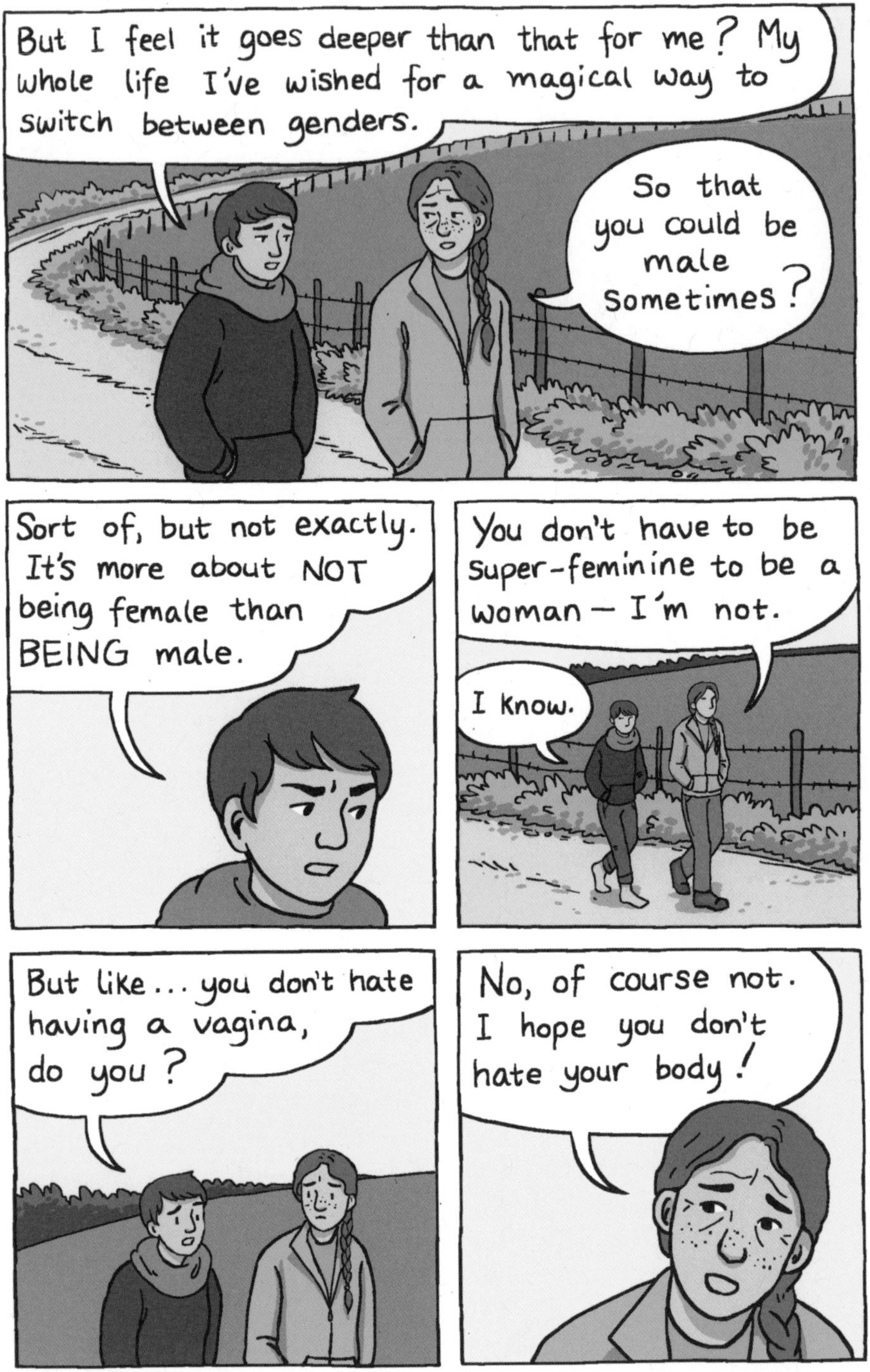
But I feel it goes deeper than that for me? My whole life I've wished for a magical way to switch between genders.
So that you could be male sometimes?
Sort of, but not exactly. It's more about NOT being female than BEING male.
You don't have to be super-feminine to be a woman — I'm not.
I know.
But like... you don't hate having a vagina, do you?
No, of course not. I hope you don't hate your body!

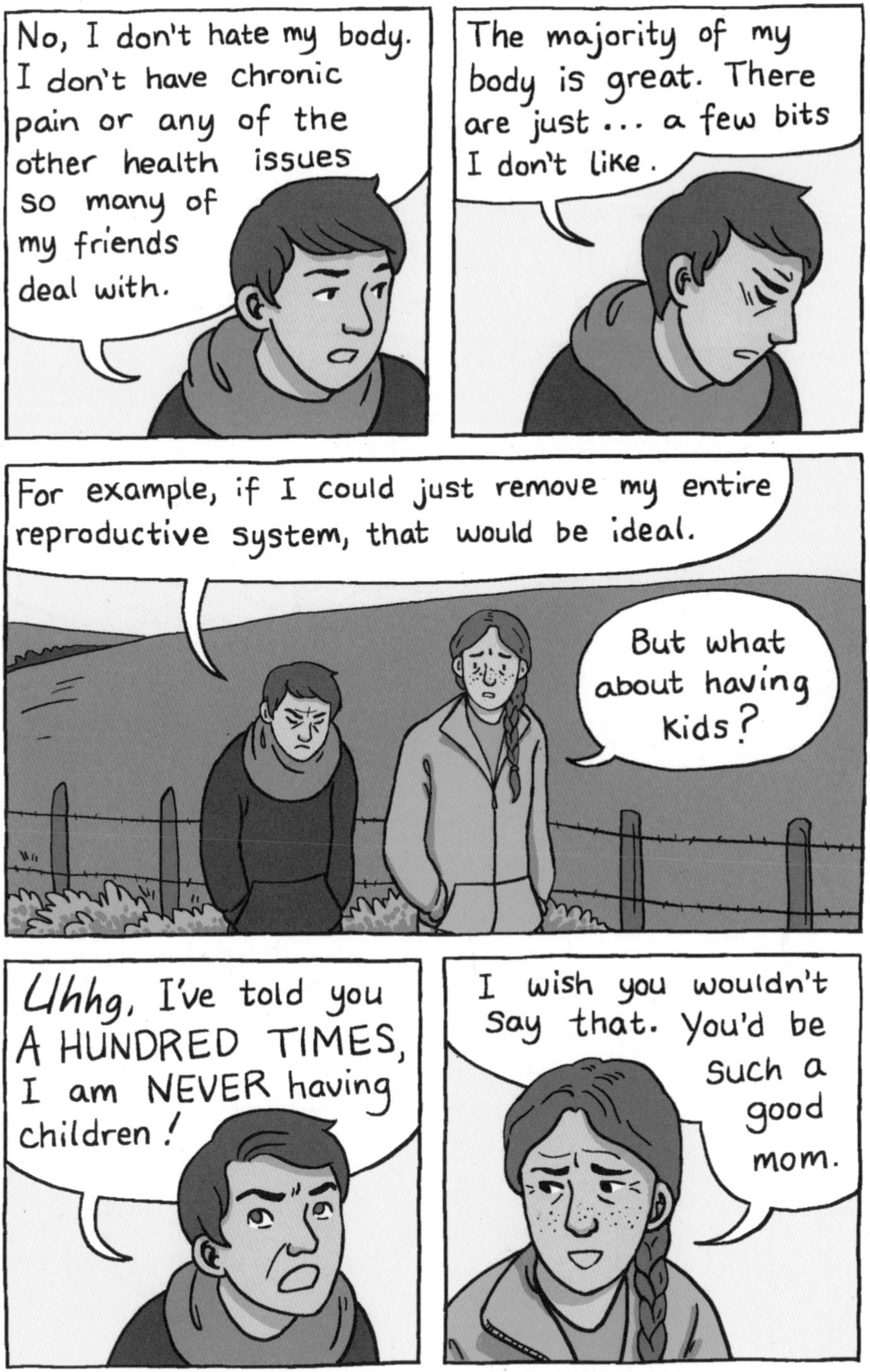
No, I don't hate my body. I don't have chronic pain or any of the other health issues so many of my friends deal with.
The majority of my body is great. There are just ... a few bits I don't like.
For example, if I could just remove my entire reproductive system, that would be ideal.
But what about having kids?
Uhhg, I've told you A HUNDRED TIMES, I am NEVER having children!
I wish you wouldn't say that. You'd be such a good mom.

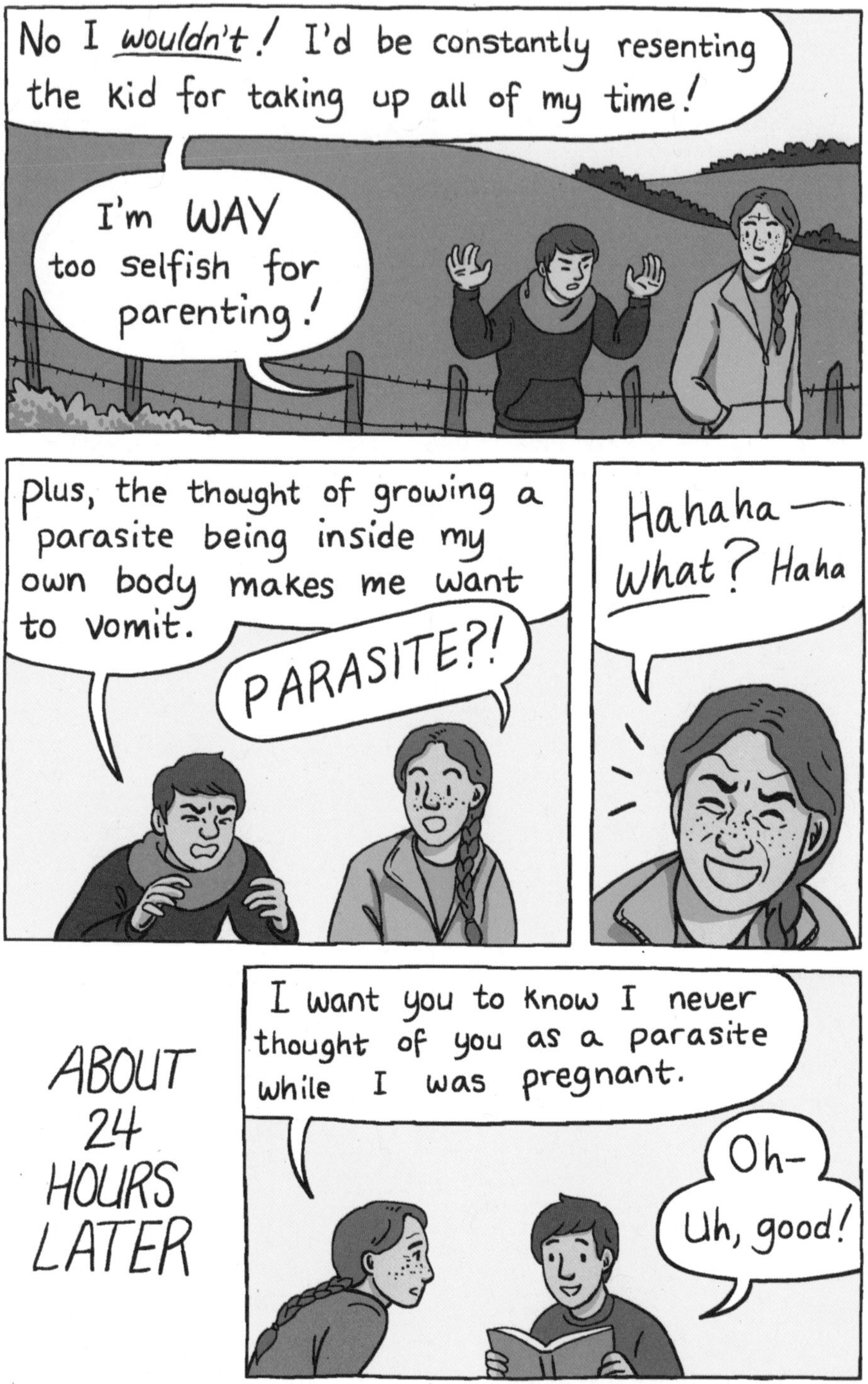

No I wouldn't! I'd be constantly resenting the kid for taking up all of my time!
I'm WAY too selfish for parenting!
plus, the thought of growing a parasite being inside my own body makes me want to vomit.
PARASITE?!
Hahaha— What? Haha
ABOUT 24 HOURS LATER
I want you to know I never thought of you as a parasite while I was pregnant.
Oh- Uh, good!

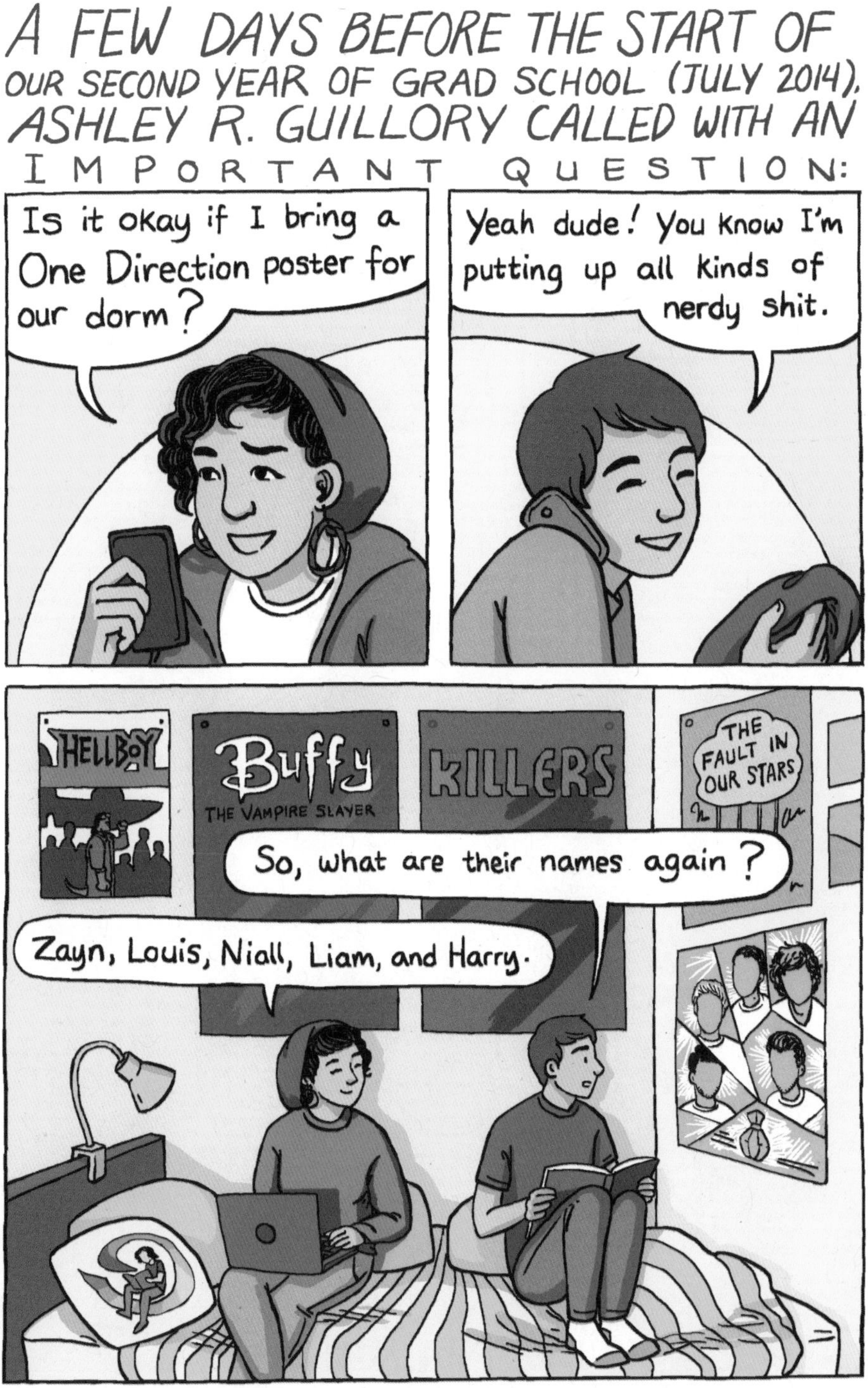
A FEW DAYS BEFORE THE START OF OUR SECOND YEAR OF GRAD SCHOOL (JULY 2014), ASHLEY R. GUILLORY CALLED WITH AN IMPORTANT QUESTION:
Is it okay if I bring a One Direction poster for our dorm?
Yeah dude! You know I'm putting up all kinds of nerdy shit.
HELLBOY
Buffy THE VAMPIRE SLAYER
KILLERS
THE FAULT IN OUR STARS
So, what are their names again?
Zayn, Louis, Niall, Liam, and Harry.

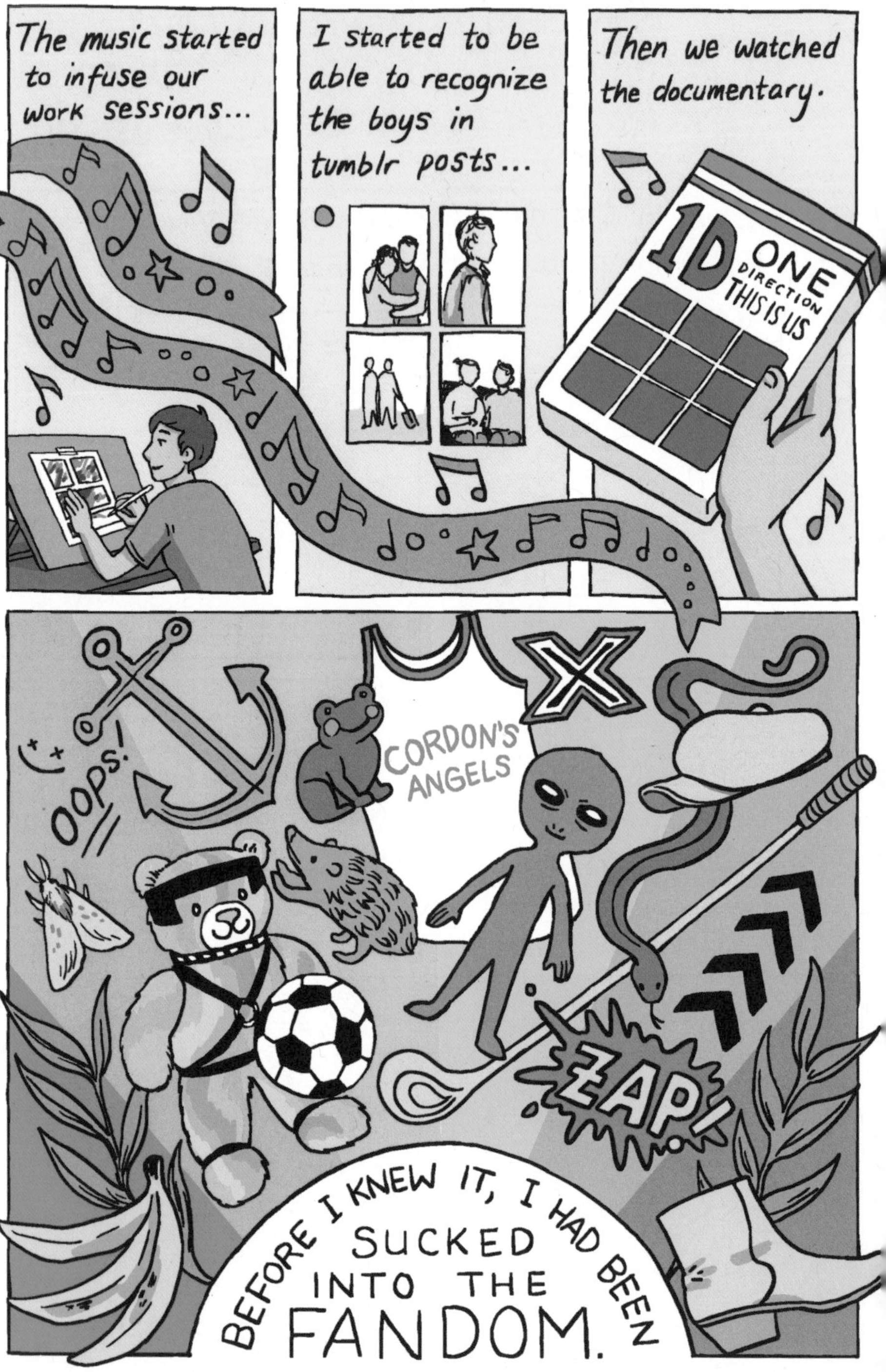
The music started to infuse our work sessions...
I started to be able to recognize the boys in tumblr posts...
Then we watched the documentary.
1D ONE DIRECTION THIS IS US
OOPS!
CORDON'S ANGELS
X
ZAP!
BEFORE I KNEW IT, I HAD BEEN SUCKED INTO THE FANDOM.

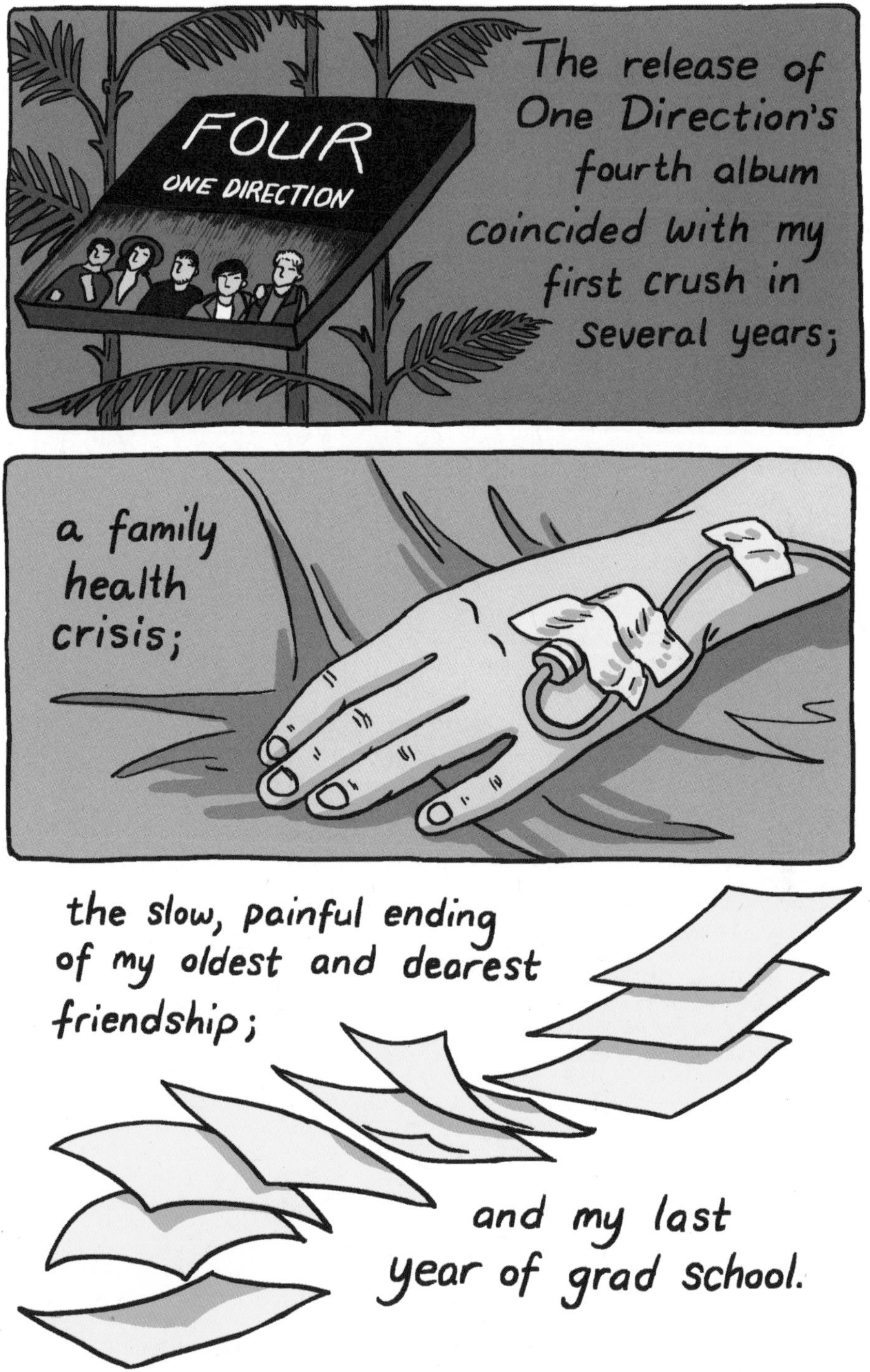

FOUR
ONE DIRECTION
The release of One Direction's fourth album coincided with my first crush in several years;
a family health crisis;
the slow, painful ending of my oldest and dearest friendship;
and my last year of grad school.

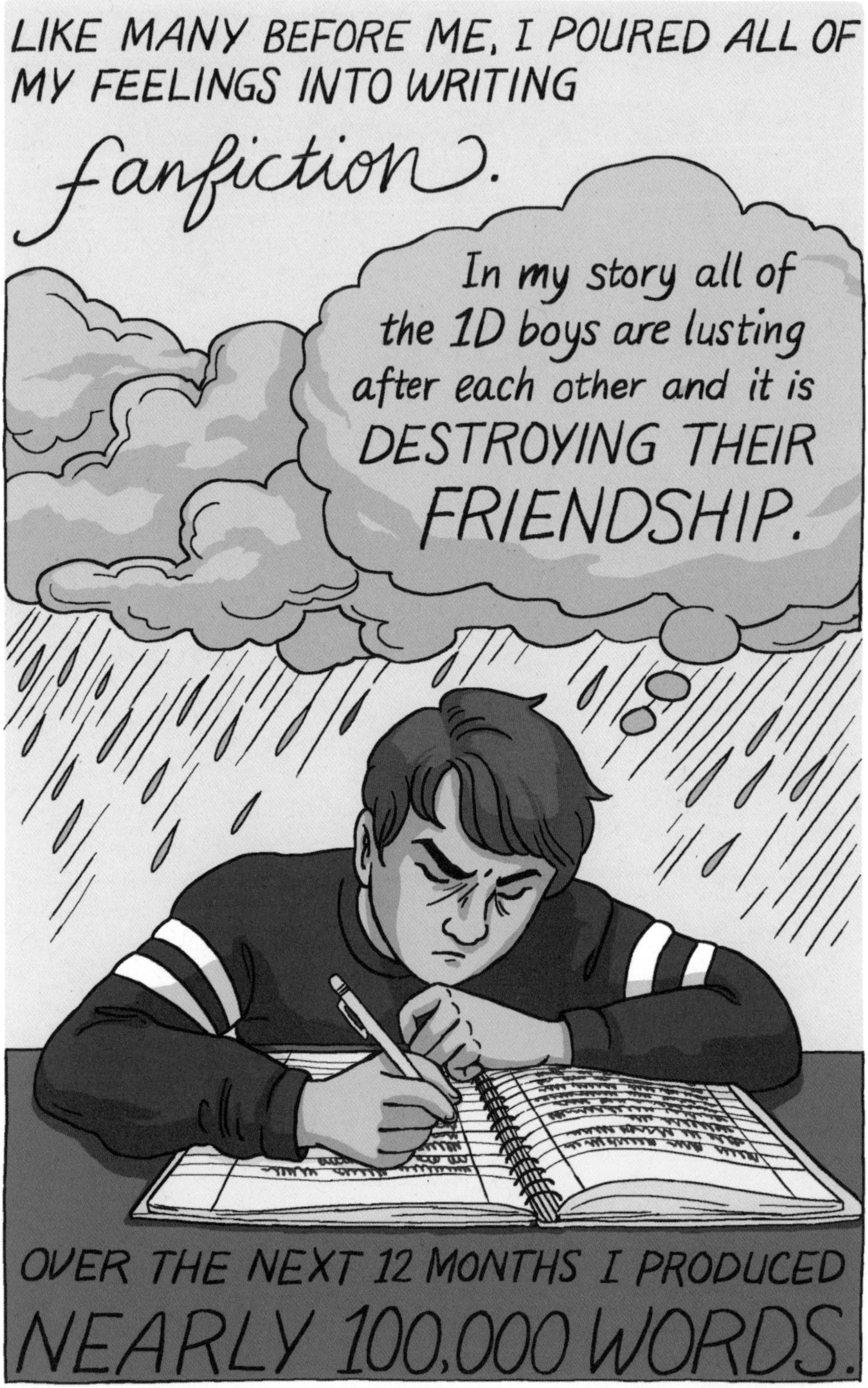
LIKE MANY BEFORE ME, I POURED ALL OF MY FEELINGS INTO WRITING
fanfiction.
In my story all of the 1D boys are lusting after each other and it is DESTROYING THEIR FRIENDSHIP.
OVER THE NEXT 12 MONTHS I PRODUCED
NEARLY 100,000 WORDS.

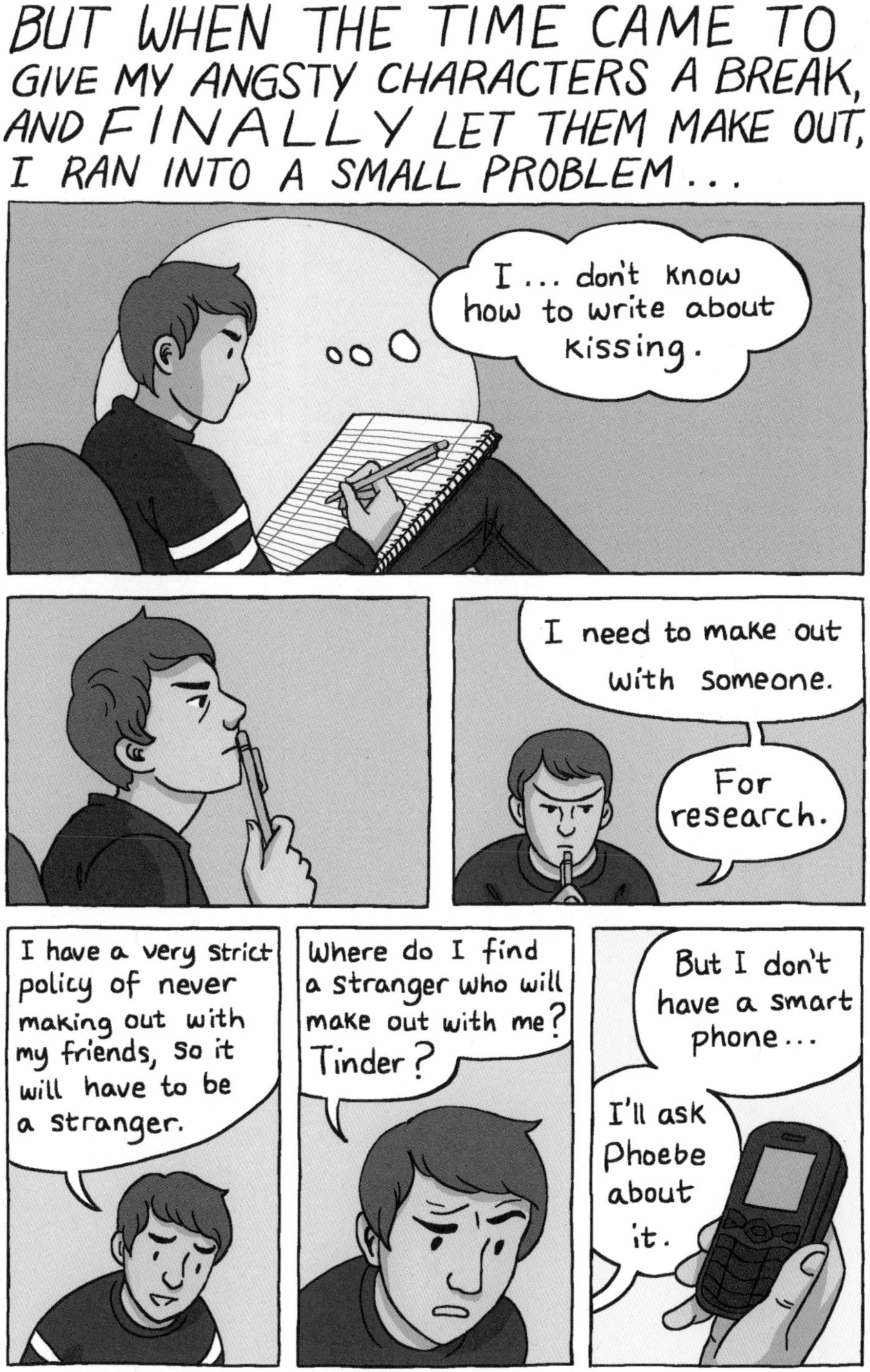
BUT WHEN THE TIME CAME TO GIVE MY ANGSTY CHARACTERS A BREAK, AND FINALLY LET THEM MAKE OUT, I RAN INTO A SMALL PROBLEM...
I... don't know how to write about kissing.
I need to make out with someone.
For research.
I have a very strict policy of never making out with my friends, so it will have to be a stranger.
Where do I find a stranger who will make out with me? Tinder?
But I don't have a smart phone...
I'll ask Phoebe about it.

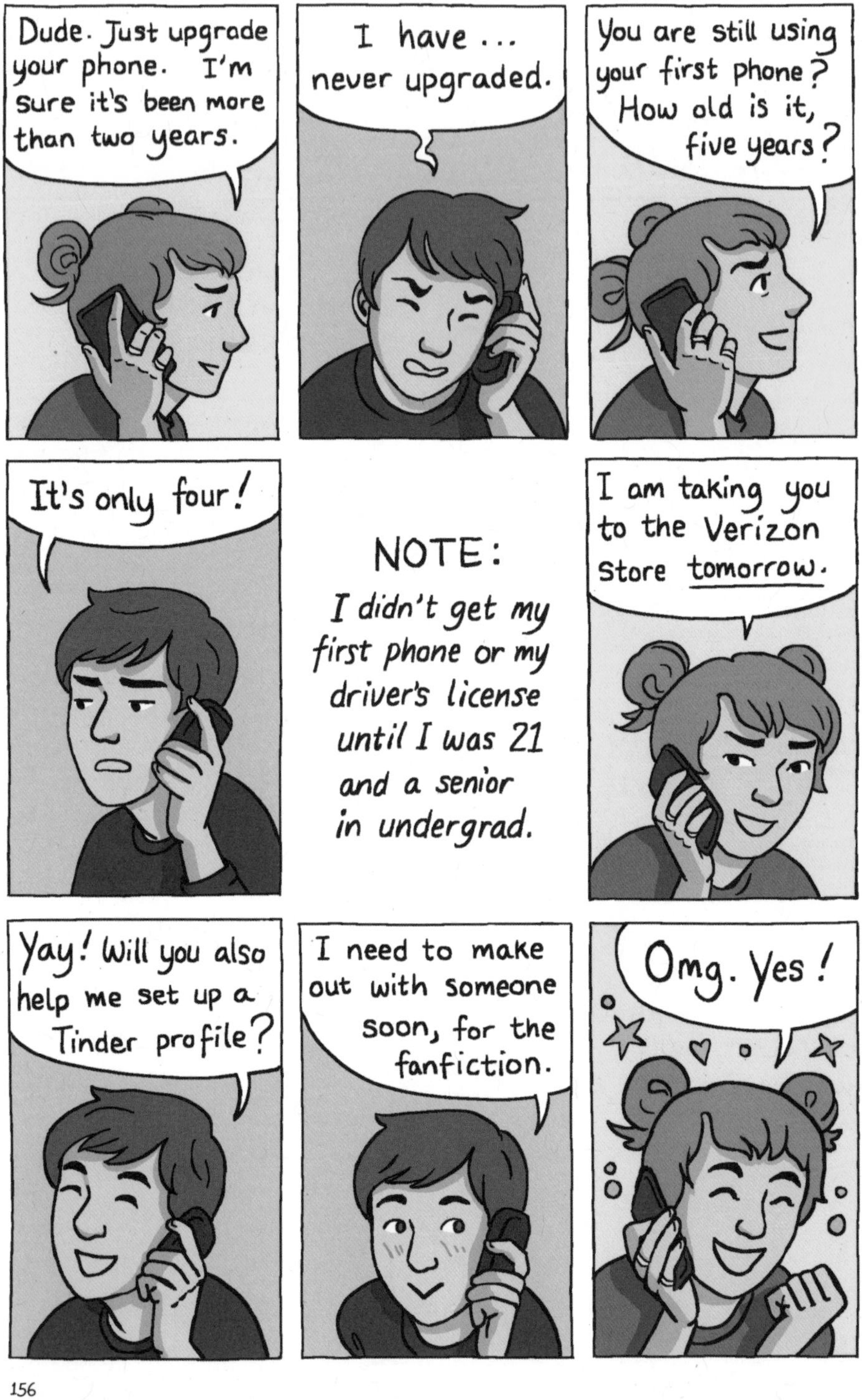
Dude. Just upgrade your phone. I'm sure it's been more than two years.
I have ... never upgraded.
You are still using your first phone? How old is it, five years?
It's only four!
NOTE: I didn't get my first phone or my driver's license until I was 21 and a senior in undergrad.
I am taking you to the Verizon store tomorrow.
Yay! Will you also help me set up a Tinder profile?
I need to make out with someone soon, for the fanfiction.
Omg. Yes!

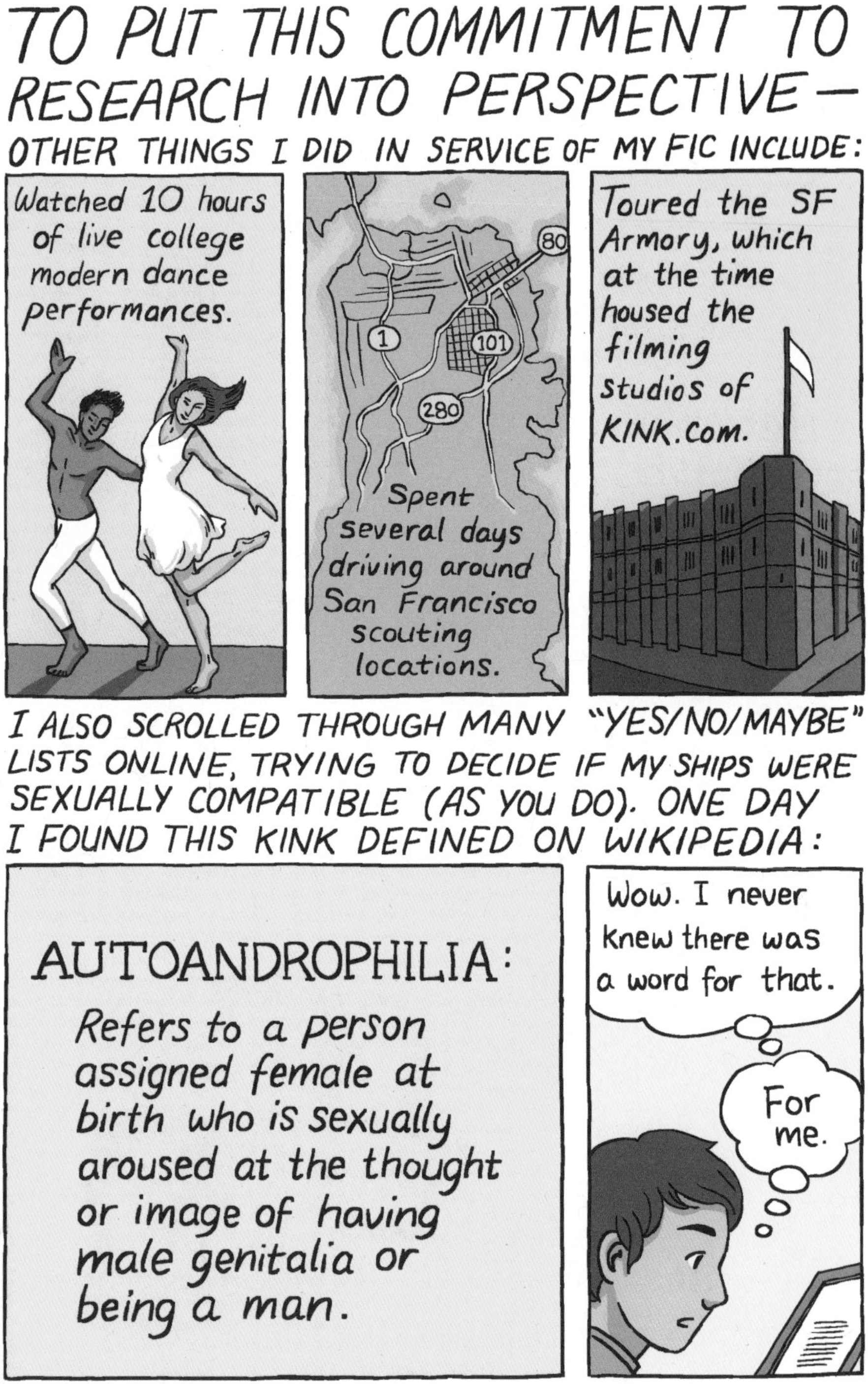
TO PUT THIS COMMITMENT TO RESEARCH INTO PERSPECTIVE—
OTHER THINGS I DID IN SERVICE OF MY FIC INCLUDE:
Watched 10 hours of live college modern dance performances.
80
1
101
280
Spent several days driving around San Francisco scouting locations.
Toured the SF Armory, which at the time housed the filming studios of KINK.com.
I ALSO SCROLLED THROUGH MANY "YES/NO/MAYBE" LISTS ONLINE, TRYING TO DECIDE IF MY SHIPS WERE SEXUALLY COMPATIBLE (AS YOU DO). ONE DAY I FOUND THIS KINK DEFINED ON WIKIPEDIA:
AUTOANDROPHILIA:
Refers to a person assigned female at birth who is sexually aroused at the thought or image of having male genitalia or being a man.
Wow. I never knew there was a word for that.
For me.

My Very Brief Tinder JOURNEY

I matched with six women.

I sent all of them a first message.

Four of them responded.

Two of those responses developed into conversations.

I asked if they wanted to meet in person, and they both said yes!

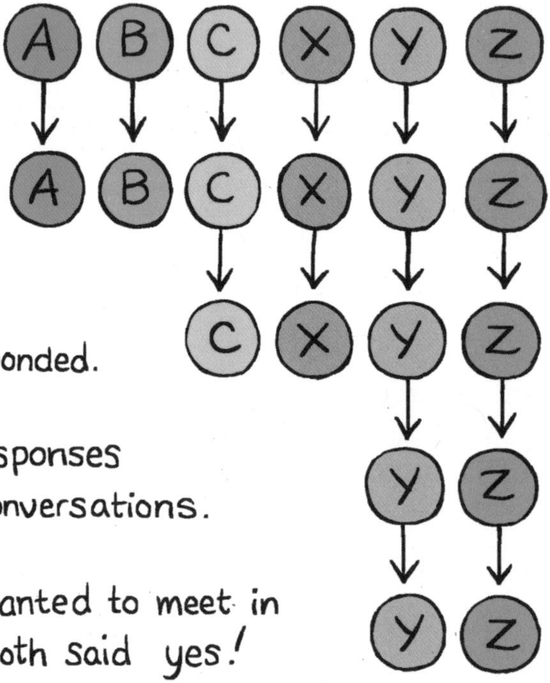

A B C X Y Z
A B C X Y Z
C X Y Z
Y Z
Y Z

SO I PICKED A TIME TO MEET
CANDIDATE Y.

She had come off as shy in our messages. I tried to get a sense of her hobbies, interests, and aspirations but she seemed hesitant to reveal them.

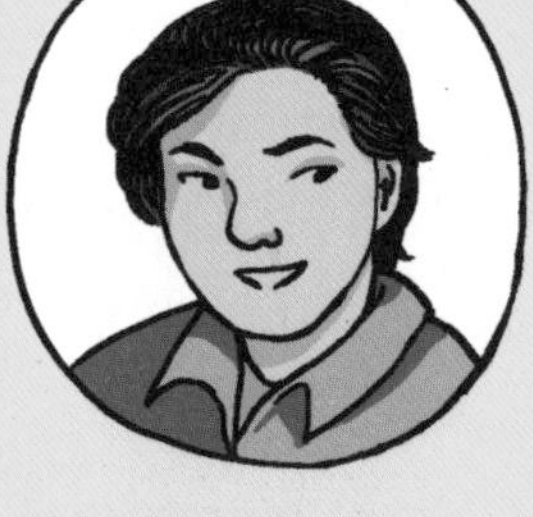

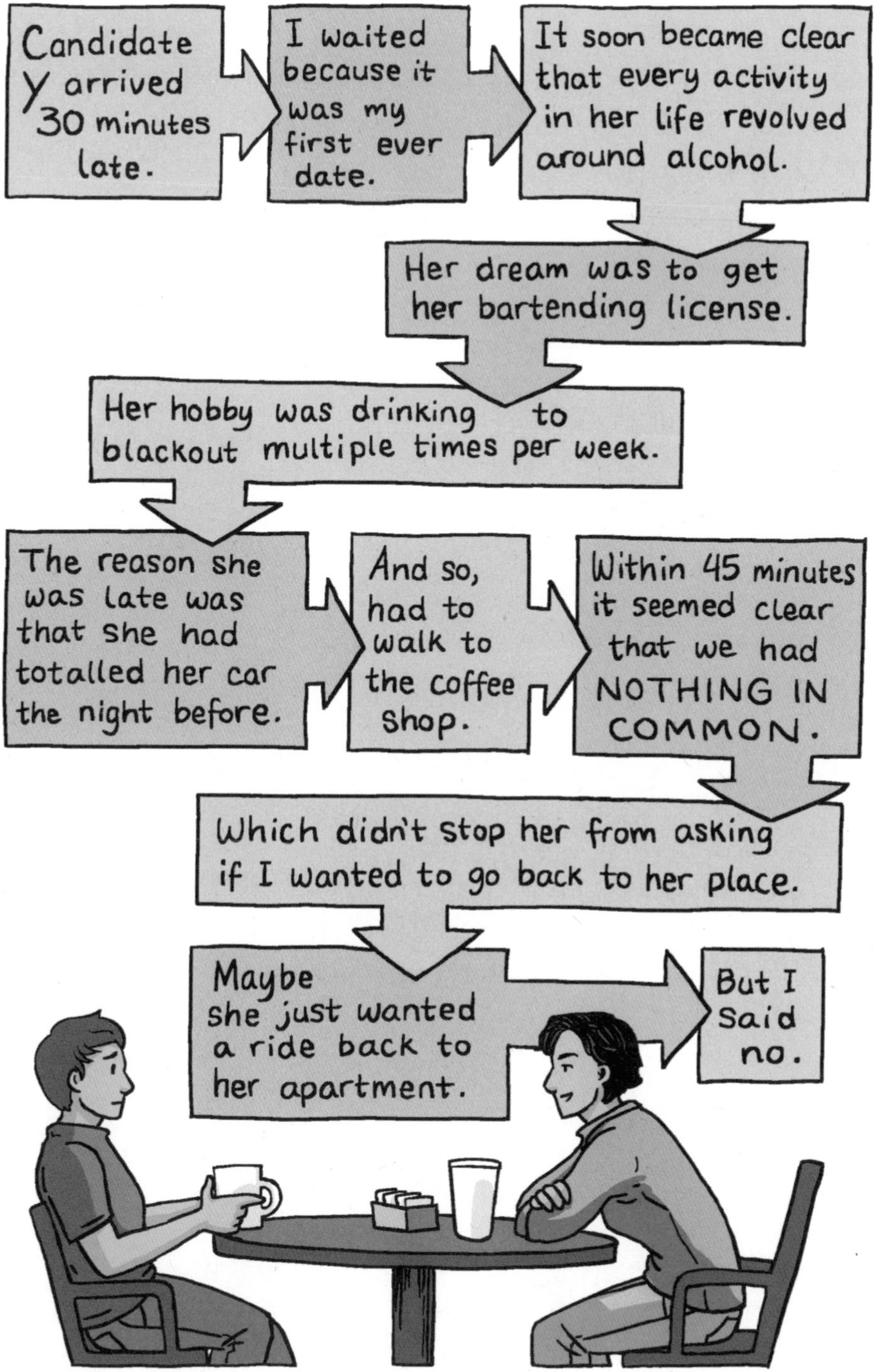
Candidate Y arrived 30 minutes late.
I waited because it was my first ever date.
It soon became clear that every activity in her life revolved around alcohol.
Her dream was to get her bartending license.
Her hobby was drinking to blackout multiple times per week.
The reason she was late was that she had totalled her car the night before.
And so, had to walk to the coffee shop.
Within 45 minutes it seemed clear that we had NOTHING IN COMMON.
Which didn't stop her from asking if I wanted to go back to her place.
Maybe she just wanted a ride back to her apartment.
But I said no.

SINCE THAT DATE CONSTITUTED 100% OF MY DATING EXPERIENCE, I WAS MORE THAN A LITTLE NERVOUS FOR MY MEETING WITH *Candidate Z.*

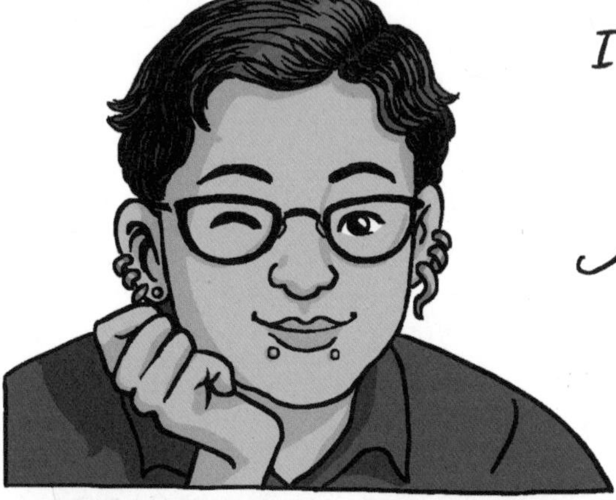

I NEEDN'T HAVE BEEN. SHE WAS AMAZING.

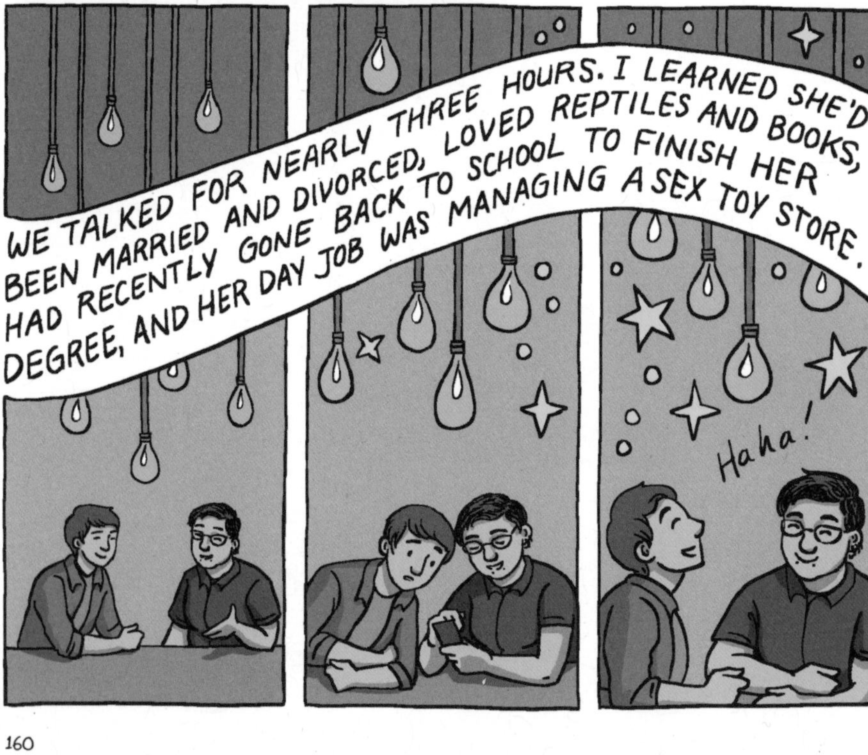
WE TALKED FOR NEARLY THREE HOURS. I LEARNED SHE'D BEEN MARRIED AND DIVORCED, LOVED REPTILES AND BOOKS, HAD RECENTLY GONE BACK TO SCHOOL TO FINISH HER DEGREE, AND HER DAY JOB WAS MANAGING A SEX TOY STORE.
Haha!

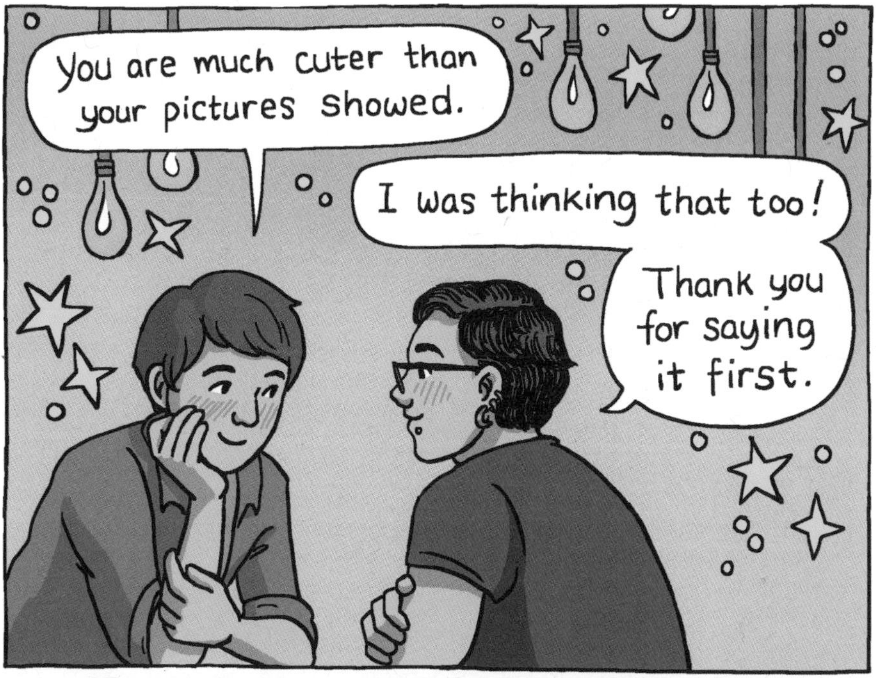
You are much cuter than your pictures showed.
I was thinking that too!
Thank you for saying it first.

AS I DROVE HOME I REMEMBER THINKING:

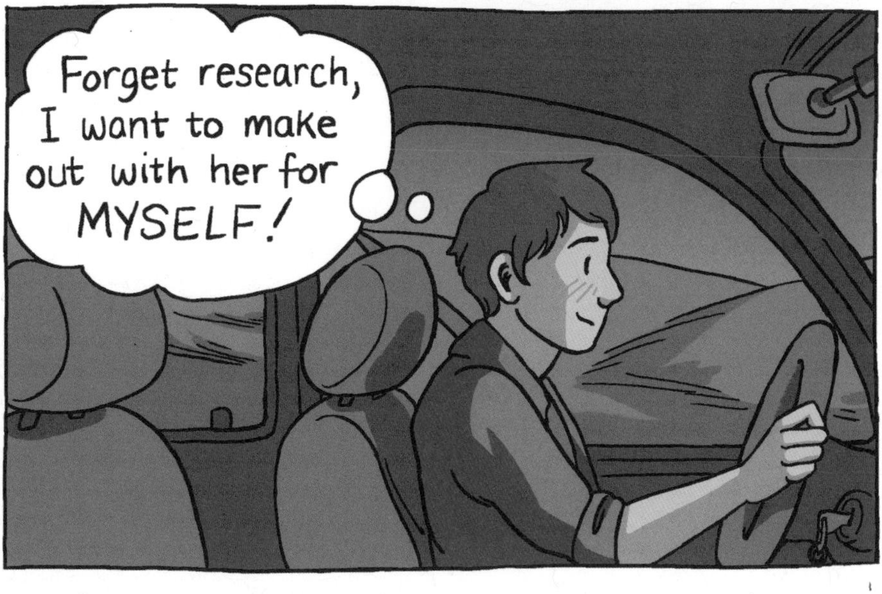
Forget research, I want to make out with her for MYSELF!

We planned a second date.

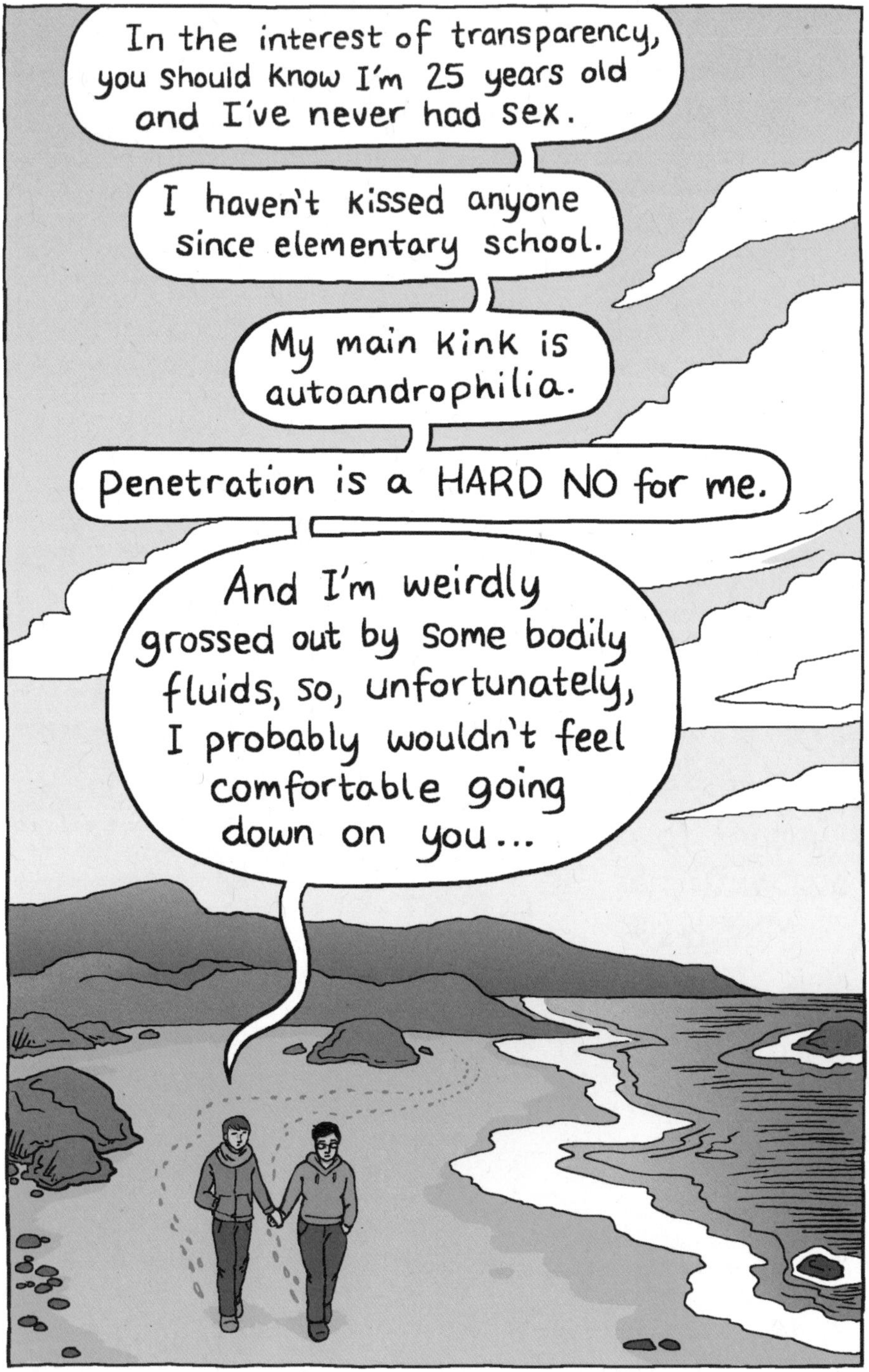
In the interest of transparency, you should know I'm 25 years old and I've never had sex.
I haven't kissed anyone since elementary school.
My main kink is autoandrophilia.
Penetration is a HARD NO for me.
And I'm weirdly grossed out by some bodily fluids, so, unfortunately, I probably wouldn't feel comfortable going down on you...

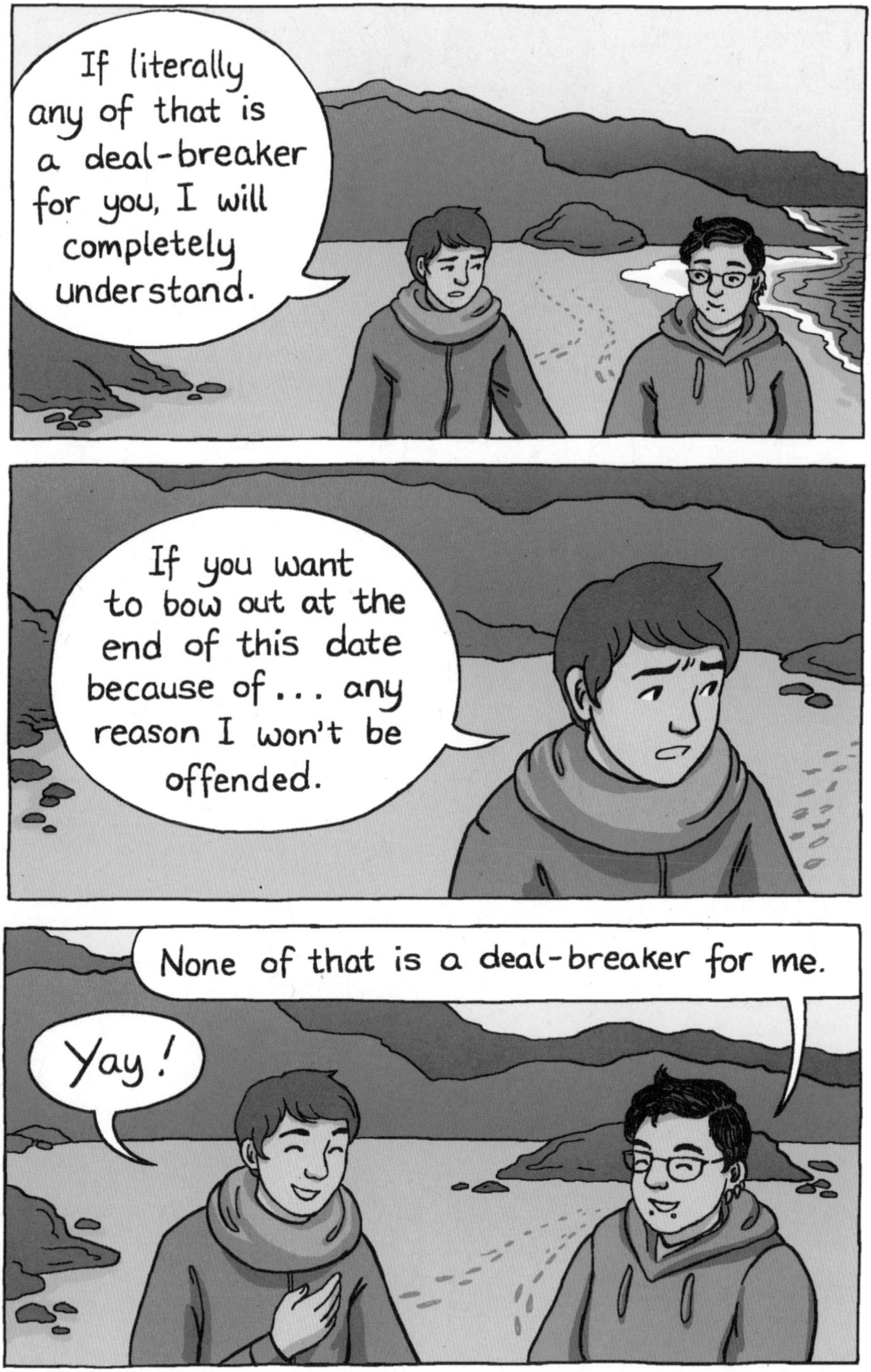
If literally any of that is a deal-breaker for you, I will completely understand.
If you want to bow out at the end of this date because of... any reason I won't be offended.
None of that is a deal-breaker for me.
Yay!

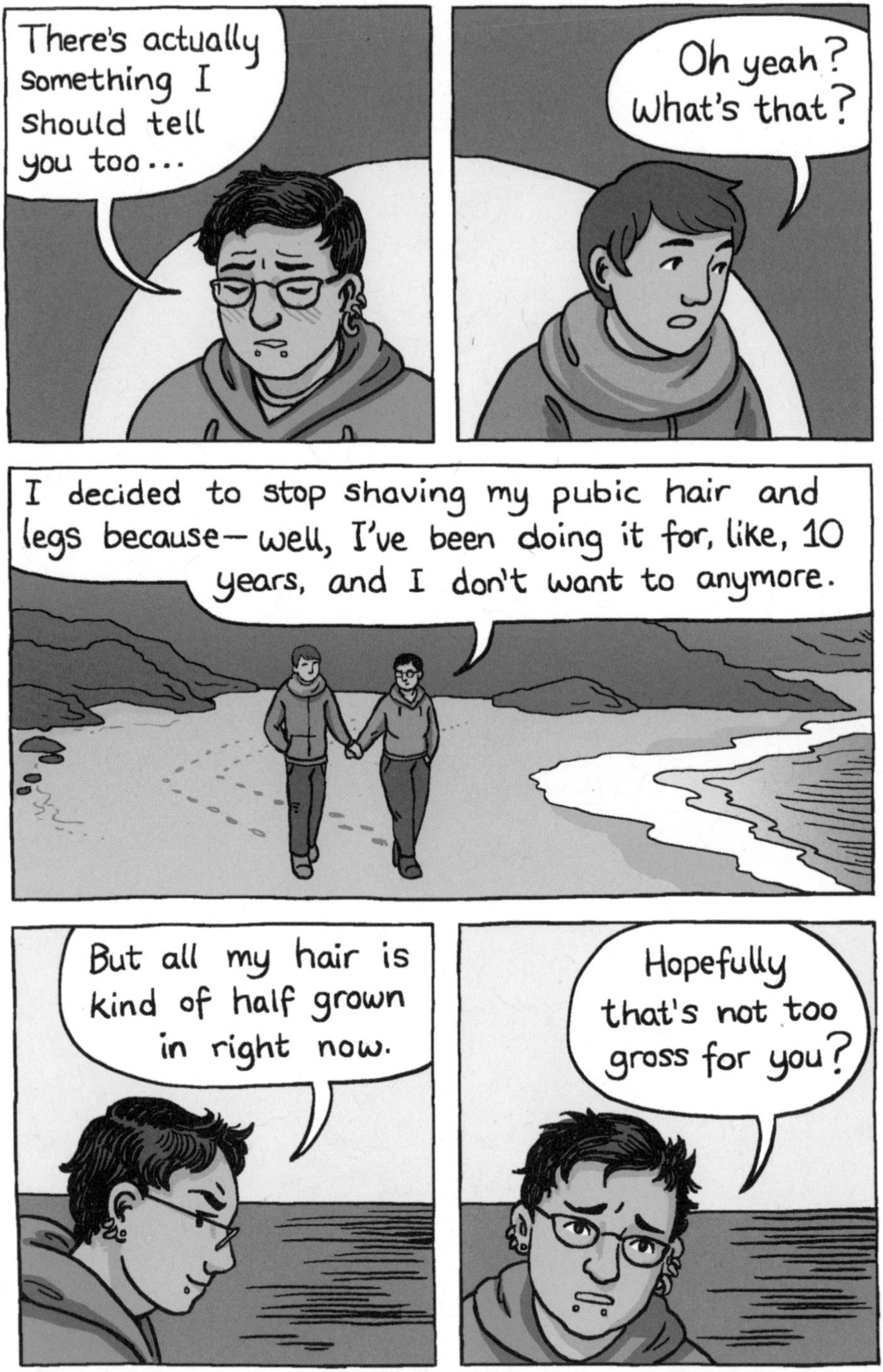
There's actually something I should tell you too...
Oh yeah? What's that?
I decided to stop shaving my pubic hair and legs because—well, I've been doing it for, like, 10 years, and I don't want to anymore.
But all my hair is kind of half grown in right now.
Hopefully that's not too gross for you?

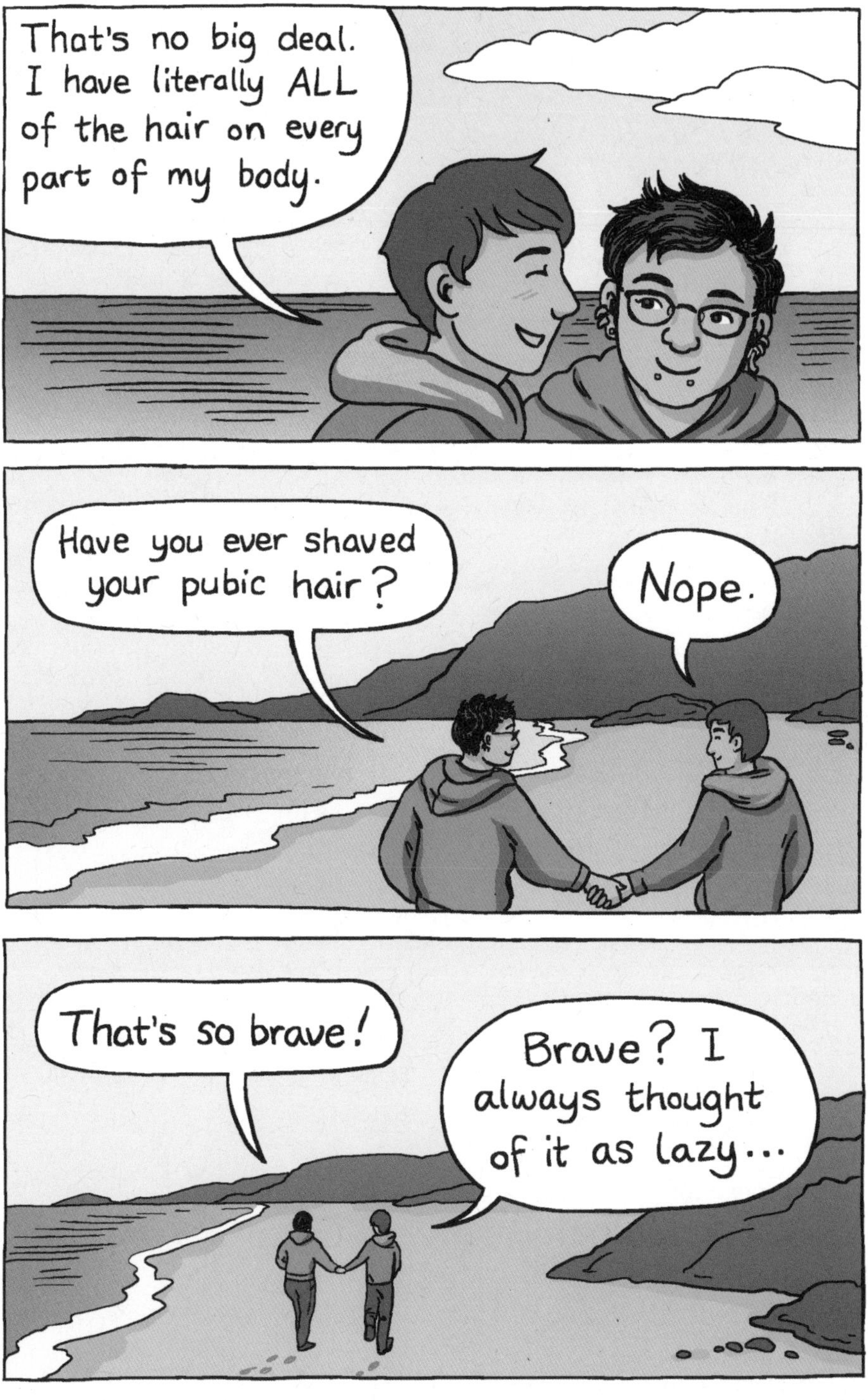
That's no big deal. I have literally ALL of the hair on every part of my body.
Have you ever shaved your pubic hair?
Nope.
That's so brave!
Brave? I always thought of it as lazy...

FAST-FORWARD: WE'VE BEEN DATING FOR TWO MONTHS. WE'VE MADE OUT, WE'VE HAD SEX, WE'VE MOVED ON TO SEXTING AT WORK.

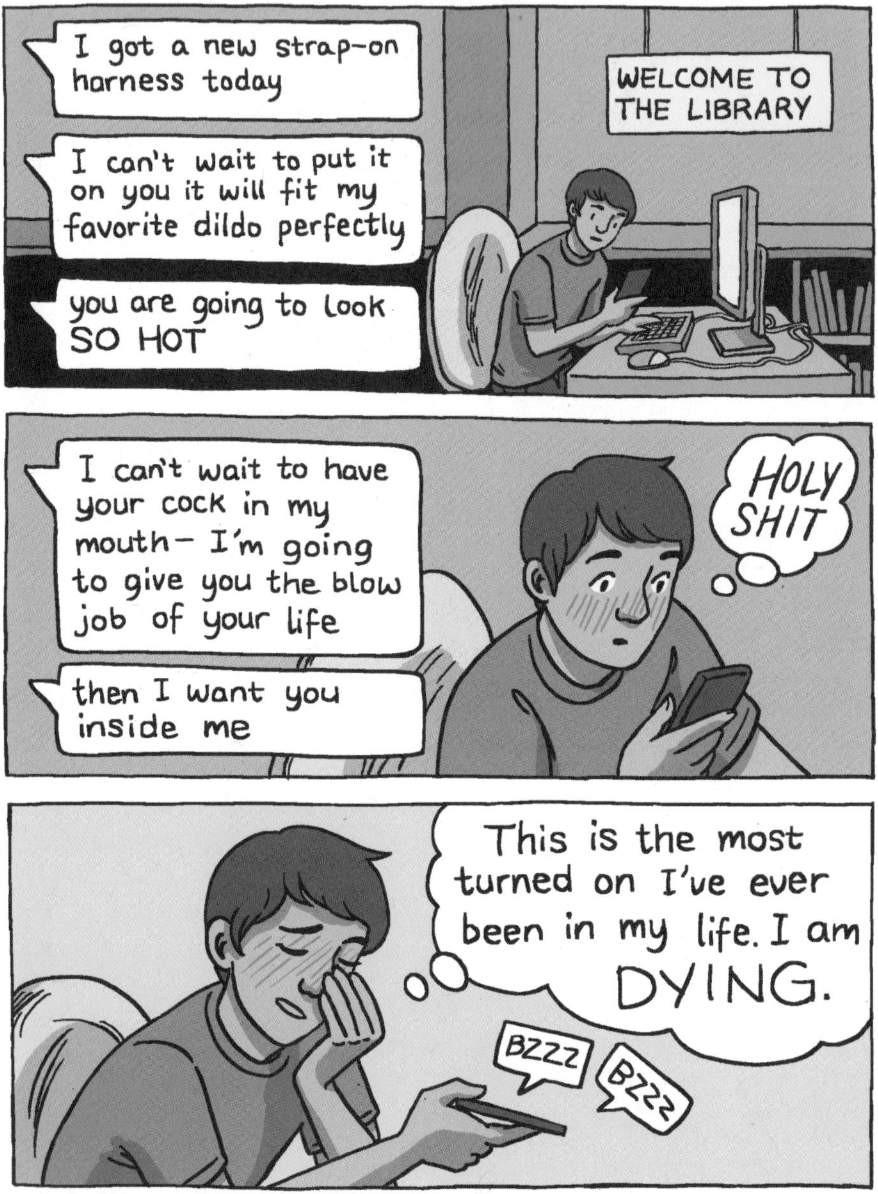
I got a new strap-on harness today
I can't wait to put it on you it will fit my favorite dildo perfectly
you are going to look SO HOT
WELCOME TO THE LIBRARY
I can't wait to have your cock in my mouth- I'm going to give you the blow job of your life
then I want you inside me
HOLY SHIT
This is the most turned on I've ever been in my life. I am DYING.
BZZZ
BZZZ

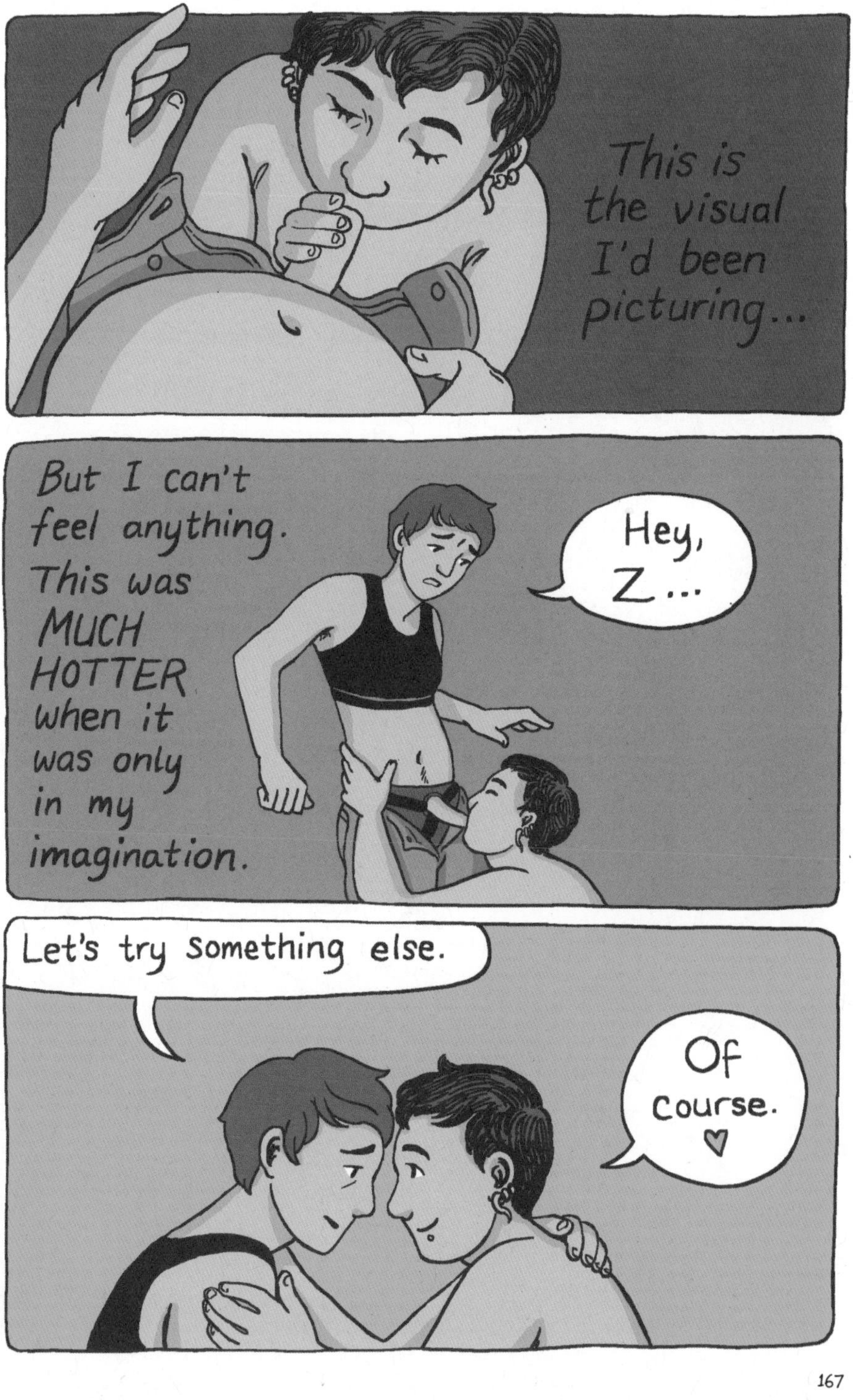
This is the visual I'd been picturing...
But I can't feel anything. This was MUCH HOTTER when it was only in my imagination.
Hey, Z...
Let's try something else.
Of course. ♡

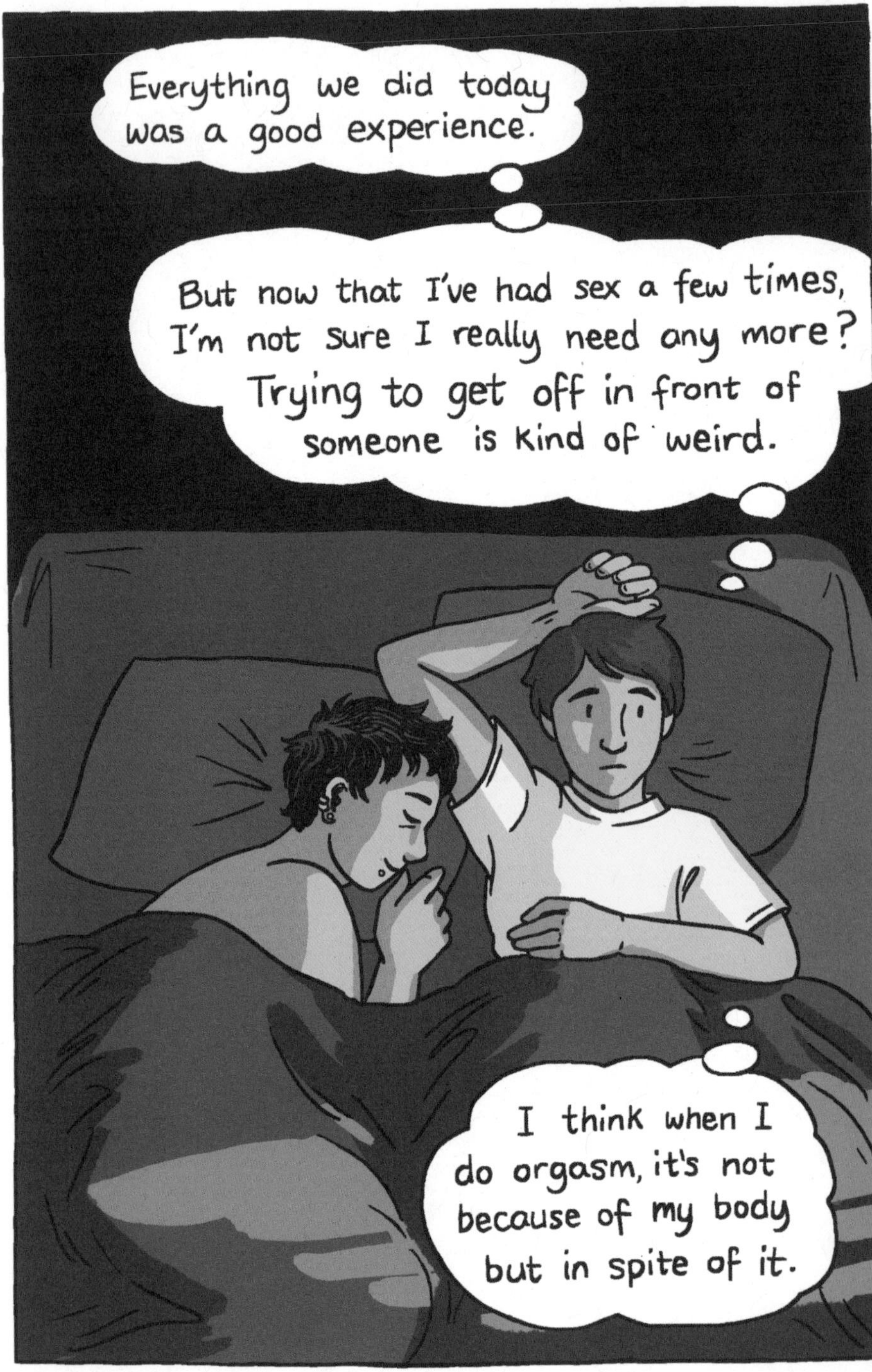
Everything we did today was a good experience.
But now that I've had sex a few times, I'm not sure I really need any more? Trying to get off in front of someone is kind of weird.
I think when I do orgasm, it's not because of my body but in spite of it.

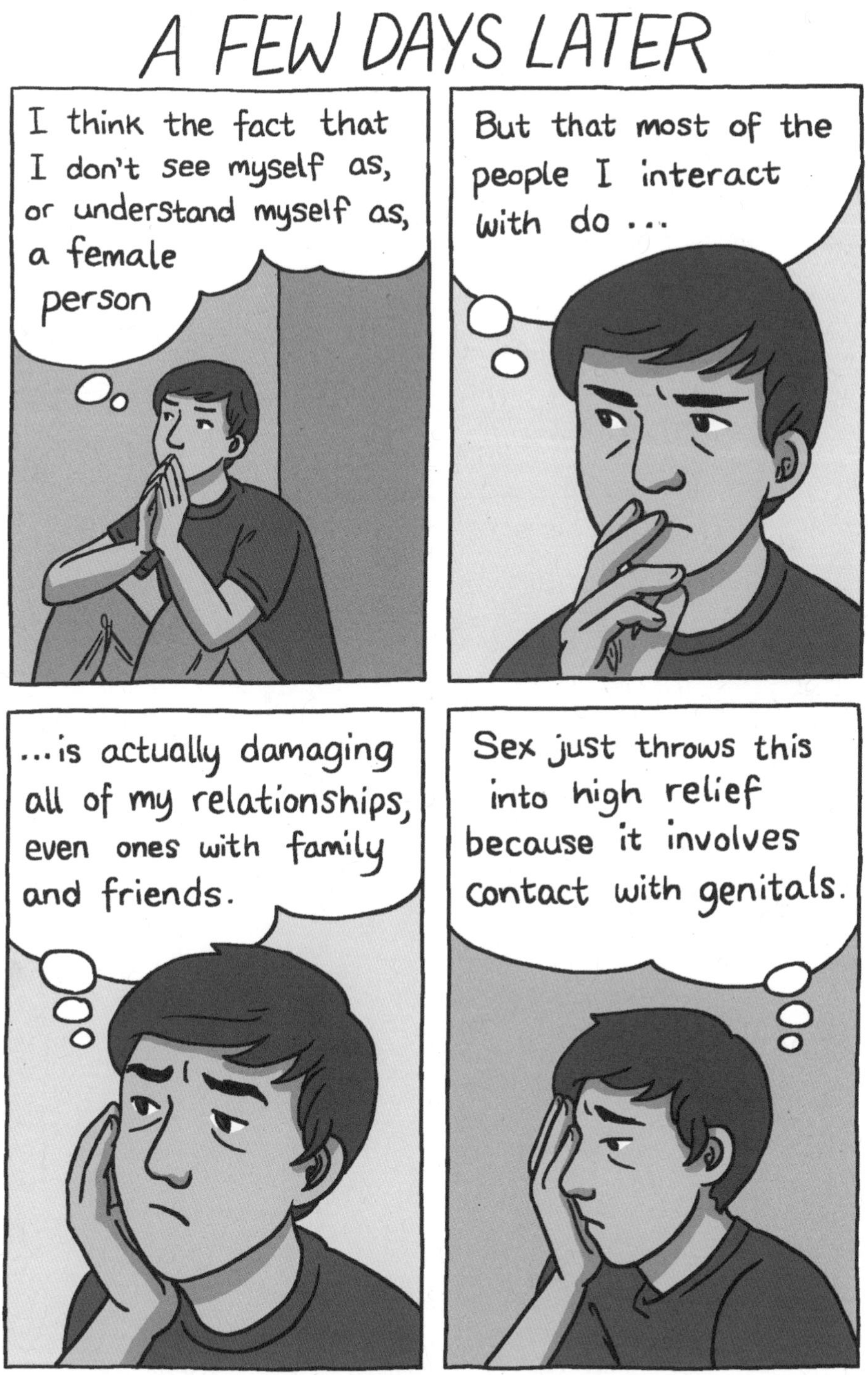
A FEW DAYS LATER
I think the fact that I don't see myself as, or understand myself as, a female person
But that most of the people I interact with do ...
... is actually damaging all of my relationships, even ones with family and friends.
Sex just throws this into high relief because it involves contact with genitals.

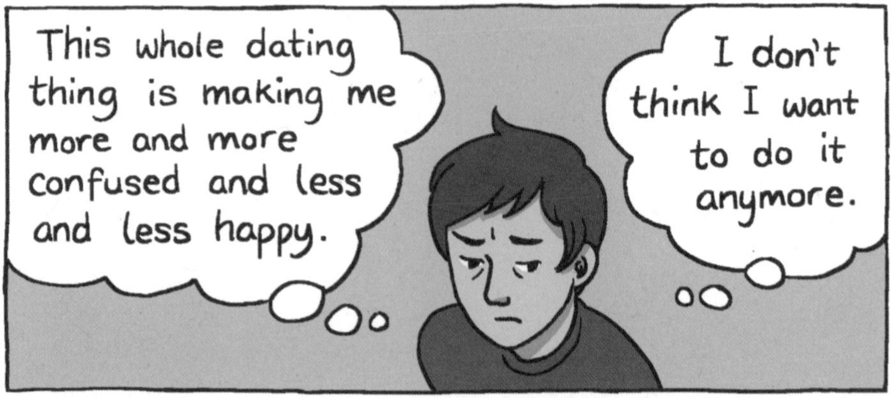
This whole dating thing is making me more and more confused and less and less happy.
I don't think I want to do it anymore.

SO WHEN SHE TOLD ME:

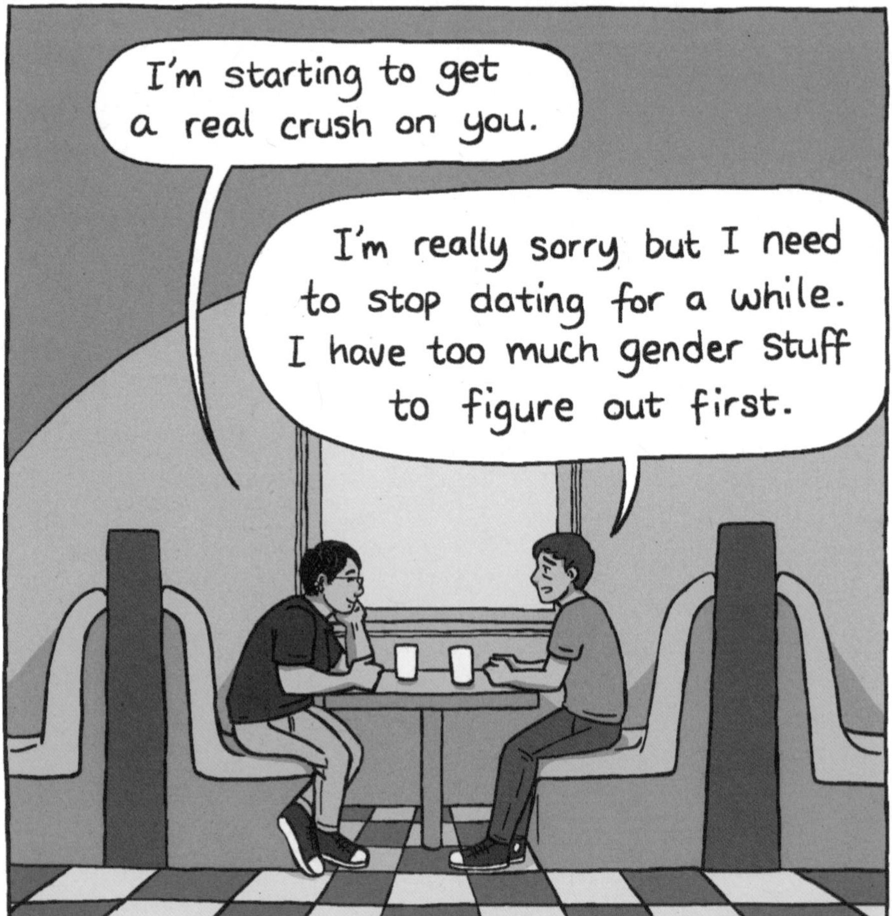
I'm starting to get a real crush on you.
I'm really sorry but I need to stop dating for a while. I have too much gender stuff to figure out first.

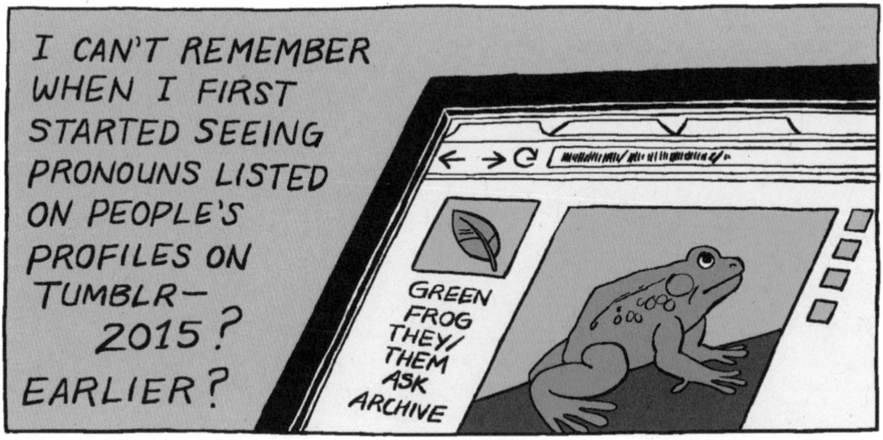
I CAN'T REMEMBER WHEN I FIRST STARTED SEEING PRONOUNS LISTED ON PEOPLE'S PROFILES ON TUMBLR— 2015? EARLIER?
GREEN FROG THEY/THEM ASK ARCHIVE

BUT THE FIRST PERSON I REMEMBER GETTING TO KNOW WHO USES THEY/THEM PRONOUNS WAS ONE OF MY CCA TEACHERS.

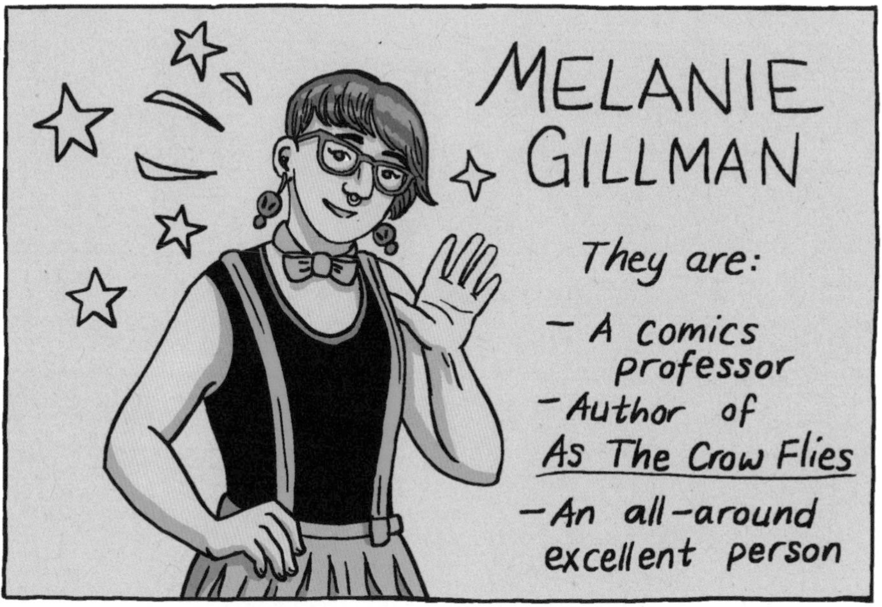
MELANIE GILLMAN
They are:
- A comics professor
- Author of As The Crow Flies
- An all-around excellent person

MY CLASSMATES AND I WERE DETERMINED NOT TO MISGENDER THEM BUT WE MADE FREQUENT MISTAKES.

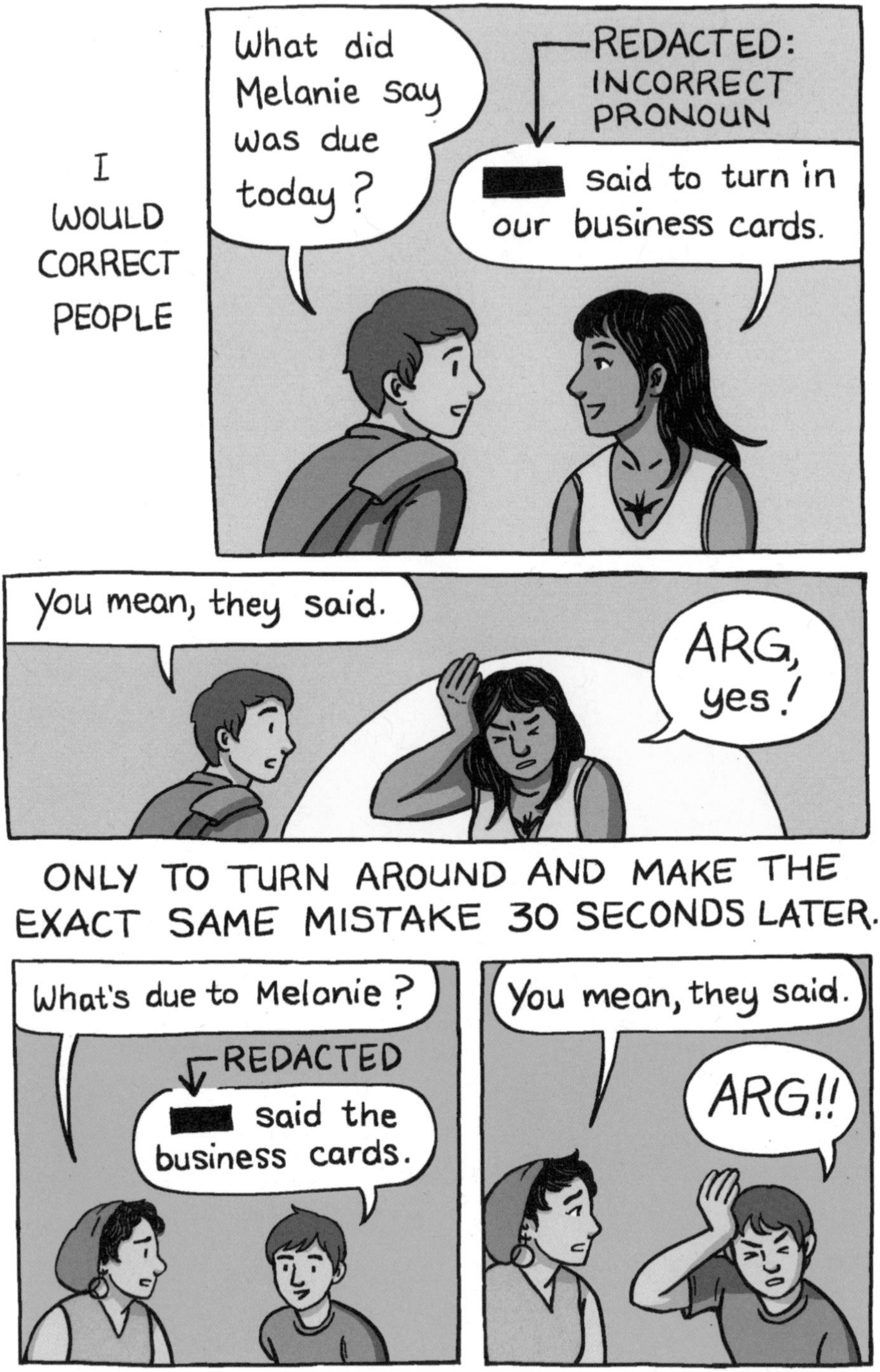
I WOULD CORRECT PEOPLE
What did Melanie say was due today?
REDACTED: INCORRECT PRONOUN
[redacted] said to turn in our business cards.
you mean, they said.
ARG, yes!
ONLY TO TURN AROUND AND MAKE THE EXACT SAME MISTAKE 30 SECONDS LATER.
What's due to Melanie?
REDACTED
[redacted] said the business cards.
You mean, they said.
ARG!!

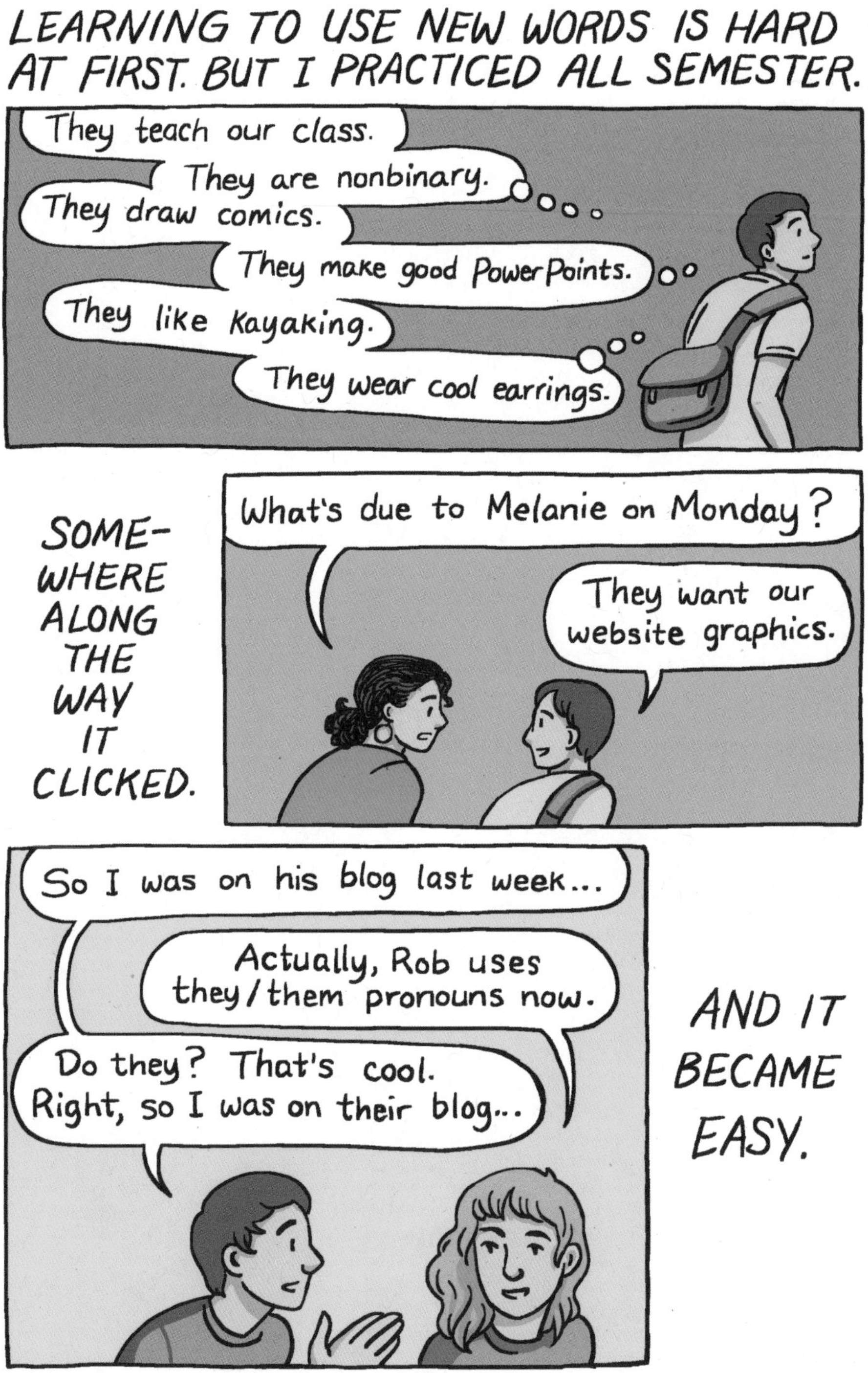
LEARNING TO USE NEW WORDS IS HARD AT FIRST. BUT I PRACTICED ALL SEMESTER.
They teach our class.
They are nonbinary.
They draw comics.
They make good PowerPoints.
They like Kayaking.
They wear cool earrings.
SOME-WHERE ALONG THE WAY IT CLICKED.
What's due to Melanie on Monday?
They want our website graphics.
So I was on his blog last week...
Actually, Rob uses they/them pronouns now.
Do they? That's cool. Right, so I was on their blog...
AND IT BECAME EASY.

AT THANKSGIVING IN 2015, MY SISTER BROUGHT HER NEW BOYFRIEND TO STAY WITH ME AND MY PARENTS FOR THE FIRST TIME.

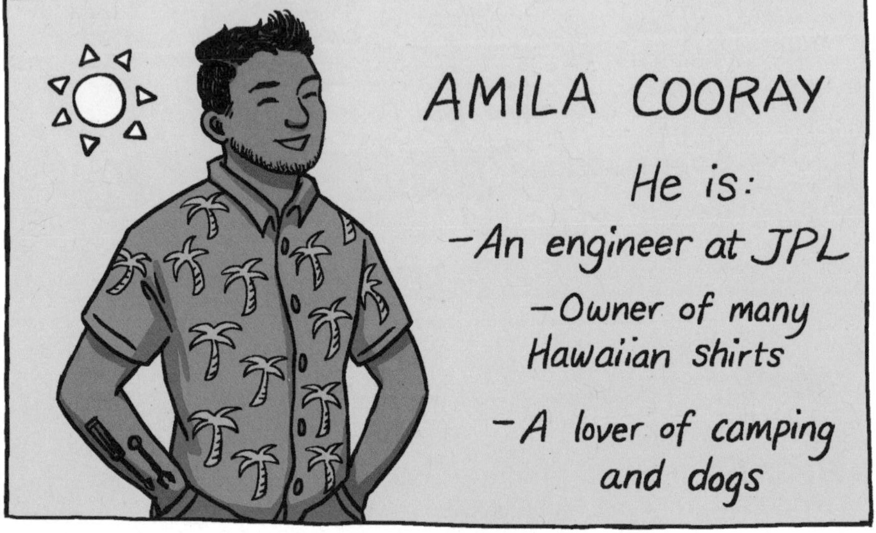
AMILA COORAY
He is:
-An engineer at JPL
-Owner of many Hawaiian shirts
-A lover of camping and dogs

AMILA IS THE FIRST PERSON I'VE WATCHED TAKE TESTOSTERONE.

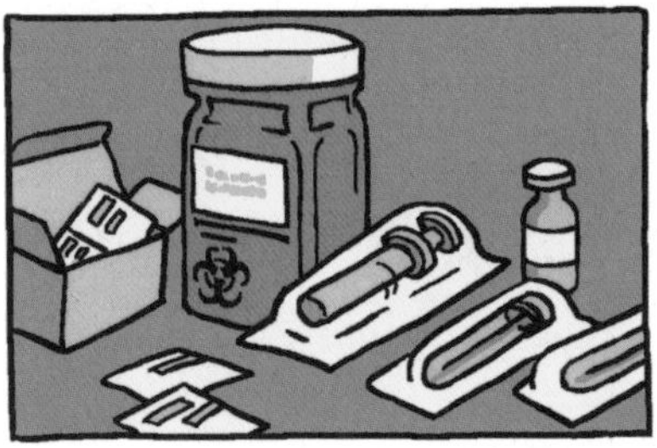

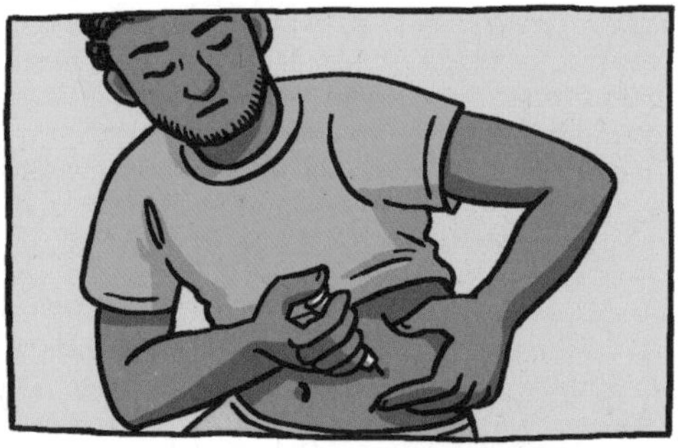

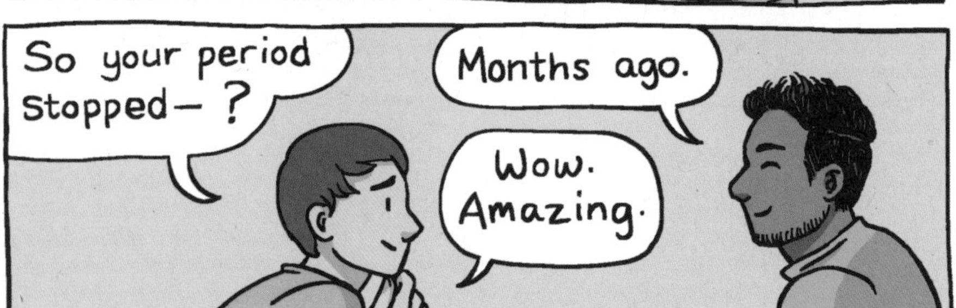
So your period stopped— ?
Months ago.
Wow. Amazing.

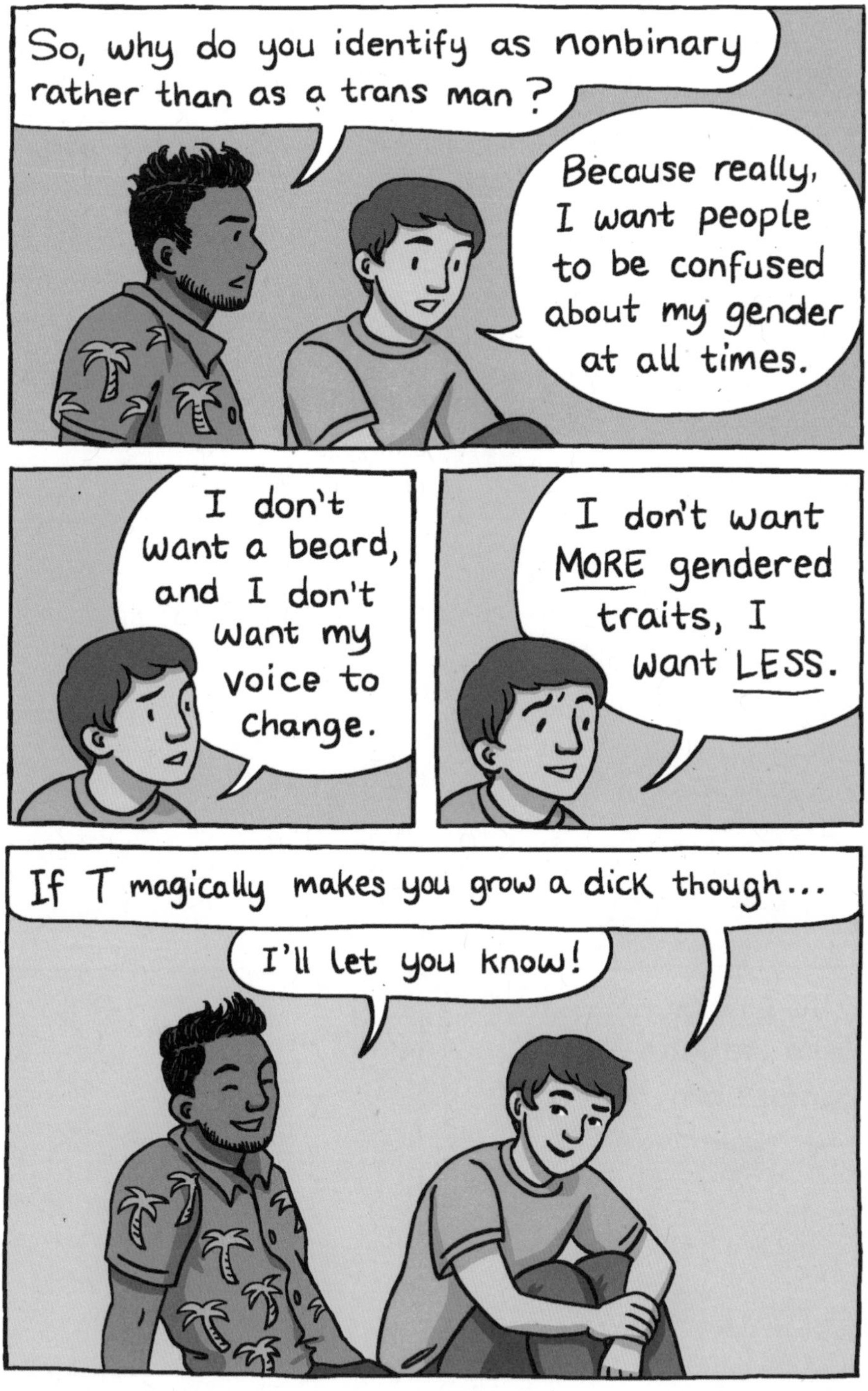
So, why do you identify as nonbinary rather than as a trans man?
Because really, I want people to be confused about my gender at all times.
I don't want a beard, and I don't want my voice to change.
I don't want MORE gendered traits, I want LESS.
If T magically makes you grow a dick though...
I'll let you know!

A FEW MONTHS AFTER BREAKING UP WITH Z, I PONDERED REOPENING TINDER.

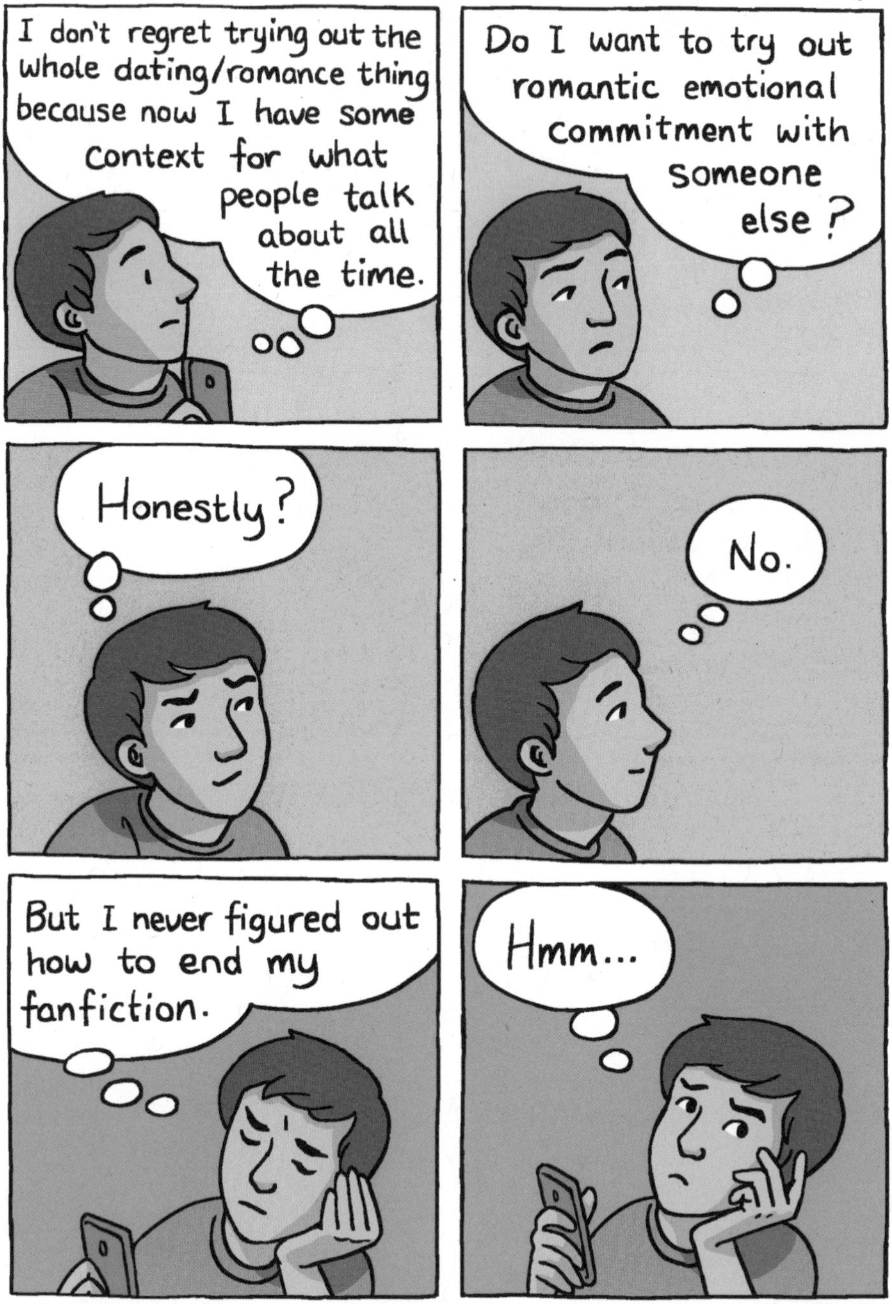
I don't regret trying out the whole dating/romance thing because now I have some context for what people talk about all the time.
Do I want to try out romantic emotional commitment with someone else?
Honestly?
No.
But I never figured out how to end my fanfiction.
Hmm...

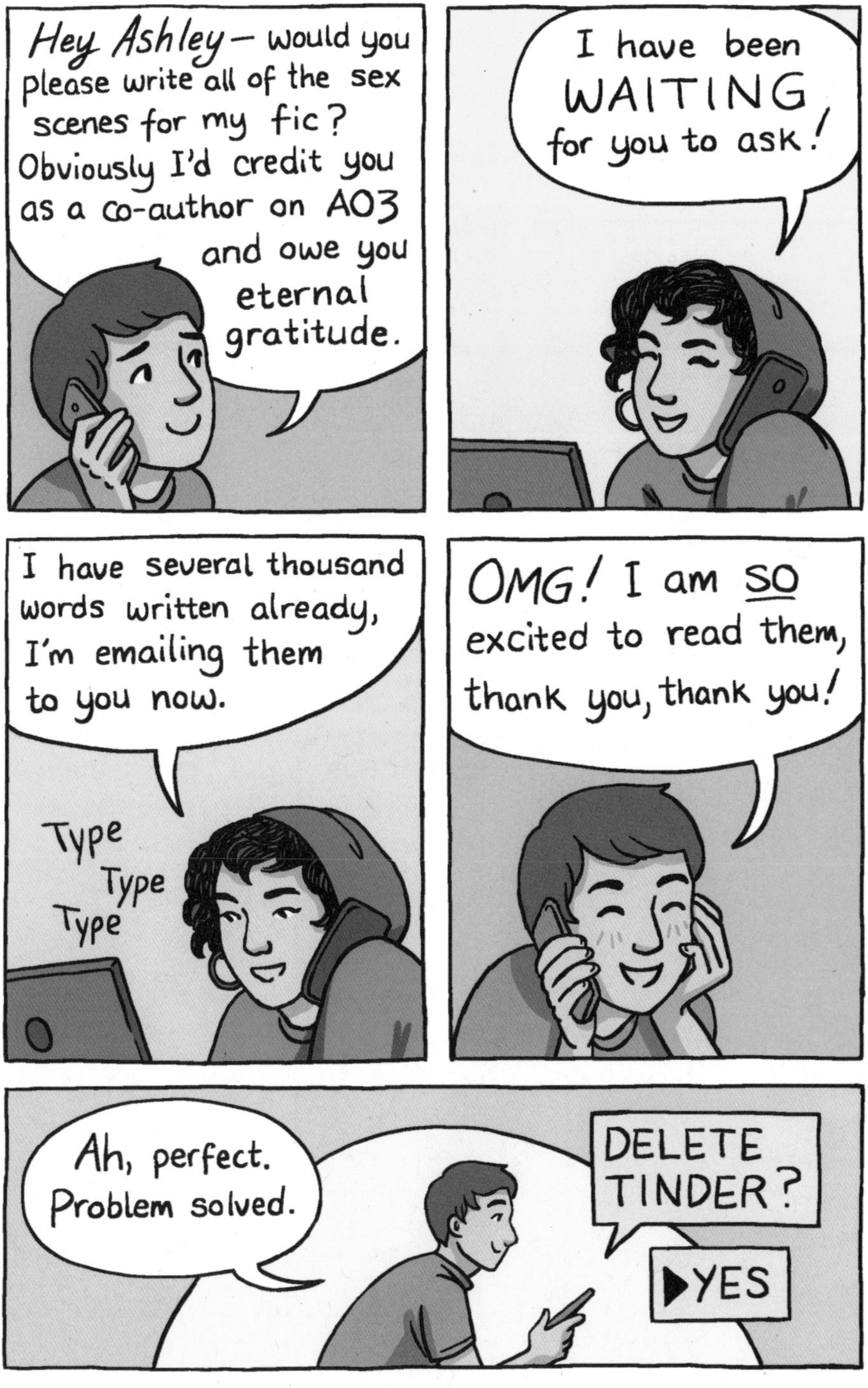
Hey Ashley— would you please write all of the sex scenes for my fic? Obviously I'd credit you as a co-author on AO3 and owe you eternal gratitude.
I have been WAITING for you to ask!
I have several thousand words written already, I'm emailing them to you now.
Type
Type
Type
OMG! I am SO excited to read them, thank you, thank you!
Ah, perfect. Problem solved.
DELETE TINDER?
▶YES

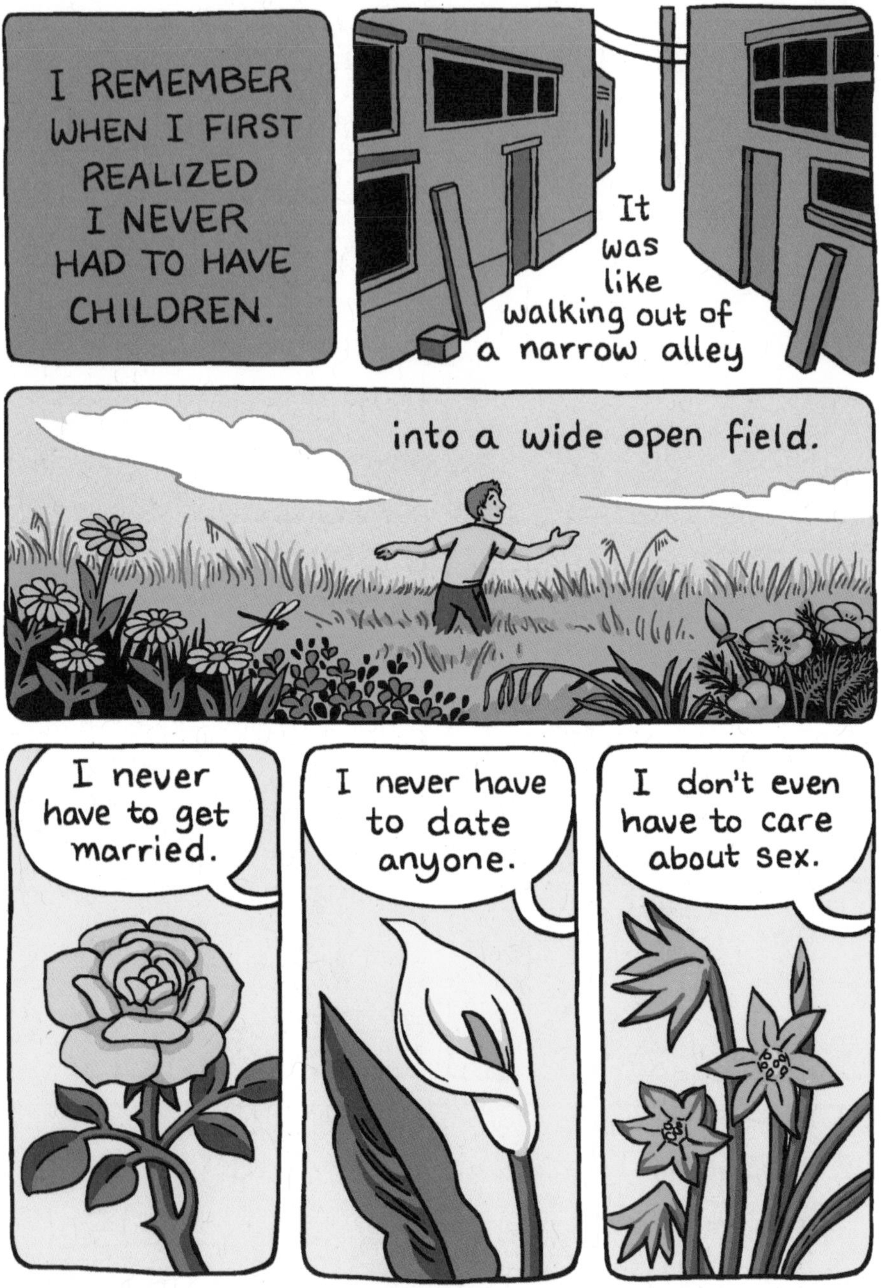
I REMEMBER WHEN I FIRST REALIZED I NEVER HAD TO HAVE CHILDREN.
It was like walking out of a narrow alley
into a wide open field.
I never have to get married.
I never have to date anyone.
I don't even have to care about sex.

THESE REALIZATIONS WERE LIKE GIFTS THAT I GAVE TO MYSELF.

There is a photo of me at about age four posing with a kitten – unaware or uncaring that my mermaid undies are also on display.

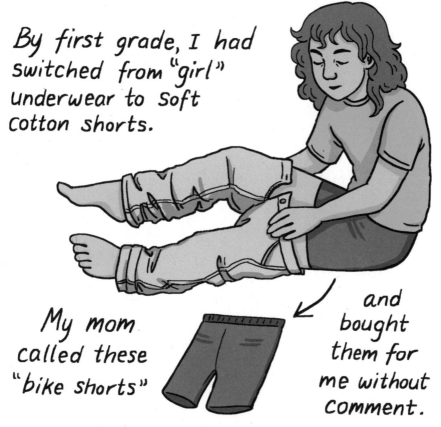

By first grade, I had switched from "girl" underwear to soft cotton shorts.

My mom called these "bike shorts"

and bought them for me without comment.

WHEN I STARTED MY PERIOD, I QUICKLY REALIZED THAT PADS AND SHORTS WERE NOT COMPATIBLE.

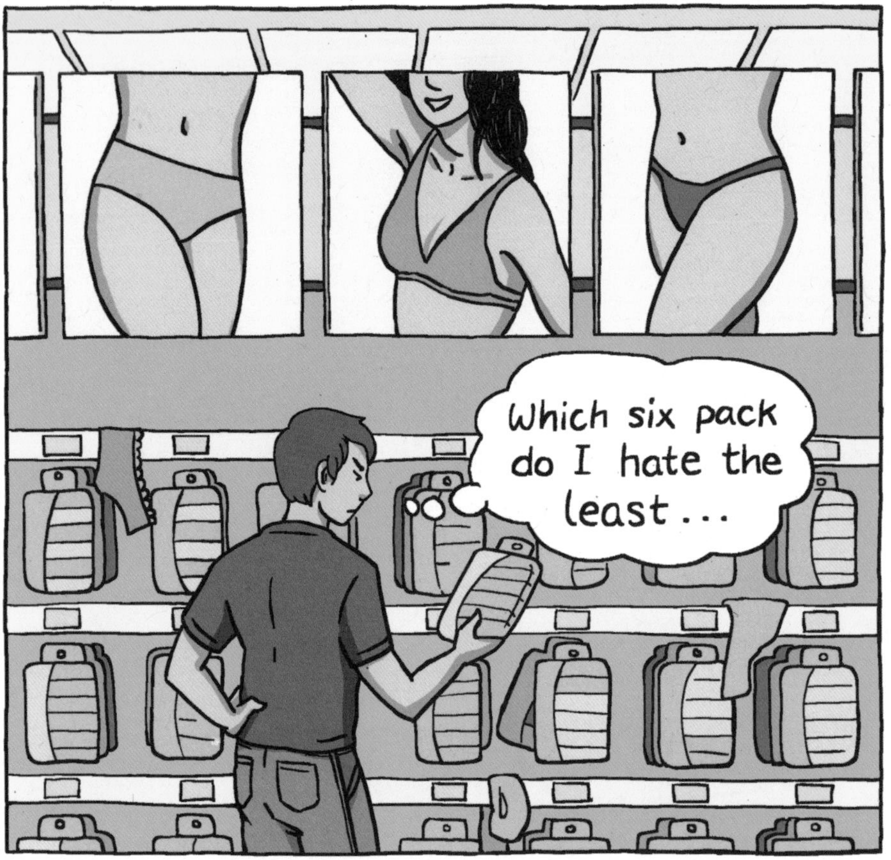
Which six pack do I hate the least...

VERY RELUCTANTLY I RETURNED TO THE "GIRLS' SECTION."

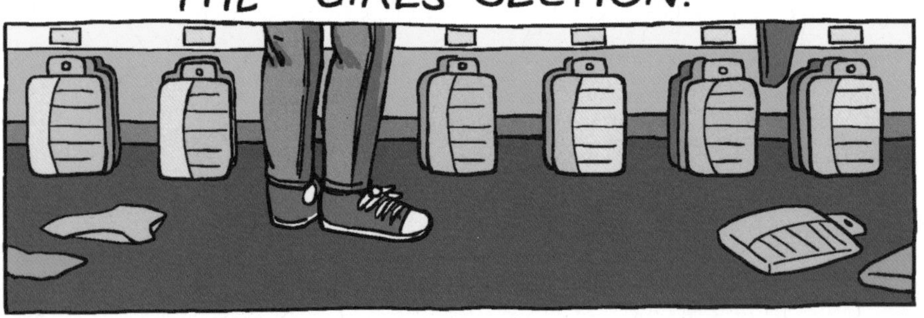

I BOUGHT ESSENTIALLY THE EXACT SAME ONES FOR 15 YEARS.

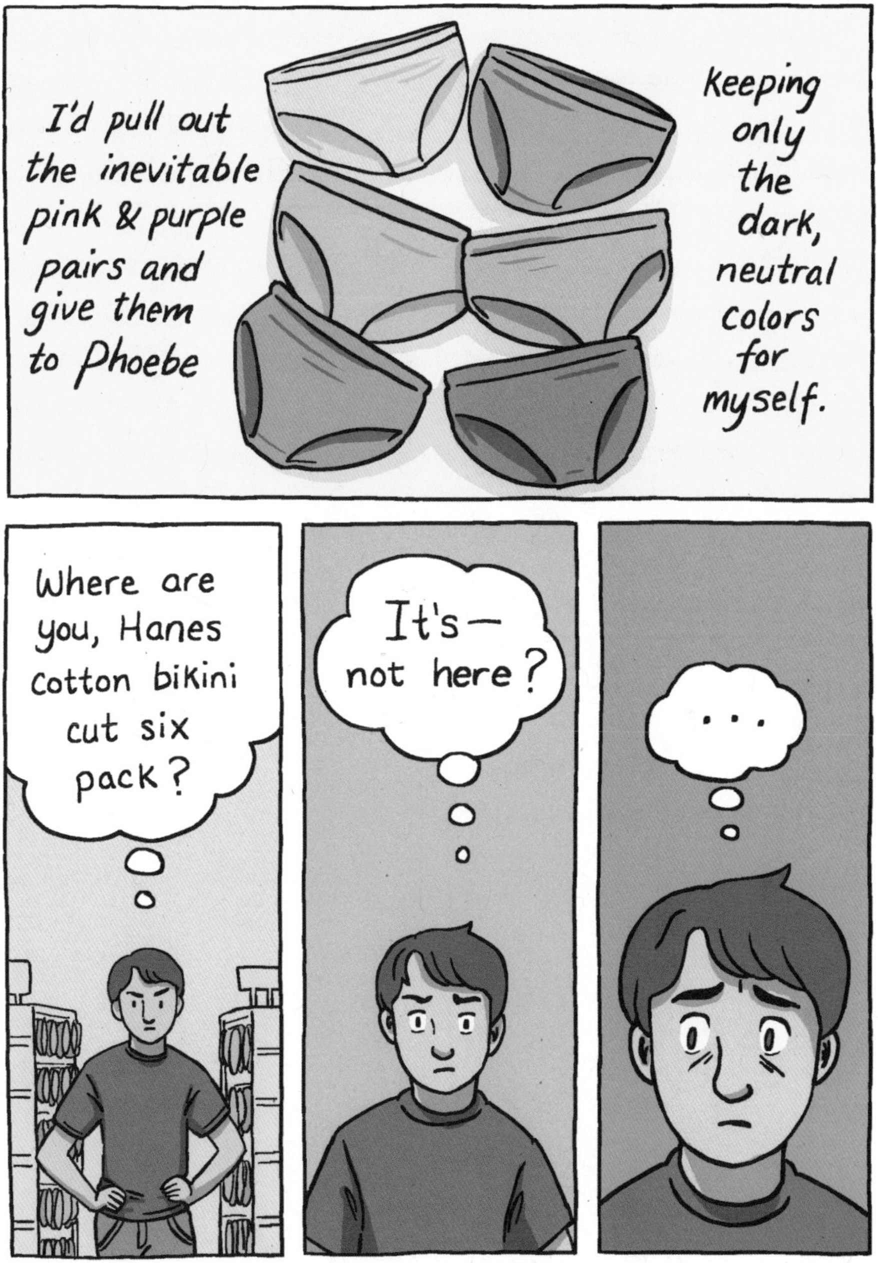
I'd pull out the inevitable pink & purple pairs and give them to Phoebe
keeping only the dark, neutral colors for myself.
Where are you, Hanes cotton bikini cut six pack?
It's— not here?
. . .

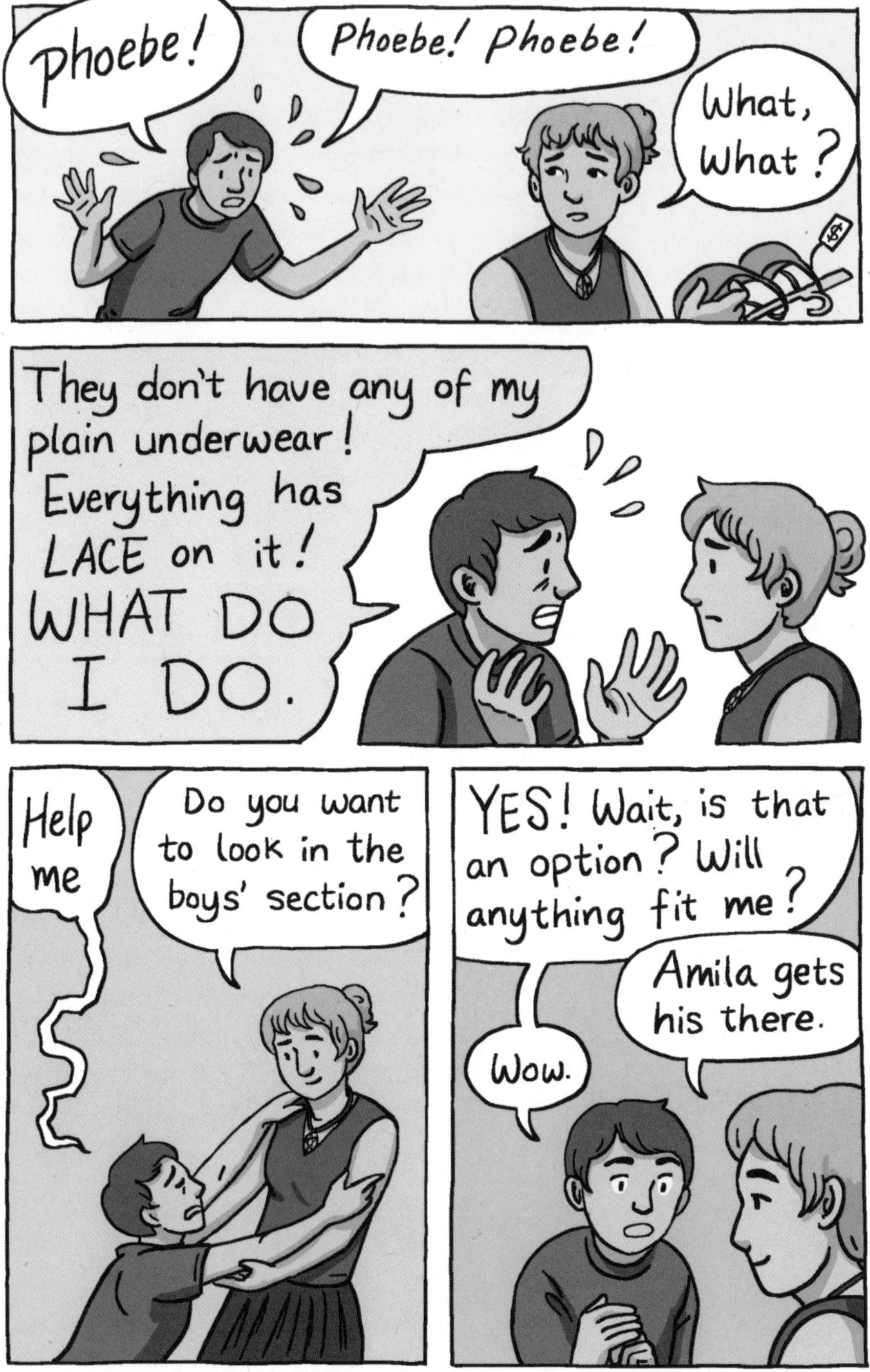
Phoebe!
Phoebe! Phoebe!
What, what?
They don't have any of my plain underwear! Everything has LACE on it! WHAT DO I DO.
Help me
Do you want to look in the boys' section?
YES! Wait, is that an option? Will anything fit me?
Amila gets his there.
Wow.

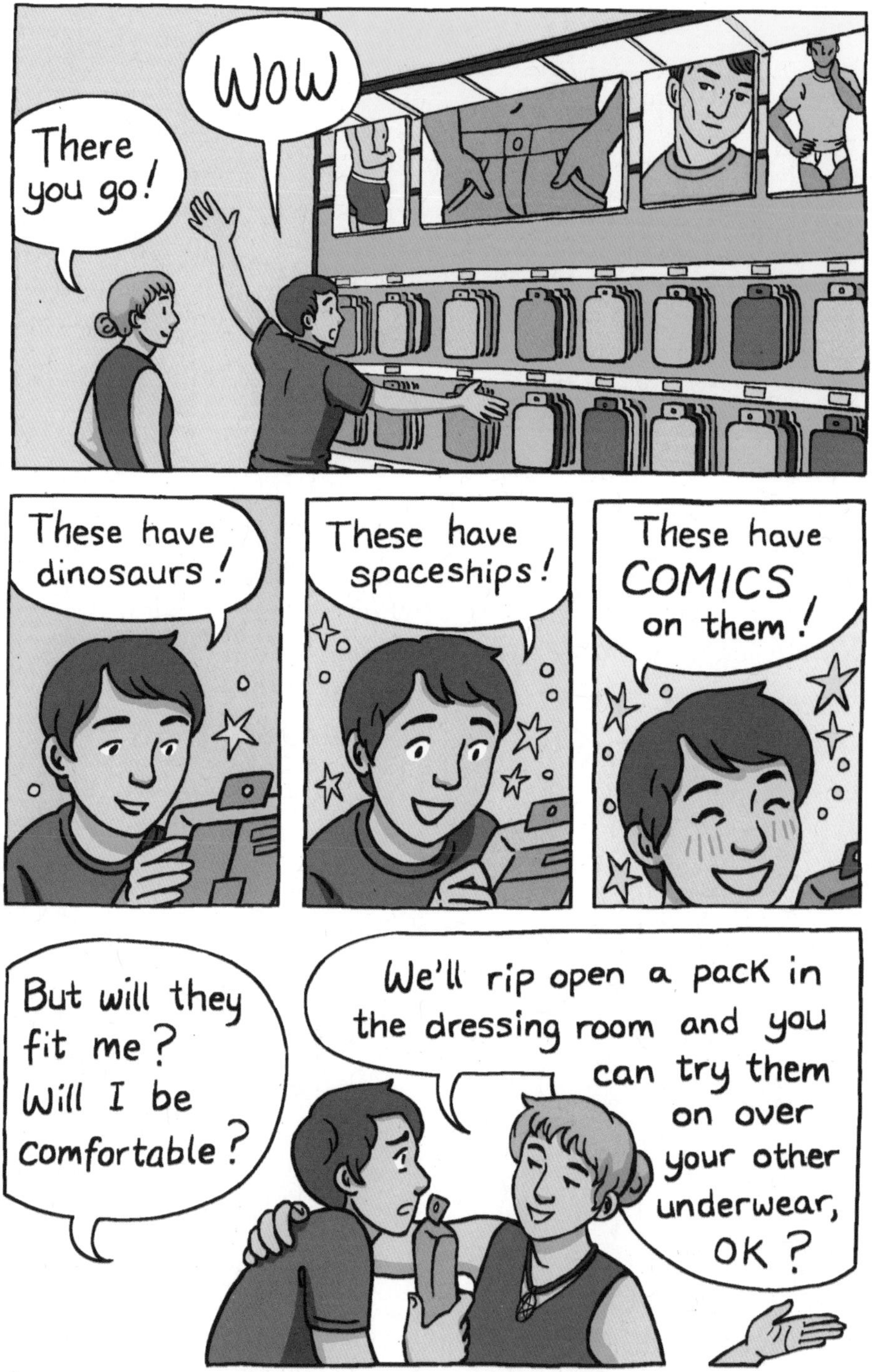
There you go!
WOW
These have dinosaurs!
These have spaceships!
These have COMICS on them!
But will they fit me? Will I be comfortable?
We'll rip open a pack in the dressing room and you can try them on over your other underwear, OK?

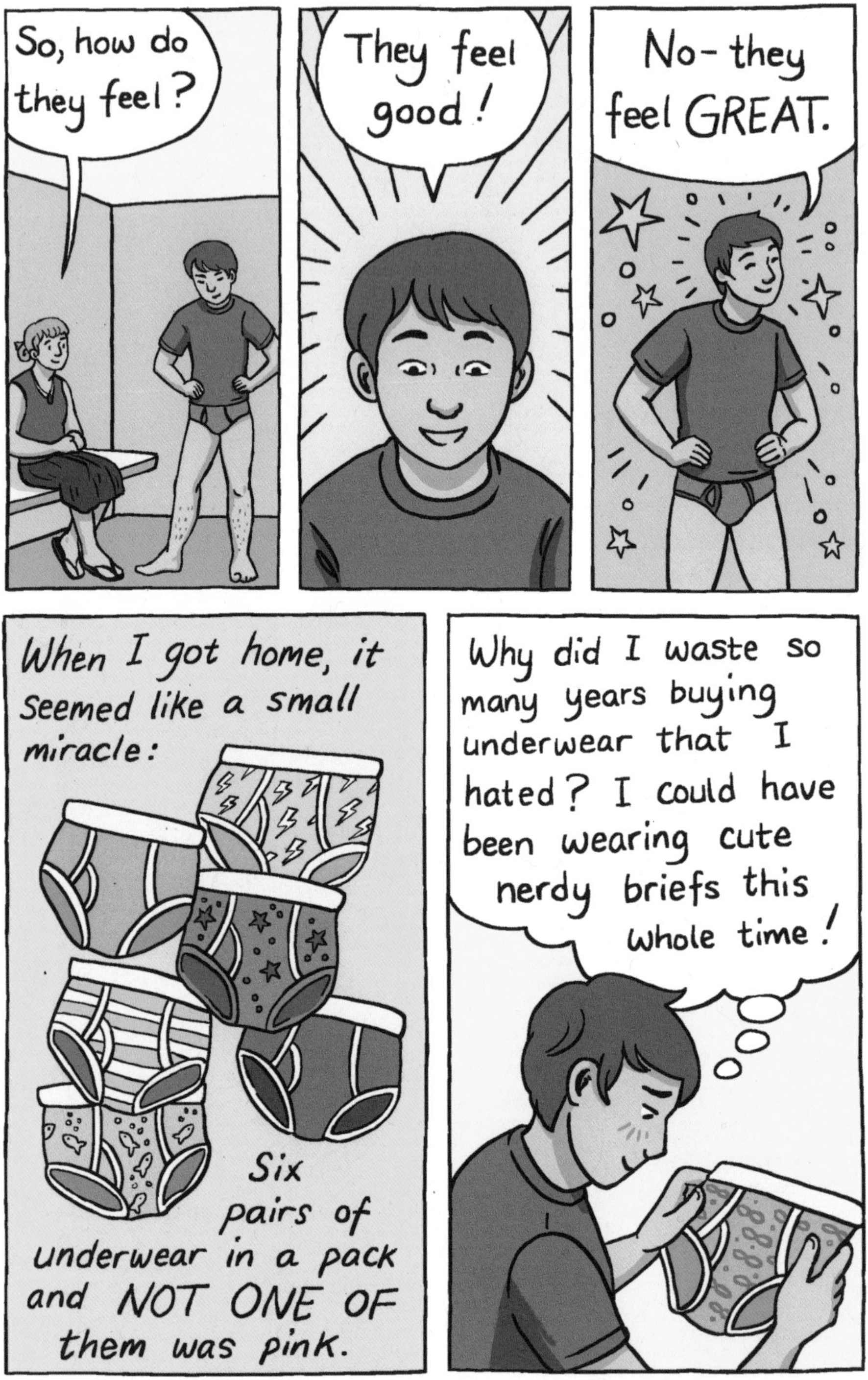
So, how do they feel?
They feel good!
No- they feel GREAT.
When I got home, it seemed like a small miracle:
Six pairs of underwear in a pack and NOT ONE OF them was pink.
Why did I waste so many years buying underwear that I hated? I could have been wearing cute nerdy briefs this whole time!

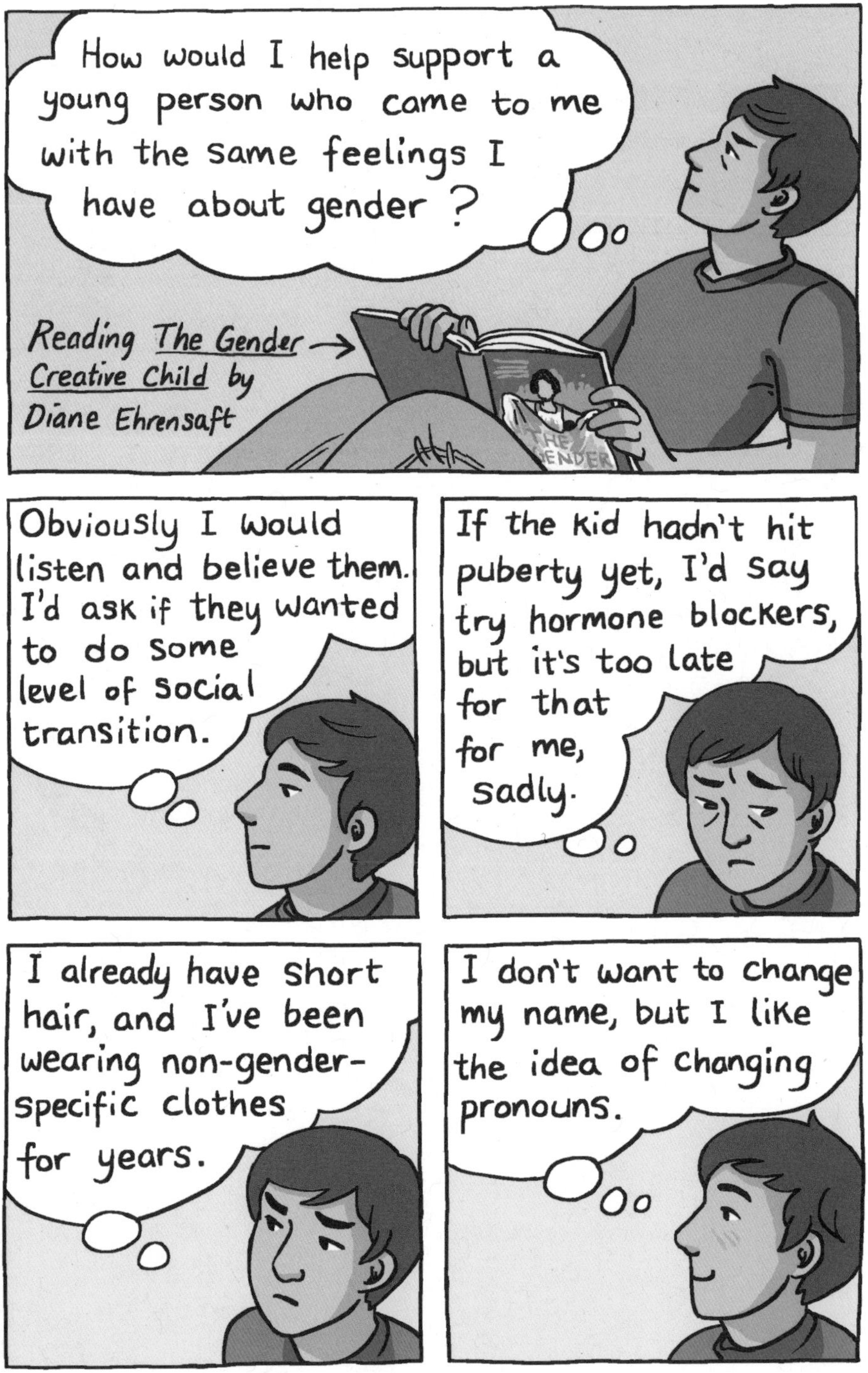
How would I help support a young person who came to me with the same feelings I have about gender?
Reading The Gender Creative Child by Diane Ehrensaft
THE GENDER
Obviously I would listen and believe them. I'd ask if they wanted to do some level of social transition.
If the kid hadn't hit puberty yet, I'd say try hormone blockers, but it's too late for that for me, sadly.
I already have short hair, and I've been wearing non-gender-specific clothes for years.
I don't want to change my name, but I like the idea of changing pronouns.

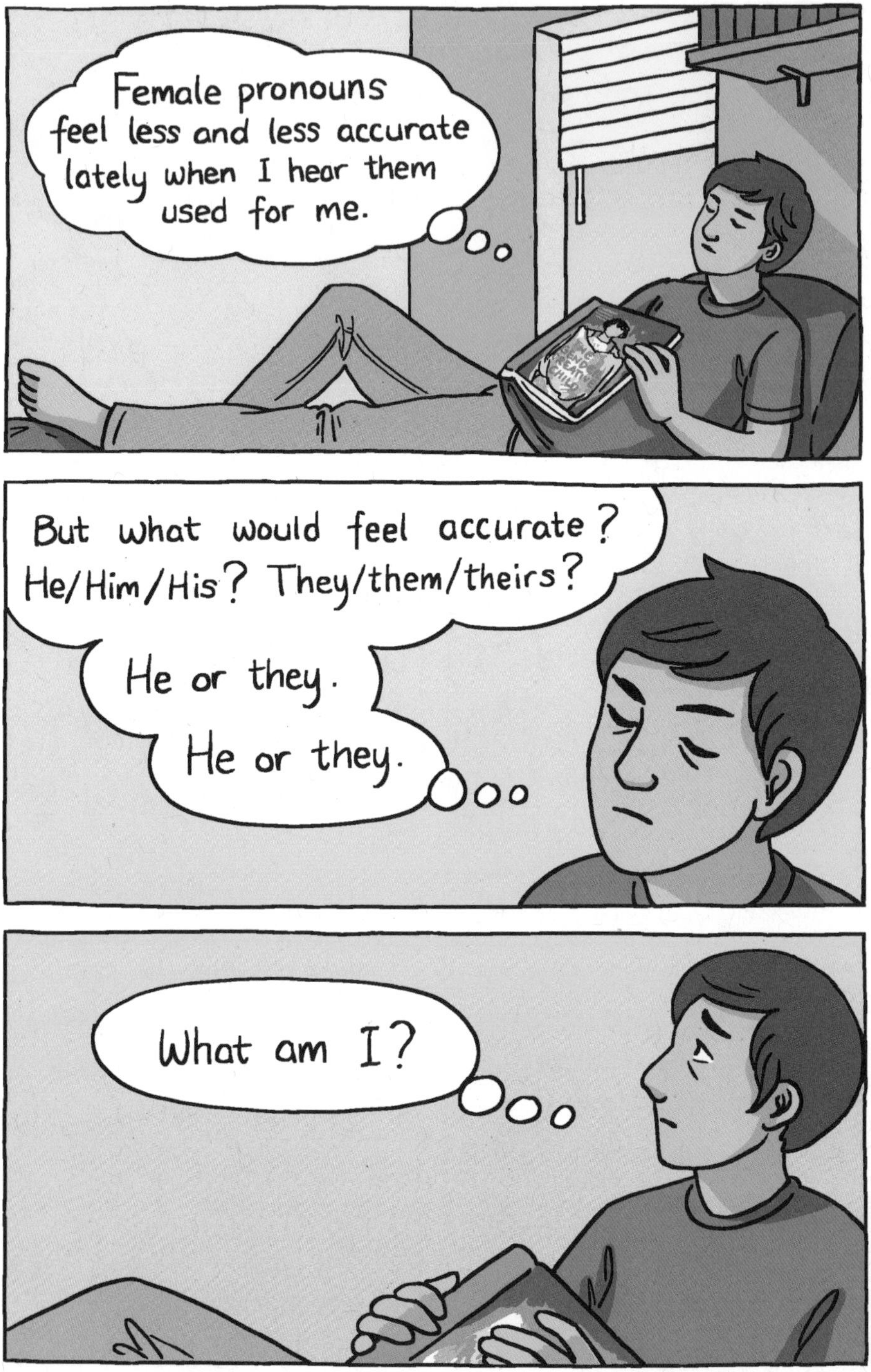
Female pronouns feel less and less accurate lately when I hear them used for me.
But what would feel accurate? He/Him/His? They/them/theirs?
He or they.
He or they.
What am I?

I FIRST MET JAINA BEE AT GALEN'S FAMILY'S ANNUAL NEW YEAR'S EVE PARTY IN 2003 WHEN I WAS 14.

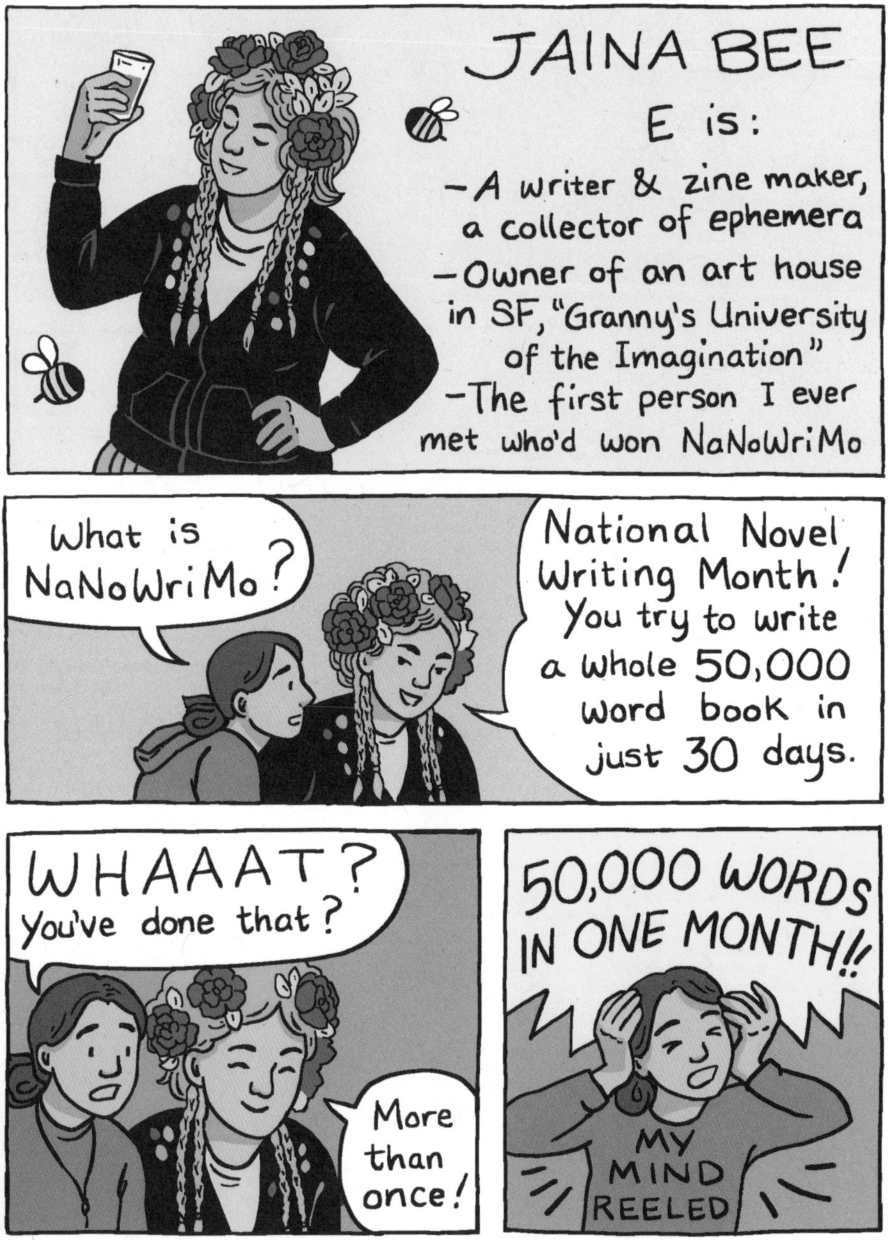
JAINA BEE
E is:
–A writer & zine maker, a collector of ephemera
–Owner of an art house in SF, "Granny's University of the Imagination"
–The first person I ever met who'd won NaNoWriMo
What is NaNoWriMo?
National Novel Writing Month! You try to write a whole 50,000 word book in just 30 days.
WHAAAT? You've done that?
More than once!
50,000 WORDS IN ONE MONTH!!
MY MIND REELED

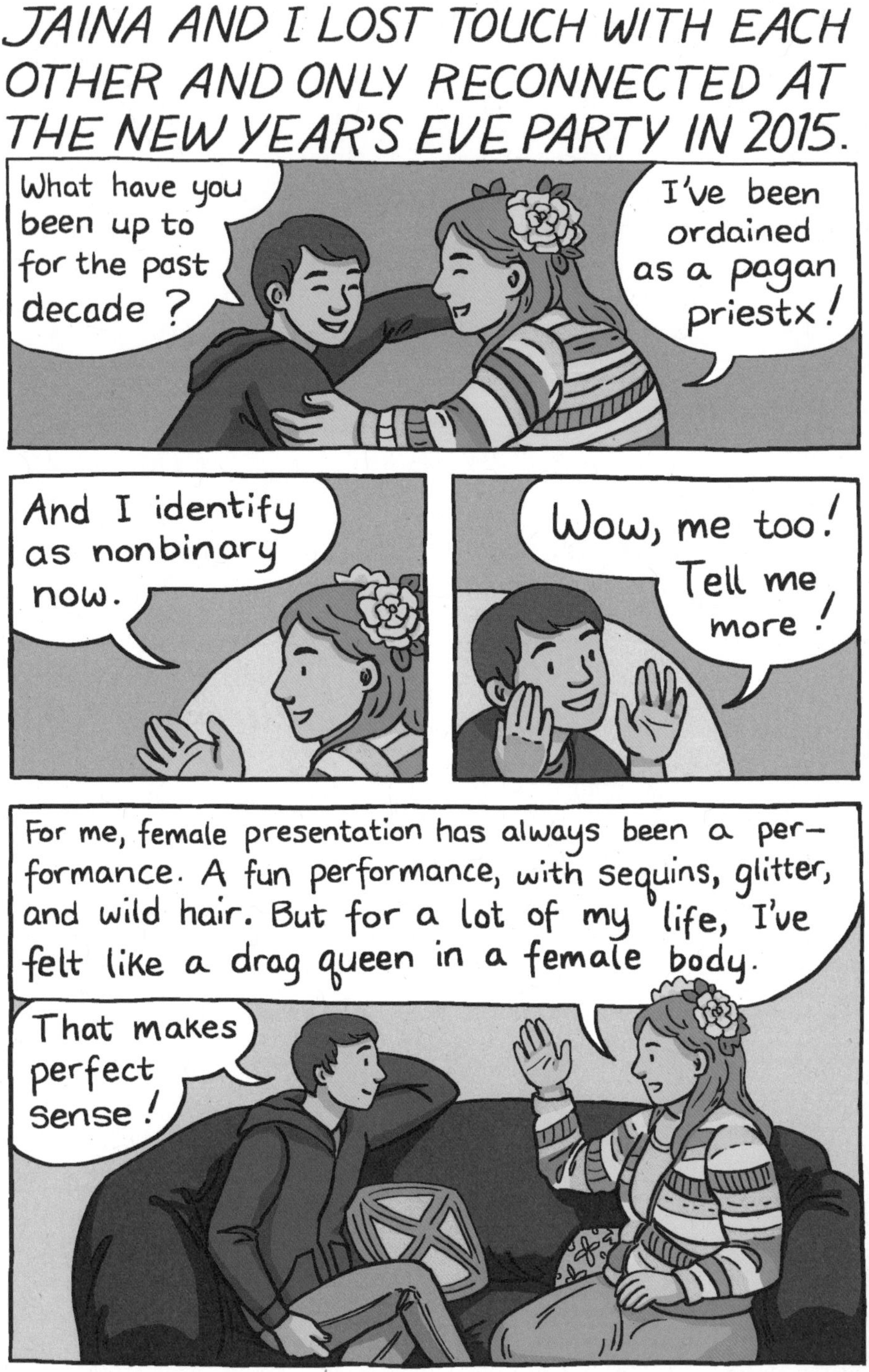
JAINA AND I LOST TOUCH WITH EACH OTHER AND ONLY RECONNECTED AT THE NEW YEAR'S EVE PARTY IN 2015.
What have you been up to for the past decade?
I've been ordained as a pagan priestx!
And I identify as nonbinary now.
Wow, me too! Tell me more!
For me, female presentation has always been a performance. A fun performance, with sequins, glitter, and wild hair. But for a lot of my life, I've felt like a drag queen in a female body.
That makes perfect sense!

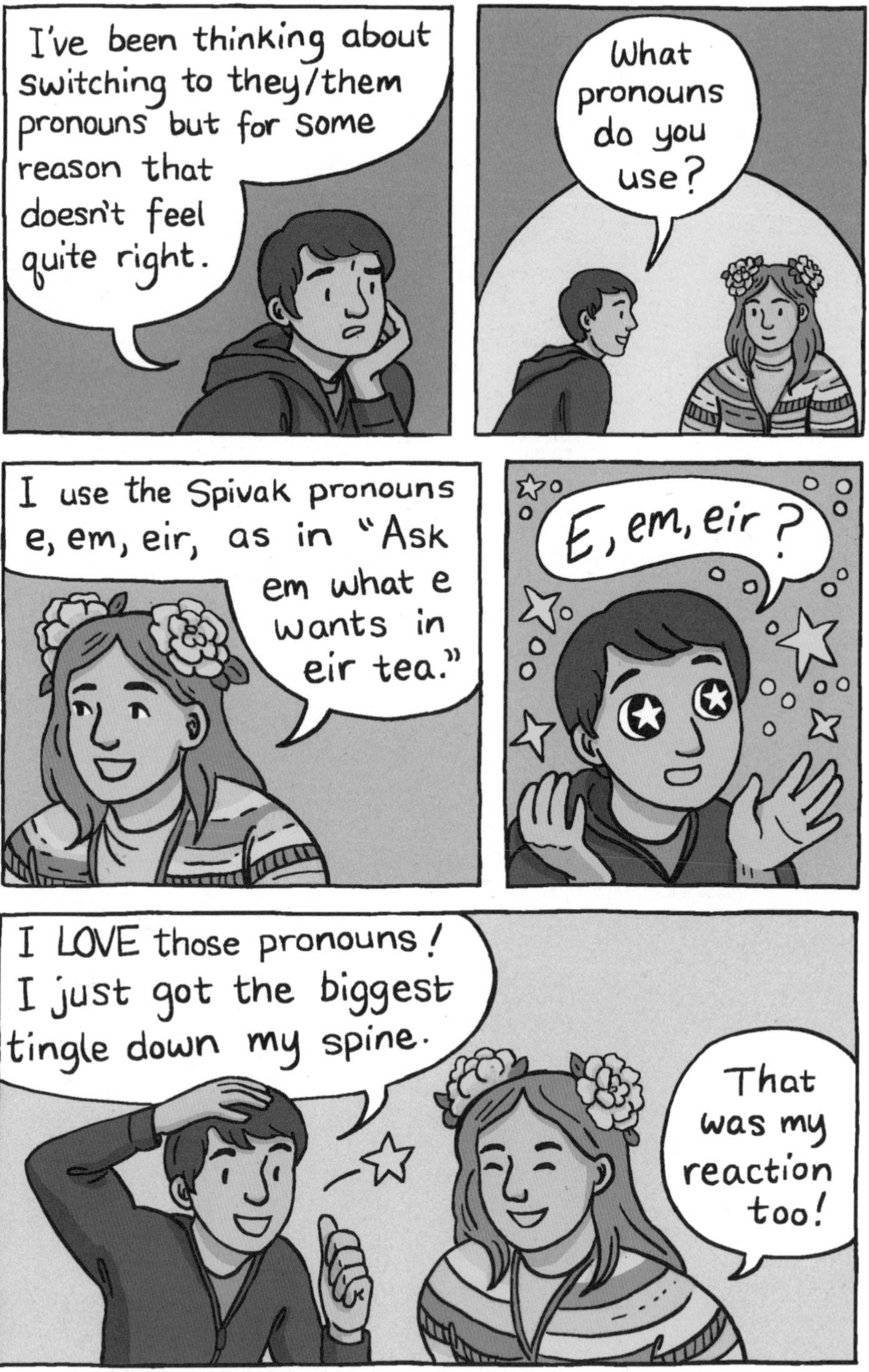
I've been thinking about switching to they/them pronouns but for some reason that doesn't feel quite right.
What pronouns do you use?
I use the Spivak pronouns e, em, eir, as in "Ask em what e wants in eir tea."
E, em, eir?
I LOVE those pronouns! I just got the biggest tingle down my spine.
That was my reaction too!

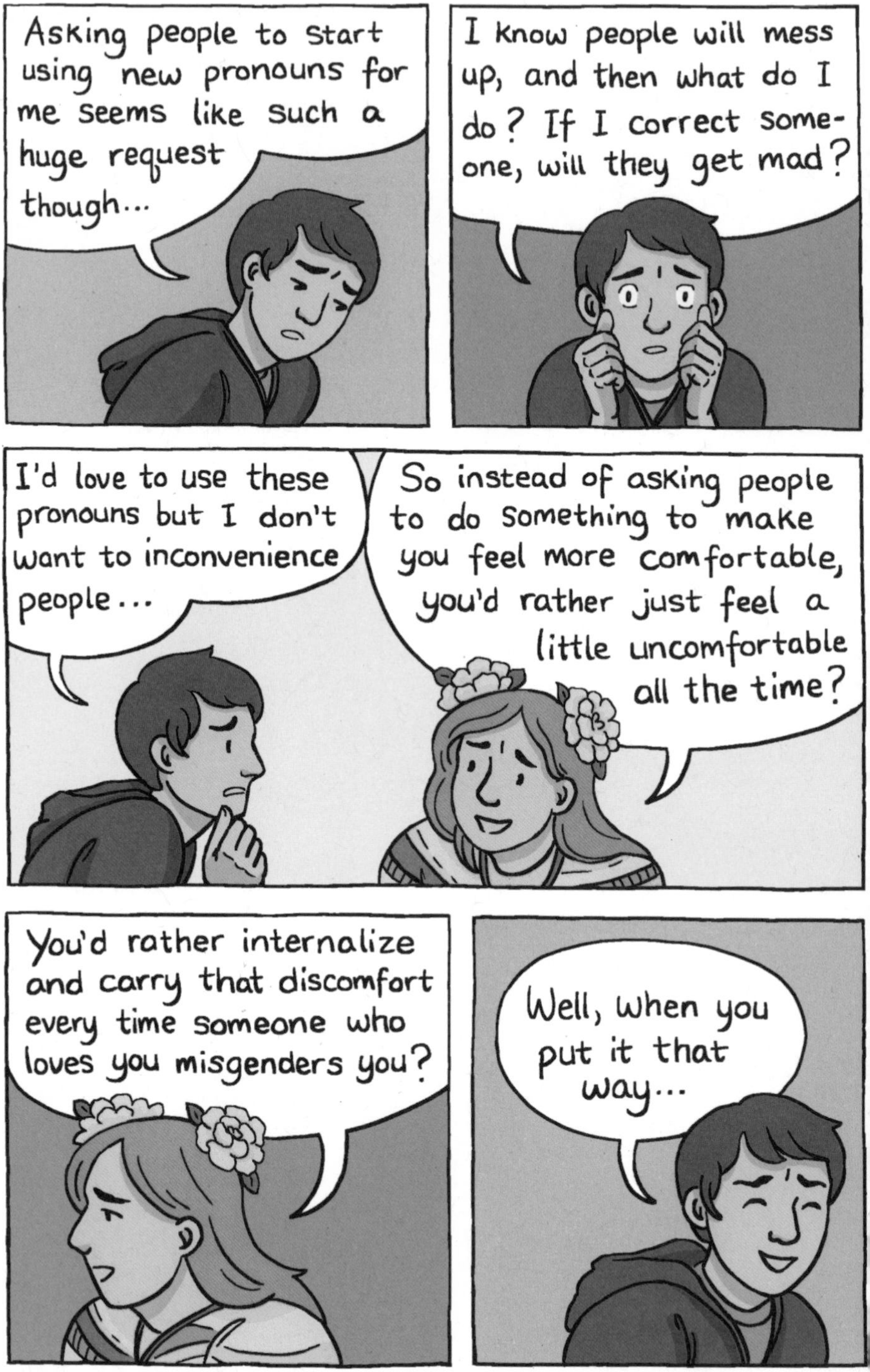
Asking people to start using new pronouns for me seems like such a huge request though...
I know people will mess up, and then what do I do? If I correct some-one, will they get mad?
I'd love to use these pronouns but I don't want to inconvenience people...
So instead of asking people to do something to make you feel more comfortable, you'd rather just feel a little uncomfortable all the time?
You'd rather internalize and carry that discomfort every time someone who loves you misgenders you?
Well, when you put it that way...

AS I PONDERED A PRONOUN CHANGE, I BEGAN TO THINK OF GENDER LESS AS A SCALE AND MORE AS A LANDSCAPE.

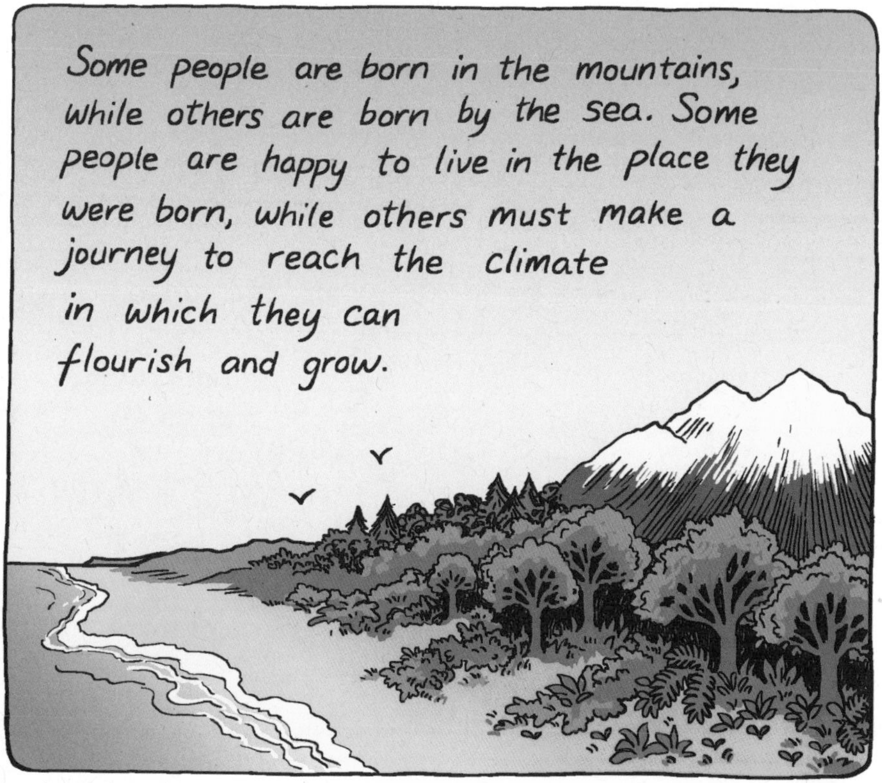
Some people are born in the mountains, while others are born by the sea. Some people are happy to live in the place they were born, while others must make a journey to reach the climate in which they can flourish and grow.

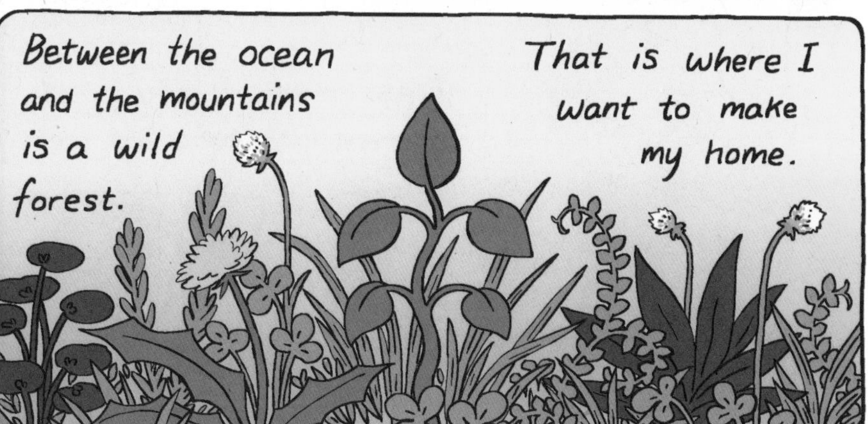
Between the ocean and the mountains is a wild forest.
That is where I want to make my home.

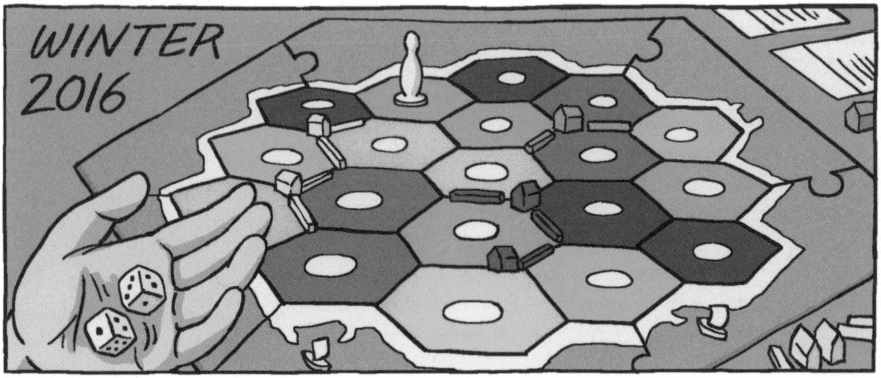
WINTER
2016

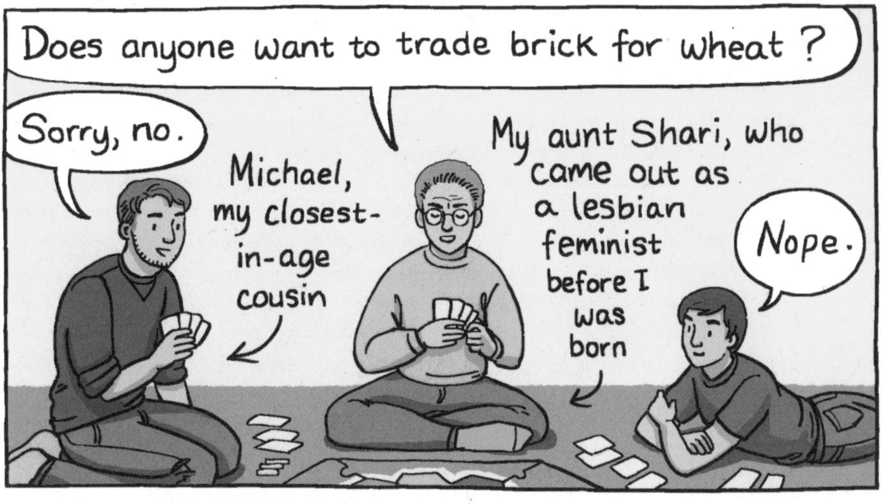
Does anyone want to trade brick for wheat?
Sorry, no.
Michael, my closest-in-age cousin
My aunt Shari, who came out as a lesbian feminist before I was born
Nope.

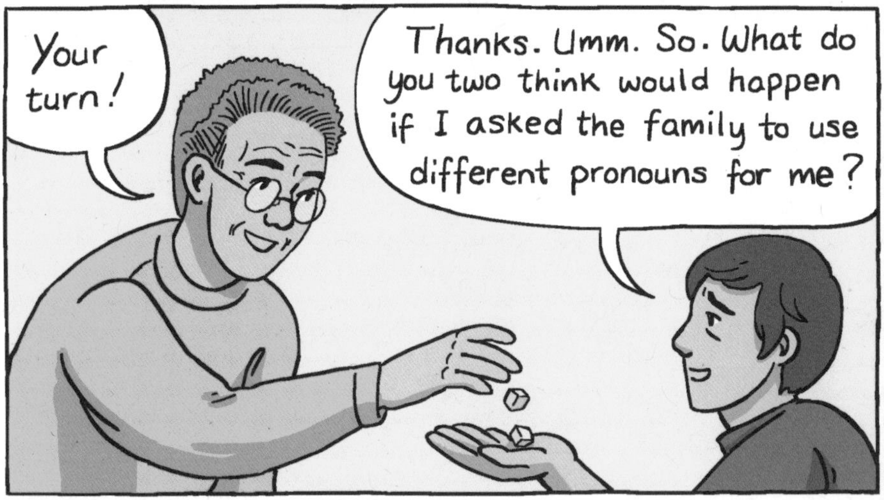
Your turn!
Thanks. Umm. So. What do you two think would happen if I asked the family to use different pronouns for me?

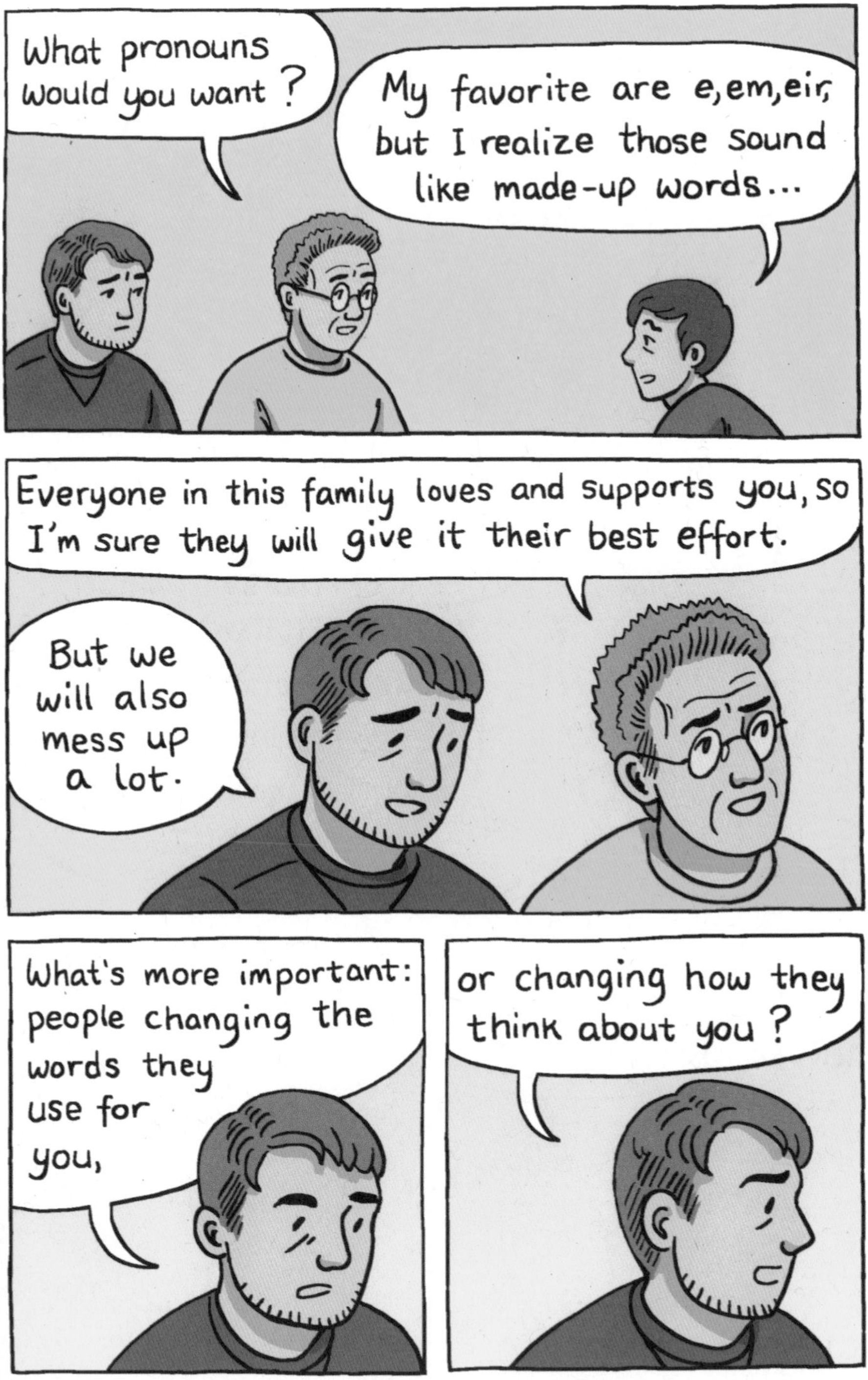
What pronouns would you want?
My favorite are e, em, eir, but I realize those sound like made-up words...
Everyone in this family loves and supports you, so I'm sure they will give it their best effort.
But we will also mess up a lot.
What's more important: people changing the words they use for you,
or changing how they think about you?

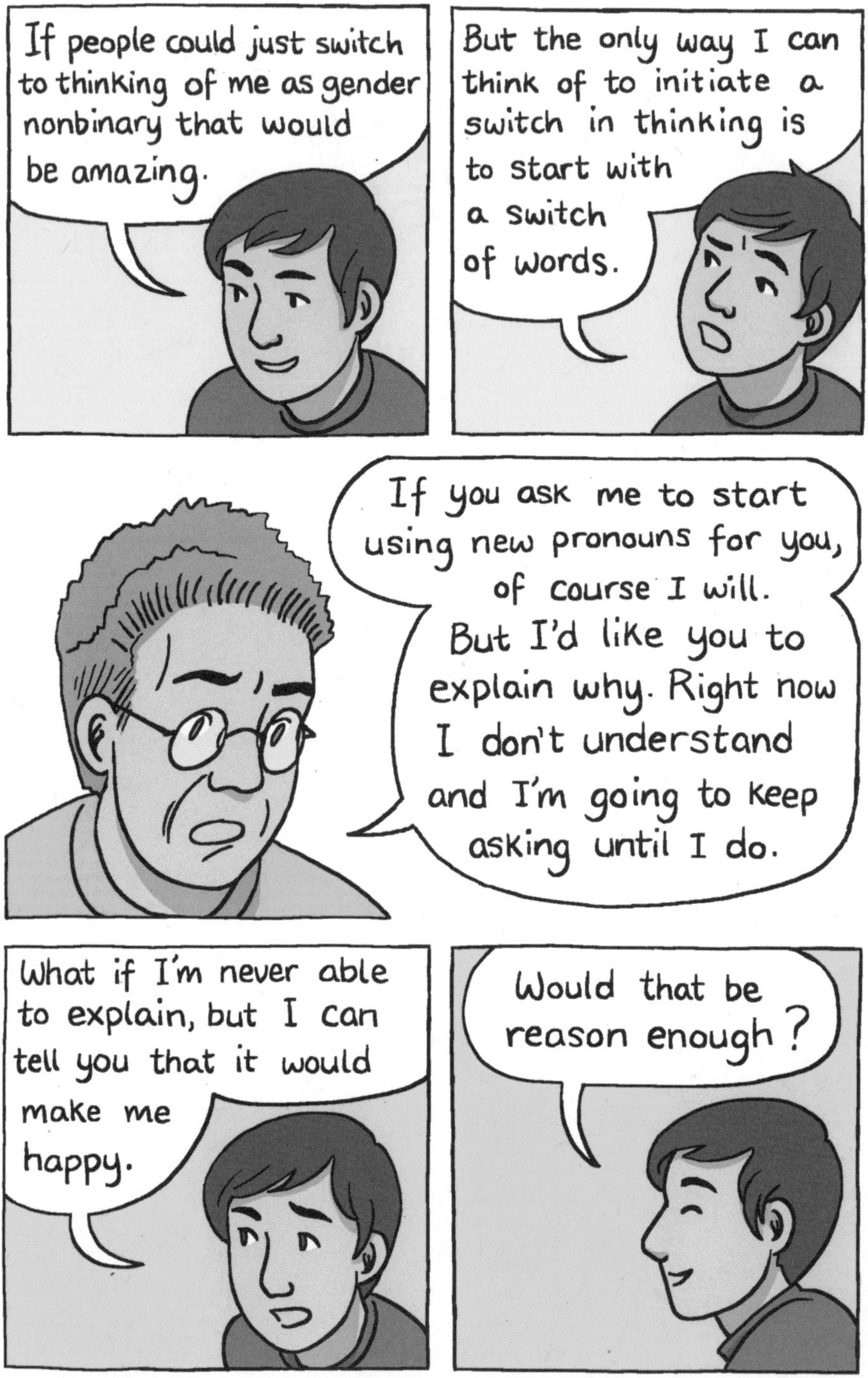
If people could just switch to thinking of me as gender nonbinary that would be amazing.
But the only way I can think of to initiate a switch in thinking is to start with a switch of words.
If you ask me to start using new pronouns for you, of course I will. But I'd like you to explain why. Right now I don't understand and I'm going to keep asking until I do.
What if I'm never able to explain, but I can tell you that it would make me happy.
Would that be reason enough?

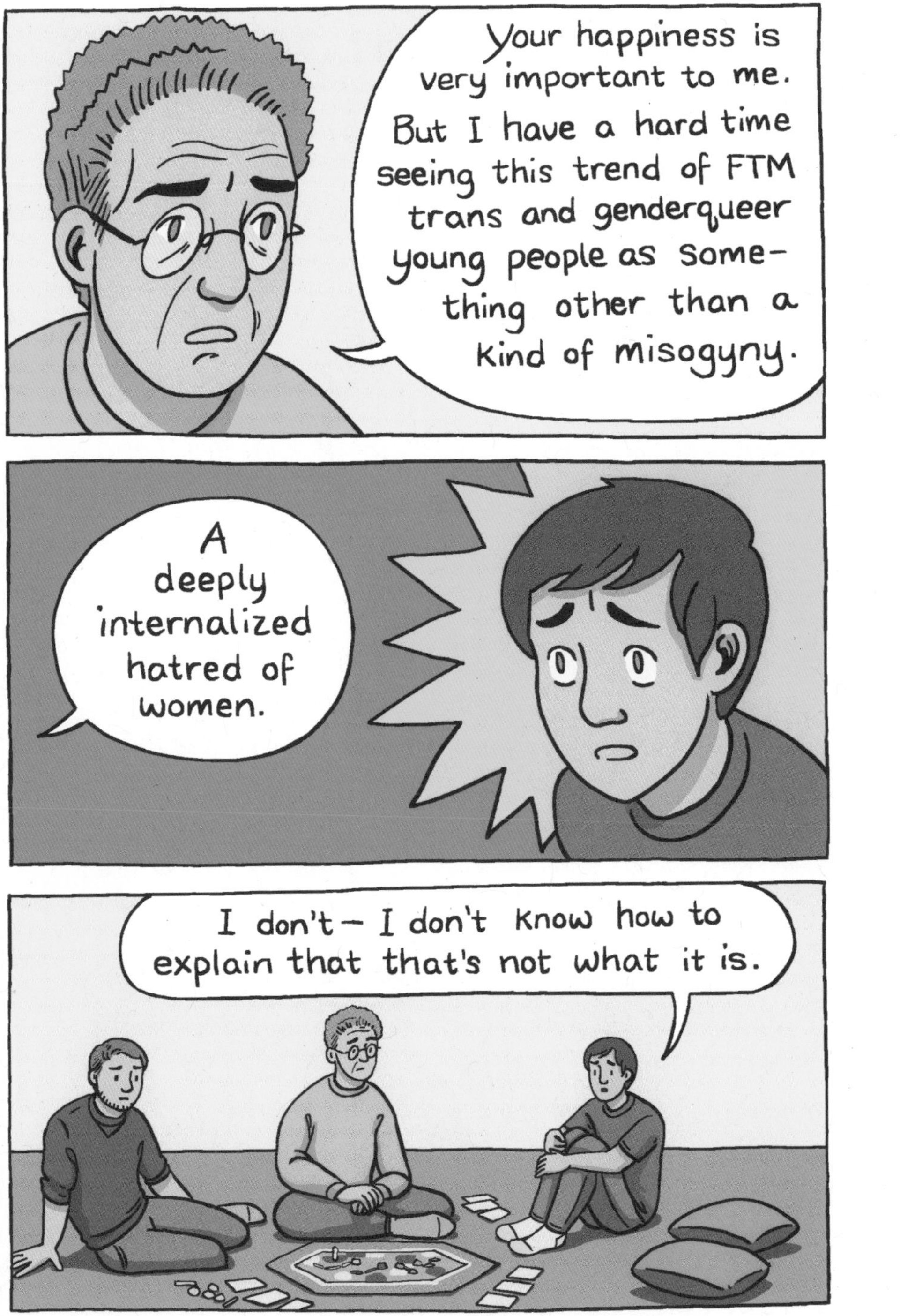
Your happiness is very important to me. But I have a hard time seeing this trend of FTM trans and genderqueer young people as some-thing other than a kind of misogyny.
A deeply internalized hatred of women.
I don't— I don't know how to explain that that's not what it is.

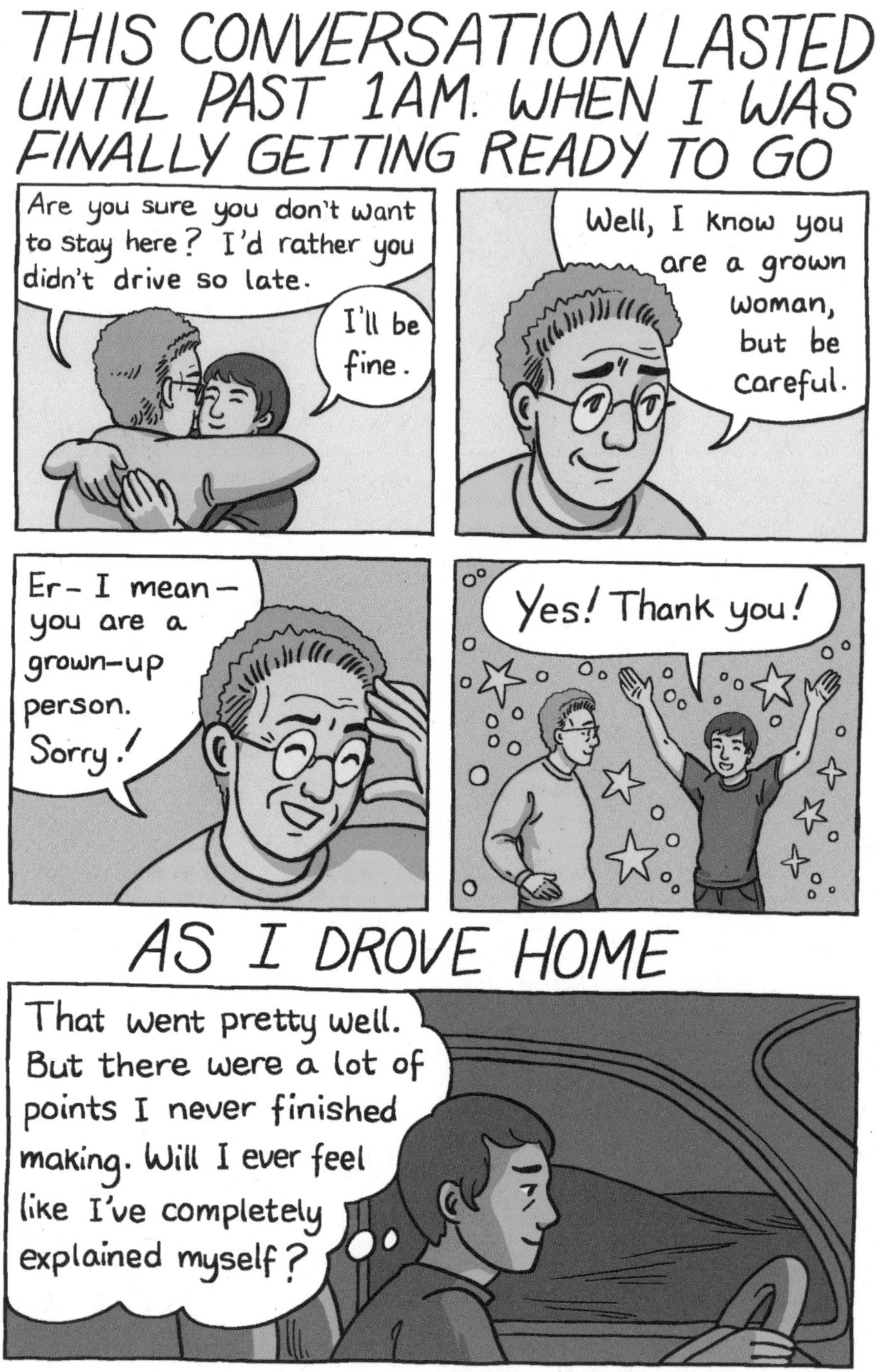
THIS CONVERSATION LASTED UNTIL PAST 1AM. WHEN I WAS FINALLY GETTING READY TO GO
Are you sure you don't want to stay here? I'd rather you didn't drive so late.
I'll be fine.
Well, I know you are a grown woman, but be careful.
Er– I mean– you are a grown–up person. Sorry!
Yes! Thank you!
AS I DROVE HOME
That went pretty well. But there were a lot of points I never finished making. Will I ever feel like I've completely explained myself?

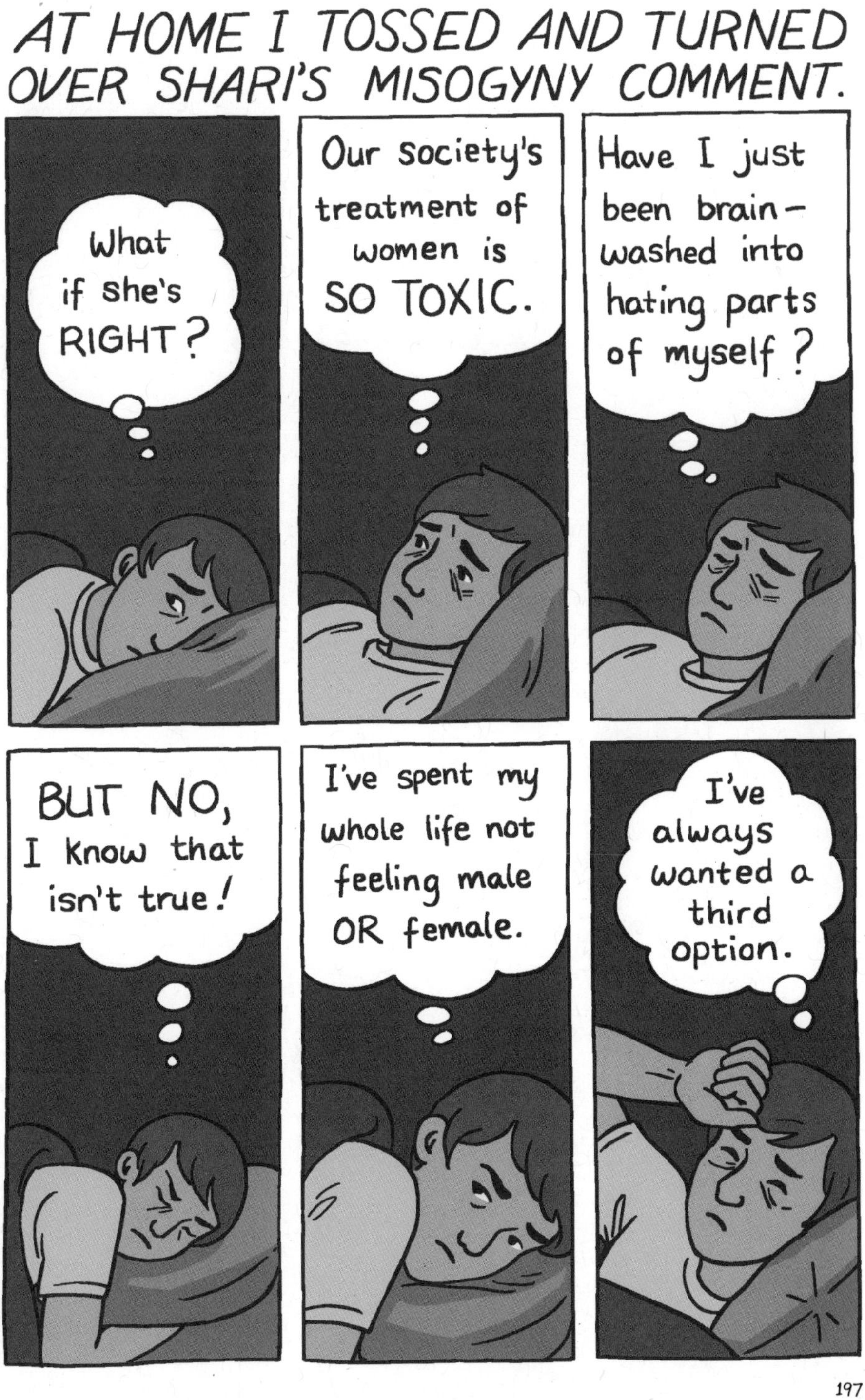
AT HOME I TOSSED AND TURNED OVER SHARI'S MISOGYNY COMMENT.
What if she's RIGHT?
Our society's treatment of women is SO TOXIC.
Have I just been brain-washed into hating parts of myself?
BUT NO, I know that isn't true!
I've spent my whole life not feeling male OR female.
I've always wanted a third option.

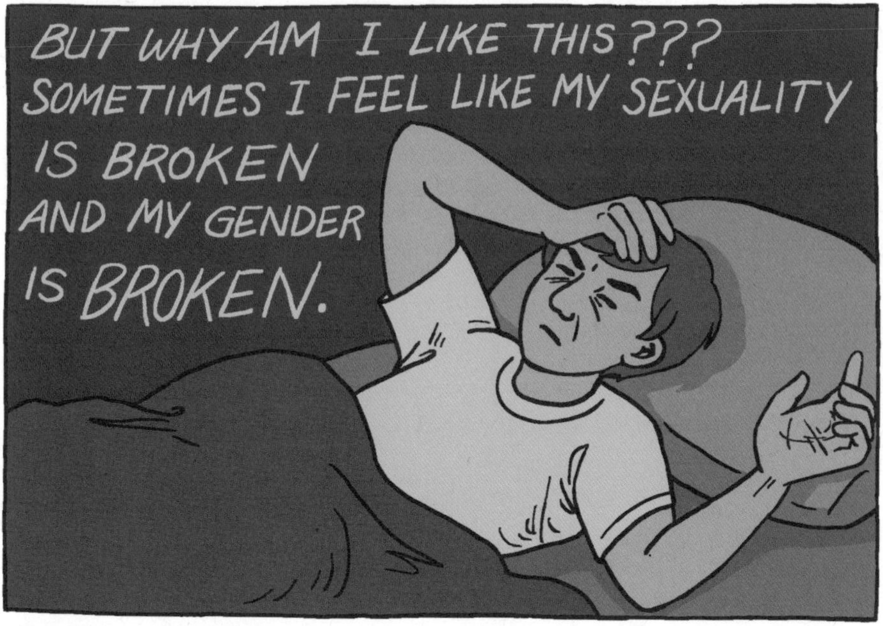
BUT WHY AM I LIKE THIS???
SOMETIMES I FEEL LIKE MY SEXUALITY IS BROKEN
AND MY GENDER IS BROKEN.

I feel like there are all these wires in my brain which were supposed to connect

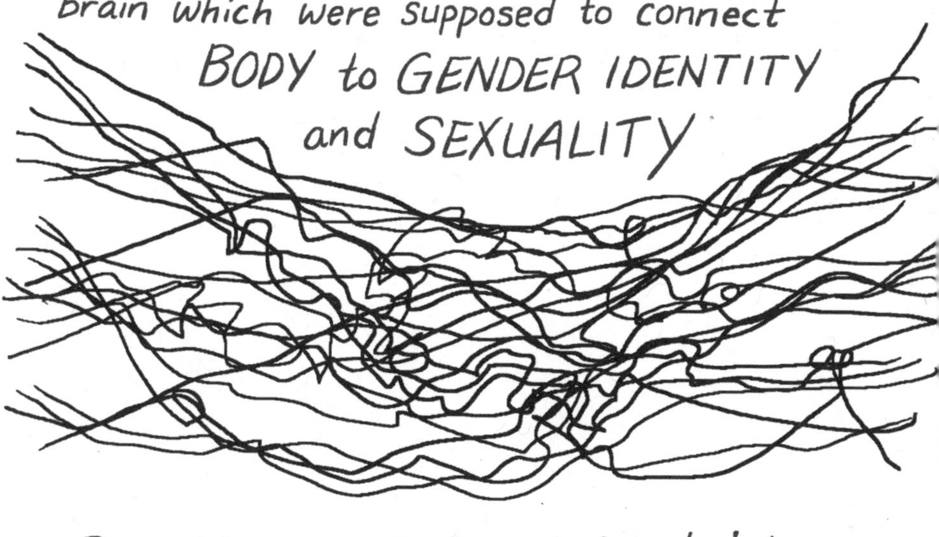
BODY to GENDER IDENTITY
and SEXUALITY

But they've all been twisted into a HUGE SNARLED MESS.

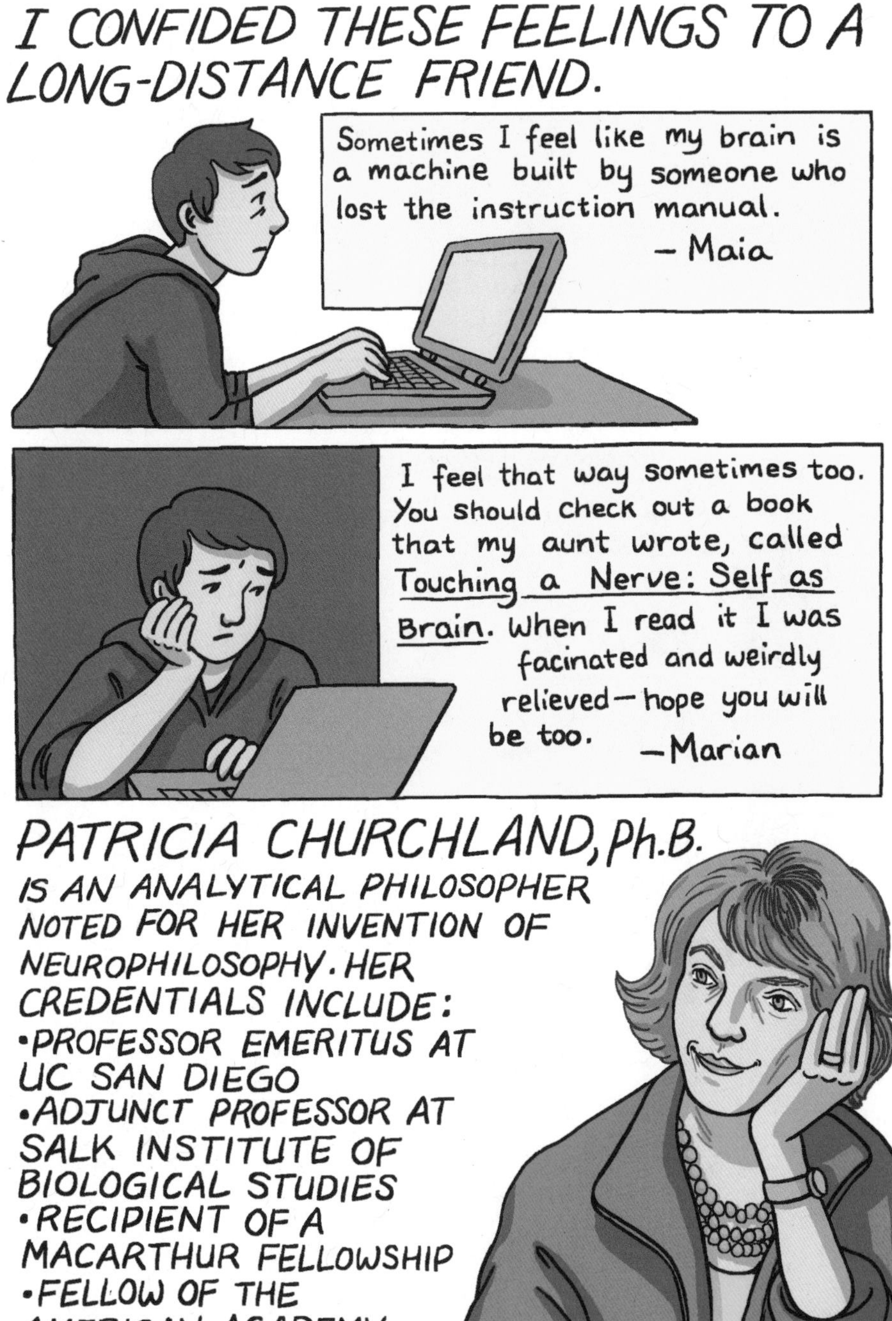
I CONFIDED THESE FEELINGS TO A LONG-DISTANCE FRIEND.
Sometimes I feel like my brain is a machine built by someone who lost the instruction manual. —Maia
I feel that way sometimes too. You should check out a book that my aunt wrote, called Touching a Nerve: Self as Brain. When I read it I was facinated and weirdly relieved—hope you will be too. —Marian
PATRICIA CHURCHLAND, Ph.B.
IS AN ANALYTICAL PHILOSOPHER NOTED FOR HER INVENTION OF NEUROPHILOSOPHY. HER CREDENTIALS INCLUDE:
•PROFESSOR EMERITUS AT UC SAN DIEGO
•ADJUNCT PROFESSOR AT SALK INSTITUTE OF BIOLOGICAL STUDIES
•RECIPIENT OF A MACARTHUR FELLOWSHIP
•FELLOW OF THE AMERICAN ACADEMY OF ARTS & SCIENCES

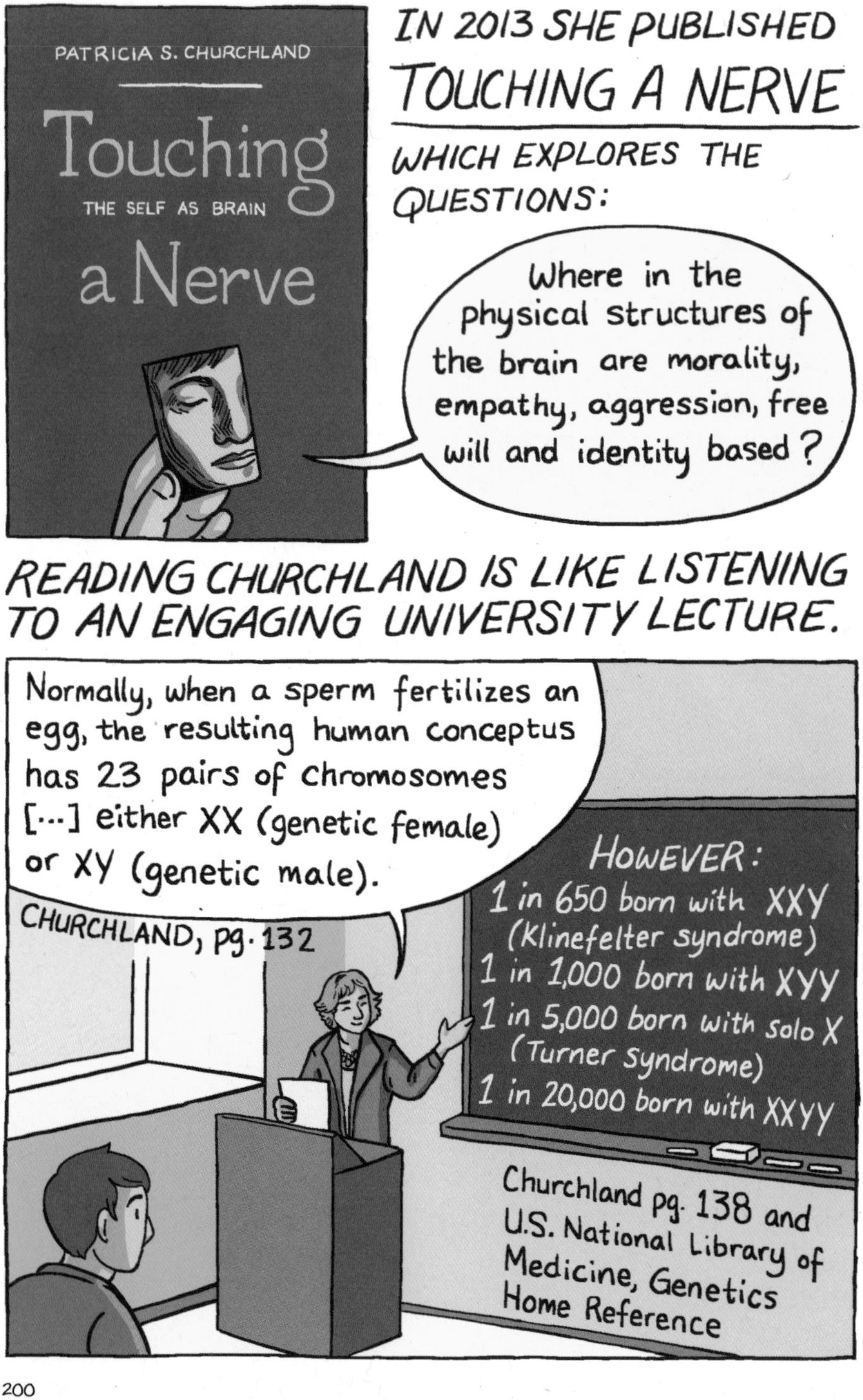
PATRICIA S. CHURCHLAND
Touching a Nerve
THE SELF AS BRAIN
IN 2013 SHE PUBLISHED TOUCHING A NERVE WHICH EXPLORES THE QUESTIONS:
Where in the physical structures of the brain are morality, empathy, aggression, free will and identity based?
READING CHURCHLAND IS LIKE LISTENING TO AN ENGAGING UNIVERSITY LECTURE.
Normally, when a sperm fertilizes an egg, the resulting human conceptus has 23 pairs of chromosomes [...] either XX (genetic female) or XY (genetic male).
CHURCHLAND, pg. 132
HOWEVER:
1 in 650 born with XXY (Klinefelter syndrome)
1 in 1,000 born with XYY
1 in 5,000 born with solo X (Turner syndrome)
1 in 20,000 born with XXYY
Churchland pg. 138 and U.S. National Library of Medicine, Genetics Home Reference

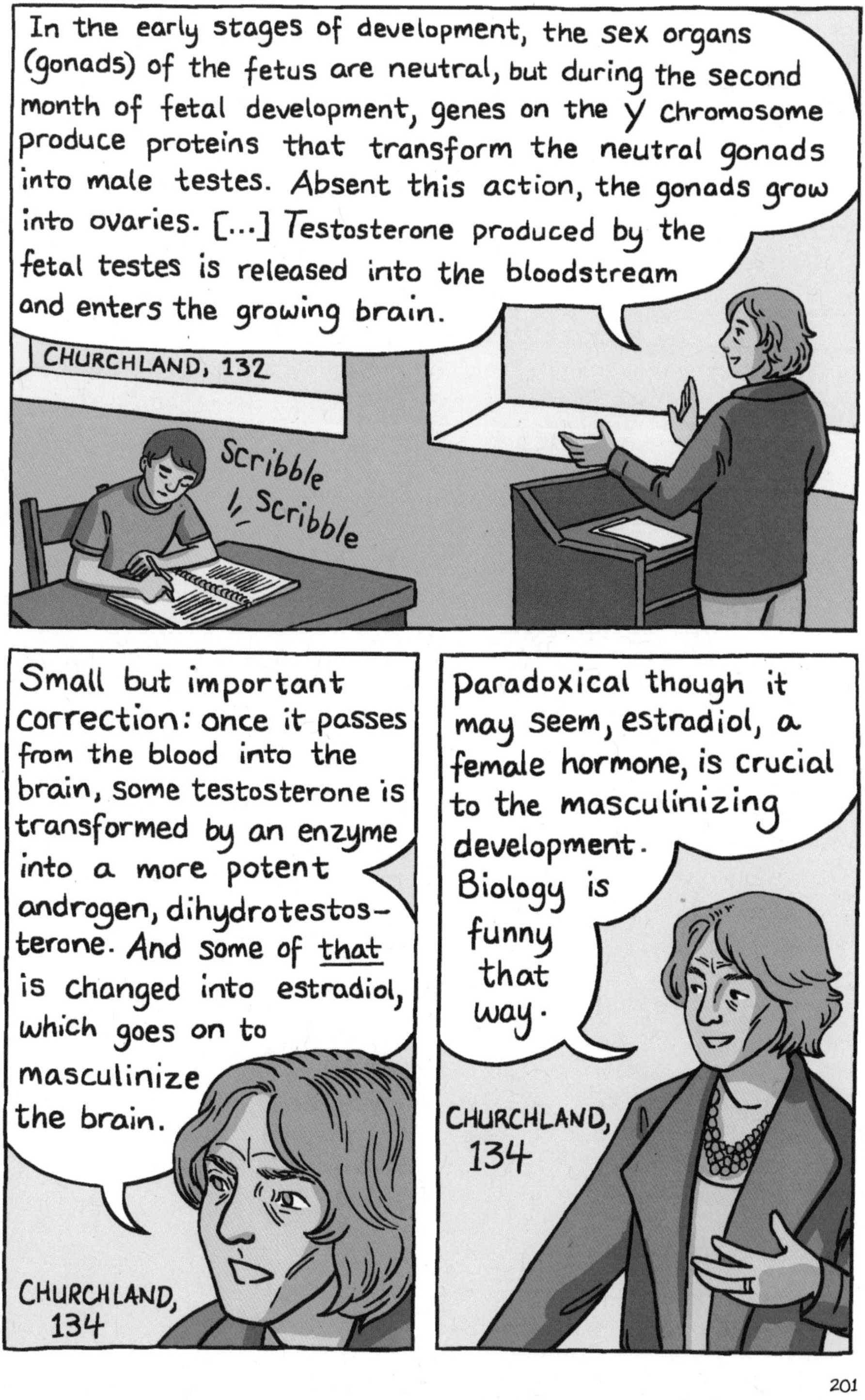
In the early stages of development, the sex organs (gonads) of the fetus are neutral, but during the second month of fetal development, genes on the Y chromosome produce proteins that transform the neutral gonads into male testes. Absent this action, the gonads grow into ovaries. [...] Testosterone produced by the fetal testes is released into the bloodstream and enters the growing brain.
CHURCHLAND, 132
Scribble
Scribble
Small but important correction: once it passes from the blood into the brain, some testosterone is transformed by an enzyme into a more potent androgen, dihydrotestosterone. And some of that is changed into estradiol, which goes on to masculinize the brain.
CHURCHLAND, 134
Paradoxical though it may seem, estradiol, a female hormone, is crucial to the masculinizing development.
Biology is funny that way.
CHURCHLAND, 134

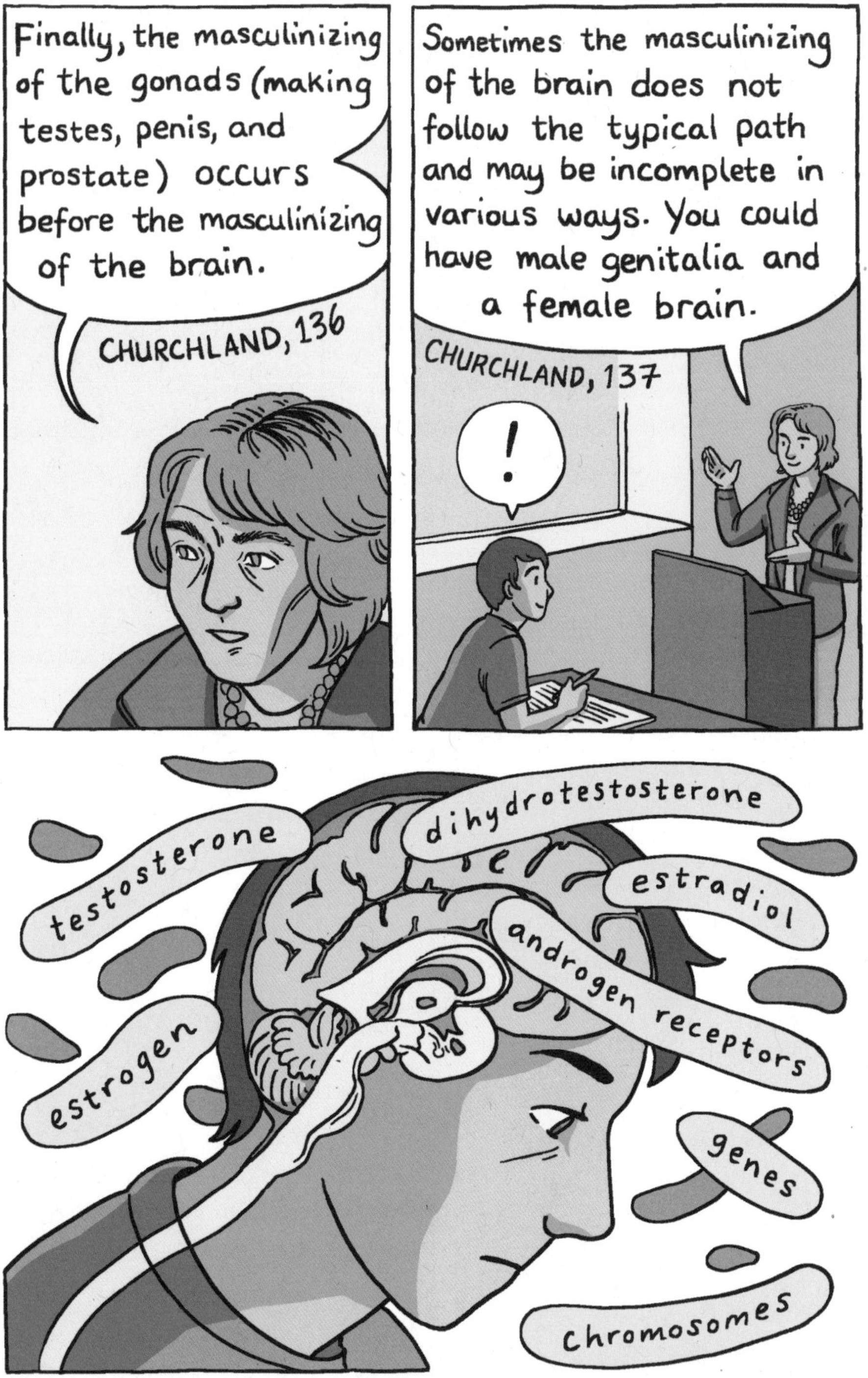
Finally, the masculinizing of the gonads (making testes, penis, and prostate) occurs before the masculinizing of the brain.
CHURCHLAND, 136
Sometimes the masculinizing of the brain does not follow the typical path and may be incomplete in various ways. You could have male genitalia and a female brain.
CHURCHLAND, 137
!
testosterone
dihydrotestosterone
estradiol
androgen receptors
estrogen
genes
chromosomes

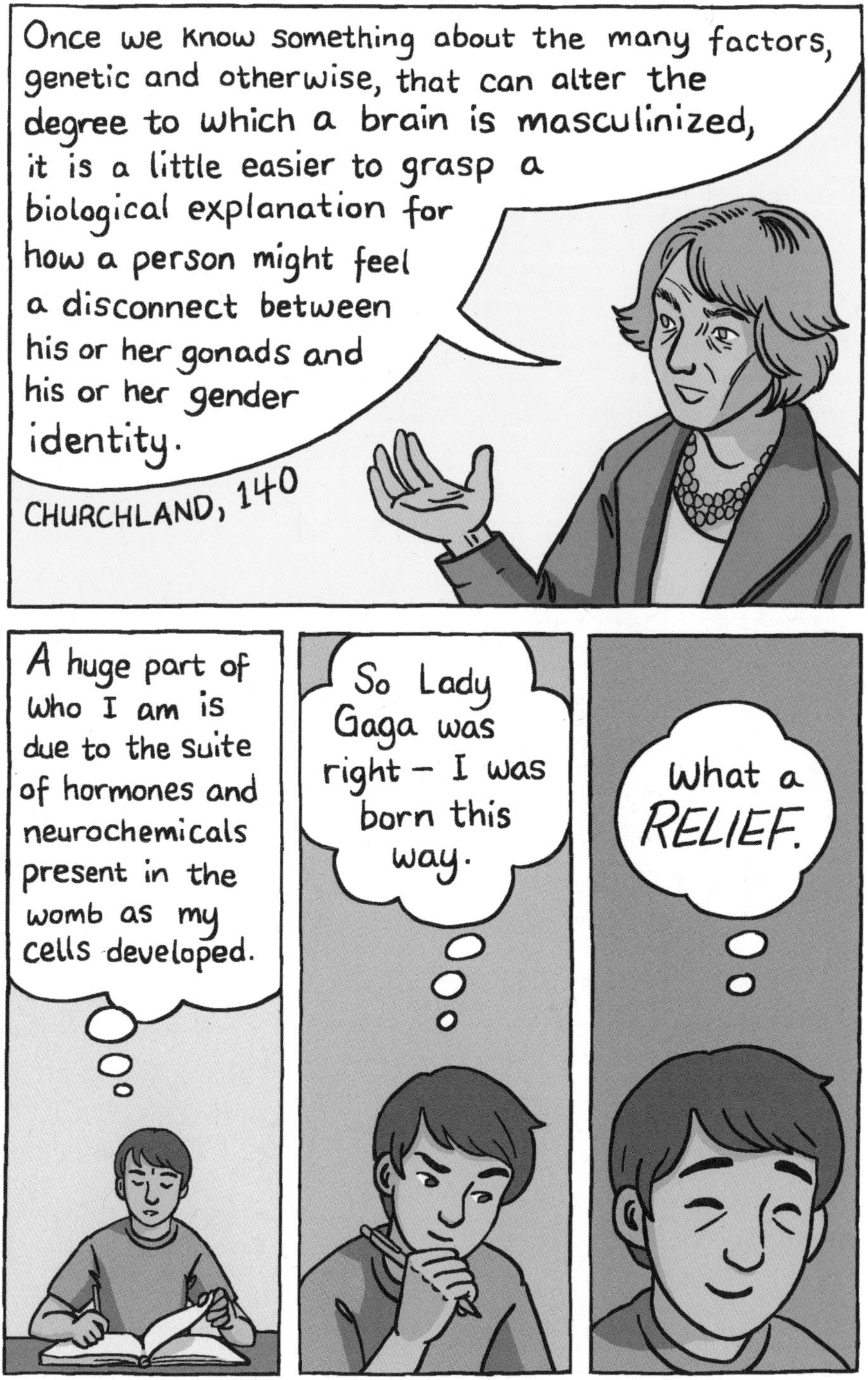
Once we know something about the many factors, genetic and otherwise, that can alter the degree to which a brain is masculinized, it is a little easier to grasp a biological explanation for how a person might feel a disconnect between his or her gonads and his or her gender identity.
CHURCHLAND, 140
A huge part of who I am is due to the suite of hormones and neurochemicals present in the womb as my cells developed.
So Lady Gaga was right – I was born this way.
What a RELIEF.

IN THE SUMMER OF 2016, I TABLED AT THE QUEER COMICS EXPO IN SAN FRANCISCO.

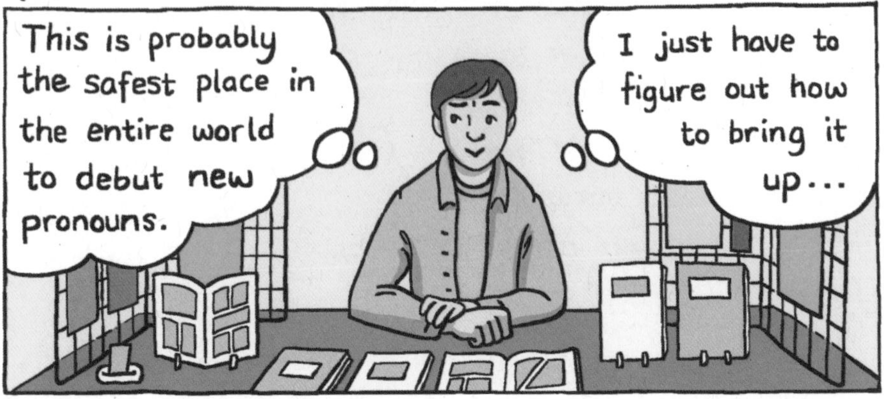
This is probably the safest place in the entire world to debut new pronouns.
I just have to figure out how to bring it up...

LATER, I FOUND SCOUT TRAN'S PRONOUN PATCHES AT THE DEGENDERETTE BOOTH.

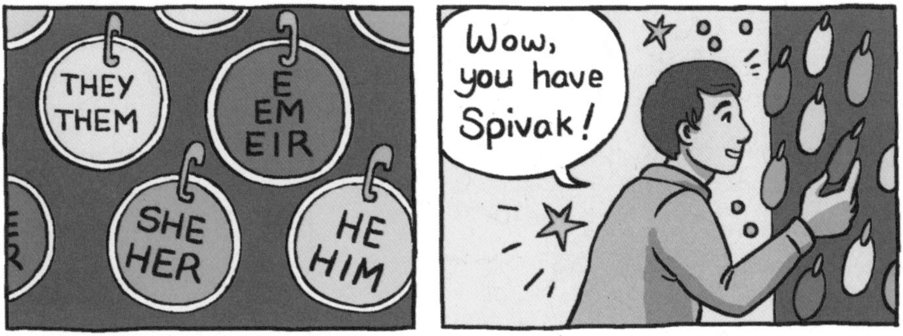
THEY THEM
E EM EIR
SHE HER
HE HIM
Wow, you have Spivak!

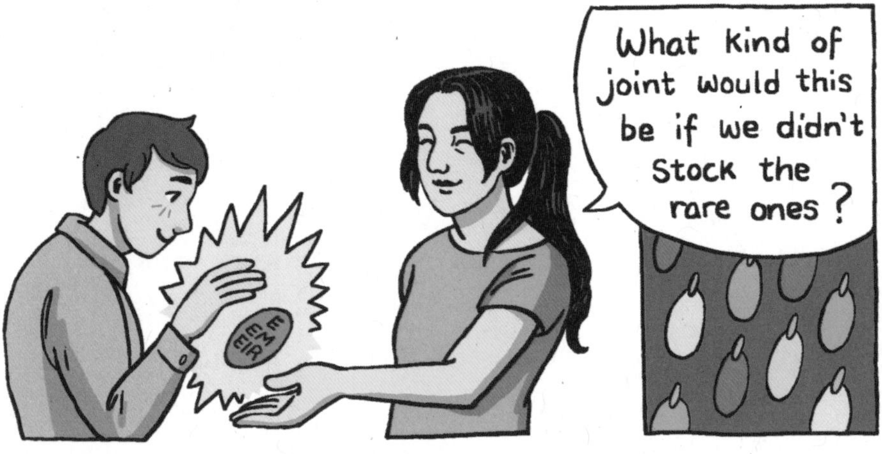
E EM EIR
What kind of joint would this be if we didn't stock the rare ones?

I HAD TO SIT WITH THE PATCH IN MY HAND FOR 20 MINUTES BEFORE I WAS ABLE TO PUT IT ON.

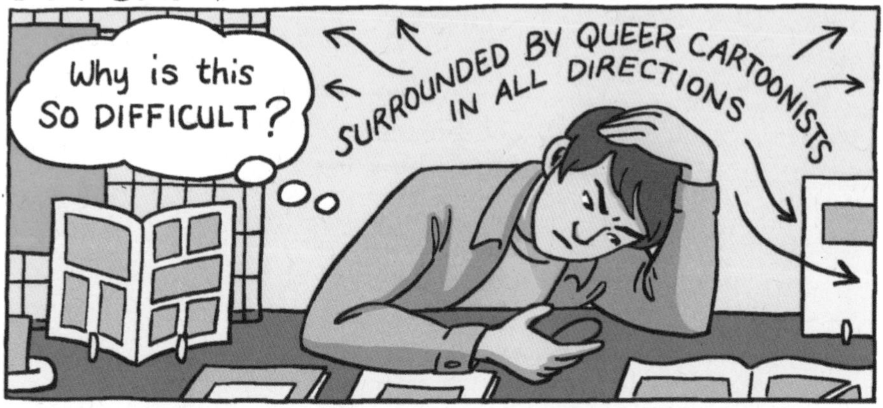
Why is this SO DIFFICULT?
SURROUNDED BY QUEER CARTOONISTS IN ALL DIRECTIONS

LATER, WHILE WEARING IT:

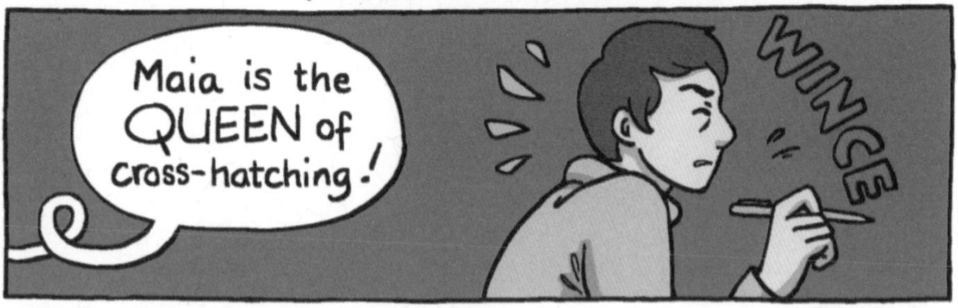
Maia is the QUEEN of cross-hatching!
WINCE

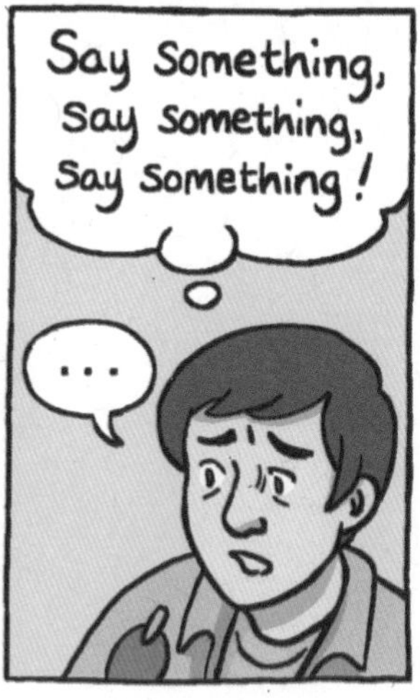
Say Something, Say Something, Say Something!
...

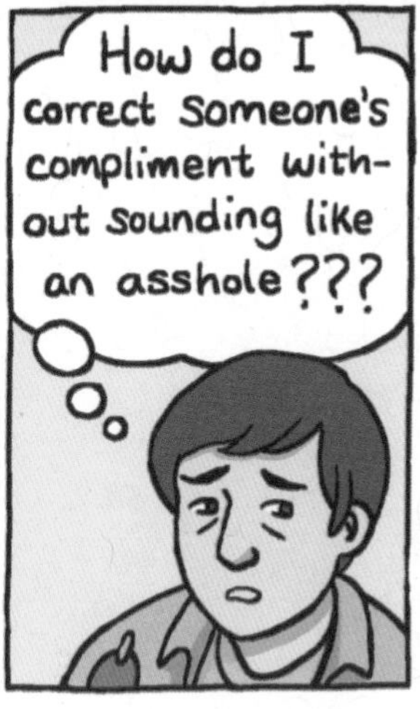
How do I correct Someone's compliment with-out sounding like an asshole???

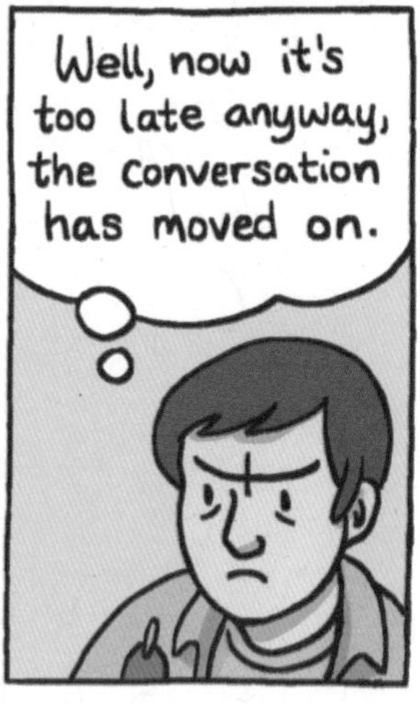
Well, now it's too late anyway, the conversation has moved on.

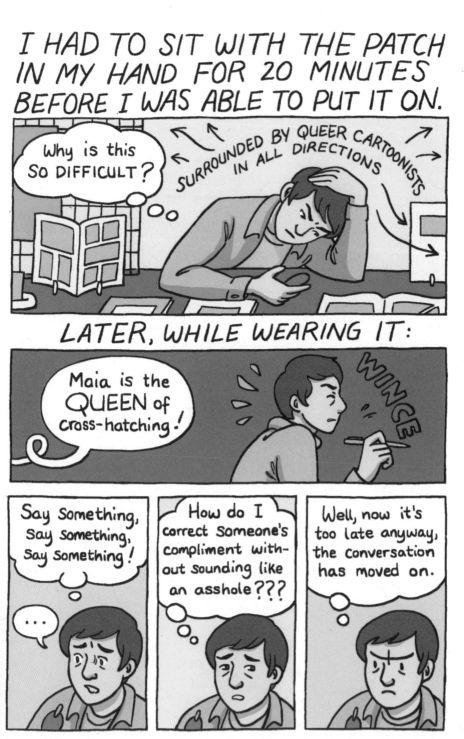

SHORTLY AFTER, AT AN ART OPENING:

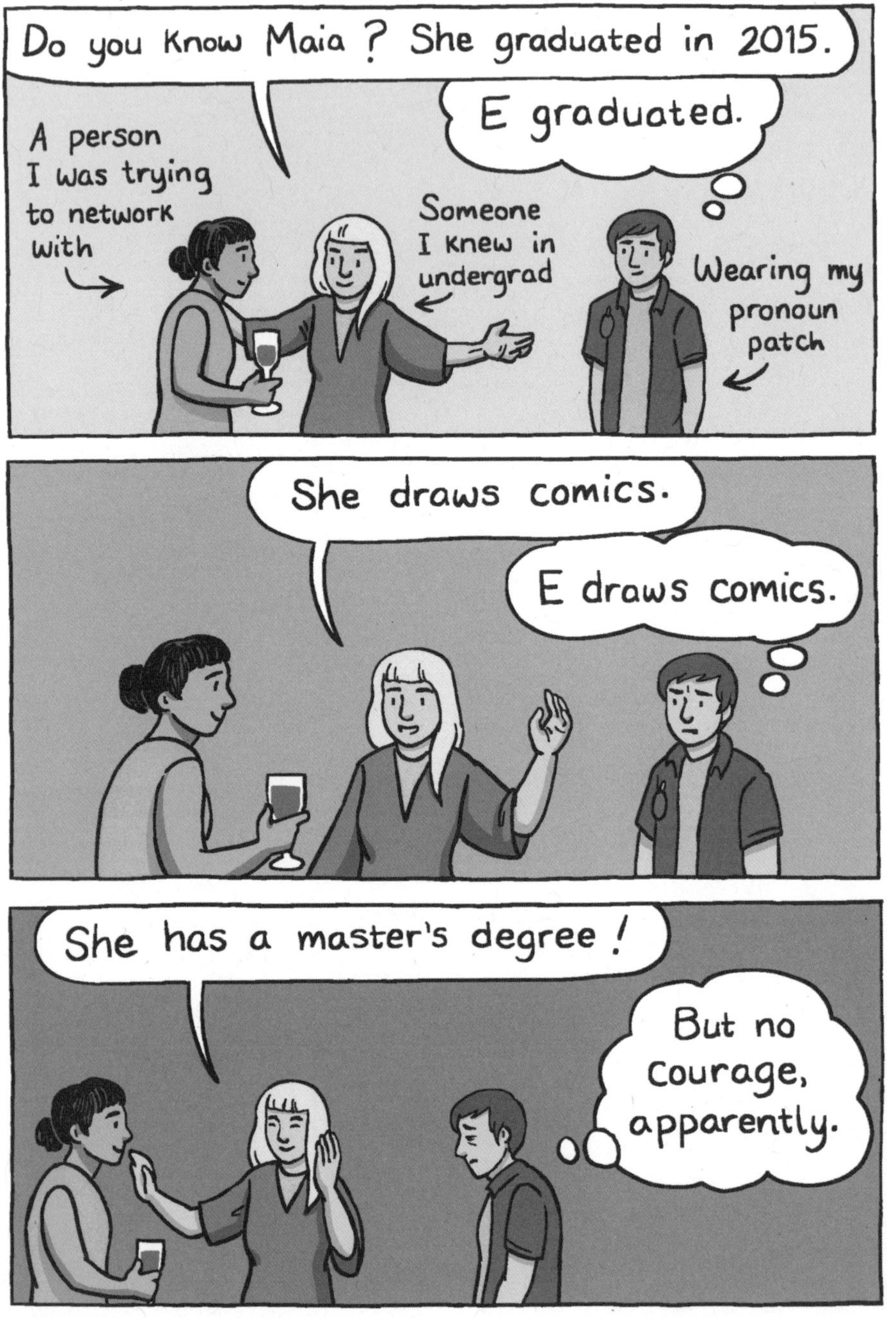
Do you know Maia? She graduated in 2015.
E graduated.
A person I was trying to network with
Someone I knew in undergrad
Wearing my pronoun patch
She draws comics.
E draws comics.
She has a master's degree!
But no courage, apparently.

I FOUND MYSELF TURNING TO METAPHORS OF MILD PHYSICAL PAIN AS I TRIED TO ARTICULATE WHY I WANTED NEW PRONOUNS.

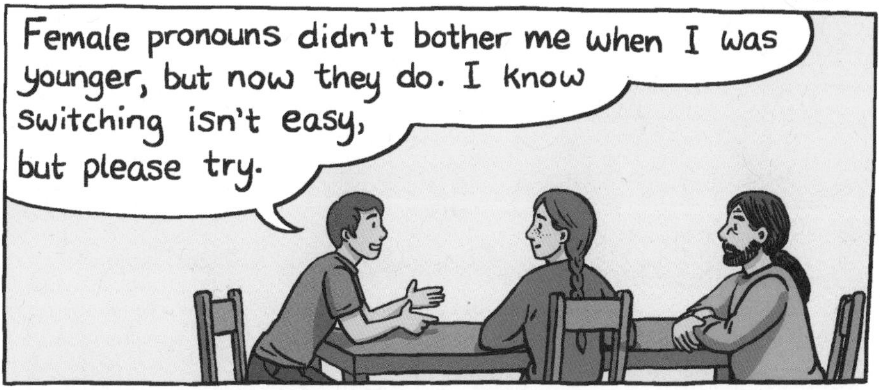
Female pronouns didn't bother me when I was younger, but now they do. I know switching isn't easy, but please try.

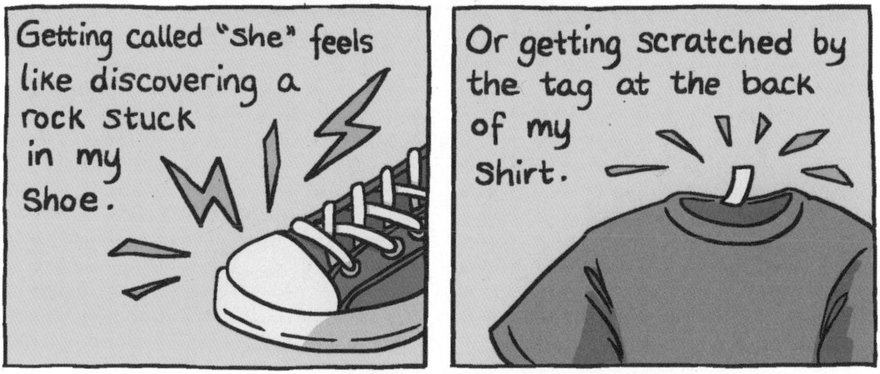
Getting called "she" feels like discovering a rock stuck in my shoe.
Or getting scratched by the tag at the back of my shirt.

A SMALL SPIKE OF SOLVABLE DISCOMFORT.

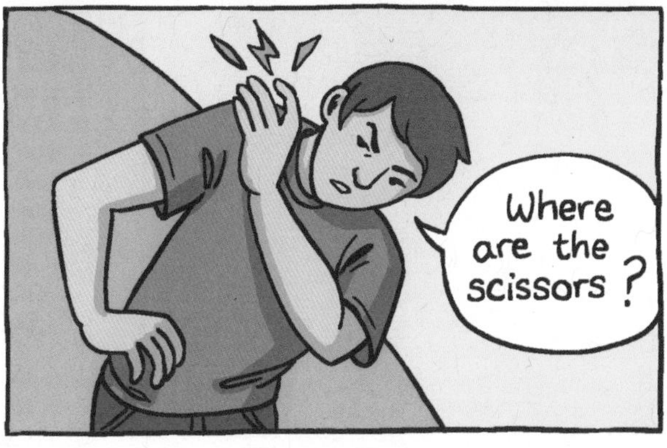
Where are the scissors?

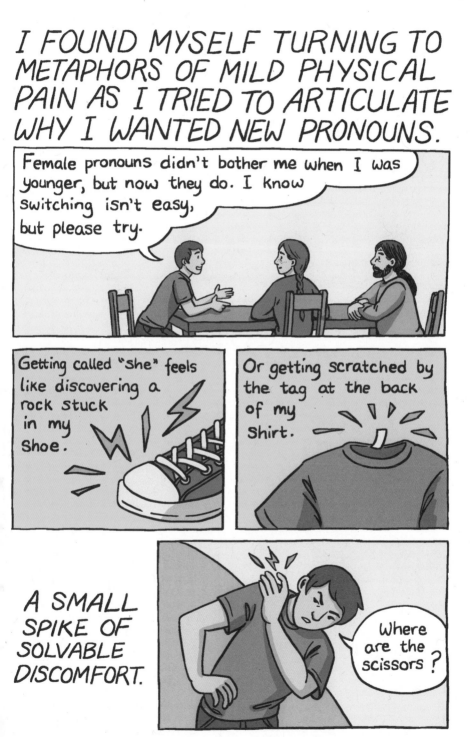

ALSO IN 2016, ASHLEY AND I WERE INVITED TO SIGN AT A PUBLISHER'S BOOTH AT COMIC CON FOR THE FIRST TIME.

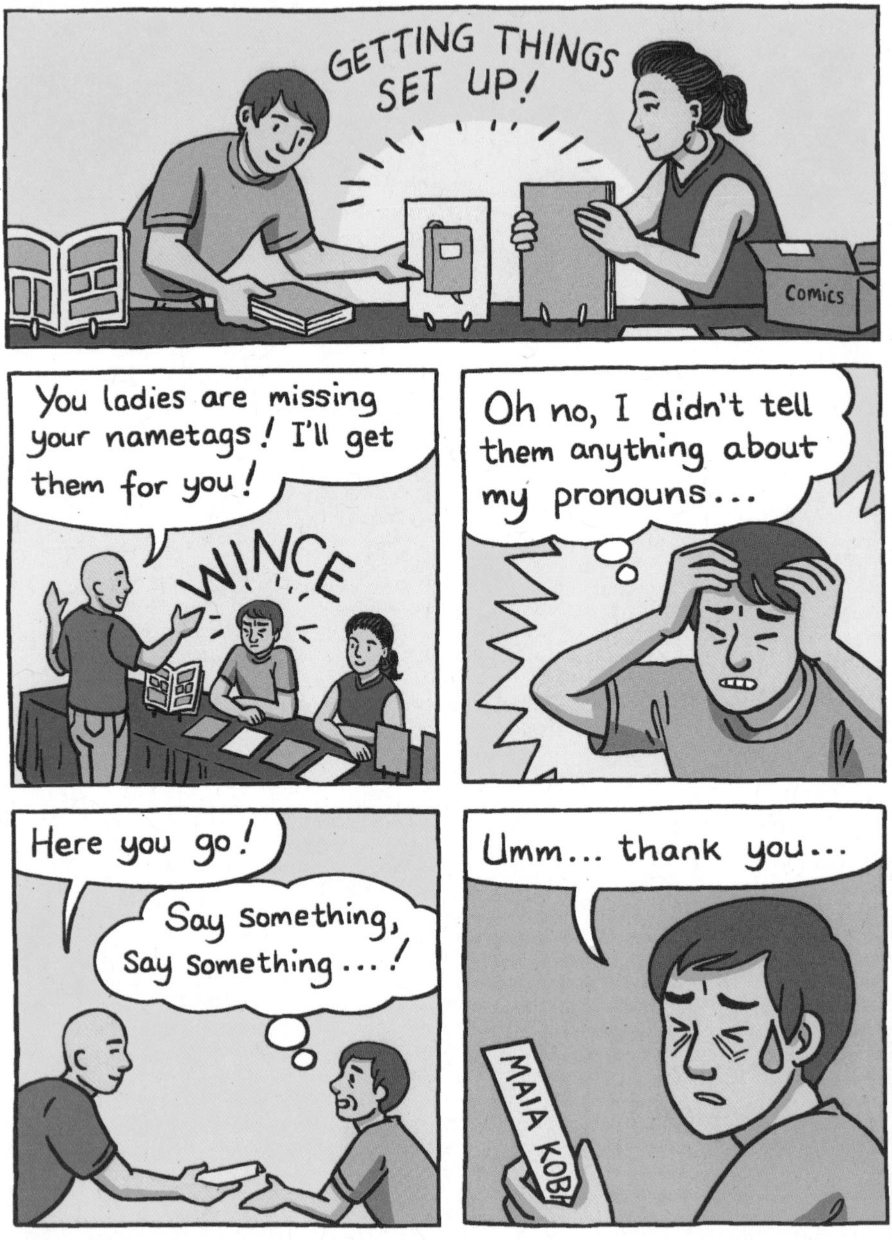
GETTING THINGS SET UP!
COMICS
You ladies are missing your nametags! I'll get them for you!
WINCE
Oh no, I didn't tell them anything about my pronouns...
Here you go!
Say something, say something...!
Umm... thank you...
MAIA KOBA

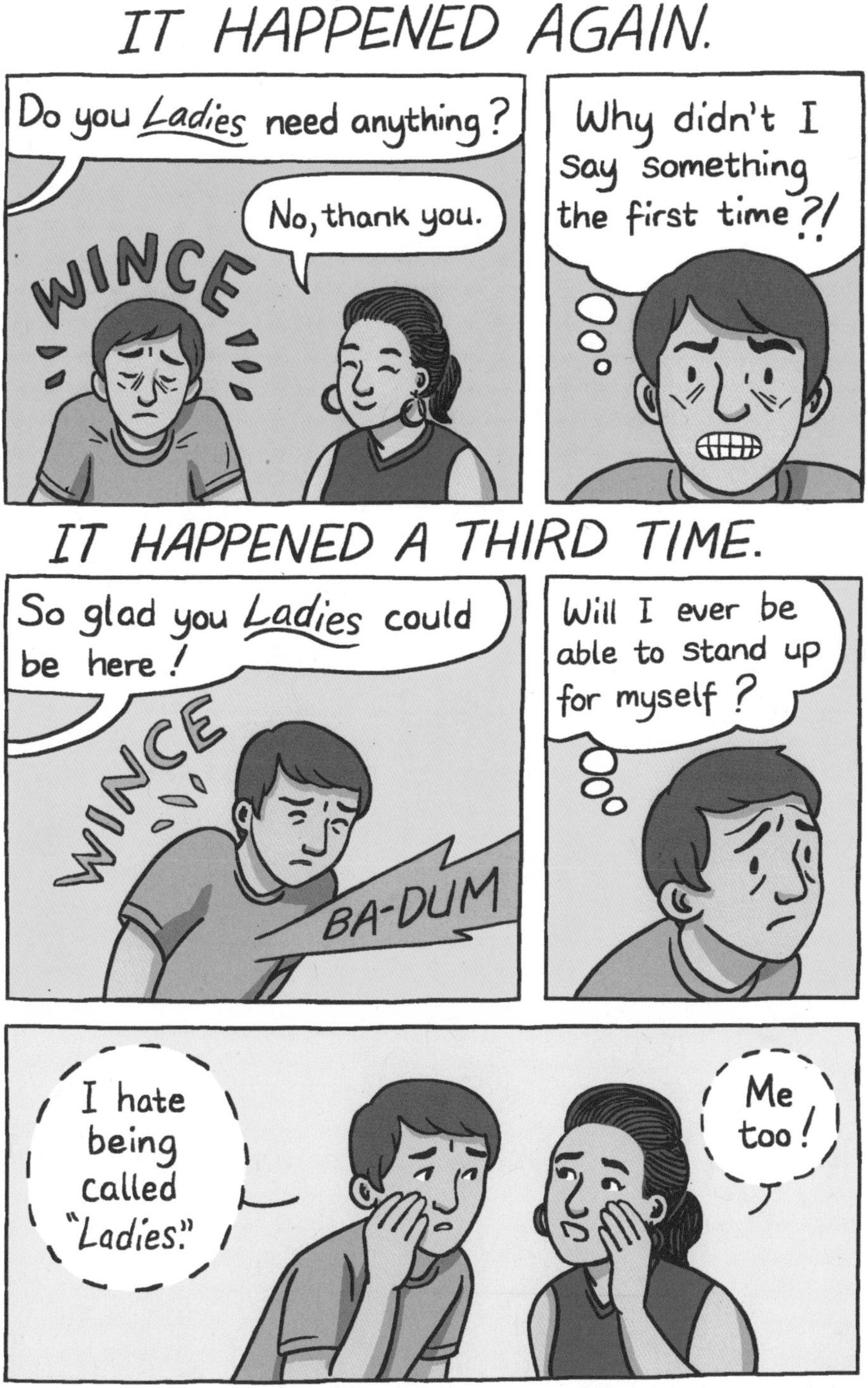
IT HAPPENED AGAIN.
Do you Ladies need anything?
No, thank you.
WINCE
Why didn't I say something the first time?!
IT HAPPENED A THIRD TIME.
So glad you Ladies could be here!
WINCE
BA-DUM
Will I ever be able to stand up for myself?
I hate being called "Ladies."
Me too!

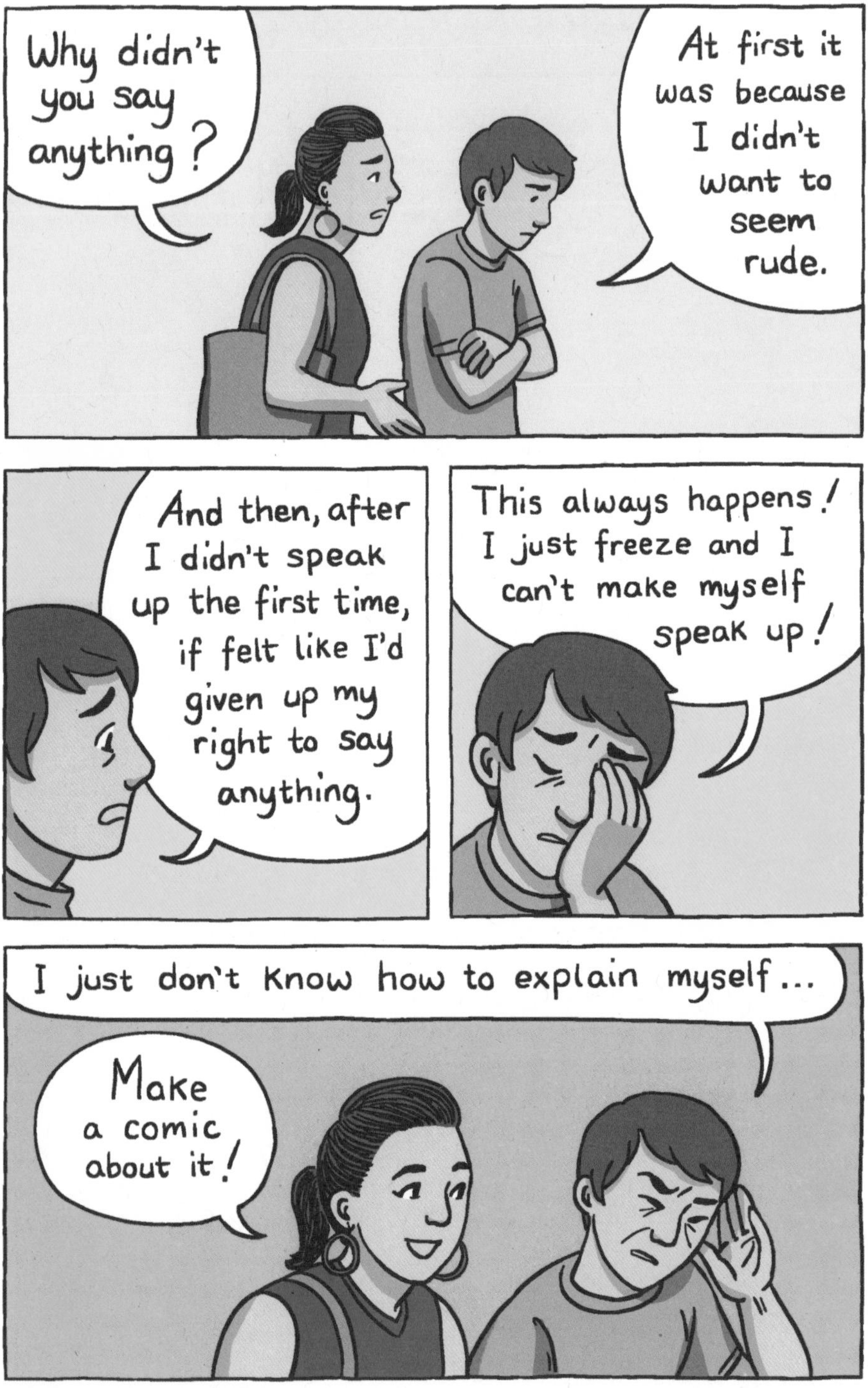
Why didn't you say anything?
At first it was because I didn't want to seem rude.
And then, after I didn't speak up the first time, if felt like I'd given up my right to say anything.
This always happens! I just freeze and I can't make myself speak up!
I just don't know how to explain myself...
Make a comic about it!

PHOEBE & AMILA CAME TO STAY IN WINTER 2016. ON CHRISTMAS EVE:

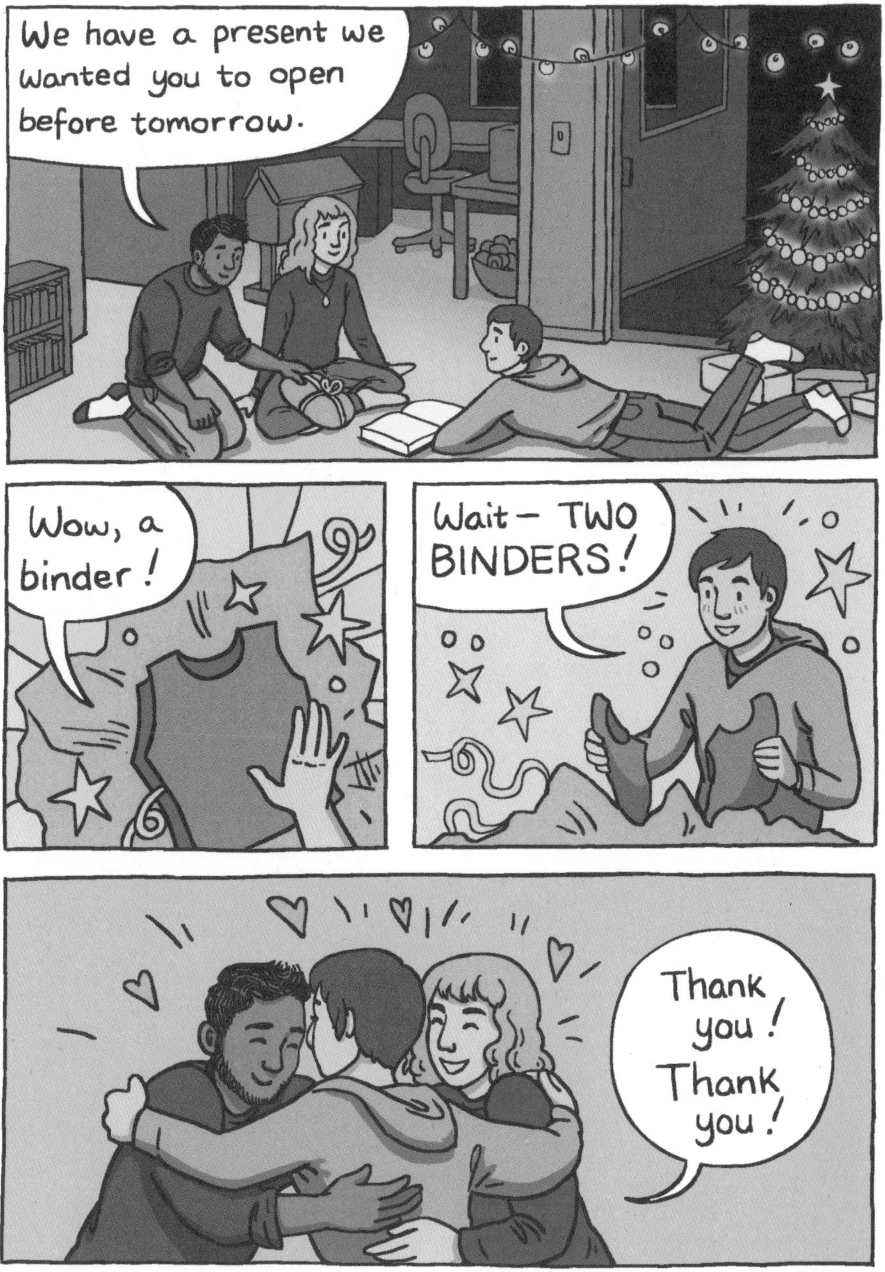
We have a present we wanted you to open before tomorrow.
Wow, a binder!
Wait— TWO BINDERS!
Thank you! Thank you!

IN JANUARY, I WORE A BINDER TO WORK FOR THE FIRST TIME

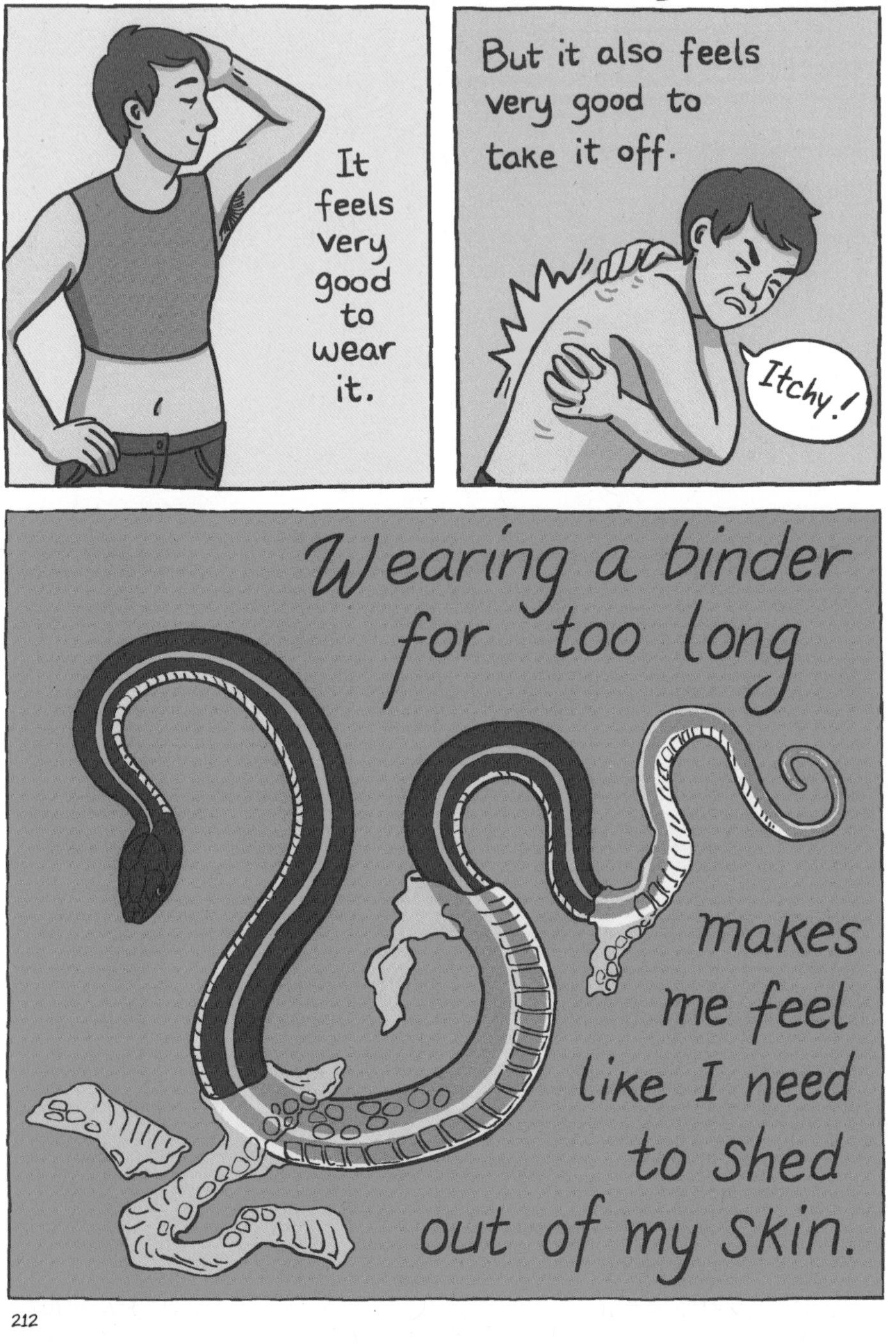
It feels very good to wear it.
But it also feels very good to take it off.
Itchy!
Wearing a binder for too long
makes me feel like I need to Shed out of my skin.

AS SENIORS IN HIGH SCHOOL,
I REMEMBER ALL OF MY CLASSMATES PLANNING WHAT TATTOOS THEY WANTED AS SOON AS THEY TURNED 18.

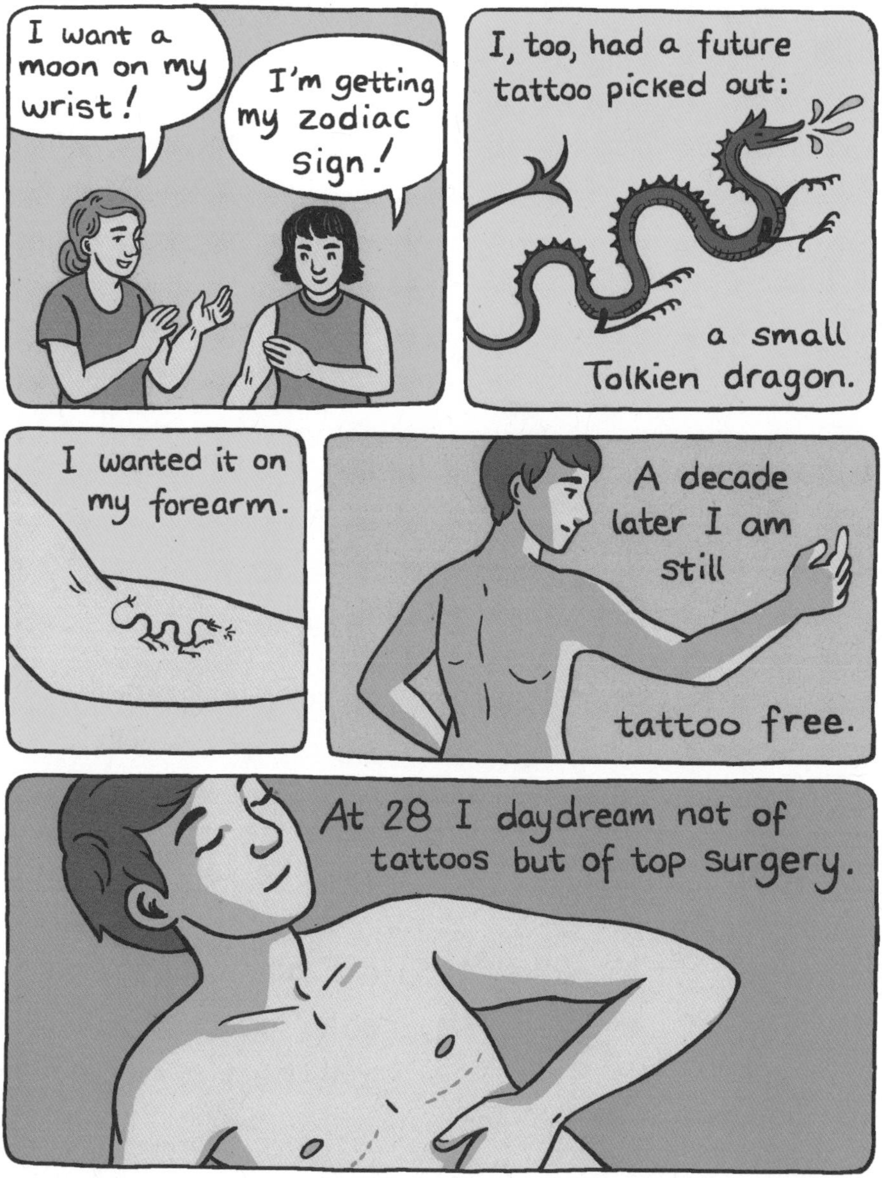
I want a moon on my wrist!
I'm getting my zodiac sign!
I, too, had a future tattoo picked out:
a small Tolkien dragon.
I wanted it on my forearm.
A decade later I am still
tattoo free.
At 28 I daydream not of tattoos but of top surgery.

MY PARENTS ARE GETTING A LITTLE BETTER WITH MY PRONOUNS BUT THEY STILL SLIP UP

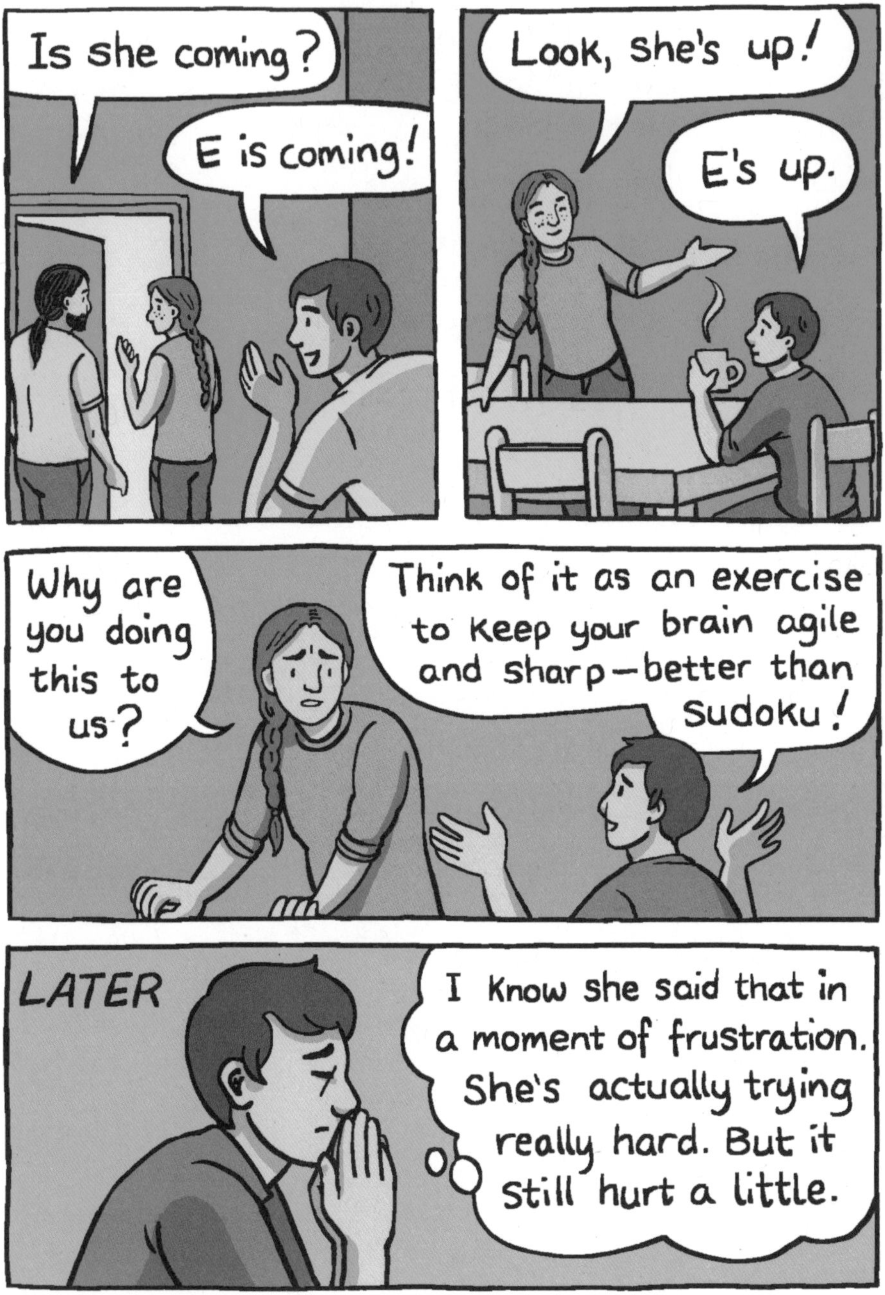
Is she coming?
E is coming!
Look, she's up!
E's up.
Why are you doing this to us?
Think of it as an exercise to keep your brain agile and sharp—better than Sudoku!
LATER
I know she said that in a moment of frustration. She's actually trying really hard. But it still hurt a little.

THE FIRST TIME I SAW MYSELF REFERRED TO AS "E" IN A WORK EMAIL

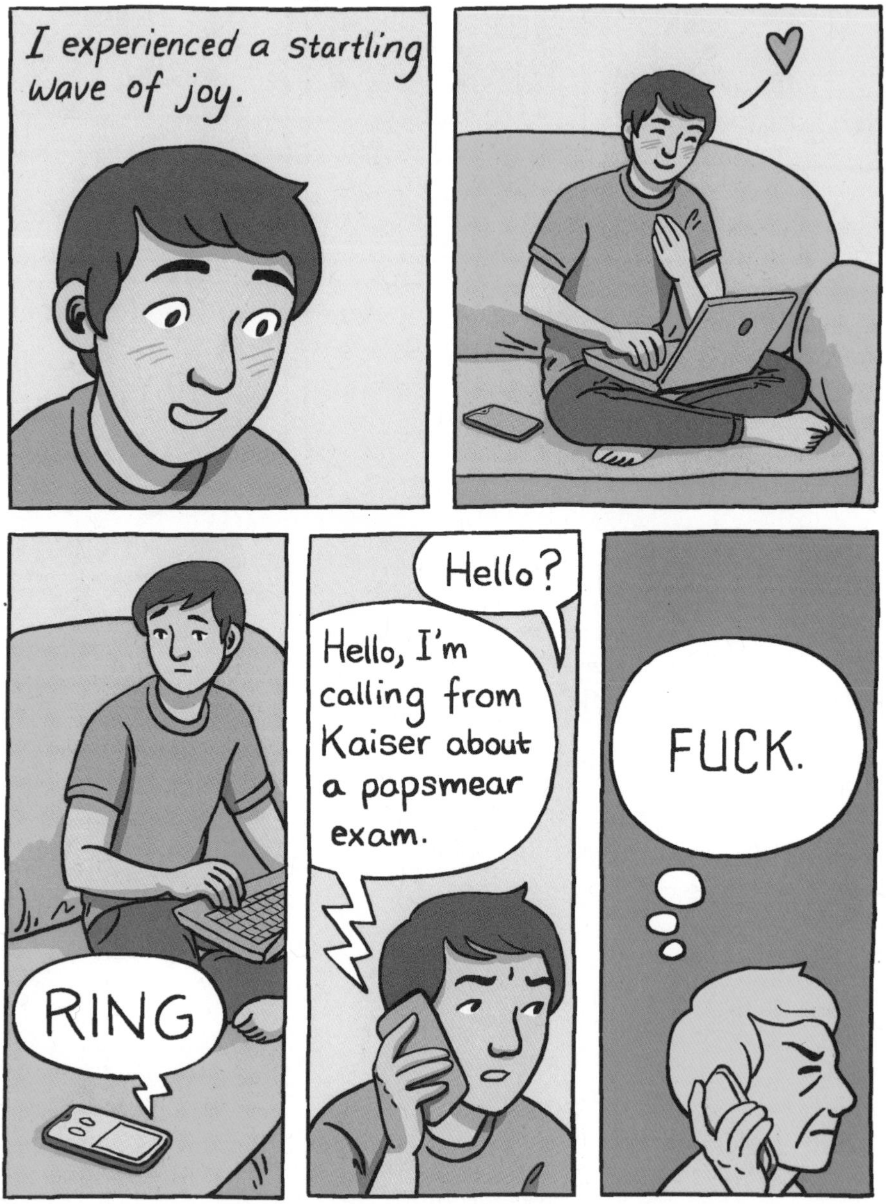

I experienced a startling wave of joy.
RING
Hello?
Hello, I'm calling from Kaiser about a papsmear exam.
FUCK.

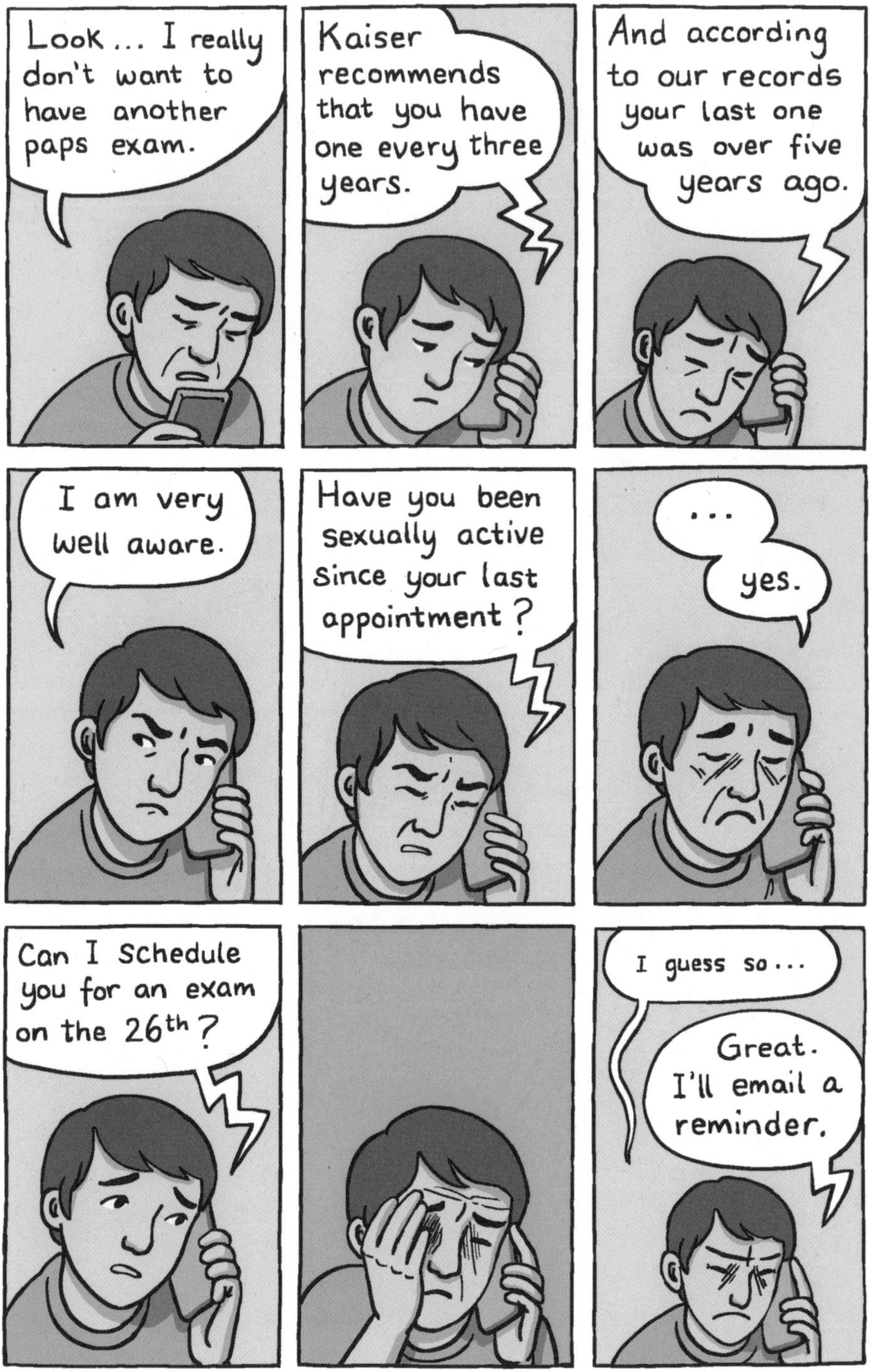
Look... I really don't want to have another paps exam.
Kaiser recommends that you have one every three years.
And according to our records your last one was over five years ago.
I am very well aware.
Have you been sexually active since your last appointment?
...
yes.
Can I schedule you for an exam on the 26th?
I guess so...
Great. I'll email a reminder.

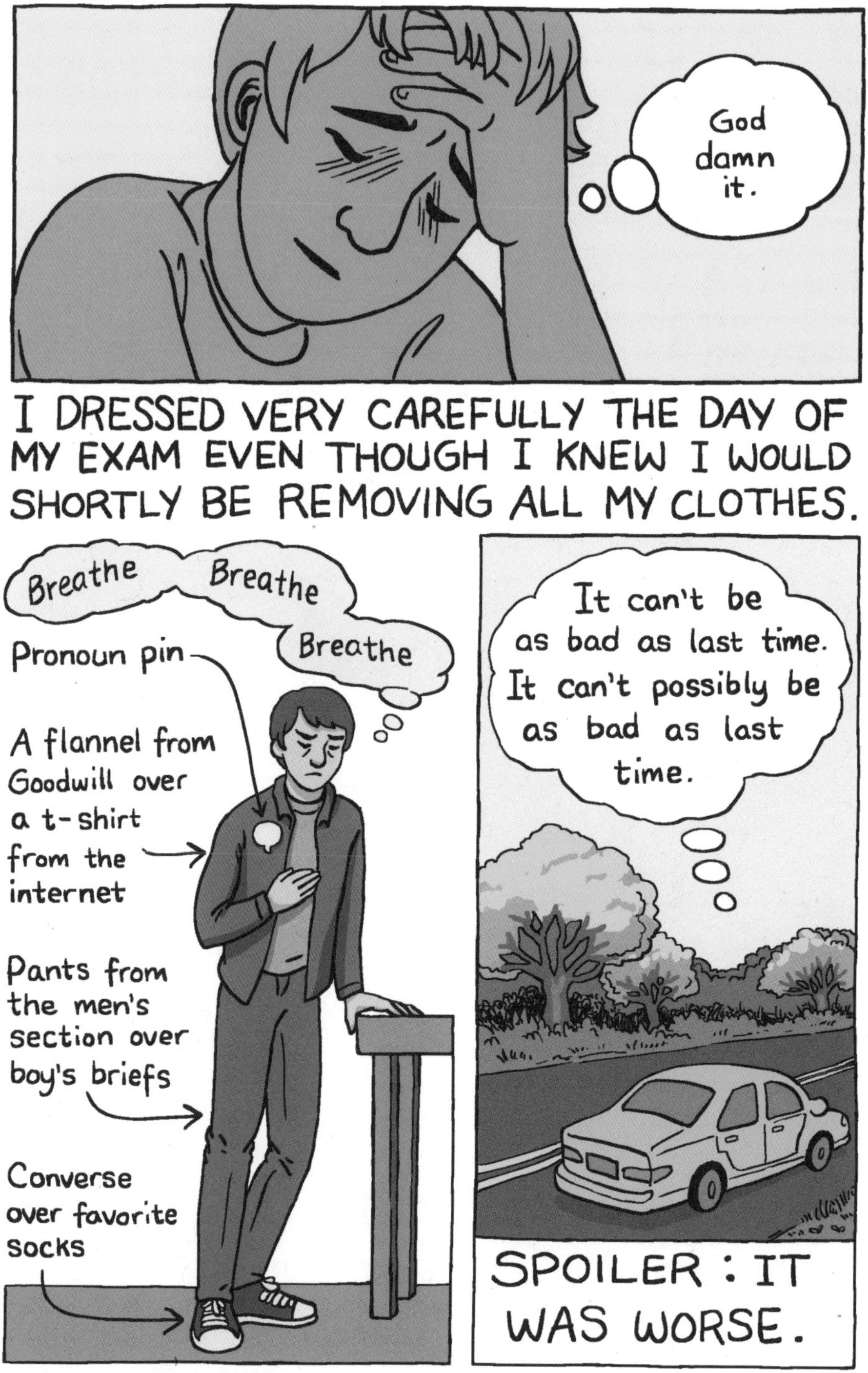
God damn it.
I DRESSED VERY CAREFULLY THE DAY OF MY EXAM EVEN THOUGH I KNEW I WOULD SHORTLY BE REMOVING ALL MY CLOTHES.
Breathe Breathe Breathe
Pronoun pin
A flannel from Goodwill over a t-shirt from the internet
Pants from the men's section over boy's briefs
Converse over favorite socks
It can't be as bad as last time. It can't possibly be as bad as last time.
SPOILER : IT WAS WORSE.

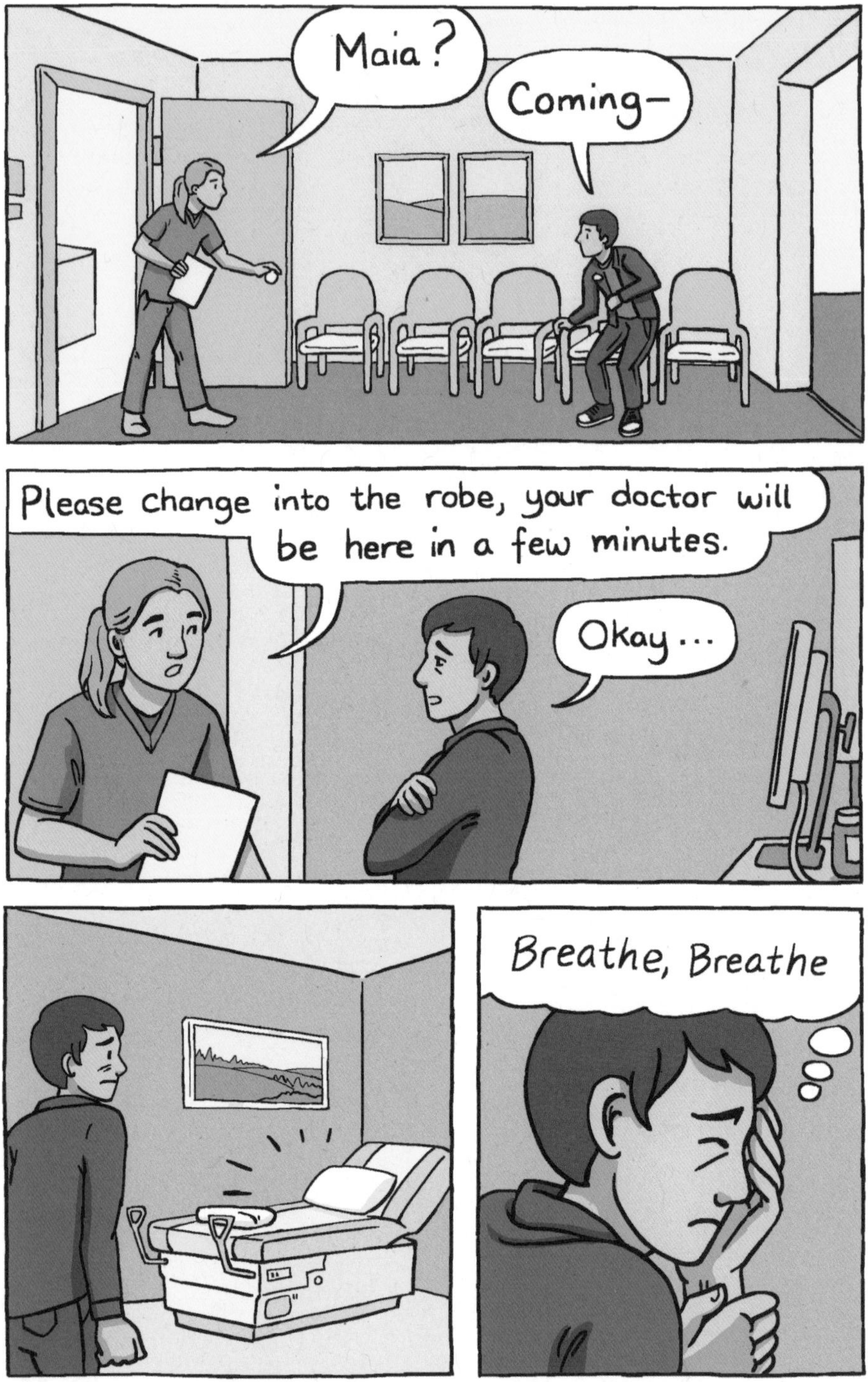
Maia?
Coming–
Please change into the robe, your doctor will be here in a few minutes.
Okay...
Breathe, Breathe

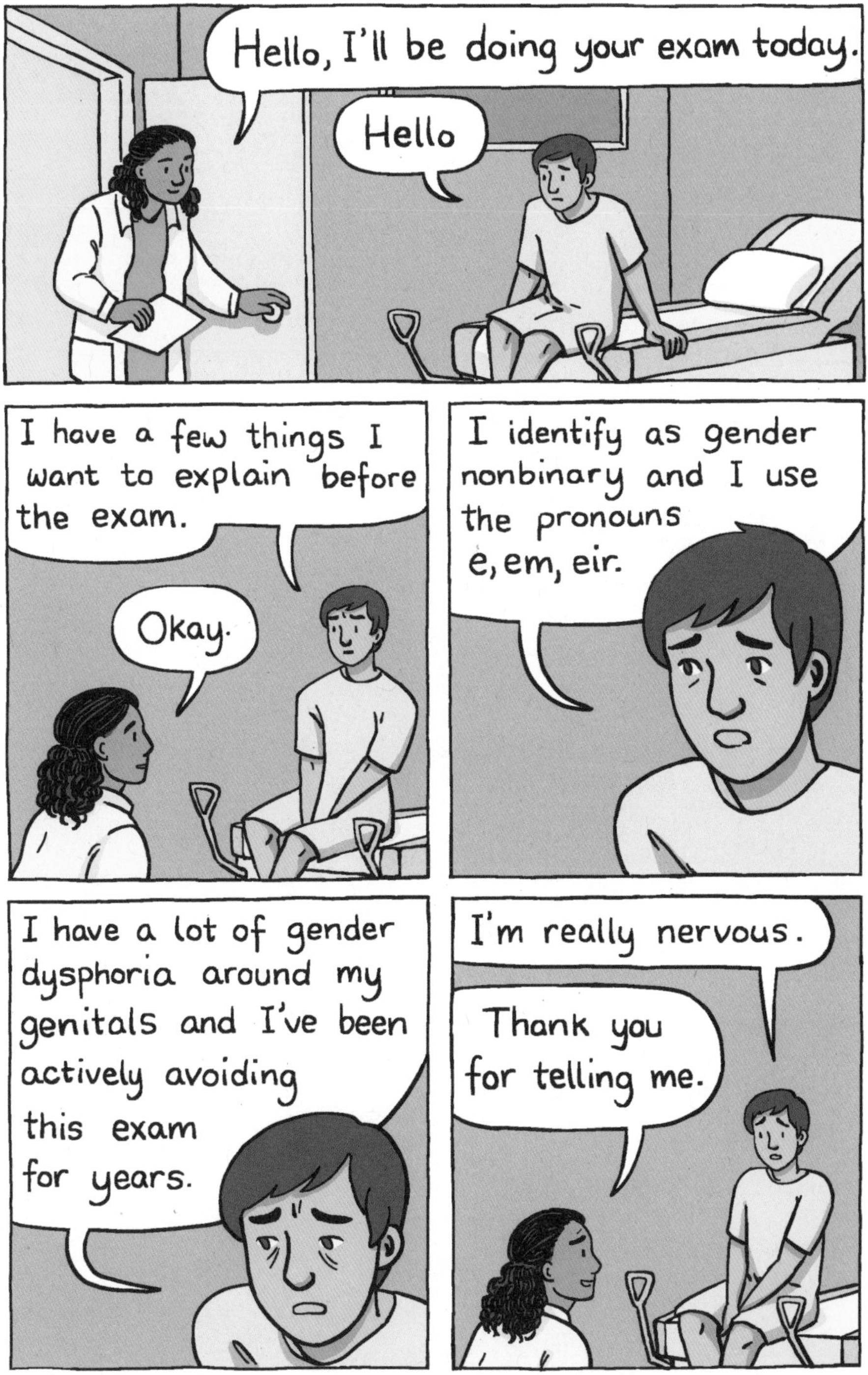
Hello, I'll be doing your exam today.
Hello
I have a few things I want to explain before the exam.
Okay.
I identify as gender nonbinary and I use the pronouns e, em, eir.
I have a lot of gender dysphoria around my genitals and I've been actively avoiding this exam for years.
I'm really nervous.
Thank you for telling me.

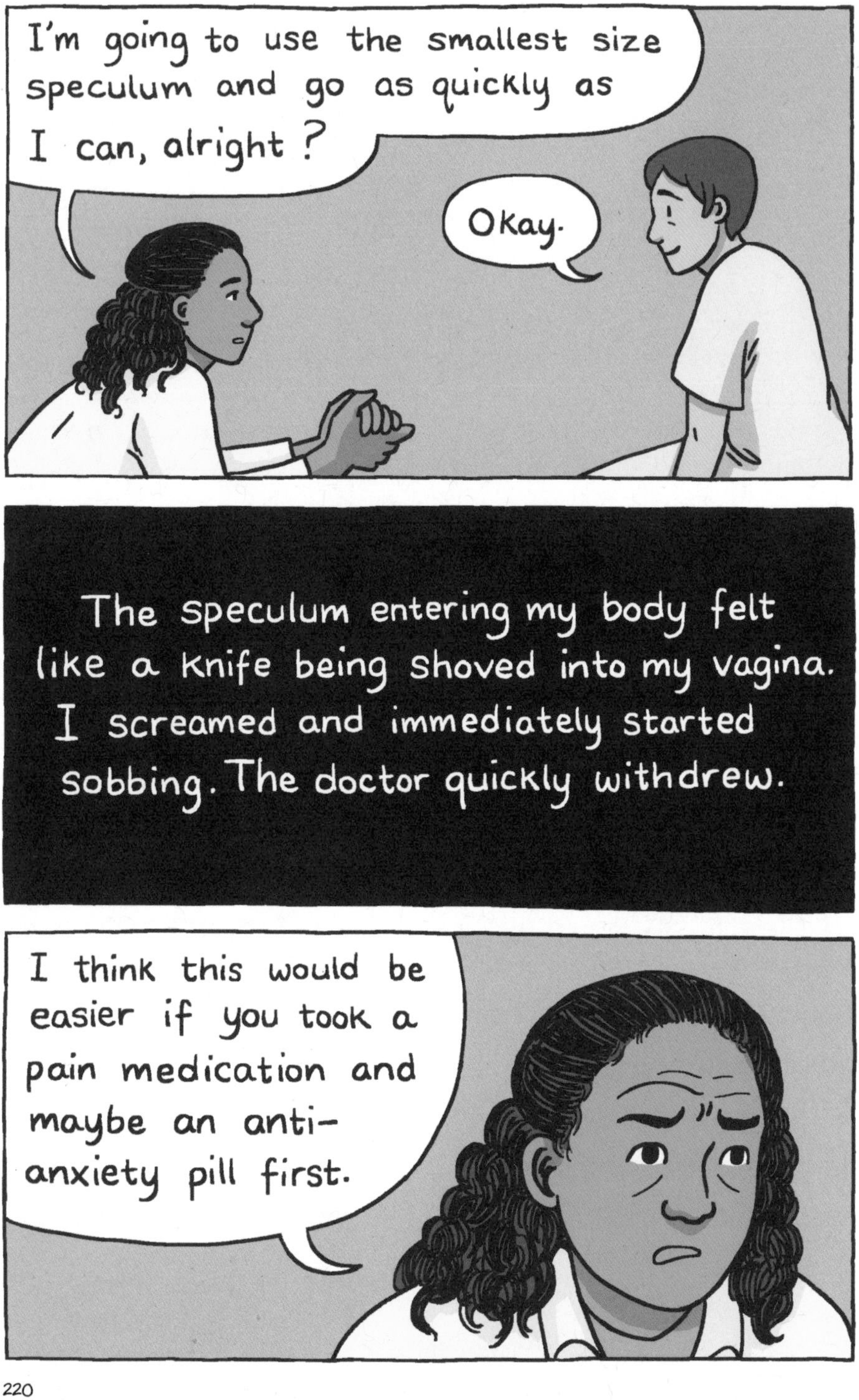
I'm going to use the smallest size speculum and go as quickly as I can, alright?
Okay.
The speculum entering my body felt like a knife being shoved into my vagina. I screamed and immediately started sobbing. The doctor quickly withdrew.
I think this would be easier if you took a pain medication and maybe an anti-anxiety pill first.

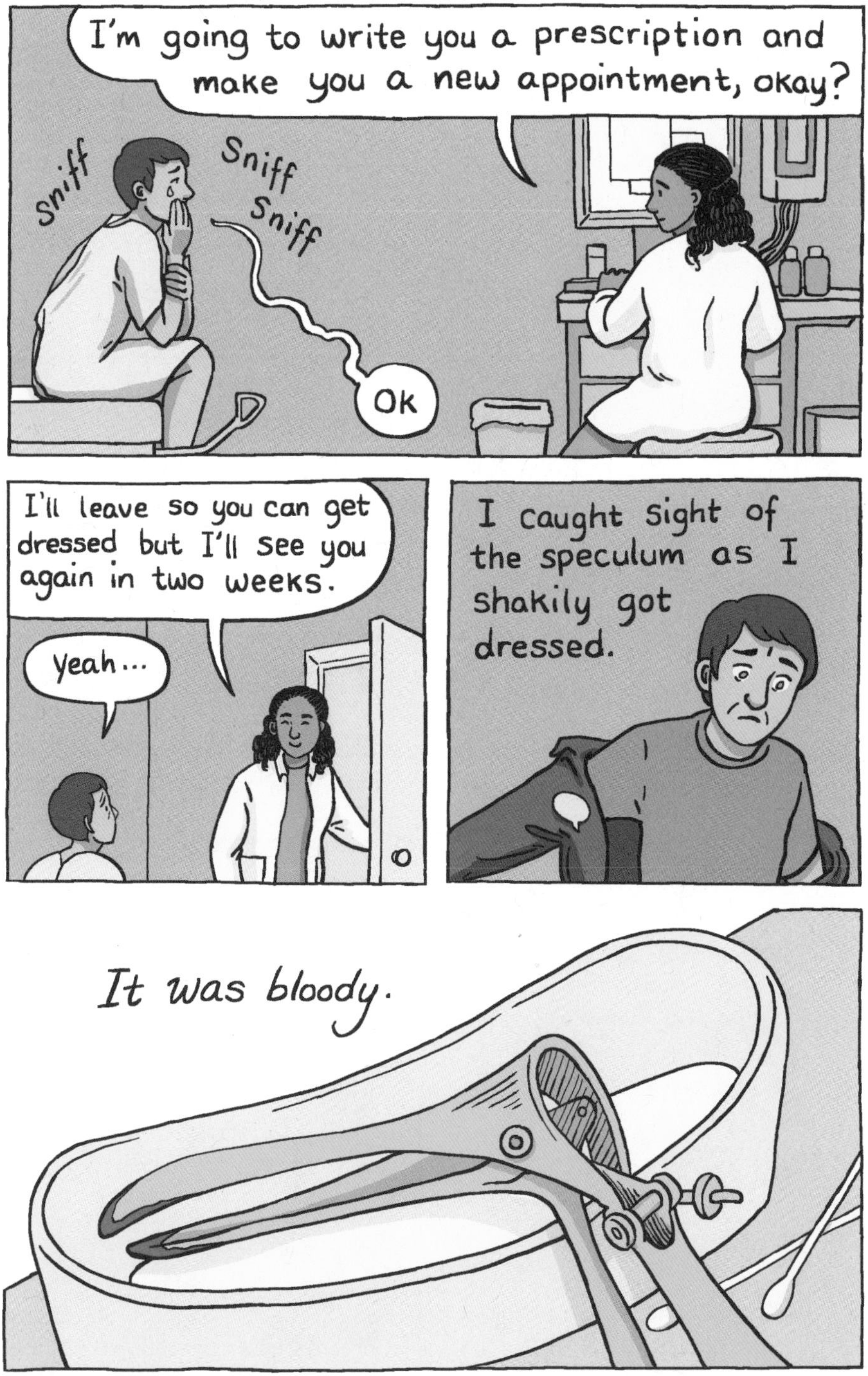
I'm going to write you a prescription and make you a new appointment, okay?
Sniff
Sniff
Sniff
Ok
I'll leave so you can get dressed but I'll see you again in two weeks.
yeah...
I caught sight of the speculum as I shakily got dressed.
It was bloody.

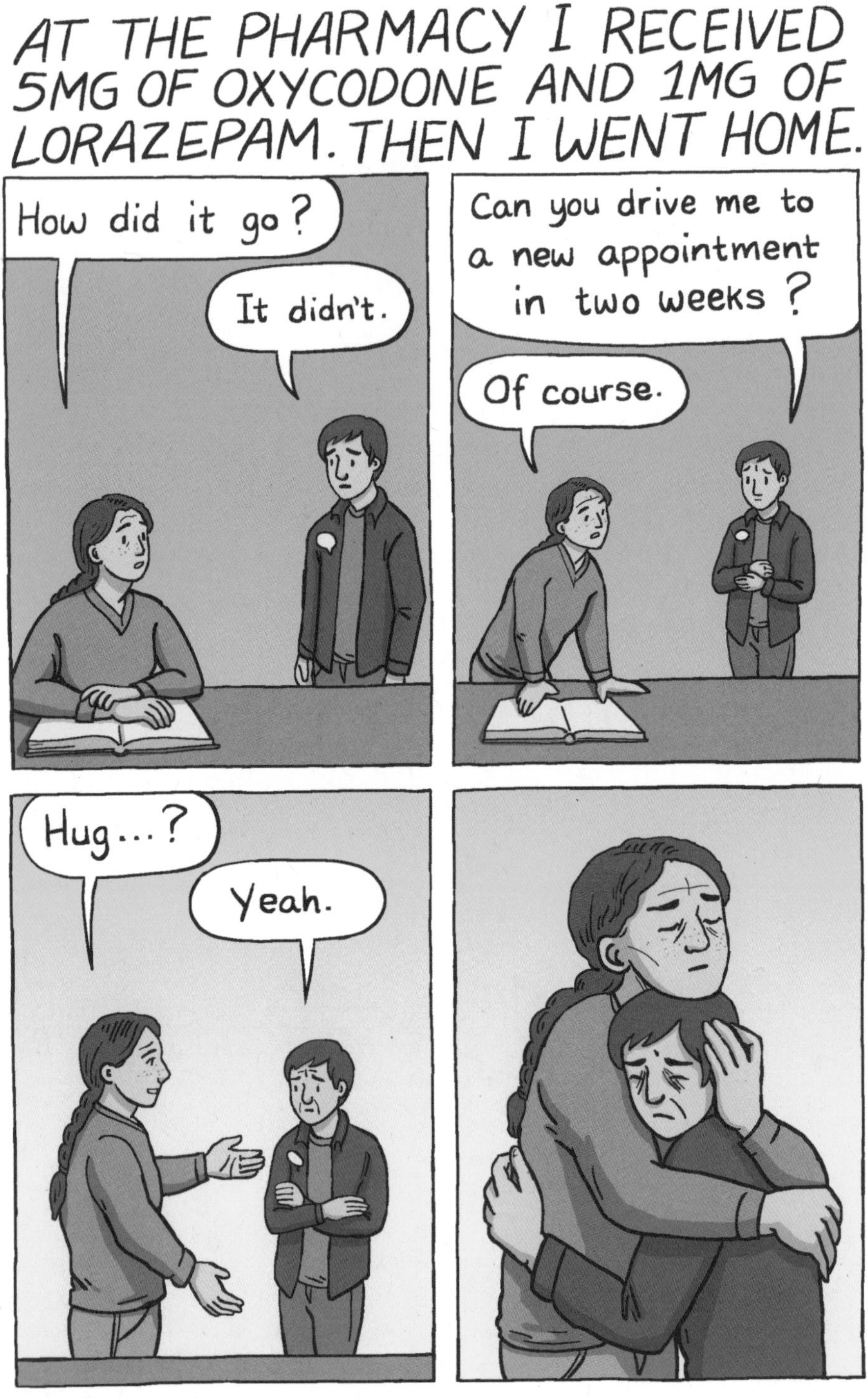
AT THE PHARMACY I RECEIVED 5MG OF OXYCODONE AND 1MG OF LORAZEPAM. THEN I WENT HOME.
How did it go?
It didn't.
Can you drive me to a new appointment in two weeks?
Of course.
Hug...?
Yeah.

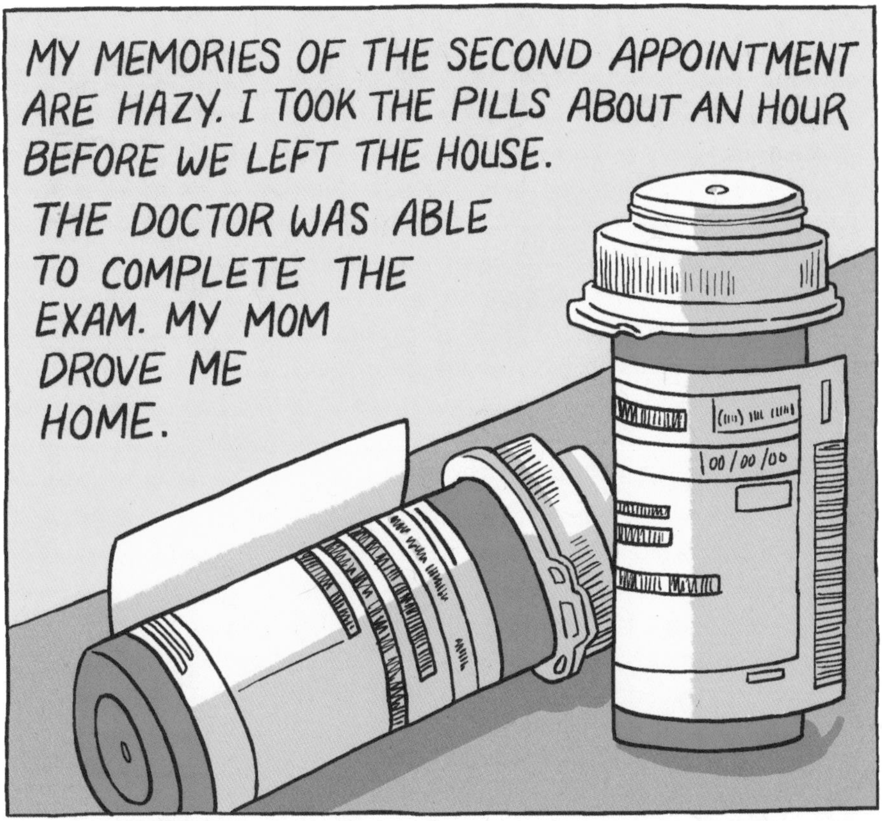
MY MEMORIES OF THE SECOND APPOINTMENT ARE HAZY. I TOOK THE PILLS ABOUT AN HOUR BEFORE WE LEFT THE HOUSE.
THE DOCTOR WAS ABLE TO COMPLETE THE EXAM. MY MOM DROVE ME HOME.
00/00/00

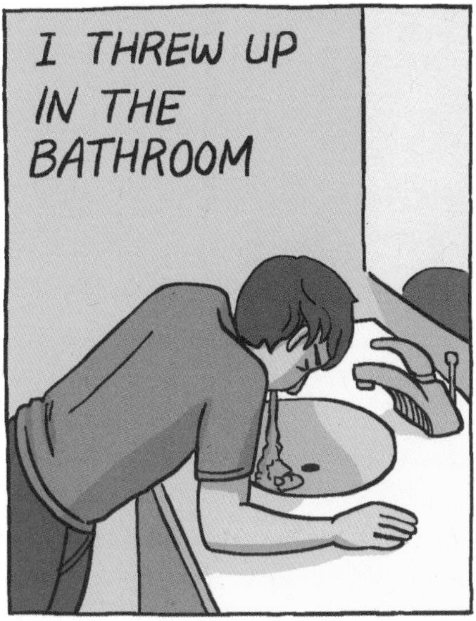
I THREW UP IN THE BATHROOM

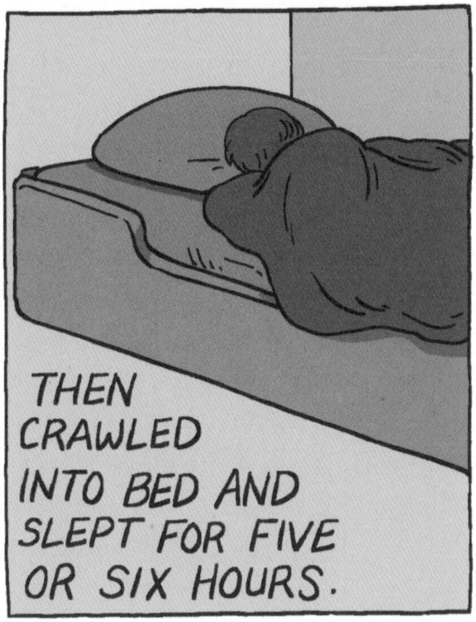
THEN CRAWLED INTO BED AND SLEPT FOR FIVE OR SIX HOURS.

A FEW WEEKS LATER

I RECEIVED A VERY SHORT LETTER FROM MY DOCTOR: THE RESULTS OF MY EXAMINATION WERE NORMAL. NOTHING TO REPORT.

IN SPRING 2017, I ATTENDED A MARCH FOR TRANS RIGHTS IN MY MIDDLE-SIZED LIBERAL HOMETOWN.

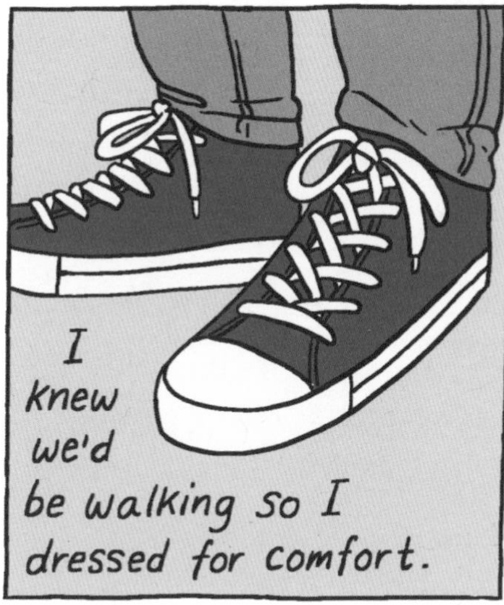
I knew we'd be walking so I dressed for comfort.

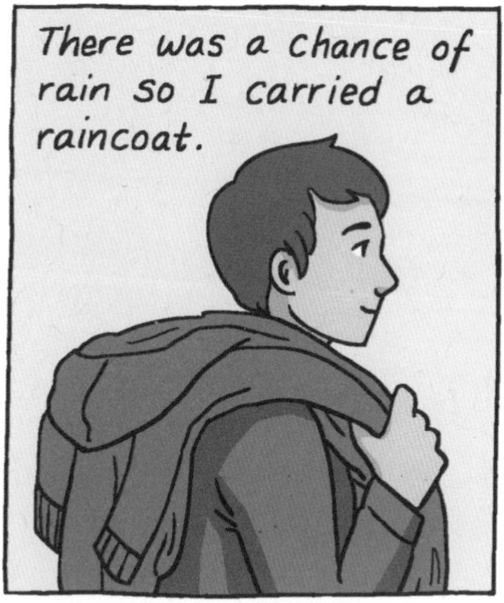
There was a chance of rain so I carried a raincoat.

WHEN I ARRIVED IT SEEMED LIKE EVERYONE HAD DRESSED UP EXCEPT ME.

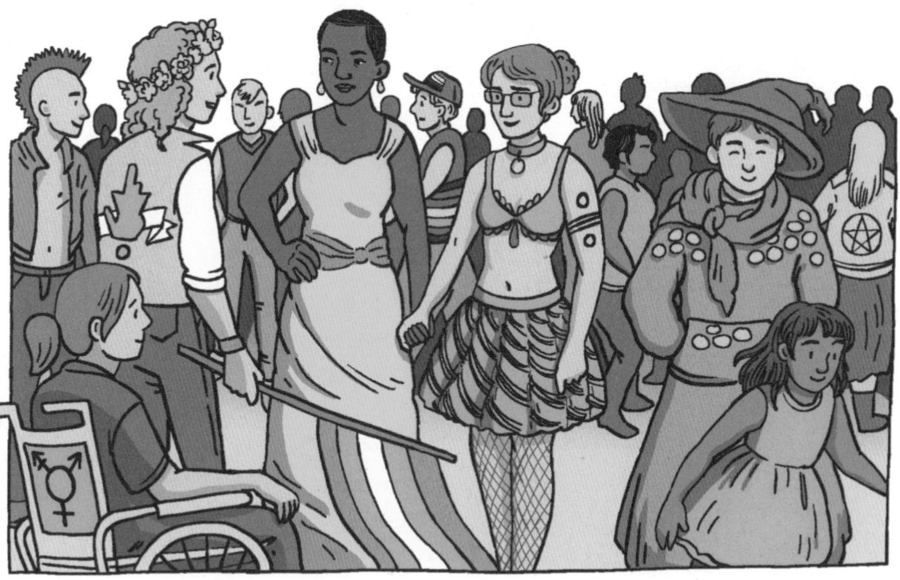

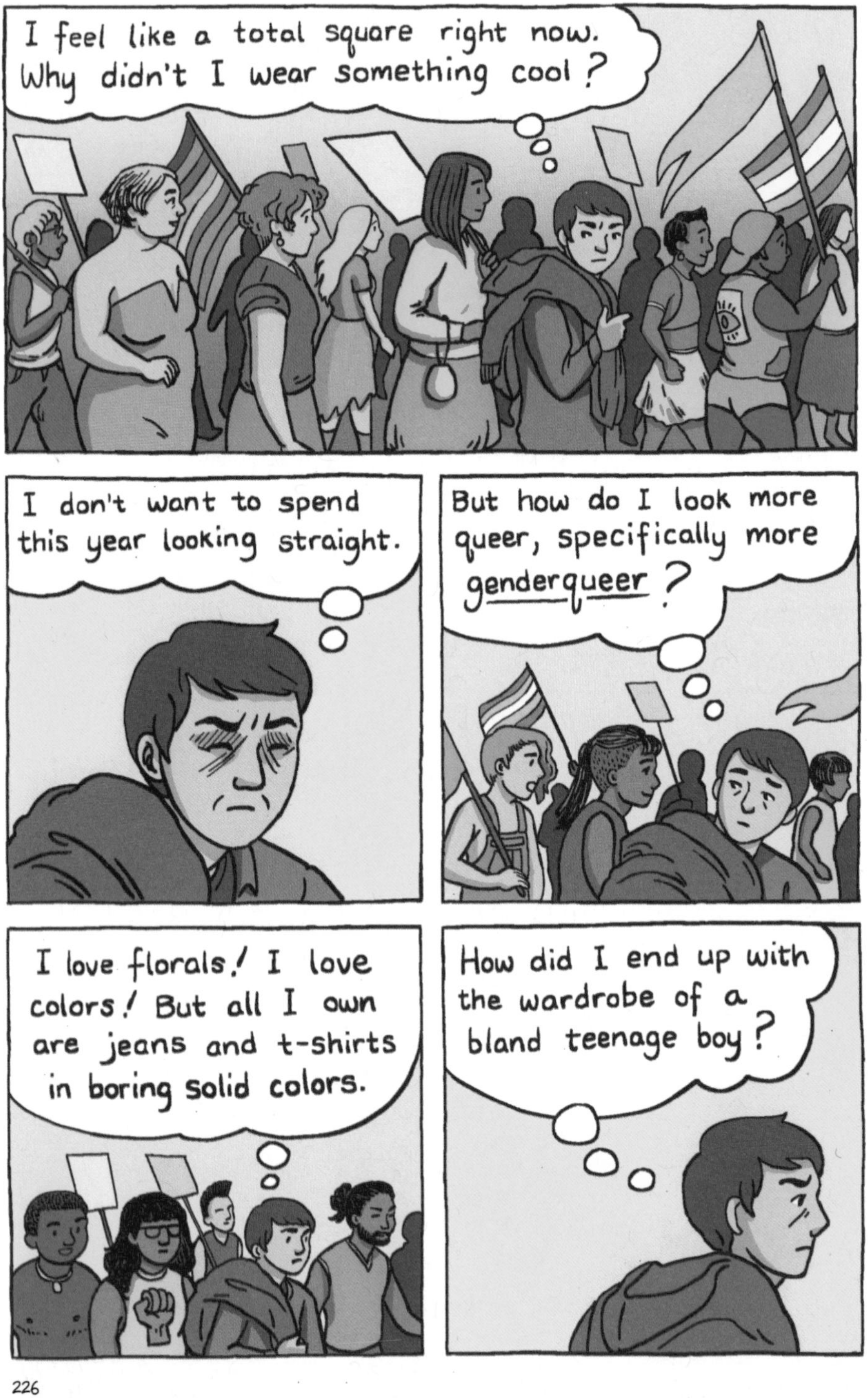

I feel like a total square right now. Why didn't I wear something cool?
I don't want to spend this year looking straight.
But how do I look more queer, specifically more genderqueer?
I love florals! I love colors! But all I own are jeans and t-shirts in boring solid colors.
How did I end up with the wardrobe of a bland teenage boy?

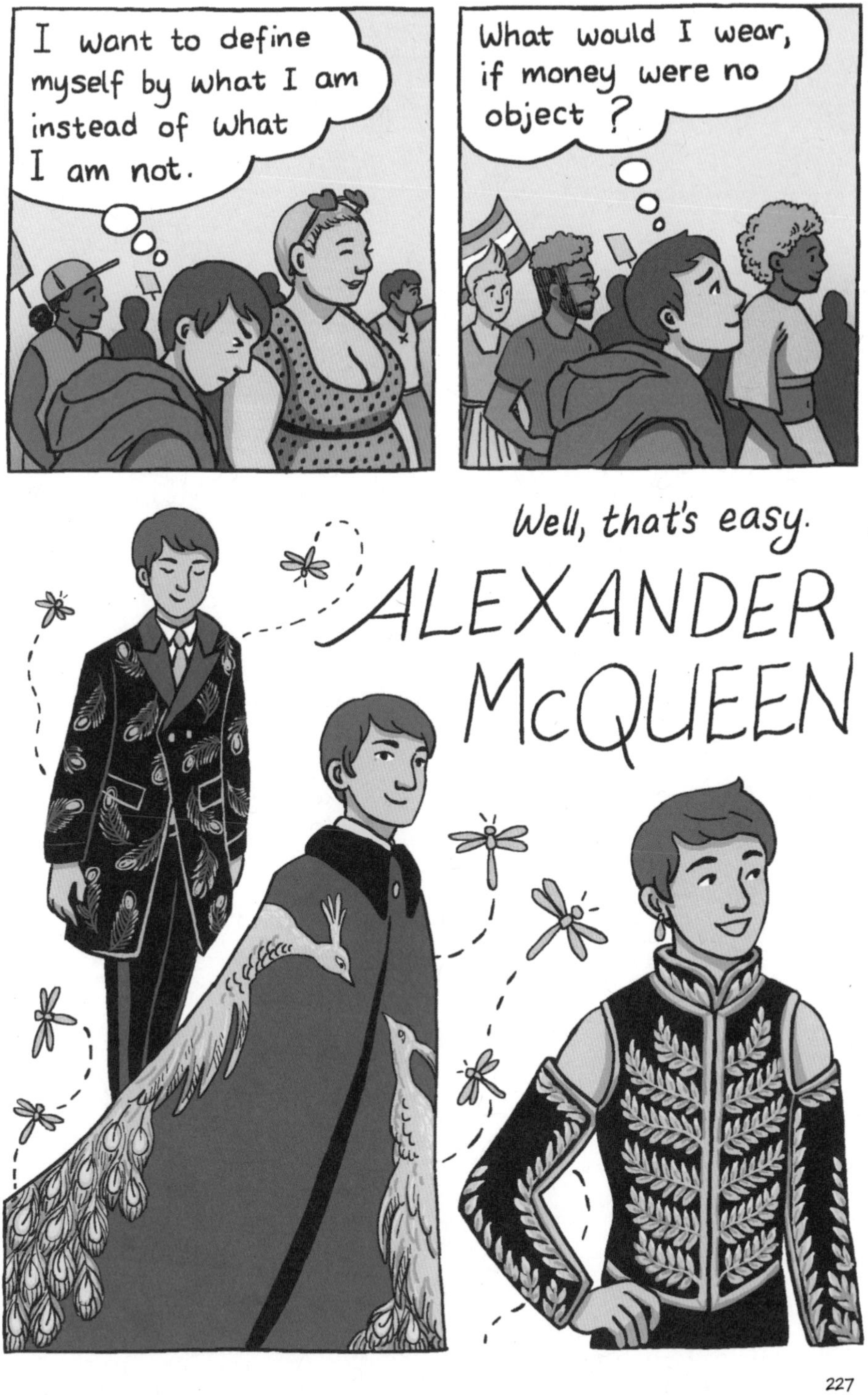
I want to define myself by what I am instead of what I am not.
What would I wear, if money were no object?
Well, that's easy.
ALEXANDER McQUEEN

IN AN EFFORT TO ACHIEVE THE HIGH-FANTASY-GAY-WIZARD-PRINCE LOOK OF MY DREAMS, I BEGAN GIVING MYSELF STRICT SHOPPING GUIDELINES.

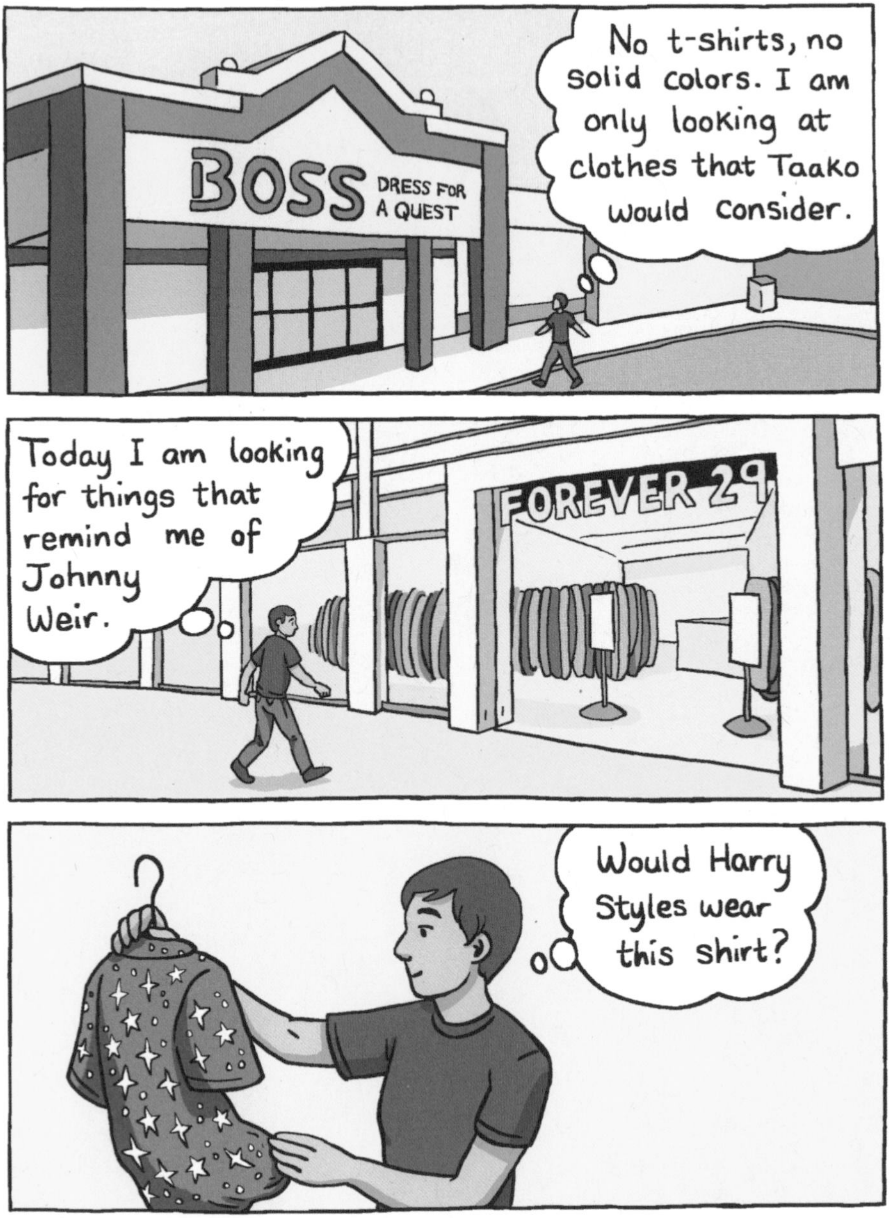
BOSS
DRESS FOR A QUEST
No t-shirts, no solid colors. I am only looking at clothes that Taako would consider.
Today I am looking for things that remind me of Johnny Weir.
FOREVER 29
Would Harry Styles wear this shirt?

SLOWLY I BEGAN TO COLLECT THINGS THAT FELT QUEER & MAGICAL

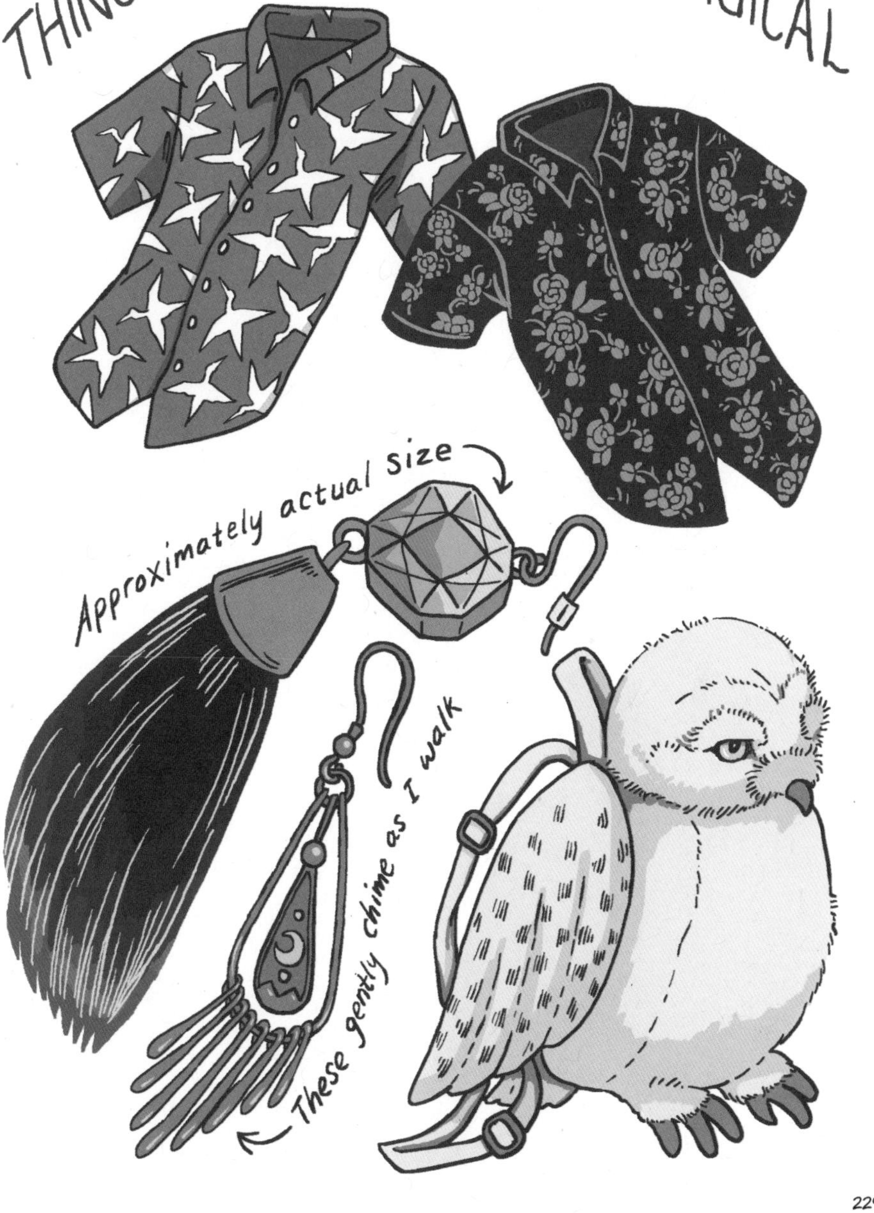
Approximately actual size
These gently chime as I walk

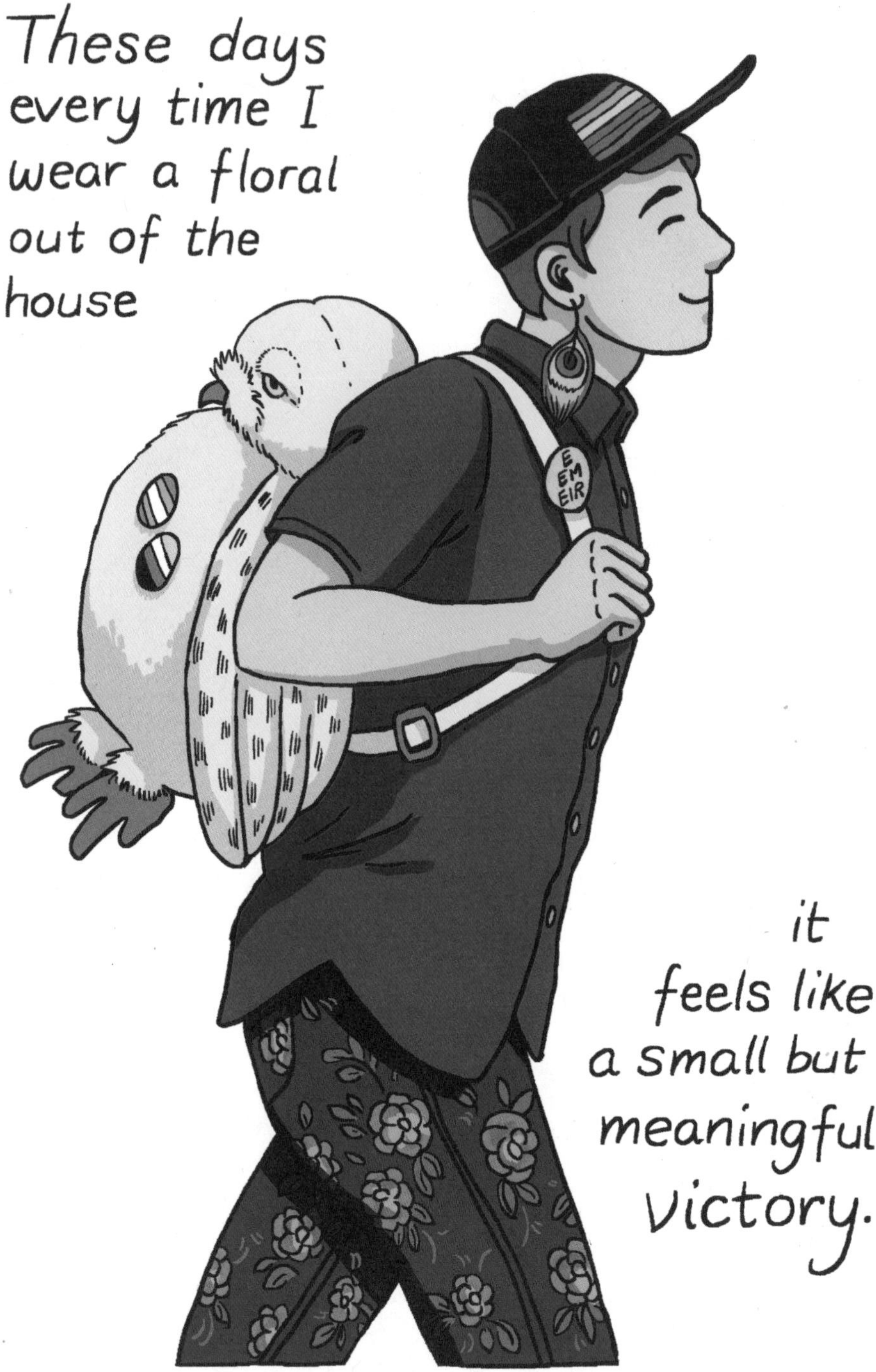
These days every time I wear a floral out of the house
E EM EIR
it feels like a small but meaningful victory.

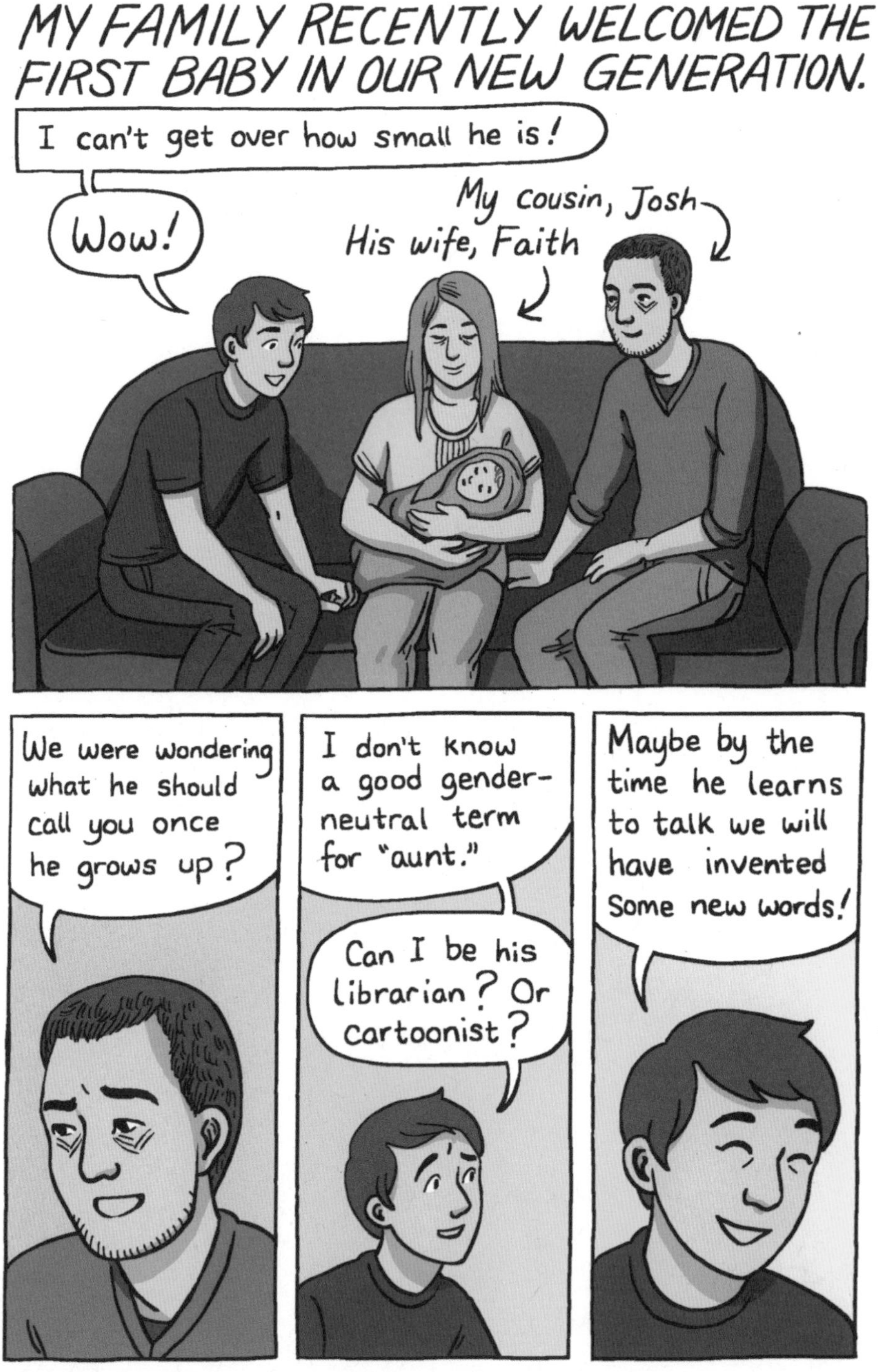
MY FAMILY RECENTLY WELCOMED THE FIRST BABY IN OUR NEW GENERATION.
I can't get over how small he is!
Wow!
My cousin, Josh
His wife, Faith
We were wondering what he should call you once he grows up?
I don't know a good gender-neutral term for "aunt."
Can I be his librarian? Or cartoonist?
Maybe by the time he learns to talk we will have invented some new words!

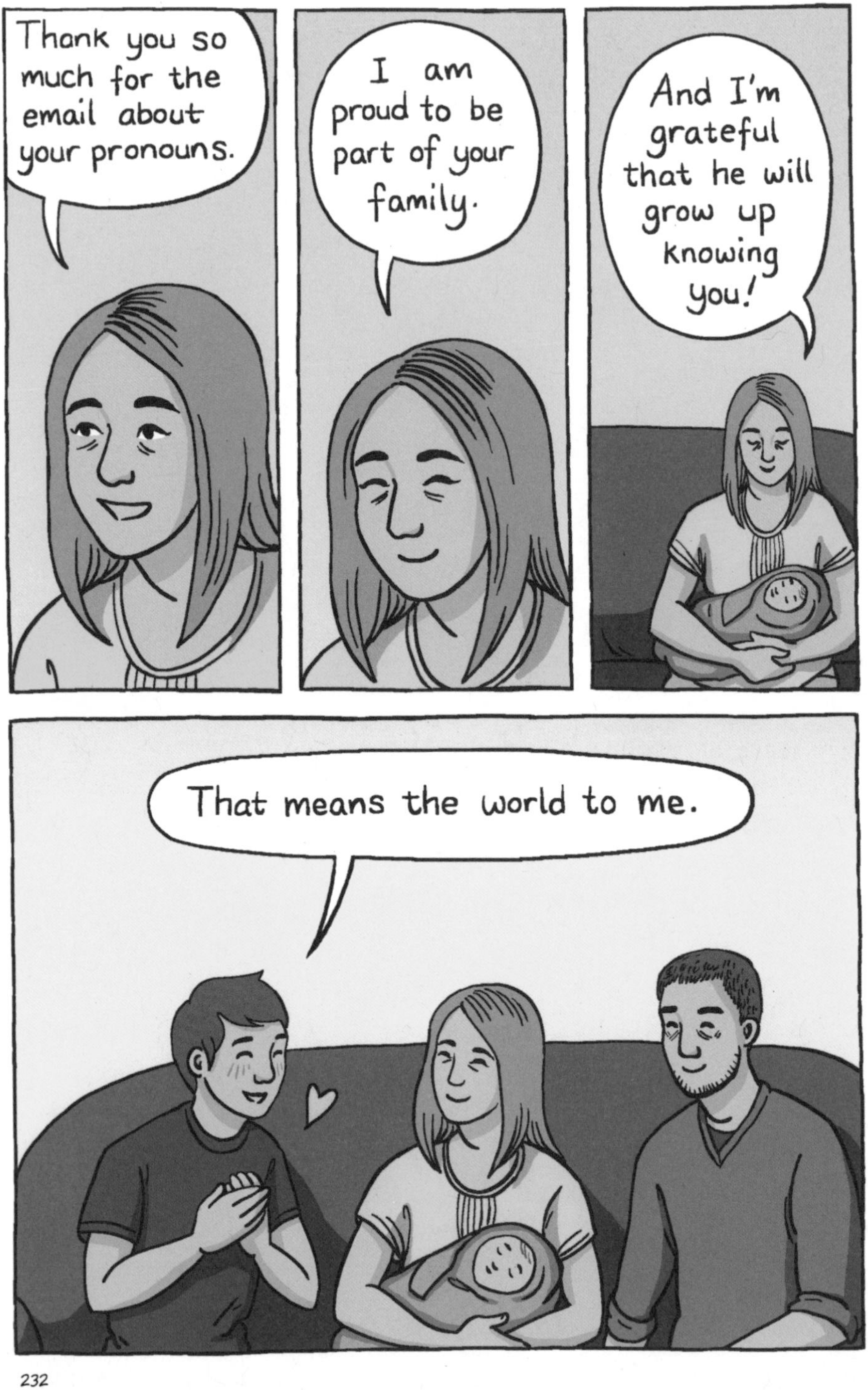
Thank you so much for the email about your pronouns.
I am proud to be part of your family.
And I'm grateful that he will grow up knowing you!
That means the world to me.

IN FALL 2017 I STARTED TEACHING SINGLE-DAY COMICS WORKSHOPS TO JUNIOR HIGH KIDS AT LOCAL LIBRARIES.

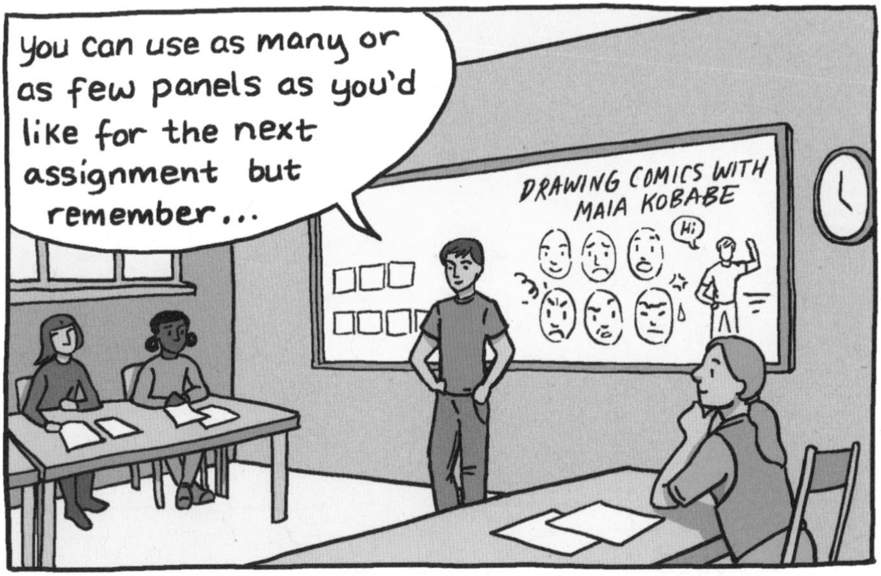

You can use as many or as few panels as you'd like for the next assignment but remember...
DRAWING COMICS WITH MAIA KOBABE
HI

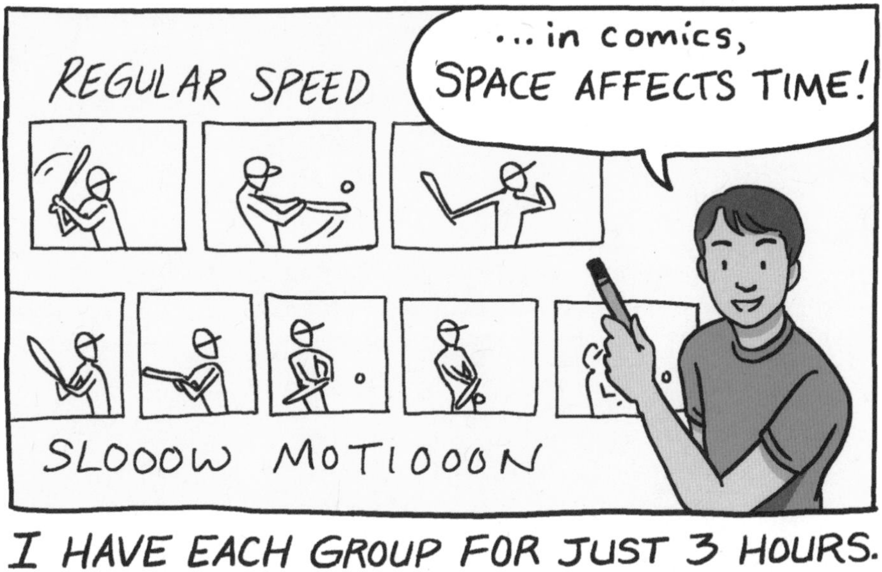

REGULAR SPEED
...in comics, SPACE AFFECTS TIME!
SLOOOW MOTIOOON

I HAVE EACH GROUP FOR JUST 3 HOURS.

I PACK IN AS MUCH AS I CAN.

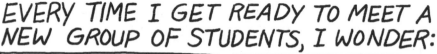

EVERY TIME I GET READY TO MEET A NEW GROUP OF STUDENTS, I WONDER:

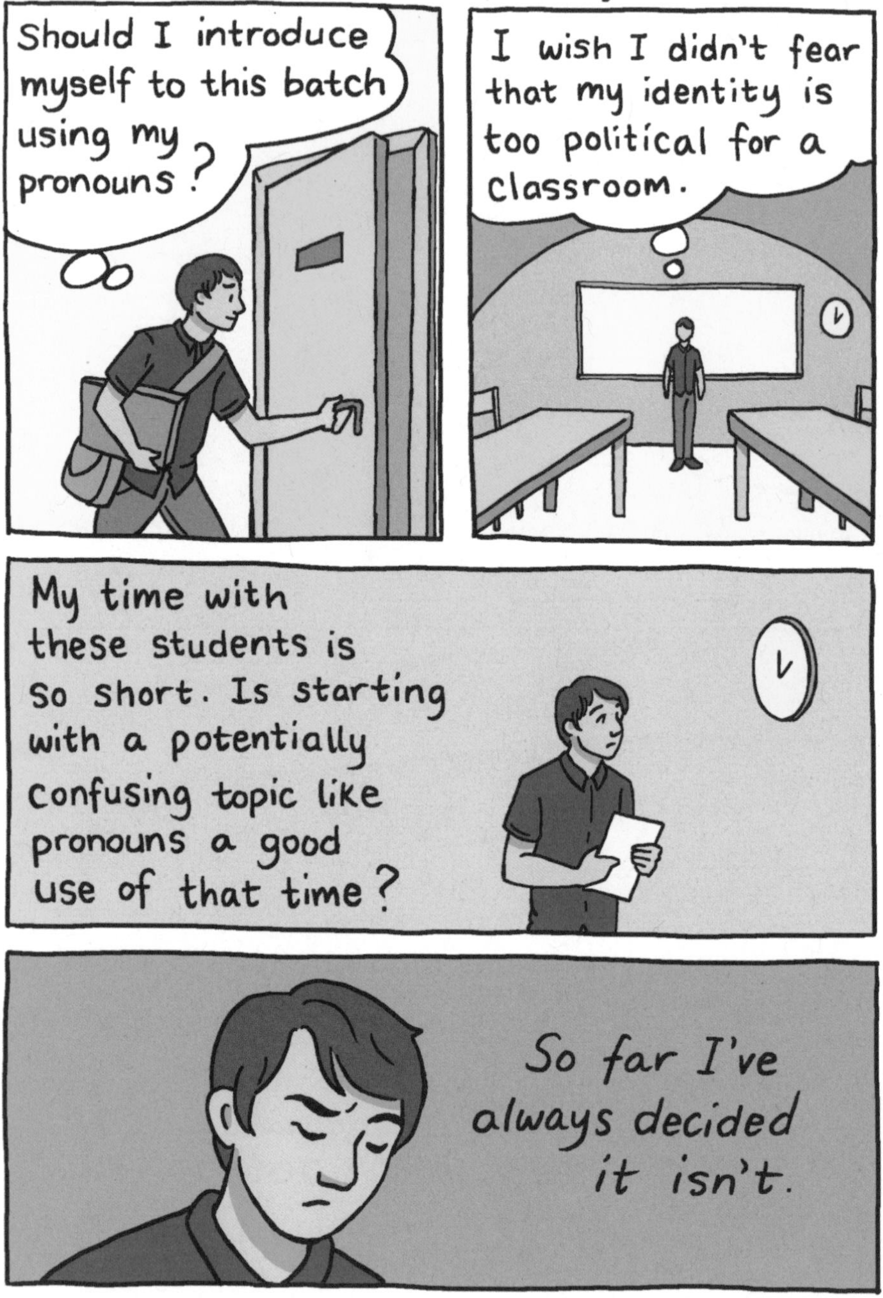

Should I introduce myself to this batch using my pronouns?
I wish I didn't fear that my identity is too political for a classroom.
My time with these students is so short. Is starting with a potentially confusing topic like pronouns a good use of that time?
So far I've always decided it isn't.

DURING THE SNACK BREAK OF A RECENT CLASS A MOM CAME UP TO ME:

My daughter loves to draw! I'm so glad she's getting to see a female artist role model.

When I was a girl I had no role models who looked like me... There were no women doctors, no professors, no CEOs...

I WANTED TO SAY:

I never saw role models like myself either! I didn't even meet another out nonbinary person until grad school.

But I feared that the truth would ruin her moment.

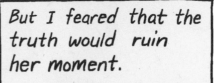

I KEPT QUIET.

THE KIDS I TEACH ARE PRIMARILY A.F.A.B. AND THEY RANGE IN AGE FROM 11 TO 14.

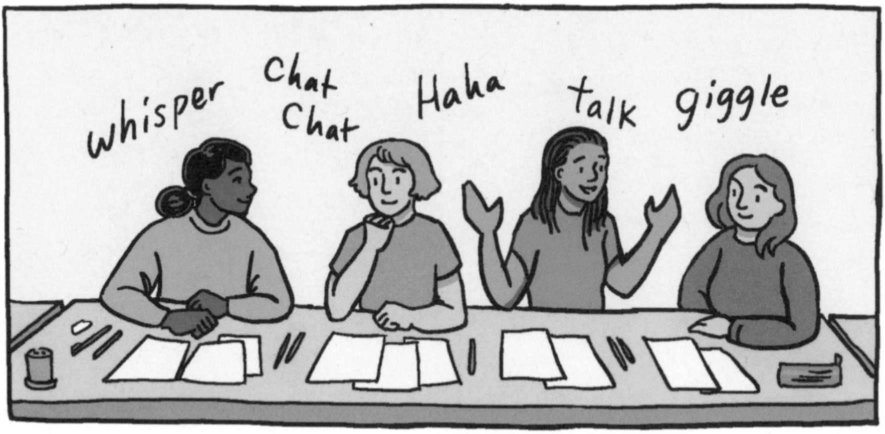
whisper
Chat
Chat
Haha
talk
giggle

Those were my first big years of gender confusion, but I doubt anyone would have guessed just by LOOKING AT ME.

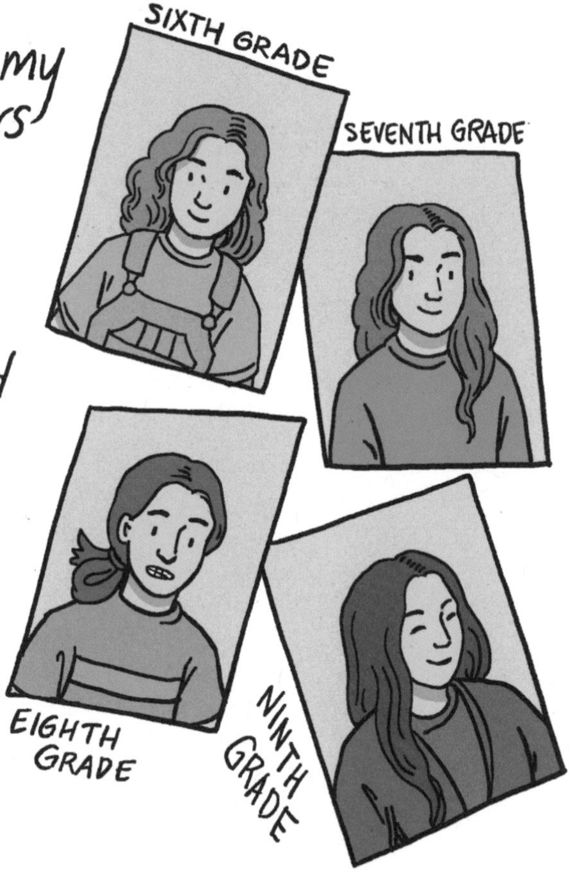
SIXTH GRADE
SEVENTH GRADE
EIGHTH GRADE
NINTH GRADE

LOOKING AROUND MY CLASS TODAY:

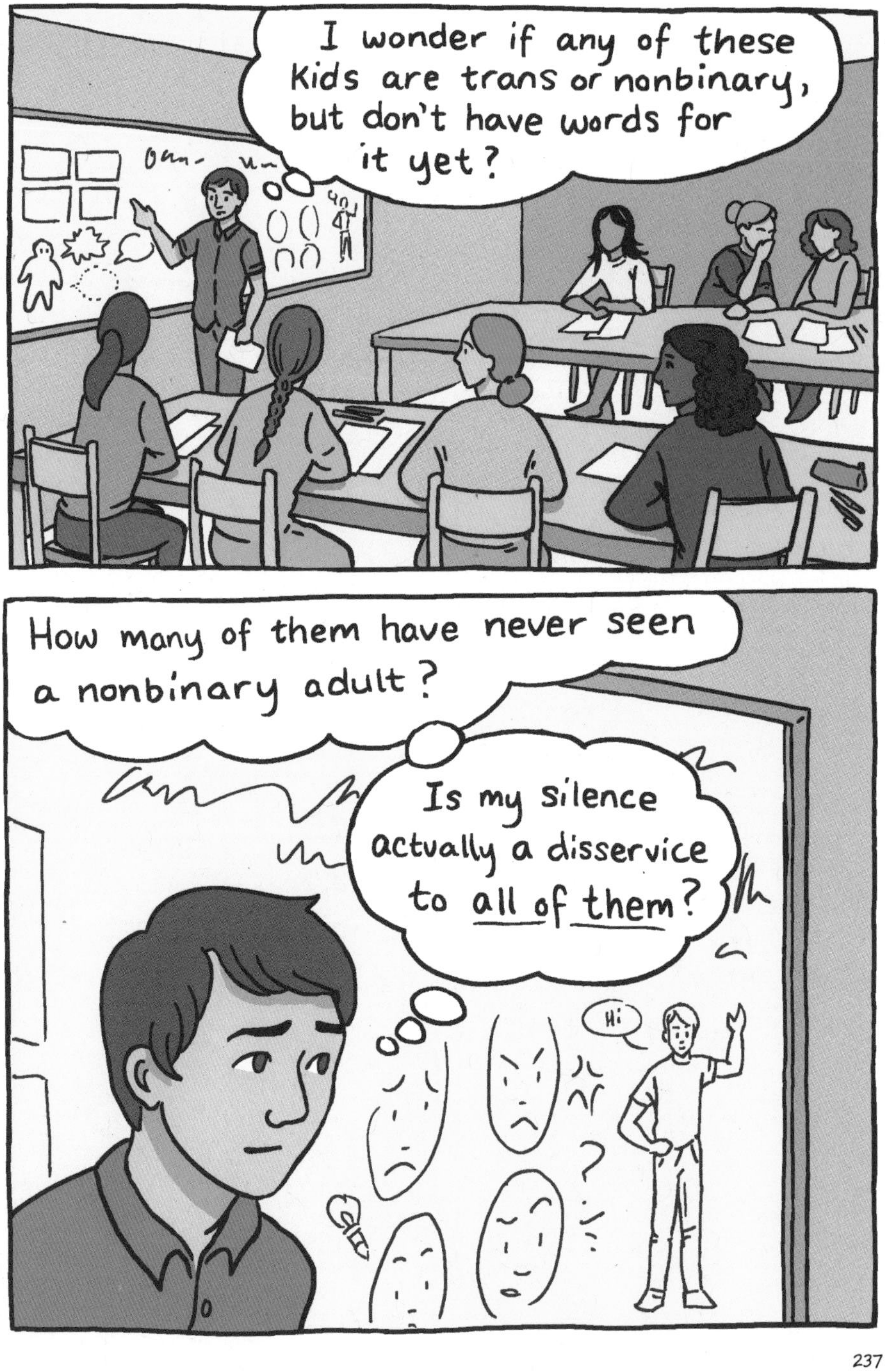
I wonder if any of these kids are trans or nonbinary, but don't have words for it yet?
How many of them have never seen a nonbinary adult?
Is my silence actually a disservice to all of them?
Hi

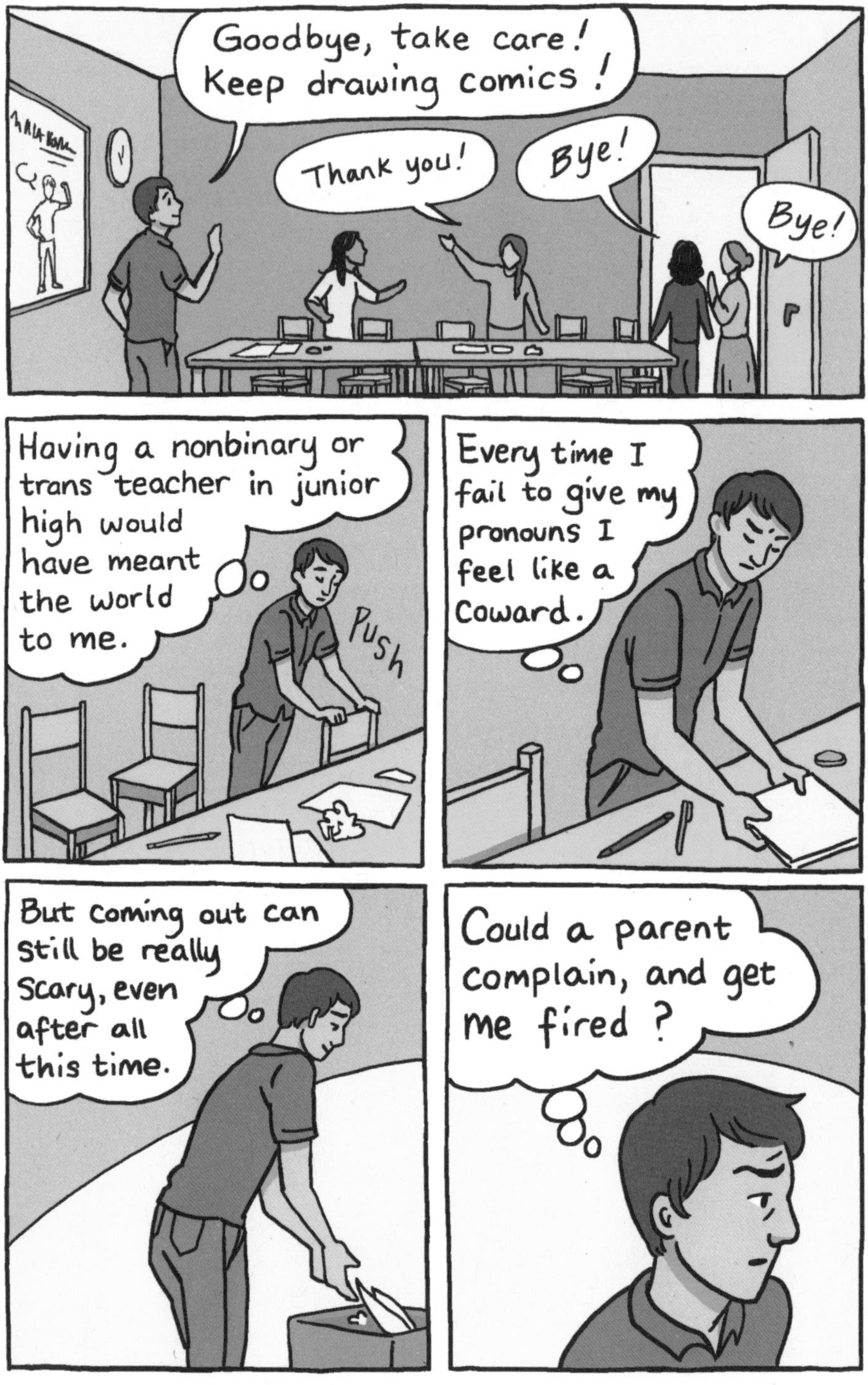
Goodbye, take care! Keep drawing comics!
Thank you!
Bye!
Bye!
Having a nonbinary or trans teacher in junior high would have meant the world to me.
PUSH
Every time I fail to give my pronouns I feel like a coward.
But coming out can still be really scary, even after all this time.
Could a parent complain, and get me fired?

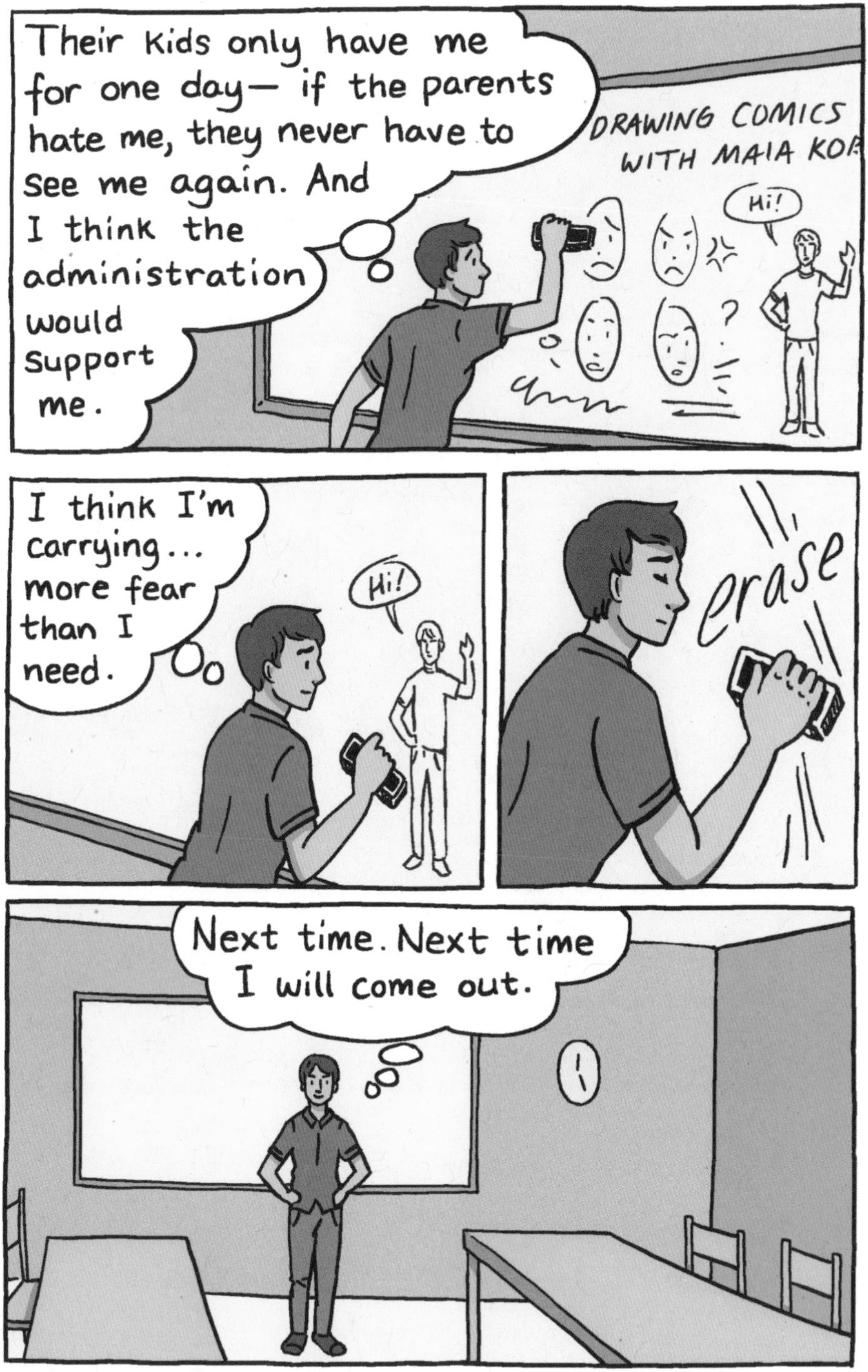
Their kids only have me for one day— if the parents hate me, they never have to see me again. And I think the administration would support me.
DRAWING COMICS WITH MAIA KO
Hi!
I think I'm carrying... more fear than I need.
Hi!
erase
Next time. Next time I will come out.

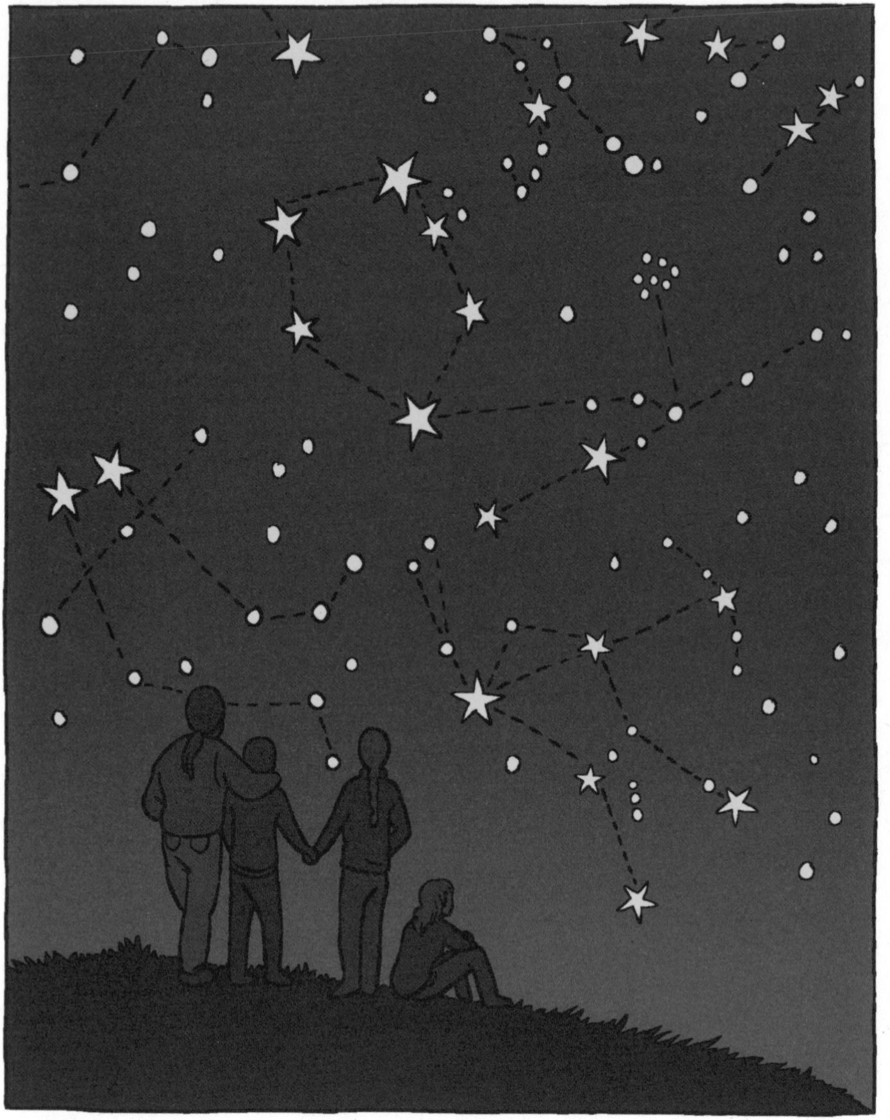

A note to my parents:

Though I have struggled with being your daughter,
I am so, so glad that I am your child.

–MK